Acclaim for R

KA

"Magnificent . . . Calasso has done for Hindu mythology what *The Marriage of Cadmus and Harmony* did for Greek mythology: he has written a book that reads simultaneously like a novel and a sacred text, that ties together all the fragments of Hindu mythology into a continuous, readable, intensely detailed story." —*The New Republic*

"All is spectacle and delight, and tiny mirrors reflecting human foibles are set into the weave, turning this retelling into the stuff of literature." —*The New Yorker*

"Marvelously lyrical . . . we can experience the kind of excitement that must have been felt in ancient times by those who first heard these captivating tales."
—*The Philadelphia Inquirer*

"Moving, exhilarating, extraordinary . . . an astonishing synthesis of myths and legends, philosophical inquiry and speculative narrative. . . . Calasso's erudition is enriched by a pointillist ability to retell ancient stories in a way that captures our contemporary imaginations."
—*The Washington Post Book World*

"In Calasso's retellings, the ancient stories' visionary energy flares in a modern idiom. . . . One closes the book with the sense of having tasted a way of thinking about the world that, despite being magical, probes the most fundamental questions about mortality, desire, time, selfhood and cosmos." —*San Francisco Chronicle*

Also by Roberto Calasso

The Marriage of Cadmus and Harmony
The Ruin of Kasch

Roberto Calasso

KA

Born in Florence, Roberto Calasso lives in Milan, where he is publisher of Adelphi. He is the author of *The Ruin of Kasch* and *The Marriage of Cadmus and Harmony*, which was the winner of France's Prix Veillon and the Prix du Meilleur Livre Etranger.

KA

Stories of the Mind and Gods of India

Roberto Calasso

Translated by Tim Parks

Vintage International
Vintage Books
A Division of Random House, Inc.
New York

FIRST VINTAGE INTERNATIONAL EDITION,
NOVEMBER 1999

 Published in the United States by Vintage Books, a division of Random House, Inc., New York, and simultaneously in Canada by Random House of Canada Limited, Toronto. Originally published in Italy as *Ka* by Adelphi Edizioni, S.P.A., Milan, in 1996. This translation first published in hardcover in the United States by Alfred A. Knopf, Inc., New York, in 1998.

The Library of Congress has cataloged the Knopf edition
as follows:
Calasso, Roberto.
Ka / Roberto Calasso ; translated by Tim Parks. —
1st American ed.
p. cm.
Includes bibliographical references.
ISBN 0-679-45131-5
1. Mythology, Greek—Fiction. 2. Mythology, Hindu—Fiction.
I. Title. II. Parks, Tim.
PQ4863.A3818K3 1998
98087763
CIP

Vintage ISBN: 0-679-77547-1

Author photograph by Giorgio Magister

www.vintagebooks.com

Printed in the United States of America

For Joseph

The world is like the impression left by the telling of a story.

Yogavāsiṣṭha, 2.3.11

Ideae enim nihil aliud sunt, quam narrationes sive historiae naturae mentales.

Spinoza, *Cogitata metaphysica*, 1.6

Contents

I

Suddenly an eagle darkened the sky. Its bright black, almost violet feathers made a moving curtain between clouds and earth. Hanging from its claws, likewise immense and stiff with terror, an elephant and a turtle skimmed the mountaintops. It seemed the bird meant to use the peaks as pointed knives to gut its prey. Only occasionally did the eagle's staring eye flash out from behind the thick fronds of something held tight in its beak: a huge branch. A hundred strips of cowhide would not have sufficed to cover it.

Garuḍa flew and remembered. It was only a few days since he had hatched from his egg and already so much had happened. Flying was the best way of thinking, of thinking things over. Who was the first person he'd seen? His mother, Vinatā. Beautiful in her tininess, she sat on a stone, watching his egg hatch, determinedly passive. Hers was the first eye Garuḍa held in his own. And at once he knew that that eye was his own. Deep inside was an ember that glowed in the breeze. The same he could feel burning beneath his own feathers.

Then Garuḍa looked around. Opposite Vinatā, likewise sitting on a stone, he saw another woman, exactly like his mother. But a black bandage covered one eye. And she too seemed absorbed in contemplation. On the ground before her, Garuḍa saw, lay a great tangle, slowly heaving and squirming. His perfect eye focused, to understand. They were snakes. Black snakes, knotted, separate, coiled, uncoiled. A moment later Garuḍa could make out a thousand snakes' eyes, coldly watching him. From behind came a voice: "They are your cousins. And that woman is my sister, Kadrū. We are their slaves." These were the first words his mother spoke to him.

Vinatā looked up at the huge expanse that was Garuḍa and said: "My child, it's time for you to know who you are. You have been born to a mother in slavery. But I was not born into slavery. I and my sister Kadrū were brides of Kaśyapa, the great *ṛṣi*, the seer. Slow, strong, and taciturn, Kaśyapa understood everything. He loved us, but apart from the absolute essentials took no care of us. He would sit motionless for hours, for days—and we had no idea what he was doing. He held up the world on the shell of his head. My sister and I longed to be doing something with ourselves. An angry energy drove us from within. At first we vied for Kaśyapa's attention. But then we realized that he looked on us as clouds do: equally benevolent and indifferent to both. One day he called us together: it was time for him to withdraw into the forest, he said. But he didn't want to leave without granting us a favor. Immediately we thought of ourselves all alone, amid these marshes, these woods, these brambles, these dunes. Kadrū needed no prompting: she asked for a thousand children, of equal splendor. Kaśyapa agreed. I too was quick to decide: I asked for just two children, but more beautiful and powerful than Kadrū's. Kaśyapa raised his heavy eyelids: 'You will have one and a half,' he said. Then he set off with his stick. We never saw him again."

Vinatā went on: "My child, I have kept watch over your egg for five hundred years. I didn't want the same thing to happen to you as happened to your brother Aruṇa. Impatience got the better of me, and I opened his egg too soon. Only then did I understand what a *ṛṣi* from a distant land, a pale and angular seer, will say one day: that impatience is the only sin. Thus was the lower half of Aruṇa's body left unformed. No sooner had he seen me than my first child cursed me. I would be my sister's slave for five hundred years. And at the end of that time I would be saved by my other child, by you. This said, Aruṇa ascended toward the sun. Now you can see him cross the sky every day. He is Sūrya's charioteer. He will never speak to me again."

Vinatā went on: "We were the only human beings, myself and Kadrū, with a thousand black snakes about us, all of them the same, and your egg maturing imperceptibly in a pot of steaming clay. Already we loathed each other, we two sisters. But we couldn't do without each other. One evening we were squatting down on the shore of the ocean. You know that I am also called Suparṇī, Aquilina, and perhaps that's why I'm your mother. There's nothing my eye doesn't see. Kadrū has only one eye, she lost the other at Dakṣa's sacrifice—oh, but that's a story you could hardly know . . . Yet she too has very keen sight. One evening we were heading in the same direction, bickering and bored as ever, our eyes scanning the waters of the ocean, seeking out the creatures of the deep, the pearls. A diffuse glow in the depths led us on. We didn't know where it came from. Then we turned to gaze at the ocean's end, where sea joins sky. Two different lights. A sharp line separated them, the only sharp line in a world that was all vain profusion. Suddenly we saw something take shape against the light: a white horse. It raised its hooves over waters and sky, suspended there. Thus we discovered amazement. Beside the bright horse we glimpsed something dark: a log? its tail? Everything else was so distinct. That was what the world was made of, as we saw it: the expanse of the waters, the expanse of the sky, that white horse."

Garuḍa stopped her: "Who was the horse?" "I knew nothing at the time," Vinatā said. "Now I know only that this question will haunt us forever, until time itself dissolves. And that final moment will be announced by a white horse. All I can tell you now, of the horse, is what it is called and how it was born. The horse is called Uccaiḥśravas. It was born when the ocean was churned." Listening to his mother, Garuḍa was like a schoolboy who for the first time hears something mentioned that will loom over his whole life. He said: "Mother, I shall not ask you any more about the horse, but how did it happen, what was the churning of the ocean?" Vinatā said: "That's something you'll have to know about, and you'll soon understand why. You are my son—and you were born to ransom me. Children are born to ransom their parents. And there is only one way I can be ransomed by giving the *soma* to the Snakes. The *soma* is a plant and a milky liquid. You will find it in the sky; Indra watches over it, all the gods watch over it, and other powerful beings too. It's the *soma* you must win. The *soma* is my ransom."

Vinatā had withdrawn deep within herself. She spoke with her eyes on the ground, almost unaware of the majestic presence of her son, his feathers quivering. But she roused herself and began talking again, as though to a child, struggling both to be clear and to say only the little that could be said at this point: "In the beginning, not even the gods had the *soma.* Being gods wasn't enough. Life was dull, there was no enchantment. The Devas, the gods, looked with hatred on the other gods, the Asuras, the antigods, the firstborn, who likewise felt keenly the absence of the *soma.* Why fight at all, if the desirable substance wasn't there to fight for? The gods meditated and sharpened their senses, but there would come the day when they wanted just to live. Gloomily, they met together on Mount Meru, where the peak passes through the vault of the heavens to become the only part of this world that belongs to the other. The gods were waiting for something new, anything. Viṣṇu whispered to Brahmā, then Brahmā explained to the others. They had to stir the churn of the ocean, until the *soma* floated up, as butter floats up from milk. And this task could not be undertaken in opposition to the Asuras, but only with their help.

The pronouncement ran contrary to everything the Devas had previously thought. But in the end, what did they have to lose, given that their lives were so futile? Now they thought: Anything, so long as there be a trial, a risk, a task."

Vinatā fell silent. Garuḍa respected her silence for a long time. Then he said: "Mother, Mother, you still haven't told me how you became a slave to your sister." "We were looking at the white horse. The more it enchanted me, the greater the rancor I felt for my sister. I said: 'Hey, One-Eye, can you see what color that horse is?' Kadrū didn't answer. The black bandage leaned forward. Then I said: 'Want to bet? The one who gets the horse's color right will be mistress of the other.' The following morning, at dawn, we were together again, watching the sky. And once again the horse appeared against the background of sea and sky. I shouted: 'It's white.' Silence. I repeated: 'Kadrū, don't you think it's white?' To this day I have never seen such a malignant look in her eye. Kadrū said: 'It's got a black tail.' 'We'll go and see,' I said, 'and whichever of us is wrong will be the other's slave.' 'So be it,' Kadrū said.

"Then we split up. Later I learned that Kadrū had tried to corrupt her children. She had asked them to hang on to the horse's tail, to make it look black. The Snakes refused. For the first time Kadrū showed her fury. She said: 'You'll all be exterminated . . .' One day you'll realize," Vinatā went on in a quieter voice, "that nothing can be exterminated, because everything leaves a residue, and every residue is a beginning . . . But it's too soon to be telling you any more . . . Just remember this for now: Kadrū's curse was powerful. One far-off day it will happen: the Pāṇḍavas and the Kauravas will fight, almost to the point of extinction, their own and that of the peoples allied to them, so that a sacrifice of the Snakes may fail, so that people recognize that the Snakes cannot be exterminated. That will happen at the last possible moment . . . Kadrū is calamitous, her word is fatal." Vinatā's eyes were two slits. "But where was I? Now we had to get to the horse. We took flight, side by side. The creatures of the deep flashed their backs above the waters, surprised to see these two women in flight. We paid no attention. The only thing in the world that mattered to us was our game. When we reached the horse, I stroked its white rump. 'As you see,' I said to Kadrū. 'Wait,' said One-Eye. And she showed me a few black hairs her deft fingers had picked out from among all the white ones of the creature's tail. For no apparent reason, they were wrapped around a pole. Some say that those hairs were Snakes, faithful to their mother. Or that there was only one black hair, the Snake Karkoṭaka. Others say that Uccaiḥśravas has black hairs mixed in with the white. It's a dispute that will never be settled. 'I've beaten you. The sea is my witness. Now you are my slave,' said Kadrū. It was then that I sensed, in a sudden rending, what debt is, the debt of life, of any life. For five hundred years I would feel its weight."

"I'll go and win this *soma,* Mother," said Garuḍa with his most solemn expression. "But first I must eat." They were squatting down face-to-face. Garuḍa, a mountain of feathers; Vinatā, a minute, sinuous creature. "Go to the middle of the ocean," said Vinatā. "There you'll find the land of the Niṣādas. You can eat as many of them as you want. They don't know the Vedas. But remember: Never kill a brahman. A brahman is fire, is a blade, is poison. Under no circumstances, even if seized by anger, must you hurt a brahman." Garuḍa listened, ever more serious. "But what is a brahman, Mother?" he said. "How do I recognize one?" So far Garuḍa had seen nothing but black, coiled snakes and those two women who hated each other. He did not know what his father looked like. A brahman? What on earth can that be? wondered Garuḍa. "If you feel a firebrand in your throat," said Vinatā "that's a brahman. Or if you realize you've swallowed a hook." Garuḍa stared straight at her and thought: "So you can't tell a brahman until you've almost swallowed him." But already he was stretching his wings, eager to be gobbling up the Niṣādas.

9

Caught by surprise, the Niṣādas didn't even see Garuḍa coming. Blinded by wind and dust, they were sucked by the thousands into a dark cavity that opened behind his beak. They plunged down there as if into a well. But one of them managed to hang on to that endless wall. With his other hand he held a young woman with snaky hair tight by the waist, dangling in the void. Garuḍa, who was gazing ahead with his beak half open, just enough to swallow up swarms of Niṣādas, suddenly felt something burning in his throat. "That's a brahman," he thought. So he said: "Brahman, I don't know you, but I don't mean you any harm. Come out of my throat." And from Garuḍa's throat came a shrill, steady voice: "I'll never come out unless I can bring this Niṣāda woman with me, she's my bride." "I've no objections," said Garuḍa. Soon he saw them climbing onto his beak, taking care, fearful of getting hurt. Garuḍa was intrigued and thought: "Finally I'll know what a brahman looks like." He saw them sliding down his feathers. The brahman was thin, bony, dusty, his hair woven in a plait, his eyes sunken and vibrant. His long, determined fingers never let go of the wrist of the Niṣāda woman, whose beauty immediately reminded Garuḍa of his mother and his treacherous aunt Kadrū. This left him bewildered, while he reflected that quite probably he had already swallowed up thousands of women like her. But by now those two tiny beings were hurrying off, upright, agile, impatient, as if the whole world were opening before them. Garuḍa was more puzzled than ever. He felt an urgent need to talk to his father, whom he'd still not seen. As his wings stretched, another whirlwind devastated the earth.

Kaśyapa was watching a line of ants. He paid no attention to his son, nor to the crashing that announced his arrival. But Garuḍa wasn't eager to speak either. He was watching Kaśyapa, his wrinkled, polished skull, his noble arms hanging down in abandon. He studied him for a while. He thought: "Now I know what a brahman is. A brahman is one who feeds himself by feeding on himself." After a day's silence, Kaśyapa looked up at Garuḍa. He said: "How is your mother?" then immediately went on to something else, as if he already knew the answer. "Seek out the elephant and the turtle who are quarreling in a lake. They will be your food. The Niṣādas aren't enough for you. Then go and eat them on Rauhiṇa, that's a tree near here, a friend of mine. But be careful not to offend the Vālakhilyas . . ."

"Who can these Vālakhilyas be?" thought Garuḍa, flying along, the elephant and the turtle tight in his claws. "No sooner does one thing seem to get clearer than another, bigger thing turns up that's completely obscure." While Garuḍa was thinking this over, puzzled again, his wing skimmed the huge tree Rauhiṇa. "By all means rest on a branch and eat," said the tree's voice. "Before you were born you sat here on me, along with a companion of yours, exactly like yourself. Perched on opposite branches, at the same height, you never left each other. You were already eating my fruit back then. And your companion watched you, though he didn't eat. You couldn't fly about the world then, because I was the world." Garuḍa settled on a branch. Surrounded by the foliage that enfolded his feathers, he felt at home and couldn't understand why. Of his birthplace he could remember only sand, stone, and snakes. Whereas this tree protected him on every side with swathes of emerald that softened the merciless light of the sky. Hmm . . . In the meantime he might as well devour the elephant and the turtle, now on their backs on this branch that was a hundred leagues long. He concentrated a moment. He was choosing the spot where he would sink his beak—when there came a sudden crash. The branch had snapped. Shame and guilt overcame Garuḍa. He knew at once that he had done something awful, without having meant to. And it was all the more awful because he had not meant it. A vortex opened up in the tree, and Garuḍa flew out with the broken branch in his beak, the elephant and the turtle still in his claws. He was lost. He didn't know where to go. He sensed he was in danger of making a fatal mistake. From the branch came a hiss. At first he thought it was the wind. But the hissing went on, peremptory and fearfully shrill. He looked at the twigs. Upside down among the leaves, like bats, dangled scores of brahmans, each no taller than the phalanx of a thumb. Their bodies were perfectly formed and almost transparent, like flies' wings. Used as they were to hanging motionless, the flight was upsetting them terribly. Garuḍa thought: "Oh, the Vālakhilyas . . ." He was sure it was they, sure of the enormity of his crime. "Noble Vālakhilyas," said Garuḍa, "the last thing I want is to hurt you." He was answered by a mocking rustle. "That's what you all say . . ." Now he made out a voice. "The indestructible is tiny and tenuous as a syllable. You should know that, being made of syllables yourself. The tiny is negligible. So it is neglected . . ." "Not by me," said Garuḍa. And now he began to fly in the most awkward fashion, taking the greatest possible care not to shake the branch he held in his beak. Despondent, he studied the mountains, looking for a clearing large and soft enough for him to put down the Vālakhilyas. But he couldn't find one. Perhaps he would waste away in the sky, circling forever. It was then that a huge mountain, the Gandhamādana, began to take shape ahead, and Garuḍa thought that he might attempt a last exploration. He was flying around the summit, slowly and cautiously, when he recognized the polished head of his father, Kaśyapa, sitting by a pond on the slopes of the Gandhamādana. Garuḍa hovered over him, without making a sound. Kaśyapa said nothing, paid no attention, though the whole of Gandhamādana was veiled in shadow. Then he said: "Child, don't be distressed, and don't do anything rash that you might regret. The Vālakhilyas drink the sun, they could burn your fire . . ." Garuḍa was still hovering above his father, terrified. Then he heard Kaśyapa's voice change. He was speaking to the Vālakhilyas, on familiar terms, whispering. "Garuḍa is about to perform a great deed. Take your leave of him now, I beg you, if you still think well of me . . ." A little later, Garuḍa saw the

Vālakhilyas detaching themselves from the branch, like tiny, dry leaves, gray and dusty. They turned slowly in the air and slowly settled next to Kaśyapa. Soon they had disappeared among the blades of grass, heading toward the Himālaya.

Garuḍa had watched the scene unfold with overwhelming anxiety. Now he felt moved. Long after the last of the Vālakhilyas had disappeared in the vegetation, he said: "Father, you saved me." Without looking up, Kaśyapa answered: "I saved you because I saved myself. Listen to the story. One day I had to celebrate a sacrifice. I had told Indra and the other gods to find me some wood. Indra was coming back from the forest, loaded with logs. He was feeling proud of his strength, and he knew he would be back first. As he was walking along, his eyes fell on a puddle. Something was moving in it: the Vālakhilyas. They were trying to ford it, which was hard going for them. Moving in single file, they held a blade of grass on their shoulders, like a log, and at the same time were struggling to get out of the mud. Indra stopped to watch and was seized with laughter. He was drunk with himself. Just as they were about to get out, he pushed those Vālakhilyas back in the puddle with his heel. And laughed.

"The following day I got a visit from the Vālakhilyas. They said: 'We've come to give you half our *tapas*, the heat that has baked our minds since times long past. It's the purest *tapas*, never corroded by the world, never poured out into the world. Now we want to pour some into you so that you can pour out your seed and generate a being who will be a new Indra, who will be the scourge of Indra, the arrogant, the uncivilized, the cowardly Indra. Such a one shall be your son.' 'Indra was brought into the world by the will of Brahma. He cannot be ousted by another Indra,' I objected. 'Then he shall be an Indra of the birds. And he shall be the scourge of Indra.' I agreed.

"That night I felt the Vālakhilyas' *tapas* flowing into me. I became transparent and manifold, a veil and a bundle of burning arrows. Your mother, Vinatā, took fright when I came to her bed. The following morning she told me how, while pleasure had been invading her pores and curling her nails, something dark had raised her to a mattress of leaves, on the top of a huge tree—and she had seen a glow flare up from beneath. Down the trunk ran drop after drop of a clear liquid. She felt sure that that liquid came from an inexhaustible reserve."

Engrossed in his father's tale, Garuḍa had almost forgotten that he was still hovering in the air, claws sinking ever deeper into the elephant and the turtle, who had long been waiting to be eaten. Not to mention that cumbersome branch, still clenched in his beak. Garuḍa didn't dare do anything further on his own account. If he dropped the branch on one of the nearby mountains, even the most barren, and crushed so much as a single brahman, hidden in the vegetation, what then? "Thinking paralyzes," thought Garuḍa, motionless in the sky. Kaśyapa was eager to put an end to his son's wretched predicament. He would have plenty of time, billions of passing moments, to reflect on his crime: that broken branch. Now his father could help him. "Fly away, Garuḍa," he said. "Go north. When you find a mountain covered with nothing but ice and riddled with caves like dark eye sockets, you can leave the branch there. That's the only place where there's no risk of killing a brahman. And there you can finally eat up the elephant and the turtle." Garuḍa flew off at once.

"So many things happening, so many stories one inside the other, with every link hiding yet more stories . . . And I've hardly hatched from my egg," thought an exultant Garuḍa, heading north. At last a place with no living creatures. He would stop and think things over there. "No one has taught me anything. Everything has been shown to me. It will take me all my life to begin to understand what I've been through. To understand, for example, what it means to say that I am made of syllables . . ." He was even happier, drenched in joy, when a barrier of pale blue ice and snow filled his field of vision, a sight that would have blinded any other eye. The branch of the tree Rauhiṇa fell with a thud, then down plunged the elephant and the turtle just a moment before Garuḍa's beak forced a way into flesh already wrapped in a gleaming sepulchre.

"And now the theft, the deed . . . ," said Garuḍa. Around him on an endless white carpet lay the stripped remains of the elephant and the turtle. He rose in flight, off to win the *soma.*

At that very moment one of the gods noticed something odd in the celestial stasis: the garlands had lost their fragrance, a thin layer of dust had settled on the buds. "The heavens are wearing out like the earth . . ." was the silent fear of more than one god. It was a moment of pure terror. What came after was no more than a superfluous demonstration. The rains of fire, the meteors, the whirlwinds, the thunder. Indra hurled his lightning bolt as Garuḍa invaded the sky. The lightning bounced off his feathers. "How can that be?" said Indra to Bṛhaspati, chief priest of the gods. "This is the lightning that split the heart of Vṛtra. Garuḍa tosses it aside like a straw." Sitting on a stool, Bṛhaspati had remained impassive throughout, from the moment the sky had begun to shake. "Garuḍa is made not of feathers but of meters. You cannot hurt a meter. Garuḍa is *gāyatrī* and *triṣṭubh* and *jagatī.* Garuḍa is the hymn. The hymn that cannot be scratched. And then: remember that puddle, those tiny beings you found so funny, with their blade of grass . . . Garuḍa is, in part, their child."

Still raging though the battle was, its outcome was clear from the start. The gods knew they were going to lose. They hurried to get away. But what infuriated them most were the whirlwinds of dust unleashed in the heavens by every flap of Garuḍa's wings. Dust in the heavens . . . It was the ultimate humiliation . . . Even the guardians of the *soma* were overcome. In vain they loosed their arrows. Just one of Garuḍa's feathers spun majestic in the sky, severed by an arrow from Kṛśānu, the footless archer. Garuḍa took no notice of his enemies. The trial still before him was far harder. On the summit of the heavens he found a metal wheel, its sharp spokes spinning without cease. Behind the wheel he could just see a glow: a gold cup, or rather two cups, one turned upside down upon the other, their rims jagged and sharp. And these cups likewise were moving. They opened and closed in a rocking motion. When they closed, their rims fit perfectly together. Between the wheel and the cups hissed two Snakes. Garuḍa tossed dust in the Snakes' eyes and concentrated. He must slip between the wheel's blades, he would have to get his beak between the rims of the two cups, he would have to snatch the glow he had glimpsed within. Then escape. But everything had to happen in no more than the blinking of an eye. On that tiny fraction of time depended the fate of his mother, indeed of the world. Garuḍa did it. It didn't occur to him to drink the *soma* that dripped from his beak as he headed back to earth. He was thinking of the Snakes, and of his mother.

Indra tried to stop Garuḍa as he flew toward the earth. He found an accommodating and contrite expression. "There's no point in our being enemies," said Indra. "We are too powerful to be enemies," he added. Then he started to cajole: "Ask me anything you want, I have something I want to ask you: don't let the Snakes get hold of the *soma*." "But I have to ransom my mother," said the obstinate Garuḍa. "To ransom your mother all you have to do is deliver the *soma* to the Snakes. You don't have to do any more than that. But I don't want the Snakes to possess the *soma*. I'll tell you what to do . . ." "If that's how things stand . . . ," said Garuḍa. He was intimidated by Indra's self-confidence, and his reasonableness too. "After all," thought Garuḍa, "this is the king of the gods talking."

"And now tell me what you want . . . ," said Indra. He was growing insistent. "That the Snakes be my food, forever and ever," said Garuḍa. Whatever it took, he didn't want to risk swallowing a brahman again. And then he liked eating the Snakes. But now he fell silent a moment, out of shyness. He was about to announce his deepest desire, something he had never uttered before: "I would like to study the Vedas." "So be it," said Indra.

The Snakes had arranged themselves in a circle to await Garuḍa's return. They saw him coming like a black star, a point expanding on the horizon, until his beak laid down a delicate plant, damp with sap, upon the *darbha* grass. "This is the *soma*, Snakes. This is my mother's ransom. I deliver it to you. But before you drink of this celestial liquid, I would advise a purificatory bath." In disciplined devotion, the Snakes slithered off toward the river. For a moment, the only moment of tranquillity the earth would ever know, the *soma* was left, alone, on the grass. A second later Indra's rapacious hand had swooped from the heavens, and already it was gone. Gleaming with water, aware of the gravity of the moment, the Snakes could be seen returning through the tall grass. They found nothing but a place where the grass had been bent slightly. Hurriedly they licked at the *darbha* grass where Garuḍa had laid the *soma*. From that moment on the Snakes have had forked tongues.

Garuḍa said: "Mother, I've paid your ransom. You're free now. Climb on my back." They wandered over forests and plains, over the ocean, leisurely and blithe. Every now and then Garuḍa would fly down to earth to snatch bunches of Snakes in his beak. On his back, Vinatā bubbled with pleasure. Then Garuḍa took leave of his mother. He said his time had come. Once again he flew to the tree Rauhiṇa. He hid among the tree's branches to study the Vedas.

Buried deep among the tree Rauhiṇa's branches, Garuḍa read the Vedas. It was years before he raised his beak. Those beings he had terrorized in the heavens, who had scattered like dust at his arrival, who had tried in vain to fight him, he knew who they were now: with reverence he scanned their names and those of their descendants. The Ādityas, the Vasus, the Rudras. Varuṇa, Mitra, Aryaman, Bhaga, Tvaṣṭṛ, Pūṣan, Vivasvat, Savitṛ, Indra, Viṣṇu, Dhātṛ, Aṃśa, Anumati, Dhiṣaṇā, Soma, Bṛhaspati, Guṅgū, Sūrya, Svasti, Uṣas, Āyu, Sarasvatī. And others too. Thirty-three in all. But each had many names—and some gods could be replaced by others. The names whirled in silence. Perfectly motionless, Garuḍa experienced a sense of vertigo and intoxication. The hymns blazed within him. Finally he reached the tenth book of the Ṛg Veda. And here he smelled a shift in the wind. Along with the names came a shadow now, a name never uttered. What had been affirmative tended to the interrogative. The voice that spoke was more remote. It no longer celebrated. It said what is. Now Garuḍa was reading hymn one hundred and twenty-one, in *triṣṭubh* meter. There were nine stanzas, each one ending with the same question: "Who (*Ka*) is the god to whom we should offer our sacrifice?" Estuary to a hidden ocean, that syllable (*ka*) would go on echoing within him as the essence of the Vedas. Garuḍa stopped and shut his eyes. He had never felt so uncertain, and so close to understanding. Never felt so light, in that sudden absence of names. When he opened his eyes, he realized that the nine stanzas were followed by another, this one separated by a space that was slightly larger. The writing was a little more uneven, minute. A tenth stanza, without any question. And here there was a name, the only name in the hymn, the only answer. Garuḍa couldn't remember ever having seen that name before: Prajāpati.

II

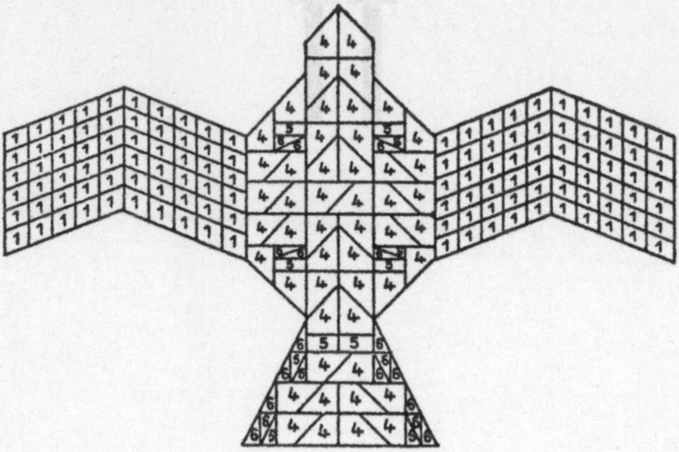

Prajāpati was alone. He didn't even know whether he existed or not. "So to speak," *iva.* (As soon as one touches on something crucial, it's as well to qualify what one has said with the particle *iva*, which doesn't tie us down.) There was only the mind, *manas.* And what is peculiar about the mind is that it doesn't know whether it exists or not. But it comes before everything else. "There is nothing before the mind." Then, even prior to establishing whether it existed or not, the mind desired. It was continuous, diffuse, undefined. Yet, as though drawn to something exotic, something belonging to another species of life, it desired what was definite and separate, what had shape. A Self, *ātman*—that was the name it used. And the mind imagined that Self as having consistency. Thinking, the mind grew red hot. It saw thirty-six thousand fires flare up, made of mind, made with mind. Suspended above the fires were thirty-six thousand cups, and these too were made of mind.

Prajāpati lay with his eyes closed. Between head and breast an ardor burned within him, like water seething in silence. It was constantly transforming something: it was *tapas.* But what was it transforming? The mind. The mind was what transformed and what was transformed. It was the warmth, the hidden flame behind the bones, the succession and dissolution of shapes sketched on darkness—and the sensation of knowing that that was happening. Everything resembled something else. Everything was connected to something else. Only the sensation of consciousness resembled nothing at all. And yet all resemblances flowed back and forth within it. It was the "indistinct wave." Each resemblance was a crest of that wave. At the time, "this world was nothing but water." And then? "In the midst of the waves a single seer." Already the waters were the mind. But why that eye? Within the mind came that split that precedes all others, that implies all others. There was consciousness and there was an eye watching consciousness. In the same mind were two beings. Who might become three, thirty, three thousand. Eyes that watched eyes that watched eyes. But that first step was enough in itself. All the other eyes were there in that "one seer" and in the waters.

The waters yearned. Alone, they burned. "They burned their heat." A golden shell took shape in the wave. "This, the one, was born from the strength of the heat." And inside the shell, over the arc of a year, the body of Prajāpati took shape. But "the year didn't exist" then. Time appeared as the organ of a single being, nesting inside that being, who drifted on the waters, with no support. After a year the being began to emit syllables, which were the earth, the air, the distant sky. Already he knew he was Father Time. Prajāpati was granted a life of a thousand years: he looked out before him, beyond the cresting waves, and far, far away glimpsed a strip of earth, the faint line of a distant shore. His death.

Prajāpati was the one "self-existing" being, *svayaṃbhū*. But this did not make him any less vulnerable than any creature born. He had no knowledge, didn't have qualities. He was the first self-made divinity. He didn't know the meters, not in the beginning. Then he felt a simmering somewhere inside. He saw a chant—and finally let it out. Where from? From the suture in his skull.

• • •

Born of the waters' desiring, Prajāpati begat "all this," *idaṃ sarvam,* but he was the only one who couldn't claim to have a progenitor—not even a mother. If anything he had many mothers, for the waters are an irreducible feminine plural. The waters were his daughters too, as though from the beginning it was important to show that in every essential relationship generation is reciprocal.

The mind: a flow restricted by no bank or barrier, crossed by flashes that fade away. A circle would have to be drawn, a frame, a *templum.* "Settle down," Prajāpati told himself. But everything pitched about. "Need a solid base," *pratiṣṭha,* he said. "Otherwise my children will wander around witless. If nothing stays the same, how can they ever calculate anything? How can they see the equivalences?" As he was thinking this, he lay on a lotus leaf, delicate and flimsy, blown along by the breeze, which was himself. He thought: "The waters are the foundation of all there is. But the waters are the doctrine too, the Vedas. Too difficult. Who of those to be born will understand? Need to hide, to cover at least a small part of the waters. Need earth." In the shape of a boar he dove into the deep. Surfacing, his snout was smeared with mud. He began to spread it out on the lotus leaf, with loving care. "This is the earth," he said. "Now I've spread it, I'll need some stones to keep it still." He disappeared again. Then he arranged a frame of white stones around the now dry mud. "You will be its guardians," he said. Now the earth was taut as a cowhide. Tired as he was, Prajāpati lay down on it. For the first time he touched the earth. And for the first time the earth was burdened with a weight.

The dried slime covering the lotus leaf set in a thin layer. Yet it sufficed to give some impression of stability. The white stones sketched out an enclosure, allowed one to get one's bearings. It was this, more than anything else, that was reassuring, that invited thought. Beneath, immediately beneath, flowed the waters, as ever.

While Prajāpati's back lay glued to the earth, time stretched out within him. One by one, his joints were coated, inside and out, by a corrosive patina: past and future.

In his solitude, Prajāpati, the Progenitor, thought: "How can I reproduce?" He concentrated inside, and a warmth radiated from within. Then he opened his mouth. Out came Agni, Fire, the devourer. Prajāpati looked. With his open mouth he had created, and now an open mouth was coming toward him. Could it really want to eat him, its own creator, so soon? He couldn't believe it. But now Prajāpati knew terror. He looked around. The earth was bare. Grasses, trees, they were only in his mind. "So who can it want to eat? There's no one but me," he repeated. Terror left him speechless. Then Prajāpati knew the first anguish and the first doubt. He must invent a food for the creature he had made if he wasn't to end up in Agni's mouth. Prajāpati rubbed his hands together to conjure up an offering. But all that appeared was some soggy stuff, matted with hairs. Agni wouldn't want that. He rubbed his hands together again—and out came a white, liquid substance. "Should I offer it? Or maybe not?" thought Prajāpati, paralyzed by terror. Then the wind rose and a light filled the sky. Agni devoured the offering and was gone.

Prajāpati sensed he had a companion, a "second" being, *dvitīya,* within him. It was a woman, Vāc, Word. He let her out. He looked at her. Vāc "rose like a continuous stream of water." She was a column of liquid, without beginning or end. Prajāpati united with her. He split her into three parts. Three sounds came out of his throat in his amorous thrust: *a, ka, ho. A* was the earth, *ka* the space between, *ho* the sky.

With those three syllables the discontinuous stormed into existence. From eight drops were born the Vasus, from eleven the Rudras, from twelve the Ādityas. The world, which didn't yet exist, was already full of gods. Thirty-one born from as many drops, then Sky and Earth: which made thirty-three. Plus there was *ka,* the space between, where Prajāpati was. Thirty-four. Silently, Vāc slipped back into Prajāpati, into the cavity that was ever her home.

When creating the gods, Prajāpati decided to issue them forth into this world because the worlds below, in the depths of the sky, were pitted and impracticable as a dense thicket. The earth had the advantage of being insignificant. Everything still to be built. There was a clearing—and the wind whistling through empty space.

But no sooner had they appeared than the gods were gone. To seek the sky? They took no notice of the Progenitor. They turned their backs on him at once. The earth was just a point of departure, beneath consideration, a desolate way station. Prajāpati was left behind, alone again, last not first. Something held him back, something still there waiting for him: Mṛtyu, Death. One of his own creatures.

In the dusty clearing, Prajāpati watched Death. Death watched Prajāpati, symmetrical, motionless as his adversary. Each was waiting for the right moment to overcome the other. Prajāpati practiced *tapas.* He generated heat within himself. Now and then, in that dark period of silent affliction, Prajāpati raised his arms. Upon which a globe of light would rise from his armpits and shoot off to bury itself in the vault of the sky. So the stars were born.

The first equivalences were the *sampads* that flashed across Prajāpati's mind as he was dueling with Death. A *sampad* is a "falling together," a chain of equivalences. How did they reveal themselves? Prajāpati was staring straight ahead, at Death. All around him, the world. The two combatants gazed at each other, studied each other. But didn't move. Each was surrounded by a supporting army. Wooden spoons, a wooden sword, sticks, bowls: such was Prajāpati's army. Frayed and frail. Around Death were a lute, an anklet, some powder puffs for making up.

How long would this tension last? As he waited, Prajāpati ran through everything that served as a frame to Death, a frame that amounts to everything that is. It was a long way to run. He penetrated the frame, in its scrolls and flourishes—and the density of decoration would sometimes hide Death from him. He thought: "This is like that, this corresponds to that, this is equivalent to that, this is that." A vibration, a tension, a euphoria flooded his mind. If this is that, then that corresponds to this other thing—he went on. Slender bonds wrapped themselves like ribbons around this and that. The bonds stretched, invisible to many, but not to the one who put them there. With a sentinel's eye, Prajāpati went on watching Death. But with the eye that wanders, that evokes images, numbers, and words, he went on getting things to "fall together," sometimes things that were far apart, getting them to coincide. And the further apart they were, the more exhilarated he felt. The existent world—prickly, numb, empty—let itself be covered, taken, gathered, enveloped, in the mesh of a fabric. Oh, still a loose mesh, for sure . . . Yet this made it all the more exciting, that the mesh was at once so loose and so fine, as though to avoid upsetting the blind breathing of the whole. But Death? Still crouched there, waiting. Prajāpati thought: "If he kills me, what will be left?" Until now, this thought had terrified him. Prajāpati knew that everything proceeded from himself. Imagining himself as not existing meant imagining all existence nonexistent. But now he looked around. Then he saw himself from without: an exhausted, weary, wrinkled old being. All about him, everything was still new, so that looking around he could now see how every dapple of vegetation, every outline of a rock, concealed a number, a word, an equivalence: a mental state that clung and mingled with another state. As if every state were a number. As if every number were a state. This was the first equivalence, origin of all others. Then Prajāpati thought: "If I were gone, perhaps these things would no longer fall together? Perhaps the *sampads* would dissolve? But how could Death hurt the equivalences? How could she strike them?" Where was their body, for her to wound? They occupied no space, they couldn't be touched. They surfaced in the mind, but where from? As he thought all this, Prajāpati felt a fever, release. He thought: "If the *sampads* elude me, who am myself thinking them, they will be all the more elusive for Death, who knows nothing of them. Death can kill me, but she cannot kill the equivalences." He wasn't aware that a clear, dry voice was issuing from his mouth. He was speaking to Death, after their long silence. Prajāpati said: "I've beaten you. Go ahead and kill me. Whether I am alive or not, the equivalences shall be forever."

In the end, Mṛtyu withdrew to the women's hut at the western edge of the sacrificial clearing. He was beaten, humiliated, but not entirely undone. Prajāpati stared out at the empty arena, the clumps of shriveled grass around the edges. He knew now that this solitude, every solitude, is illusory, is inhabited. There is always an intruder—a guest?—hiding in the women's hut.

The brahmans of the Vedic period followed the example of Prajāpati, who had dueled long with Death, vying with him in sacrifices—Prajāpati, who had been about to give up the game for lost, exhausted, inadequate, when the *sampads* flashed across his mind, numerical equivalence, geometry stamped on light, and then he saw how the vast dispersion of all that lived, but above all that died, could be articulated in relationships that did not deteriorate. What the mind sees, when it grasps a connection, it sees forever. The mind may perish, together with the body that sustains it, but the relationship remains, and is indelible. By creating an edifice of such connections, the brahmans imagined, as their forefather Prajāpati once had, that they had beaten Death. They persuaded themselves that evil was inexactitude. And thus died the more serene.

To bring forth "this," *idam*, was a long torment for Prajāpati. And likewise to have it become "all this," *idaṃ sarvam*, including the flies and the gadflies for which he was later reproached. Little by little he was overcome by a tremendous lassitude. A being would appear, and immediately some joint of his would come loose. The lymph shrank in his body like water in a puddle under a scorching sun. As his joints were coming apart, came apart, one after another, he gazed at bits of himself, spread out on the grass, like alien and incongruous objects. Suddenly he realized that all that was left of him was his heart. Beating, begrimed. As he struggled to see himself in that scrap of flesh, he realized he no longer recognized himself. He shrieked like a lunatic: "Self! Self, *ātman*!" Impassive, the waters heard him. Slowly they turned toward Prajāpati, as though to some relative fallen upon hard times. They gave him back his torso, so that it might once again protect his heart. Then they offered up a sacrificial ceremony to him, the *agnihotra*. It might turn out useful, someday, they said—if Prajāpati should ever wish to reassemble himself in his entirety.

As his children were hurrying away, Prajāpati had glimpsed a head of tawny, waving hair, a white shoulder, a shape that cast a spell. "Oh, if only she would come back . . . ," he thought. "I would like to join myself to her . . ." Everyone else had gone. Generating creatures seemed the most pointless of procedures. Before they appeared, he experienced a tension, a spasm within. But the creatures appeared only to disappear, in a cloud of dust. Then, in his loneliness, Prajāpati took a bowl and filled it with rice, barley, fruit, butter, honey. He looked like a beggar fussing with his few belongings. He offered his bowl to the void. "May that which is dear to me come back into me . . . ," he whispered. It was a windless night. Directly above the bowl he had placed on the ground trembled the light of Rohiṇī, the Tawny One, who ever so slightly shook her hair. One day they would call her Aldebaran.

One question tormented the Progenitor: Why were his children so irreverent, why had they fled from him? And the gods too, why did they pretend not to know him? There was no one to explain, everybody had gone. Prajāpati was left with the corrosive sensation—something that had always dogged him—of not really existing. He looked around in perplexity. All creatures were sure they existed except him, who had given them their existence. Without him, "this" would never have been, but now he felt superfluous in respect to the world, like milk spilled while being carried from one fire to another, milk that one then tosses away on an ants' nest. Scarcely had he given birth to the other beings when Prajāpati realized he wasn't needed.

The world was dense. Prajāpati empty, feverish. He lay on his back, unable to get up. Even his breathing grew heavier. He felt all the breaths that had animated him drift away and disappear. There were seven of them, and he bade farewell to each one, calling them by name. He felt he had "run the whole race." No one came near to moisten his lips. The gods left Prajāpati to die like an old man people have no more time for than a bundle of rags.

Of all Prajāpati's body, the only part left attached was the sacrificial stone. It alone stood upright amid the desolation. In the silence, the wind blew little eddies of sand off it. There was no end to them. That sand is what has been lost of Prajāpati, forever.

. . .

What did Prajāpati look like when he was torn apart at the joints and scattered throughout the world? To one side there was a cold, empty cooking pot.

That was Prajāpati.

When Prajāpati was exhausted, a white horse appeared, its muzzle bent to the ground. For a year it never lifted that muzzle. Slowly, from the horse's head, *aśva*, a fig tree grew, *aśvattha*. The white horse, the fig tree: Prajāpati.

The gods were too plainly present to understand their Father, Prajāpati. They existed—that was all. They told the truth. They weren't complicated enough. They didn't know the death that "doesn't die, for he is within the immortal." They didn't grasp the skein's loose end dangling from the *asat* (which, whatever it may be, is the negation of what is: *a-sat*). Prajāpati thought he would never speak to anyone now. But one day one of his sons, the most solitary and melancholy, eyes gray and distant, came to speak to the Father instead of running away from him. It was Varuṇa. He said: "Father, I want to be your pupil. I want sovereignty." At the time Prajāpati was a dry old man who talked to himself and to animals. He laughed when he heard the word "sovereignty." He said: "Son, you saw how much your brothers and sisters respected me. I was lucky they didn't trample all over me. I know only what is of no use to you people . . ." "The only thing I care about is what you know," said Varuṇa, undaunted. "Teach me for a hundred years." The years passed swiftly and were the happiest of times for Father and son. When Varuṇa went back to his brothers, they got up from their seats, baffled and afraid. "Don't be afraid, we are equals," said Varuṇa. "The sovereignty you see in me is in you too. The only difference is that you don't know it."

Prajāpati's numbers were thirteen, seventeen, thirty-four. Thirteen and seventeen were the numbers of surplus, that extra above a whole (twelve, sixteen) where Prajāpati found refuge. Everyone was careful to avoid them. Nobody wanted to meet him. Indeed, so determined were they not to that they forgot that they would meet him in those numbers. They avoided them and ignored him without even asking themselves why. But what of thirty-four? There were thirty-three gods. Prajāpati came before the gods and after the gods. In front of them and behind them. Always a little to one side. He was the shadow that precedes the body. The gods were born of him, but they didn't want to remember that "all the gods are behind Prajāpati." Transported by sacrifice, intoxicated, the gods conquered the sky, as if it had always been theirs. They didn't deign so much as a glance at the earth, where Prajāpati was left behind, a herdsman abandoned by his herd.

Unlike the gods, who have a shape and a story, or even many shapes and many stories, who overlap perhaps, perhaps merge together, or swap over, but always with names and shapes—unlike the gods, Prajāpati never lost his link with the nameless and shapeless, with that which has no identity. They didn't know what to call him, apart from Lord of the Creatures, Prajāpati—and even that was too definite. Behind that, his secret name was Ka—Who?—and that was how he was invoked. Prajāpati was to the gods as the K. of Kafka's *The Trial* and *The Castle* is to the characters of Tolstoy or Balzac. His stories were always the stories of a stranger, unknown to gods and men, the origin of gods and men.

No one was more uncertain about his own identity than Prajāpati. He who gave names to others found his own name undermined by the interrogative and indefinite: Ka. *Anirukta, aparimita, atirikta:* "inexpressible," "boundless," "overflowing": that was what they called him. Even those who knew him best never saw his extremities, which ever receded—and were finally lost in infinity. Perhaps that was another reason why none of his children thought of making a portrait of their Father. When they celebrated or invoked him, the only sound was an indistinct murmuring. Otherwise they worshiped him in silence. They said the silence belonged to Prajāpati.

Prajāpati was mind as power to transform. And to transform itself. Nothing else can so precisely be described as overflowing, boundless, inexpressible. Everything that exists had been in Prajāpati first. Everything remained attached to him. But it was an attachment that might well go unnoticed. Where was it? In the mind, buried in our being like a splinter no one can dislodge.

Although Prajāpati liked to tell himself that the gods had deserted him at once, without any consideration for their Father, there had been a moment when some of them asked him the question he least wanted to hear: "When you created us, why did you create Death immediately afterward?" On that occasion Prajāpati answered by going straight into detail and avoiding the crux of the question: "Compose the meters and wrap yourselves in them. That way you'll be rid of the evil of Death." Then he explained how the best meter for the Vasus was the *gāyatrī* and the best for the Rudras the *triṣṭubh.* These gods immediately composed the appropriate meters and wrapped themselves in them. Then the Adityas started up with the *jagatī* meter. By now they were all busy earnestly talking about problems of meter. As if the whole world were a question of alternating meters. The meters were like sumptuous garments. By wearing them, placing one over another, the shape of the body was hidden. Thus they believed they could hide their bodies from Death. Suddenly, they had the intoxicating sensation that they were sufficient unto themselves. Even their harrowed, mysterious Father ceased to be of interest. They didn't remember that Prajāpati hadn't answered their question, "Why?" And in the end even Prajāpati himself felt that he had answered the question—that he had offered the most effective help. But they deserted him all the same. Meanwhile Death could still see their bodies, as though they were immersed in transparent liquid.

Prajāpati's children thought about the Father. They hadn't wanted to know him. Now they felt his absence. His legacy to them was everything there was, but a fragmented, elusive everything. Only Death, who was part of that legacy, was everywhere. He dwelled in every moment of the year, a flood that swept over them. They tried rites, they tried the *agnihotra,* they tried sacrifices to the new moon and the full moon, offerings to the seasons, animal sacrifices, *soma.* They measured their gestures, their words. But to no end. Then they remembered how Prajāpati, the death rattle in his throat, had called upon Agni, the firstborn. The two had whispered a few words to each other, but no one had heard. Thoroughly ashamed of themselves, and taking Agni as a go-between, they went down to talk to Prajāpati.

Unrecognizable now, overgrown with vegetation, the Father said: "You do not know how to recompose me in all my forms. You go to excess or you fall short. As a result you will never be immortal." He fell silent, while the gods were overcome by despair. Then Prajāpati spoke again, with the calm, sober voice of a learned master builder. "Take three hundred and sixty border stones and ten thousand, eight hundred bricks, as many as there are hours in a year. Each brick shall have a name. Place them in five layers. Add more bricks to a total of eleven thousand, five hundred and fifty-six . . ." That day Prajāpati announced how the altar of fire was to be built.

Prajāpati's children, gods first, then men, realized that day that, in order to live, one must first of all recompose the

Father and recompose oneself, rebuild one's own body and one's own mind piece by piece. For if Prajāpati had been scattered and spread across the entire world, how could they—the dust of his bones—claim not to be scattered and spread? Only by patiently sewing, weaving, and tying things together could they expect to acquire a mind—hence a power of attention, rather than a blind vortex—and a body, rather than just limbs bereft of their lymph. This preparatory task would be *the task.* It would take time, it would take all time. Every one of the three hundred and sixty days of the year. Every one of the ten thousand, eight hundred hours of the year (if by "hour" we mean a *muhūrta,* which lasts forty-eight minutes). And then? Preparing life took up every hour life offered. When the time was up, the task began again. An empty clearing, a stick scratching marks in the earth.

This was what they must do: build a huge bird—a bird of prey: an eagle, a hawk—of bricks. How else could they conquer the sky? And here a false etymology, ever friend to thought, came to their aid. *Brick,* they said: *citi.* Bricks in layers. But what is *citi?* It's *cit,* which means "to think intensely." Every brick, baked and squared, was a thought. Its consistence was the consistency of their attention. Every thought had the outline of a brick. It wouldn't disappear, wouldn't let itself be swallowed up in the mind's vortex. Rather it became something you could lean on. Something you could place a next thought on—and slowly, crisscrossed with joints, a wall was raised. That was the mind, that was the body: the one and the other rebuilt, with wings outspread.

This is what they thought:

"True, we live in a blurred and disjointed state. True, what happens inside these boxes of bone that are our heads leaves no trace on the hard, rough material in which we move. And it's also true that unreality cloaks both ourselves and the things we touch, as if this were the normal state of being. But when we wander about this torpid plain, we do find, here and there, certain places that vibrate like nerves, certain sounds that peal with clarity, almost as though they meant something, and sometimes an emotion will flood through us, as though we had recognized something. Why so? We live in the broken body of Prajāpati, but we will always be tiny ourselves: only an immensely long voyage, if ever we could undertake such a thing, would allow us to glimpse the white cliff that is the further shore of a broken joint. If life is thus, must we then resign ourselves to this opacity, pierced through though it may sometimes be by the pinpoints of these vain reminders? We were warriors once, violent warriors. But no conquest ever helped us rend that blur. So one day we decided to concentrate all our fury in just one patient, grueling task. As long as time itself. Building the altar of fire.

"To arrange ten thousand, eight hundred bricks, one must start from the edge, from the frame of everything: of the world, of meanings. Start from the place where naturally we are. And the beginning will have something incongruous and obsessive about it: a few stones placed beside an empty clearing. But once formed, a frame evokes a center. And that was the fire of our minds: invisible right to the last step. It had to lie at the center of time, of the endless hours that surrounded it; at the center of the intense thought that made the bricks, that was those bricks laid one upon another. When they reached that point, touched that center, it would, as through a bundle of nerves, affect everything, as far as the furthest of the bricks, as far as the tip of the eagle's wing, as far as the most distant of days. That is what is meant by the altar of fire. But did this come to pass? We shall never be able to say. Why not? When we arrived at that point, time had run out, the year was gone. We would have to begin again, on another clearing, with other sticks, other bricks.

"Apart from the building of the altar of fire, no sacrifice will ever be enough to make us immortal, because each uses too many elements or too few. They don't have the right number. And the right number is the one that corresponds to the wholeness of time: ten thousand, eight hundred bricks, as many as there are hours in the year, which is Prajāpati.

"But what gives us this faith, *śraddhā*, in number and building? Seen from afar, we must look like bricklayers gone mad. From close up, we are a challenge to find a sense in what we do. There's a moment when we scatter sand on the altar. Why sand? 'It's the part of Prajāpati that was lost.' A vast and numberless part. Who could ever count it? When Prajāpati came to pieces, most of him was lost. And, 'Prajāpati is the whole *brahman*,' the texts tell us. That dust, sole inhabitant of the heavens, reminds us how much has been lost.

"We are devotees of the distinct and the articulate, but the infinite festers in our bones. We must circumscribe it, as our skin circumscribes a weave of stuff in which we might otherwise lose ourselves, and which includes, among other things, death herself. Yet this is the only way to live. We are not so ingenuous as to imagine that our building is sound. There is nothing more flimsy and fragile than sacrifice and the place of sacrifice. If it is to work, it must be wrapped in the cloud of the immeasurable and enclose the immeasurable within itself. The greatest must be contained and embraced in the smallest. Thus the sand. Thus the silence, which gives rhythm to the rites. Thus the murmuring that sometimes goes on behind. The sand, the silence, the murmuring: emissaries of the incommensurable. A gesture to that part of Prajāpati we can never reconstitute. Amorphous, inexhaustible."

In the beginning, Prajāpati didn't know who he was. Only when the gods issued from him, when they took on their qualities, their profiles, when Prajāpati himself had shared out their shapes, forgetting none, sovereignty and splendor included, only then did the question present itself. Indra had just killed Vṛtra. He was still shaken by the terror of it, but he knew he was sovereign of the gods. He came to Prajāpati and said: "Make me what you are, make me great." Prajāpati answered: "Then who, *ka*, am I?" "Exactly what you just said," said Indra. In that moment Prajāpati became Ka. In that moment he understood, understood it all. He would never know the joys of limitation, the repose in a straightforward name. Even when they had recomposed him, in the ten thousand, eight hundred bricks of the altar of fire, he would always be a shape shot through by the shapeless, if only in those porous stones, *svayamātṛṇṇa*, avid of emptiness, that were placed at the center of the altar and allowed it to breathe.

Home of the dark germination of all that is, Prajāpati could hardly have an identity comparable to those who issued from him. Yet, in time, he would take his place alongside them—a god like any other, to whom victims are sacrificed, oblations dedicated. Spared the burden of bringing it about, he observed life more calmly now. It relaxed him to mix with the other gods, to lose himself among them. He liked the lower ranks best. Life was a spectacle that no longer depended on him. He loved to watch it, but would still get pains in all his joints whenever he was grazed by the wing of a desire. Which was little more than a memory now. For even desire had migrated into innumerable others. So Prajāpati waited for the moment when he would be forgotten. It began imperceptibly: long liturgies, lists of gods, from which his name would suddenly be missing. Gestures forgotten. Offerings overlooked. Were they considered superfluous, perhaps, for a god so discreet as not to demand them? For a first, long moment, no one noticed, in the celestial crush, that Prajāpati was gone. Everything went on as it always had, no function faltered. For a long time nobody realized, until one evening, as the shadows drew in, someone began to tell the legend of the beginning. At which, once again, there emerged, if only in words, the image of an elusive, indistinct, faceless figure, who had no name, and whom they could only call Prajāpati, Progenitor.

III

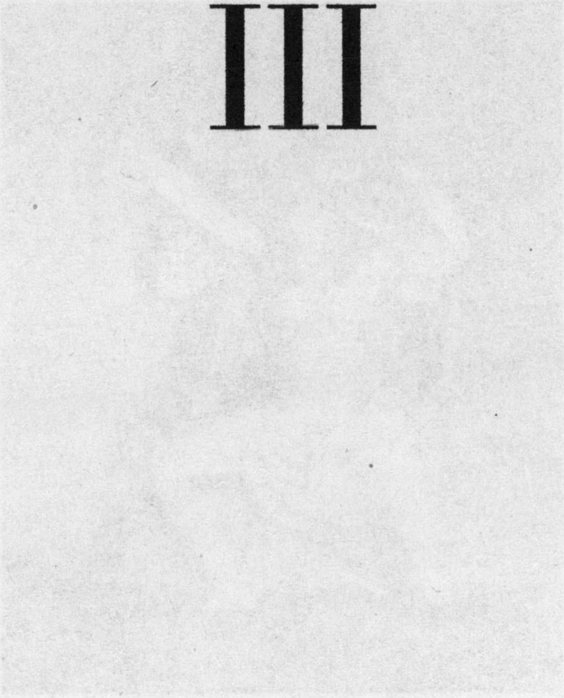

The Father saw the dawn. He saw the beauty of the Daughter rising. In the first cold light he was filled by a flame, to the tips of his fingernails. The flame beat there like a wave on rocks—then retreated. Now, in that leaden light, he wanted to go further. But was there a further? Had there ever been one? It was the body of Uṣas, Dawn, first white, now pink, that offered itself to the Father, as the light climbed upward.

The Father desired. This was no longer the heat he lived by, the furnace within that lit up the cavern of the mind. No, this heat was already darting out from his body, licking along Uṣas's soft skin. The Father got closer and closer to the Daughter, in silence. But why did Uṣas suddenly have the hide of an antelope? The Father was aware of raising antelope's hooves toward her, to caress her. A stronger light mingled with the radiance of the dawn, a light that emanated from the Father, but dazzled him too. He wasn't sure whether he was embracing Uṣas's breasts or the soft fur of an antelope. Prajāpati wrapped himself right around the Daughter, penetrated her, just as she hitherto had nestled in him. For the first time the Father's phallus opened a path into the darkness of Dawn. Neither spoke. Dawn and heat were superimposed, one on the other, coinciding, as if inside and outside were the same cloth, faintly stirred by the wind. Around them there had never been anything distinct, only now did it seem that an outline began to form. The heat grew, almost to incandescence. All that could be sensed was the breathing of Prajāpati and

Uṣas, the almost imperceptible movement of their bodies glued together.

Slowly a dark figure detached itself from the shadow, an archer. His was the first profile, of a darkness that a blade of light was carving out of darkness. He bent his bow. The more he bent it, the more the twined bodies were flooded with incandescence. Rudra yelled as he let fly his arrow. Like a flash Prajāpati withdrew from Uṣas. The arrow pierced his groin, opening a wound no bigger than a grain of barley, while his phallus squirted its seed onto the ground. Prajāpati's mouth foamed with anger and pain. On her back, almost imperceptibly, the abandoned Uṣas trembled.

Such was the scene that lies behind all other scenes, the scene every other scene repeats, alters, distorts, breaks up, reconstructs, for it is from this dawn scene that the world descends. Were there witnesses? All around was nothing but emptiness—and a gust of wind. Yet there were those who saw, silent and greedy-eyed: thirty-three (or three hundred and thirty-nine? or three thousand, three hundred and thirty-nine?) gods crowded the balconies of the sky. They exchanged glances, annoyed. They said: "Prajāpati is doing something that's never been done before." They looked around for someone able to punish him. None of the gods had the power to strike Prajāpati. They exchanged glances again, conspiracy in their eyes, all thinking the same name, never pronounced: Rudra.

The gods harbored an ancient rancor toward Prajāpati. They didn't understand this solitary, suffering father whom they were constantly obliged to heal through sacrifice. Above all they couldn't forgive him for having generated Death. For though the gods were the first to gain the sky and had fed ever since on *amṛta*, the liquid that is the "immortal," they knew that one day, however immensely far off, Death would catch up with them. They were terrified of blinking their eyelids, because they knew that anything that blinks dies. With staring eyes, they watched the hard stones of their palaces, waiting for a veil of dust to settle there, harbinger of earth and death.

When they saw how Prajāpati was gazing at Uṣas and how Uṣas was responding to that gaze, coating herself in a rosy moistness, the gods were appalled. Not because Uṣas was his daughter. All women were his daughters. But because Prajāpati was the other world. He could generate, but that was all. To touch one of his own creatures, to penetrate her: that would throw every order out of order, would negate the whole world order, of which the gods considered themselves the guardians, even in opposition to their Father.

The first thing the gods thought of was to terrify the Father. They wanted to stop him from touching the Daughter at all costs. Like shrewd surgeons they extracted the most ghastly shapes from inside themselves. Then they put them together to make Rudra. This way the Father would be forced to confront the dreadful side of existence. Infatuation wasn't everything. Prajāpati couldn't just abandon himself to that illusion, after having generated them together with Death. Rudra's sharp cry rang out. That sound that pierces all others. "You'll remember this, Father," the gods thought, pleased with their revenge.

The obscure Rudra, still lurking in that undifferentiated fullness that precedes all creation, in that state of being at once implicit and closed in upon himself, agreed to split into a double that turned to face an external progenitor, indeed his own eventual progenitor, Prajāpati. And Prajāpati opened his eyes on the indistinct, recognizing it as his own kin, the substance whence something would detach itself to exist separately. He felt his own daughter Uṣas issue forth from him, spreading first light across tremendous expanse. Then Prajāpati discovered the unprecedented pleasure of one who looks at something he does not possess. For the daughter now stretched out across all that was shapeless, was certainly not the same daughter who had dwelled within him. She was a stranger, the first foreigner. Prajāpati burned. From the tips of his toes to the hair on his head, something was rising within him, transforming and baking him, bringing his body to a state of readiness, as though for something other. Suddenly he realized that this fire was flickering out of him, toward the Daughter.

As Prajāpati moved his antelope hooves (and he hadn't even noticed the metamorphosis) toward Uṣas, fullness became aware of a breach being opened within, of an airy space, a void between the Father's body and the Daughter's. In that same void quivered Rudra's arrow, the arrow the Archer was, shortly afterward, to let fly at Prajāpati. Shortly afterward: that delay, that interval, was time, all time, all the time there would ever be, all of history, all the stories that would invisibly cloak all existence. It was the precondition of every claim to existence. That arrow reasserted, even as it punished, the breach that had been opened in fullness. It transformed the void, once and for all, into a wound.

Prajāpati's impulsive gesture, when he turned toward a still unfinished world, was a desire and a letting fly, a hiss. *Visṛj-, sṛj-:* those are its verbs. In *sṛj-* there was the letting fly, the spurting forth; in *vi-* the pervasive spreading out, in all directions. When Rudra let fly his arrow at Prajāpati, who spurted his seed toward Uṣas, this first of all actions likewise split apart. Even in the instant itself, even in that first instant, nothing would ever be *one alone.* As Prajāpati spread his seed in the void, the arrow opened a wound in his groin, a rift that looked forward to all other rifts. Through that metallic point, the barely created world penetrated the one who had created it. It turned against the

Father, injected its poison into him. To the fullness that turned impulsively outward corresponded a tiny void that was forming within that fullness.

Time entered upon the scene between the surfacing of intention and the act that followed it. As long as there is only mind, intention is action. But, as soon as there is something outside mind, Time slips in between intention and act. And then one escapes forever from the mental universe through a breach that is still open, like an open wound, in Prajāpati's groin.

Why did anything happen? Rudra, the obscure Archer, was guardian of the fullness that lacks nothing. But the fullness burned. And burning, it conceived the excitement of there being something it did lack, something on which to throw itself. Burning can easily generate hallucination. One begins to think that all does not lie within one's own fire, but that something exists outside, that an outside exists somewhere over there. A white substance, the best to burn. One day they would call it *soma.* And that becomes the object of desire, that cold, external, intoxicating being whom the fire has yet to scorch.

Fullness had to be wounded, a breach of dispossession opened. Later that breach would be encircled, closed, albeit slowly, by the same power that had produced it, the same power from which it was born—Time, he who demanded but a single idol for his celebration: the arrow. In the compact surface of existence, that breach, that void, amounted to no more than a tiny crack, no broader than a grain of barley, like the wound that Rudra's arrow opened in Prajāpati's groin and that was never to close. But the idea that in some future time that tattered edge of bleeding flesh might close was enough to suggest the possibility of a higher level of fullness, something in respect to which the fullness of the beginning seemed crude and stifled. It didn't matter whether that further fullness turned out to be—as indeed it would—unattainable. Its flickering image blotted out any desire to return to the earlier fullness.

When the *ātman*, the Self that observes the I, decided to create something distinct, a nature that would obey nature, it stretched a veil of opacity across the world. This was to be the great secret, the ultimate gamble, the novelty that would forever prevail, that the world should not communicate with the mind from which it had issued. But whether out of antique intimacy or mere amazement at the sight of that alien and, at last, unknown being, before abandoning it to its own devices, the mind went after the world, as if still in a position to caress it. Such was the incest of Prajāpati and Uṣas.

The Father lay on his back, dying. He was no longer an antelope now. He was a man again. A trickle of blood striped one thigh. The obscure Archer watched him. "Give me a name," he said. "You are Bhava, Existence," said Prajāpati, the rattle at his throat. "It's not enough," said Śarva, the Archer, "give me another name." "You are Sarva, Everything," croaked Prajāpati. The Archer demanded other names. One by one they issued in sobs from Prajāpati's mouth, which was foaming blood. "You are Pásupati, you are Ugradeva, you are Mahādeva, you are Vāstoṣpati, you are Īśāna, you are Aśani." "It's not enough," said Rudra. "You are Kumāra, Boy," was Prajāpati's last rattle. Rudra said nothing, leaning on his bow. "For every name you give me, a scale of evil falls from me," he said in a whisper. So far Prajāpati had been stunned by the Archer's ferocity. Like an evil hunter, he had shot him at the moment of utmost pleasure, utmost vulnerability. Now he was watching him die and tormenting him, insisting that the dying Father reward him with solemn names. But when Prajāpati heard him speak of this evil, he was startled: he recognized himself in the Archer. Only Prajāpati had had evil beside him like a brother, including the Evil of Death, from as far back as he could remember. What did the other gods know of that? So then Prajāpati gave up the fight, ready for the end. He could hear a confused buzzing, a chattering that came and went in waves. Half-opening his eyes, clouded with pain, he saw a number of figures busying themselves around him. They were the gods. Stooped and servile, those who had incited Rudra to wound him were examining his wound with fervor and apprehension. Their anger had been swiftly replaced by devotion. They were trying to decide how best to pull out the three-notched arrow buried in his groin. The rattle still in his throat, Prajāpati smiled to himself in contempt. "They're afraid I'll die," he thought. "They'll always be afraid I'll die, and they'll always be trying to kill me." He strained to look beyond them. Running over the ground and down to a hollow, Prajāpati's seed had formed a pond. And now that pond was surrounded by a circular wall of fire. "Other gods are about to appear . . . ," thought Prajāpati. So it was. Then the flames fell. Only here and there a few embers glowed. Prajāpati looked at them, far away, with affection: "You are the band of beautiful singers, you are the Aṅgiras . . . ," he murmured, as deft fingers slid over his belly, then the chill of a blade. They didn't pull out the arrow. They sliced into the flesh and cut away a tiny scrap, along with the metallic point.

•

"Wherever life is felt more acutely, that is Rudra," said a western dancer. The gods thought so too, and were afraid of Rudra. They would see him arrive, suddenly, from the north, a shadowy figure, cloaked in dark gowns, glowing embers in his eyes. Shrewd and smooth-tongued, they praised him, and kept out of his way. The important thing was never to use his name. When pressed, they used the adjective "rudric" rather than the name. They never invited him to their sacrifices. (And what else was life?) They were afraid something irreparable might happen in his presence, afraid the fire might flare up and engulf them all. The gods knew the risks of intensity, because they were intensity itself. They shrank from anything that might shake the world's cage too fiercely. Even the seers were startled when Rudra appeared, for his mere presence aroused the gravest of suspicions, a fear that had dogged them from the beginning: that sacrifice might not be enough, that it might not be able to draw the whole of reality into itself. At the same time, they called Rudra "King of the Sacrifice." Why? Again suspicion was at work. Perhaps, outside their rites, their meters, their calendar of ceremonies, another sacrifice was going on, silently, constantly, in the veins of all that is, in the name of Rudra. But how to distinguish such a thing from profusion and massacre?

They were always speaking of the dawn, as if they had never seen anything else. Though in India dawns are brief. The difference between the shortest and longest days is hardly considerable: just four hours. Were they remembering the dawns of another country, a northern homeland, whence they had once descended? Uṣas is everywhere in the Ṛg Veda. Her name occurs three hundred times. There are twenty hymns in her praise. Some say they are among the oldest. Some say they are among the finest. Nor did they fulfill the function of forming the accompaniment to an offering, since no material oblations were made to Uṣas. The poetic word wrapped around her as though around itself. And no offering to any god could serve its purpose unless Uṣas was witness to it. Recipient of words alone, Uṣas was the precondition of every offering: that flaring up of consciousness that occurs when Uṣas steps forward, uncovering herself.

"True with the true, great with the great, goddess with goddesses, venerable with the venerable," she would appear from afar, head high, "bright beacon of the immortal," dripping moisture, on a chariot drawn by pink horses, laden with ritual offerings. Always powdered with the same makeup, "like women on their way to an assignation," she bathed standing up, the better to be seen, white, gleaming, born from black, buzzing around men like a fly. Why? To awaken them. Awakening: this was the "fine virtue" of Uṣas, her impalpable gift, as the gifts she received were likewise impalpable: mere words arranged in meters. Never the slaughtered animal, never the libation. Just words.

Uṣas has a prefix peculiar to herself: *prati-*, which is a "coming to meet" someone, a stepping forward, face-to-face, from the furthest distances. The hymn singers never wearied of praising Uṣas's breasts. "Young and brazen, forward she comes": thus Uṣas appears. And what is her first gesture? "She bares her breasts, like a loose woman." Or, with an observation that was also an invitation, they remarked: "Girl full of smiles, bare your breasts when you shine in the east"; "You bare your breasts to make yourself beautiful." If Uṣas was slow to make the gesture, the singers were quick as chroniclers to remind: "Going to meet men, like a beautiful young woman, she pops out her breasts."

Awakening is a vision that comes forward. It is the first image that adheres to the mind, flood tide of fullness, of a taste hitherto unknown. It is Uṣas who welcomes the *pūrváhūti,* the "first ritual call," which is also the "first thought," *pūrvácitti.* There's a race to be the first one to think of her. And to receive grace is to be the first one she thinks of. Here the goddess is subject and object, coupling without end. Since she is the first, Uṣas is the unique, she from whom all others issue, to whom they return, but she is also—immediately—multiple, surrounded by emulators and look-alikes. She appears "from day to day bearing her many names." There is no Uṣas without *uṣásaḥ,* countless "Dawns bearing happy names," which echo her, disperse her, until you ask: Which one is Uṣas?

. . .

Thirteen times the Ṛg Veda speaks of a goddess who is *svásṛ*, "sister." Eleven of those times it means Uṣas. Intimate with everyone, no other divinity could boast such an abundance of kinfolk. She was reputed to have many lovers, and often enough they were her brothers—Agni? Pūṣan? Sūrya? the Aśvin twins? She was the only goddess of whom such stories were told. One day the young Śunaḥśepa found himself tied to a sacrificial stake. His father had sold him for a hundred cows so that he could be sacrificed instead of someone else. The appointed time drew near. Then the Aśvin twins suggested he invoke Uṣas. Śunaḥśepa remembered a hymn that had been dear to him, that he had sung many times, thinking of Uṣas, of the lover he had always desired, never believing she would be his. Śunaḥśepa said: "What mortal can presume to possess you, immortal Uṣas, you who love as you will? Who will you choose from among us, o radiant one?" He went on invoking her. Verse after verse, the cords that bound him came undone.

Uṣas and Sandhyā, the two fatal maidens, were Dawn and Dusk. Why was their beauty thought to be superior to any other that would ever be? Those two moments, the unfettering and the fading of the light, this entry into the manifest and retreat from it, were articulation itself, were "connection," *bandhu*. But not the usual connection, between two similar and manifest beings, or between two equally visible shapes. Here what emerged was the connection between the manifest and the unmanifest, between two worlds that might have remained forever separate—but which now came together, surfaced together in the bodies of those two girls who look back and flee. This connection tended to become something else too: a coupling. Everybody wanted to couple with Uṣas, with Sandhyā, because coupling is the image of connection: not the other way around. Uṣas and Sandhyā were the image of supreme connection. The first particle of the invisible that penetrated them was time.

. . .

Every morning, at first light, they evoked Uṣas, strung together her sixteen epithets, sang in many meters of her gifts, of the endless extravagance they expected from her, a punctual prodigality. These words were to waken her, so that Uṣas might waken them. Each act could find a meaning only if preceded by that other act, awakening, which anchors the mind to what is, existence. But beneath the surface they harbored a dark and growing rancor toward that girl with the copper hair, who brushed against them only to desert them. At every blinking of an eyelid they remembered that Uṣas mocked them as she played, that she always won, then ran off with the prize, with life. Or they thought of her as Varuṇa's spy, doing his job for him, since everybody knows that for Varuṇa "the blinkings of a man's eyelids are numbered." To awaken means to blink one's eyelids. But the gods do not blink. That was all it took to seal the fate of men who do not want to die. One day someone would avenge them of the wrong done by the fatal maiden with the copper hair. It happened once—and never ceased to happen, right up to Gilda and beyond.

Indra knew the hiding place where the Cows, the Dawns, the Waters, lay concealed. He crouched down in deep dark, waiting to pounce. The dazzling lights of Uṣas's chariot had barely taken shape when he attacked. He waved a lethal weapon, quite out of proportion with his adversary, that nimble, ivoried chariot, counterpoint to its rider's ornaments. And Uṣas was already fleeing, hitting high notes of terror. Was it a comedy? Was it a play? Grimly, Indra unleashed his rage on the empty chariot. He split through yoke and shaft. He was like a crazed warrior, tormented by some pain no one understood. And awkward too, in the fury of blows he rained down on that sumptuous and delicate object.

It wasn't a sight to be proud of, Uṣas's flight, as trembling and terrified she stumbled over her embroidered robes while Indra's lightning split her chariot. And the rabble of men whose bigoted blah-blah had egged Indra on looked at once laughable and dire. Thus was established the model of all moral zeal. Later to receive its official seal in Upper Iran, cradle of the Āryas, in the place and in the language, Avestic, where for the first time they sought to split the cosmos in two, dividing it up into Good Creation and Bad Creation. Upon which the beautiful and heedless Uṣas was transformed into an evil demon they called Bušyanstā, she who says to men: "Not yet, not yet." For centuries afterward poet upon poet would evoke the "rosy-fingered" Dawn. They forgot that the girl had suffered persecution at the hands of gods and men. She was the first to meet that fate henceforth reserved for beautiful women: beatings and banishment.

"Indra's quarrel with Uṣas. A strange myth. No motive is ever suggested," remarks a puzzled Geldner in a note on the only Vedic hymn in which Indra's attack on Uṣas's chariot is briefly described. "A mythical element which only appears outside of the hymns to Uṣas, and always abruptly, unexpectedly, like an erratic block, such is the image of Indra splitting Uṣas's chariot," remarks a puzzled Renou. Why on earth should Indra, the liberator, attack Uṣas, whom he had liberated? What respect did he hope to gain among men with that cowardly, incongruous deed? There was a dark story, behind it all, which no one has told. Dark as Dawn. "Which is the dark face of Dawn?" asked Ānanda K. Coomaraswamy, in the manner of the *ṛṣis.* And the answer could hardly be other than dark, imperceptible as the blinking of an eyelid.

Bespattered with the blood and seed of the Father, no sooner was she separated from him than Uṣas fled south, "like an outcast." As she ran she sobbed: "All my seductions have come to naught." Words no one paid any attention to. The eyes of the gods were fixed on the Archer and the dying Father, who were about to speak to each other. At this point Uṣas was no longer the Dawn of exalted hymns, resounding each morning in the mouths of men who, freshly awakened, called on Uṣas to waken them. She was just an antelope running off into the woods, waiting for the hunter who would shoot her down.

The antelope was the first being to be wounded, when Rudra's arrow buried itself in Prajāpati's groin. So it was also the first being to be hunted and sacrificed. There was a knowledge of the gods—and a knowledge of the sacrificers. A knowledge of the Archer and a knowledge of the witnesses. The wheel of time would go on turning to the point where the last, and hitherto mute, knowledge would speak: that of the victim. The target stood erect, alone. The Bodhisattva was the victim who freed himself from the sacrificial stake. Where did he run to? Toward the awakening. That was the target that spills blood no more. That was the goal of Siddhārtha, "He who has reached the goal."

"Where the black antelope ranges by nature, that should be known as the country fit for sacrifices; and beyond it is the country of the barbarians," say the Laws of Manu. Antelope: the prey par excellence, of hunter and predator. At a certain point in their history, it occurred to men that they might climb up a level, might increase their powers, if they were to imitate those they had always fled from: the predators. Thus, having long thought of themselves as antelopes, men began to kill antelopes, to hunt them. The antelope was the first being in whose regard they felt guilty: killing the antelope, they were killing themselves, as once they had been. The whole forbidding structure of Vedic sacrifice is founded on the recognition of that guilt and it is dedicated as much to the antelope as to the gods. They thought of the antelope as an animal that could not be sacrificed, yet sacrifice had meaning only in relation to the antelope. Unless the skin of a black antelope was laid out on the ground, there could be no sacrifice. The sacrifice rested on that skin, on the side of the fur: the black hairs were the Vedic meters. And those undergoing initiation, the *dīkṣitas,* would gird their loins with a black antelope skin, as if at every moment to recall, indeed to absorb through their pores, something of the substance of that being whose wanderings and flight marked out the borders of the territory where sacrifice took place—civilization—beyond which lay an unknown land, merely wild, that hemmed it in on every side.

One day Uṣas became the Buddha. The powers of the world—the desire and the wound—come to a stop there where all that is left of the antelope is a hoofprint. The Buddha remembered as much when he came to Sārnāth, drawn by an episode from one of his earlier lives. The king of Vārāṇasī hunted a great many antelopes in his park. Many died in ditches where the vultures and jackals devoured them. The king of the stags made a pact with the king of Vārāṇasī. Every day he would hand over one antelope, who would be chosen by drawing lots. One day the lot fell on a pregnant antelope. No one was willing to take her place. Then the Bodhisattva, who was an antelope, offered to take her place and went to show himself to the cooks. The knife fell from the cook's hand. On seeing what had happened, the king of Vārāṇasī granted all the antelopes their freedom. Instead of being called Antelope Park, his park became Grace-Done-to-Antelopes.

If the Buddha is he who leads toward awakening, his Vedic precursor was the young woman who comes forward, "like a girl without a brother who walks toward the men," visible from afar: Uṣas, sovereign of awakening. Before it became a noun, *bodhi,* the "awakening," which was Buddha's revelation—and which the fainthearted translate as "illumination"—was actually an imperative—"Awaken!"—issued from the lips of Uṣas. But there was a duplicity about Uṣas that enchanted men and distressed them. The Buddha wanted to put an end to it. And this, not the awakening, was the novelty of his doctrine. "Awakening," the word that describes the act that is peculiar to Uṣas, can be said in two ways, which alternate constantly in the hymns addressed to her: *bodháyantī, jaráyantī.* But a second meaning lurks in *jaráyantī:* "making one grow old." With awakening, with that which brings things into existence, comes time, which makes them disappear. What brings to existence and what causes to disappear, the two impalpable powers, which precede all others, to which all others return, appeared together, every morning, in the form of the one who is "the most beautiful of all," and behind whom one might glimpse a never-ending procession of copies, all equally beautiful. And, alongside, countless faces watching them: the dead, the unborn. "The mortals who saw the first Dawn shine forth have departed. Now she lets us gaze upon her. And behold the approach of those who shall see her in times to come."

Horror-struck, Uṣas fled south—and no one paid any attention. She was an antelope hurrying back to hide in the forest. But she knew that the forest was still part of the scene. As she ran, a gesture of defiance began to take shape within. To exit from the scene. To find a place where Prajāpati's embrace and Rudra's arrow could never reach her. But how was such a thing conceivable? No one saw Uṣas when, on reaching the horizon, she pressed on into the sky. For a long time she kept on running across dark plains. Occasionally she recognized rivers and animals to each side. She passed the Kṛttikās, the wet and glistening Pleiades. But already she knew where she was going to stop: further on, in the light of Aldebaran, of Rohiṇī, she too an antelope, she too a dawn. Copper-Hair returned to Copper-Hair.

There are only so many gestures one can make, but meanings are innumerable. So the same stories are repeated, with variations, so that each time we may discover, in one slow rotation, a new earth and a new sky of meanings. And it was precisely there, in the sky, that that rotation was first observed. There was a time when Orion had risen in the dawning of the spring equinox, beginning of every beginning, first moment of time. It shone brightly and soon disappeared, swamped by the sunlight. But the seers saw how through the centuries Orion was slowly moving—and how Aldebaran was approaching the place where it had been. They recognized the precession of the equinoxes long before Hipparchus gave it its name and consigned it to science. And they found all the actors in the drama up there. They saw the precession of crimes in the sky. In the beginning the guilt lay with Prajāpati, who was Orion, whom they called the Antelope, Mṛga. In the end, as the equinoctial point shifted, it was in the hunter himself, the Archer, Rudra, who was Sirius. But now the arrow was loosed not by a god, in perfect wakefulness, but by a man, Pāṇḍu, a hunter king who mistakenly, carelessly, shot two antelopes, one a brahman, the other his spouse, as they coupled.

There is a strip of sky that is the Place of the Hunter. It lies between Sirius and the Pleiades, Betelgeuse and Aldebaran. In the middle shines Orion. It is that area of the heavens between Gemini and Taurus, on the edge of the Milky Way. From places as far away as Greece and Guyana, people have looked up and seen it as the scene of a hunt, the trail of a desperate chase. Here and there, to the sides of the trail, you could see bright bones and shreds of flesh. And an antelope or a girl in flight. Or a huge man, shot through by a young huntress: Artemis. The arrow was always loosed from the point where Sirius shines, always buried itself in Orion: another great hunter, shot by mistake, or inscrutable calculation.

Aldebaran, Betelgeuse: between these enchanting names lies the Place of the Hunter. A bloody, feverish story has embedded itself in the sky. It reminds us that it will go on happening forever. But at its edges we find these names, which dissolve in the mind and dissolve the mind. They are the fragrance of sound. If every word conceals the killer of the thing, still without redress since time immemorial, these names emanate a substance that is soft and bright, a substance we would seek in vain among the things that are. Perhaps it is here that a hint of redress may be found.

When Uṣas took her place in the sky, when her moist body was stretched over Rohiṇī's, the primordial scene once again found its home, there where it had all happened, motionless on the backdrop of the night. Beyond, blazed the awesome light of Orion. Uṣas immediately recognized it as Prajāpati's head. Below flashed the three-notched arrow, buried in the three stars of Orion's girdle. And still further away was a light that wounded, the light of Sirius, the Archer. Once again they formed the triangle of desire and punishment.

IV

It takes millions of years for the gods to pass from one aeon to the next. A few centuries for mankind. The gods change their names and do the same things as before, with subtle variations. So subtle as to look like pure repetition. Or again: so subtle as to look like stories that have nothing to do with those that came before them. For men, what change are the names, and likewise the literary genres in which deed and variation are accomplished. Thus Prajāpati became Brahmā. Thus Rudra became Śiva. Thus, from the allusive cipher of the Ṛg Veda and the abrupt, broken narratives of the Brāhmaṇas, stories picked up only to be hurriedly dropped, one passed to the ruthless redundance of the Purānas, their incessant dilution, their indulgence in hypnotic and hypertrophic detail. Narration once again became the receptacle of every form, every calculation, every duty. A huge and divine novel unfolded, slowly. And the demands on the listener changed too. There was a time when he'd been obliged to solve abrupt enigmas, or find his head bursting. Now he could heap up rewards merely by listening to the stories as they proliferated. The shift had to do with a growing weariness: the era of the *bhakti* had begun, the era of obscure and pervasive devotion, where the pathos of abandoning oneself to a belief prevailed over the transparent perception of the *bandhus*, of the connections woven into all that is.

. . .

There came a moment when Brahmā believed his work on earth was done. He had created everything out of his mind: the entire inventory of beings, from microbe to mountain, stretched away before him. But there was a false note. It all looked like an enameled court painting. Everything moved, everything looked normal. But nothing decayed. Nor grew. Was all to remain intact forever? Was this the earth it behooved Brahmā to create? The god smiled a sad smile of solitary soliloquy. He knew it was not.

Brahmā's creation suffered from this weakness: all were born exclusively of the mind, and worse still, no one died. Faced with such a world, at once rowdy and inert, a stifled, menacing anger slowly brewed up in its creator, an anger that seemed eager to unleash itself in a final conflagration. Brahmā sat apart from it all, his legs crossed, gazing at the world with the contempt of a father reflecting on the mediocrity of his son. In each separate element he recognized a sense of all-pervading fatuity. So Śiva was doing no more than showing mercy when he suggested to Brahmā what was missing, that figure who alone could save the world from a brusque and spiteful end: Mṛtyu, Death.

"Anger rushes out at the world from the orifices of your body, sets it ablaze, scorches its mane. Thus it is flat and arid once again. But still inhabited by these multitudes of men who don't know what to do with themselves. Why reduce the life you have invented to such pettiness? Let men die. And, since among ourselves everything happens many times, they can die many times and live many times. That way they need no longer be humiliated by this endless life, which only oppresses the earth with its weight." Thus spoke Śiva to Brahmā one day when his benevolent side was uppermost.

Grimly, Brahmā agreed. The earth was spared his flames. There was a moment of suspension, as if everything had stopped breathing. Then a girl appeared, a dark girl, dressed in red with large earrings. Crouched on the ground, the two gods gazed at her. Then Brahmā spoke: "Mṛtyu, Death, come here. You must go forth into the world. You must kill my creatures, the scholars and the muddlers. You must have but one rule: that there be no exceptions." The girl gazed at the god in silence, her fingers nervously twisting a garland of lotus flowers. Then she said: "Progenitor, why have you chosen me to do something that is against every law? And why should I do this and nothing but this? I shall burn on an everlasting pyre of tears." Brahmā said: "No prevaricating. You are without stain and your body blameless. Go . . ." Death stood before Brahmā in silence, her shoulders slumped.

Death was stubborn and refused to obey Brahmā's order for some time. In Dhenuka, surrounded by ascetics she should already have slaughtered, she stood on one foot for fifteen million years. No one took any notice. She was one of the many who went there in retreat. Puzzled, Mṛtyu meditated.

Brahmā reminded her of her duty. But Death just changed the foot she was standing on—and went on meditating for another twenty million years. Then for another few million she lived with the wild beasts, ate nothing but air, sank under the waters. Then she lay on Mount Meru for a long time, like a log. More millions of years passed. One day Brahmā went to see her: "My daughter, what is going on? A few moments or a few million years won't change anything. We're always back where we started. And I'll say it again: 'Do your duty.' " As if those millions of years hadn't gone by and she were resuming the conversation after no more than a moment or two, Mṛtyu said: "I'm afraid of breaking the law." "Don't be afraid," said Brahmā. "No judge could ever be as impartial as yourself. And I can't see why you should cry as much as you do either: your tears will gouge ulcers in the bodies you must kill. Better kill them quickly, without dragging it out so long." Then Death lowered her eyes and went forth silently into the world. She tried to keep the tears from her eyes, as a last sign of benevolence toward the creatures she was slaying.

Brahmā, god of *sva-*, of whatever functions from itself and in itself, self-created and self-generating as he was, constrained to concern himself only with himself, encountered, from his autistic existence beyond the cosmos (with respect to which the cosmos is but a toy), no small number of difficulties in his dealings with the earth. He would generate sons, observe their exultant youth, their erect phalluses—and so invite them to procreate. But at this point his sons would disappear. They retreated into the forest to meditate, like coy young maidens, as if, even before existing, the world had wanted nothing better than to be reabsorbed into the mind. Then Brahmā was seized by an awesome rage. What was this? Was the machine of creation that had produced billions of worlds to break down before the laughable little labor that was coitus? What were those strapping lads of his so frightened of (what was he, the self-created god, frightened of?), what was stopping them from approaching a woman's vulva?

Brahmā was sometimes an inept and hesitant creator. More than any other god, he suffered the consequences of his origin. Male reduction of the immense neuter, of the *brahman* that embraces all, nourishes all, and is the sense of all, Brahmā was forced to have a story, and hence a pitiful limitation. But at the same time, something of the amorphous still clung to him, and left him awkward: he would make an effort, stir something up, but they were only attempts at action, so that when he remembered the boundless vastness from which he had sprung, he was ashamed of them. What chiefly remained to him of the self-sufficient mental power of his origin, antecedent to every existence, was a certain reluctance, sometimes a repugnance for creation. And in particular for that creation which was irremediable: sexual creation. Yet, paradoxically, he was adored as a creator god.

If it was a question of creating from the mind, on the other hand, that was a game he loved to play. Or rather, that was what he normally did, and never tired of. Thus appeared the plants and the ghosts, the shadows and the dusk, the Snakes and the Genies who drink down words. But Brahmā still knew nothing of the creation that is born of "coupling and emotion."

He felt he wasn't the right god to take it on, and thus delegated the task to thousands of his born-of-the-mind sons, *mānasaputras.* But he soon realized that something held them back from touching the matter of the world. The words of Nārada, the most indiscreet and subtle of the *ṛṣis,* were enough to deter them. Nārada said: "How can you create when you know nothing as yet? First travel around the earth, get the measure of it, then you will be able to create with discernment." Brahmā's sons agreed and, as though relieved of a silent torment, set off on their way. No one has seen them since.

"Having created his born-of-the-mind sons, the Lord Brahmā was not satisfied with his work." Something was missing, an essential flavor. Brahmā began to invoke a name (Gāyatrī? Śatarūpā? Sāvitrī? Sarasvatī?—it was hard to make it out from that vague murmuring), until his breast opened and a female being slithered out onto the ground. Already disapproving of their progenitor's absorption, his torpid delirium, his sons stood in a circle around him and watched. When they saw the girl, they immediately thought her their sister. Meanwhile Brahmā's voice had grown clearer. He stared at the girl as if nothing else existed, and said: "What beauty! What beauty!" Brahmā's sons watched him with contempt. Why was their father being so undignified? The girl, in the meantime, greeted the father and began to circle around him with ceremonial step. It was the first circumambulation, *pradakṣiṇa,* something practiced ever since in every temple in India. Śatarūpā's step was slow, but to follow her Brahmā would have to turn his head. He could not bear to lose sight of her even for an instant. At the same time, he felt the malevolent eyes of his sons converging on him like so many pinpricks. So Brahmā sprouted a new head on each side, as Śatarūpā made her circumambulation around him. When she had finished, two brothers came to her sides, their faces grim and severe. Śatarūpā understood that she must obey. They took her wrists and told her to climb up to the sky with them. When they were already in flight, a fifth head sprouted from Brahmā's skull, looking up toward Śatarūpā, until the girl was no more than a small, dark speck in the blue. When even that speck had gone, Brahmā felt lonely and quite worn out. He closed his eyes, ten of them now, and once again was aware of the hateful presence of his disapproving sons. "Go . . . Go . . . ," he said in a hiss. He heard a muddled shuffling, and hoped he would never have to see them again.

For a long time Brahmā stood motionless, eyes still closed. He felt his body emptied of the awesome *tapas* that until now had brought forth his creatures. As for the outside world, he knew that only one of his born-of-the-mind sons was still wandering around out there, a troublesome presence in the desert. That was Kāma, Desire, with his blossoming arrows. Suddenly Brahmā opened his eyes so that they poured forth rage. Kāma was before him, careless, and for that reason alone, mocking. Brahmā told him: "Now you're satisfied, because thanks to your arrows you have made me ridiculous in the eyes of your brothers. And you mocked me, because Śatarūpā slipped away. You take pleasure in destroying me. But now the time has come for me to curse you. One day you will meet someone who will answer your arrows, and reduce you to ashes."

For a long time Brahmā was alone, motionless. His only care was to hide his fifth head under his thick, black hair, twisting it into a bun on the top of his head. None of his born-of-the-mind sons had reappeared. Nor did Brahmā want them back. One memory obsessed him—and every so often he would still say to himself: "What beauty! What beauty!" When one day he found himself once again face-to-face with Śatarūpā, he thought it must be another of the mental images that tormented him. Without realizing, he had stretched out a hand, while Śatarūpā made the same gesture toward him. Their fingertips touched. In that instant, and it was like a shock, a revelation, Brahmā understood what contact is. So he got to his feet and without a word began to walk beside her. He was looking for a delightful, hidden place, where the intrusive gaze of his sons could never find him. They reached a pond. Brahmā asked Śatarūpā to lie down on a lotus petal. Then he lay beside her. Slowly the petal closed around them. There they stayed, for a hundred years of the gods, loving each other the way common people do. Thus they conceived Manu, who founded the society of men.

Brahmā's fifth head would not always be hidden under a bun of raven hair. Sometimes people would catch a glimpse of something white, shiny even, behind those thick locks. And there were those who thought they had seen a horse's head. Soon Śiva was to cut that head off. The reason for his anger is still a matter of controversy. Was it Brahmā's desire for his daughter—or for the wives and daughters of the gods, or just in general for the first female creature he saw, who must have seemed irresistible to him if he couldn't take his eyes off her, if he spent his seed without even touching her? Alternatively, some said that that fifth head unleashed a thirst-quenching energy, *tejas,* that shook the world. Or again it seems that the fifth head may have directed some arrogant remarks at Śiva, who already had five heads himself and perhaps didn't appreciate the idea of another being's diminishing his uniqueness and usurping his sacred number five. In order to maim Brahmā, Śiva took the form of the Tremendous, Bhairava. Using the nail of his left thumb, he severed the fifth head. So precise and so sharp was the cut that Brahmā stiffened, amazed, heads gazing in all four directions, as if nothing had happened. Śiva immediately tried to hurl Brahmā's fifth head far away. Then he realized that it had stuck to the palm of his hand. Meanwhile the contents of the head poured out, leaving just the bony top of the skull, like a bowl, firmly stuck to his hand. Śiva saw what was coming: to expiate his crime, the first and most serious of crimes, for in striking Brahmā he had struck at every future brahman, he would have to wander about for years, gathering food in that bowl, the *kapāla*, which would constantly and inescapably remind him of what he had done. That's why they called him Kapālin, He-who-holds-the-bowl.

Brahmā was gloomy, oppressed. Those sons born-of-the-mind seemed such vacuous and cowardly beings. They would never understand what it means, what it might mean, *to exist*—the gamble of it, the incongruity, the elusiveness, the muddle, the folly. They were born of the mind, they had lightness and mobility, but no more consistency than a will-o'-the-wisp. The danger was that the world would never be any more than, as it were, a strip of light cloth, flimsy and fluttering in the wind, offering no resistance.

But what else could he contrive? Brahmā plunged into himself and sensed that melancholy that comes of understanding too much and not knowing whom to say it to. And it was precisely his awareness of this that dazzled him. That was what was missing: someone who would understand. Then from the thumb of his right hand gushed forth Dakṣa. He sat in front of Brahmā and gazed at him with a grave, composed expression, at once knowing and taciturn. One day Dakṣa's enemies would say that he had a face for every occasion. Brahmā looked on him with affection, as if they were old friends. His eyes rested on his long, thin, nimble fingers. In those fine bones, all ready to fashion an invisible object, he recognized the nervature of the mind. Intelligence could now undertake its first unnatural mission: to create through sex.

. . .

Aware of his own unsuitability for and incommensurability with the affairs of the world, and at the same time of the need to create it according to an order, Brahmā decided to delegate the more delicate and revelatory episodes, those that would bear witness to his presence as far as mankind was concerned, to a priest, to the priest, Dakṣa the brahman, since it was in him that Brahmā once again gave way to *brahman* and hence also, in freeing himself from the awkwardness of his divine person, became once again rightness itself: Dakṣa, "he who is skillful," *dexter.* The ongoing quarrel with Śiva, the burden of sexual creation, the orthodox practice of sacrifice: all these responsibilities fell on Dakṣa's shoulders. A long, emaciated figure, eyes sunk in deep hollows, long veins in wiry arms, a bony wrist but steady, a white tunic that fell stainless to his ankles—such was Dakṣa when he appeared in the world, and as such he has never left it.

Still callow, but loyal, Dakṣa began his work as Brahmā's substitute by procreating male children. He used his bed as a workshop. He paid no attention to pleasure, because it would have slowed him down. A thousand sons the first time, a thousand the next, always from the same wife, the robust Vīriṇī, strong enough to hold up the three worlds. The sons looked like young heroes, but then they would disappear. They followed the wind, to gain knowledge (they said), they hid in the forest to meditate, they set out in their brothers' footsteps. Any direction was fine, so long as they didn't have to mate. Then Dakṣa saw that history could only be born from women, and he generated sixty daughters.

Dakṣa gave twenty-seven daughters to Soma; he gave thirteen daughters to Kaśyapa; he gave Smṛti to Aṅgiras; he gave Khyāti to Bhṛgu; he gave Anasūyā to Atri; he gave Ūrjā to Vasiṣṭha; he gave Prīti to Pulastya; he gave Kṣamā to Pulaha; he gave Sannati to Kratu. All seers, *ṛṣis* of the first or second list, as they say, according to the age of the tradition that concerned them. All eminent practitioners of *tapas,* all theoreticians of sacrifice, all counselors of the king. His daughters well settled, Dakṣa's mission was accomplished. Now history's wheel could start to turn. But that, in the end, was of no interest to him.

Much time had been dedicated to studying his future sons-in-law, much time had gone into gathering information about them. What was essential, for Dakṣa, was that each of his sixty daughters should marry someone of their father's own level, someone with whom he, Dakṣa, could talk for long hours, sitting by the fire, of ritual-related inexactitudes. That was what mattered. Then, one day, from the bellies of his daughters, all kinds of different creatures would be born, parrots and snakes, the four-legged and the fish. But all would be able to boast an irreproachable ancestry.

The wives of Soma took their place in the sky as the dancing troop of the twenty-seven Nakṣatras, the houses of the moon; the descendants of Kaśyapa alone accounted for the entire gamut of gods and demons; from Aditi, the Boundless, were born the twelve Ādityas, the gods of whom one immediately thinks when one thinks of the gods: Viṣṇu, Indra, Vivasvat, Mitra, Varuṇa, Pūṣan, Tvaṣṭṛ, Bhaga, Aryaman, Dhātṛ, Savitṛ, Aṃśa; but from Diti, likewise one of Dakṣa's daughters and Kaśyapa's wives, would be born the Daityas, while from Danu, another of Dakṣa's daughters and Kaśyapa's wives, would be born the Dānavas; all demons, the most obdurate enemies of the gods, half brothers who would hound each other for thousands of years. Dakṣa contemplated them all with pleasure: this was creation, these the flavors with which it would be composed, on which it must feed, this the stock to which all must be traced back: his own, the branch of Dakṣa, the perfect priest, executor of those works that Brahmā was reluctant to perform himself.

Thus recounted Kaśyapa: "The gods detached themselves from the mind, not the mind from the gods. What happened before the birth of the gods, before we *ṛṣis* were charged by Brahmā to set in motion sexual creation (and there was something incongruous about this: our all turning up together as suitors in one huge palace, its corridors shrill with female voices: and then our becoming, we of all people, the first fathers of families, distracted, capricious, and refractory as we sometimes were, we who were better suited to niceties ceremonial than to matters domestic), was no more than a war within the mind, something that, however many names there may already have been, was fought out ever and only between two actors: the mind and everything without.

"Nothing enchants the mind more than the existence of the outside world, of something that resists it and will not obey. Pampered by its own omnipotence, its own capacity to connect and identify everything with everything, the mind needs an obstacle, at least as big as the world—and desires it. To pursue that obstacle and penetrate it: here was a challenge that could thrill and uplift, the riskiest challenge of all. It was the pursuit of the antelope. It has never stopped."

Thus recounted Atri: "Why does sex exist? In the beginning we didn't even know what it was. Born-of-the-mind of Brahmā, accustomed to the multiplication of fleeting images, we were bewildered when Brahmā announced that it would be our task to initiate a new mode of creation. And he said something about the female body. The wedding feast was drawing to a close, and we still hadn't touched Dakṣa's daughters. Soon we found ourselves lying in our beds, and for the first time we were not alone. With great naturalness and gravity, we discovered—and they too discovered—what it was we must do. Brahmā hadn't even mentioned the pleasure. It took us by surprise.

"A few thousand years went by. We had become masters of pleasure. One day when he had called us all together, we asked Brahmā: 'What's this pleasure for?' Brahmā smiled a somewhat embarrassed smile, as when he had called us to Dakṣa's house. He answered: 'To preserve the world's gloss.' We asked no more, because the gods love whatever is secret. But we began to go around and around those words in our minds. 'Pleasure is *tapas* of the without,' said Vasiṣṭha, the most authoritative among us. 'The world is like a cloak we must put on, otherwise it would grow dusty. If *tapas* always drew us back, to the formless place from whence we came, the world would wither too soon. It is well that our wives trouble us, it is well that kings put their daughters in our beds, it is even well that the Apsaras come and make fools of us, play those tricks of theirs, at once so infantile and so effective . . . Every time we give in to them, we help the world to refresh its gloss.' "

V

The Dakṣa household looked like an aviary. Sixty daughters and even more maids. Just one man, the austere father, immersed in his rites. There was an air of expectancy, preparations for the party, whisperings that some powerful *ṛṣis,* were already on their way, from the Himālaya, from the banks of the Sindhu and the Sarasvatī. The maids brought word of the suitors, who was the most handsome, who the strongest, who the most rigorous at *tapas.* Even King Soma was expected, from the moon. Dakṣa knew perfectly well, having spent a long time over the matter, which daughter was destined for which *ṛṣi.* Everything was going ahead according to plan. But behind the habitual severity, there was a shadow in his eyes. All the time, obsessively, Dakṣa was thinking of just one of his daughters, the one he'd always watched, and not just with a father's affection either, the only one he would speak to, at night, when all the other women slept: Satī, She-who-is.

It had been difficult, indeed tortuous, to bring Satī into the world. She-who-is, she who would one day become the concretion of reality, seemed unable to make her appearance. Until then, birth had never happened as a result of sex. Brahmā went on generating his born-of-the-mind children but was unable to overcome his perplexity. There was something unsatisfying about that world before the world. It began to look as though there might be another level of reality to discover: more opaque perhaps, perhaps less meaningful, but then again perhaps more appealing too. There Satī would be born—and one day the place would be called "reality" without further specification. One day everything would become so opaque that nobody would remember what had come before that level of reality. The thing now was to reach that level, by cunning. But Brahmā couldn't act alone. He needed a minister, who would be forever the minister: Dakṣa.

Dakṣa had a long face, furrows on each side of a hooked nose, hollow cheeks, serious, protruding eyes, and a thick, pendulous lower lip. His bearing was noble, studied, severe. But he could not efface a look of animal affliction that hung around him, an invisible burden that weighed on his mind. There were moments when you might even have imagined that Dakṣa's eyes, well practiced as they were in the art of concealment, concealed, among so much else, an intense, perhaps violent, sensuality. His features were haunted by an underlying resignation to something yet to happen, the kind of look you see in those goats who graze alone.

What was the difference between Satī and his other daughters? wondered Dakṣa. Why did the mere fact of his looking at her touch him in the only spot where he felt entirely vulnerable? She was no more beautiful than the others; just—perhaps—her face had something more serious about it. Something hidden too. And something that filled Dakṣa with amazement: a lofty sadness, for which there was no apparent reason. As if, with Satī, one sensed what the mind is like when it is internalized, concealed. Something the world knew nothing of as yet, thought Dakṣa. And he remembered the vacuous motley of his brothers, who had disappeared.

Before Satī was born, reality was less real. Dakṣa sensed that at once—and made no remark. Watching the girl grow up, he tried not to distinguish her from the other fifty-nine. But often he would feel how she followed him with her eyes, peered at him from behind doors as he celebrated the rites. Satī reminded Dakṣa of his secret. Before being a priest and the head of a family, with wife and servants, Dakṣa had been a solitary fanatic; with no experience of women, he obstinately pursued a single, never-confessed, desire: that Devī, the Goddess, she who lives in the body of Śiva, should reveal herself to him.

One day, when quite unusually he had surrendered to drowsiness, a condition akin to illness for Dakṣa, he saw the darkness grow bright and throb. There were two points of light, in the darkness: a blue lotus flower—that was what it was—and the sparkle of a blade. They moved ever so slowly: until finally Dakṣa saw the hands that held them and two other hands, unburdened in the air. Then he glimpsed the body of the Goddess. She was crouched on a lion, as if since time began that lion had been the earth. Suddenly Dakṣa felt more watchful than he had ever been. He felt the bold rashness of a warrior, something quite out of character for him. He said, "O thou, Devī, Dark One, I beg you to be born as my daughter. I beg you to find once more, through me, the one in whom you are." Those last few words were to torment Dakṣa, for years. He knew he had spoken two sentences to the Goddess, but the second had been lost, like something spoken in a dream, though what did remain, etched in his memory, was the conviction that those words were the most important of his life. Dakṣa would never cease to search for them.

Satī's maid curtsyed before Dakṣa and said: "Master, I feel it's my duty to tell you that Satī, my mistress, is odd. All her sisters are passing around miniatures of the *ṛṣis* and King Soma—and trying to guess who will marry whom. They invent charades where they dress up as *ṛṣis* and play out the scenes of their future lives. They laugh—and sometimes they're sad and cry. But Satī keeps herself to herself. While her sisters squabble, she doesn't seem to care at all. She hasn't tried on any new clothes. She hasn't asked for a new makeup box. She wanders around the gardens for hours. But I know what she does there, I've caught her at it more than once. Satī sings—or rather she hums. And the songs are always about a dark man. His name is Śiva. Or if she doesn't sing she draws. Always the same face, a frightening face. Or she practices *tapas*, something no one has taught her. Or whispers, as if there were a ghost beside her. Master, it was my duty to tell you all this."

Dakṣa and Vīriṇī, their faces noble and time-worn, though with something gloomy about them too, an expression almost of dismay, sat by the fire after their daughters and servants had gone to bed. Dakṣa said: "This man who has come, this stranger, this woman-stealer, this enemy of our rules and rites, this wanderer who loves the ashes of the dead, who speaks of things divine to the lowest of the low, this man who sometimes seems crazy, who has something obscene about him, who grows his hair long as a girl's, who bedecks himself with bones, who laughs and cries for no reason, why should I give my daughter Satī to him of all men, why should I give She-who-is to someone who, every time I see him, seems to me the opposite of everything I wanted to be myself, of everything I want life to be? Why did I compose so many rites, so many signs, so many words, why did I generate She-who-is, just to have everything stolen from me one day by the one who is its living negation?"

When the suitor stepped forward, Dakṣa, the impeccable priest, devotee of ritual precision, considered him with contempt: he was a wild beggar, with sweaty pigtails, cloaked in the stench of the pyres. One long, strong hand held Satī's tight, the other fiddled with a necklace of bone. Beside him, the unrecognizable Satī was barely covered by filthy rags, while her skin—Dakṣa was shocked to notice—seemed to have turned darker. Her eyes were bright and radiated happiness: shut up in her rooms, practicing *tapas* as a child, she had always dreamed of a man like this who would carry her off. She stroked Śiva's blue neck, mixed her oils with the ash that covered his chest like soft armor. They set out at once for the highest mountains. They had no home, nor even shelter. The beasts welcomed them and guided them. Then left them alone.

Satī had the feeling that this was the first time her body had really existed. It wasn't as if Śiva was penetrating her but as if he opened himself up to her like a huge cavity, welcoming her into himself. The contact with the surface of his body absorbed her into it. Enchanted in the darkness, Satī touched Śiva's walls. She pressed on toward the center of him, as though toward the glow of a fire in the depths of a cave. She was lost, but felt she was about to find herself. Or rather: she felt that what was happening was a return.

Śiva and Satī's embrace lasted twenty-five years, without his ever emptying his seed into her. Like a tethered elephant, Śiva couldn't move without brushing against Satī's body. When they spoke, they joked. Using moss, Śiva drew on Satī's breasts, sketching what looked like bees buzzing around a lotus. If Satī looked in the mirror, Śiva hid behind her so that Satī thought she was alone. Then one of Śiva's eyes popped up in the mirror.

One day Satī wanted to free herself from that endless embrace. "I want you to explain what the Self is," she said. "Ever since I was a little girl, I've practiced *tapas,* looking not for freedom but for slavery. All I wanted was to get your attention. Now you are my husband and I have been taught that you are release itself. During the marriage ceremony a brahman whispered to me that you had only accepted me because you were devoted to your devotees. But what does this devotion mean? I want knowledge." Śiva said: "In eras of weakness, such as the present, devotion is a name for knowledge. Learned men have identified nine types of devotion. One devotion is listening to my stories. But it is also devotion to water the *bilva* tree. Something that never occurred to those learned men." Śiva rambled on and on about devotion with a vague, vacant expression. Satī's face darkened. Her body closed up like a box, cheek on knees drawn tight to her breast. She tried to see Śiva as a stranger, a beguiling intruder. "Why do you keep talking about devotion, and never mention knowledge and detachment?" said Satī. "Because they're out of date now," said Śiva, and he laughed. "But I know that the ancients spoke of nothing but knowledge," said Satī stubbornly. "Right, the ancients," said Śiva, hardly paying attention. "But does devotion bring us release?" insisted Satī. "Devotion helps," said Śiva, less and less interested. "Devotion to you doesn't satisfy me," said Satī. "You don't need it. You are me. That is knowledge. Just three words," said Śiva. "And who are you?" said Satī, suddenly gentle, eyeing her lover. "I am that," said Śiva. "What is *that*?" Satī insisted like an obstinate child. "That which tells us we're talking. But we mustn't talk too much," said Śiva, and, as hundreds of times before, he began to slip the bracelets from Satī's wrists.

When she went for walks in the woods and glades of Mount Kailāsa, when Śiva was unapproachable, that is, immersed in *tapas*, Satī became aware of how she would soon feel a wedge of grief piercing her breast. She thought of her father, of Dakṣa. She knew that Dakṣa hated Śiva. She had always known. In that palace in the distant plain, a dogged mind was keeping track of her every moment, abhorring every gesture of love she made, shivering every time Satī's body brushed against Śiva's. She remembered how as a girl she had hardly ever touched her father's body. Eye contact had been enough for both of them. The only part of him she remembered touching was his hand, nervous and clawlike as it led her to some ceremony or other. But what else would it touch her for? Her father lived for ceremonies. It was as if he were always officiating. His anger, which could be terrible, was only ever roused when someone made some mistake in the liturgy.

Now there was nothing but silence between them. But one day a Yakṣa, one of the many Genies who visited the slopes of Kailāsa, mentioned a story that she immediately sensed would prove fatal. He thought Satī already knew it. So his tale was all the more cruel. There had been, the Genie said, a grand sacrifice. All the *ṛṣis* were there. Likewise Śiva. Finally Dakṣa arrived, solemn and severe as ever. Everybody stood up. Except Śiva. Upon which, claimed the Genie, Dakṣa had been seized by fury and said terrible things. That Śiva had the eyes of a monkey, that they were not worthy to meet the gazelle's eyes of his daughter. That giving Satī to Śiva had been like giving the fragrant word of the Vedas to a wretched outcaste. Satī hadn't wanted to hear more. She pretended she knew the story, which actually Śiva had kept hidden from her. She felt such a sharp desire to return to her father, to look once again into his deep-set eyes. When, as a little girl, she would meet those eyes, even if only obliquely or at a distance, she felt something slide across her skin, like a soft ribbon it seemed sometimes, sometimes like a noose. She would tell him in a few brusque words that all his rites did not add up to knowledge.

Satī felt sure that Dakṣa's aversion to Śiva was not reciprocated. Śiva—she thought—couldn't have an aversion to anything in the world. Aversion was something too weak for him. In theological terms, Satī was right, but there was an episode she knew nothing of that dated back to before the time Śiva appeared in her life. It had happened one day when Śiva, like Brahmā, had decided he would create new beings. But immediately he had felt a pang of nostalgia. For water, for motionlessness. He went down into a lake and stood on the bottom. A stake. Meantime, Dakṣa got down to it. If the world was empty of beings, he would make it his business to procreate. He was the officious priest, busying himself around the altar of the vagina. Beings were born.

When Śiva came out of the lake, still heedless, his mind elsewhere, he heard a rustling in the forest, a hush of voices. There were already plenty of beings about. Dakṣa had tricked him. He had dared to forestall Śiva. "Since you have been so zealous as to help me and even carry out my work before I could do it myself," Śiva said cuttingly, "one day it will be my pleasure to help you complete your work."

On another occasion Satī noticed some unusual movement on the slopes of Kailāsa. Processions of Genies, gods and demigods were floating down on the breeze. Where were they going? she asked, admiring the sumptuous clothes and jewels of the goddesses. Dakṣa has announced a great sacrifice," they said. "We're all invited. All your sisters will be there. Twenty-seven of them are already on their way down from the moon. We'll see you there," they said and went off on their chariots.

Then Satī asked Śiva if they had been invited to Dakṣa's sacrifice. "No," Śiva said. Dakṣa didn't invite me because, when I roam the world, I use the dome of what was once one of his father Brahmā's heads as a bowl." "I'll go anyway," said Satī. "You're a god, so you have to be invited. But I'm just a woman, and I don't need an invitation to go and see my family. I feel homesick for the land where I was born. It's hard to bear the beauty of life with you. Let me go and chat with my sisters awhile. The only company I have here are Nandin the bull and the snakes you coil around your neck and arms." "If you go, no good will come of it," said Śiva calmly, but he looked away, because the attar of sadness was sifting down on his eyes, like rain on a lake: "You say you have made of me the one who inhabits half of your body. Grant me this boon, let me go," said Satī. "I can't keep you," said Śiva.

Satī felt a sullen resentment toward Śiva that had her weeping tears of rage. He had never spoken to her like that, tight-lipped and toneless. And at the same time Satī felt a nagging rancor toward Dakṣa. Her father, her husband: they'd staked out her entire mind. Or were they two lovers, fighting it out to the death inside her? That was another thing that made her weep with rage. She decided to leave without saying good-bye. She walked along feverishly, at once gloomy and defiant. But soon she heard a bustling sound behind her. Śiva's servants were escorting her. Mirrors, birds, white sunshades, fans, garlands, chariots, cymbals and flutes: caught up together in a cloud, all these things were following her.

But Satī wanted to be alone when she reached the house where she was born, when she crossed the threshold of the place of sacrifice. She entered in silence, superimposed herself on the silence. Terrified as they were of Dakṣa, none of the celebrants dared so much as nod to her. Only her mother and sisters flocked around like a swarm of birds. They sobbed and laughed, having all been convinced that they would never see her again. Face set in an expression of severity, Satī looked more than ever like her father. Her cheeks were white as white. Refusing the place of honor Vīriṇī had immediately offered her, Satī looked around, with the eyes of one long accustomed to taking in every detail of the ceremony.

The offerings for the gods had been laid in a line side by side. One for each god, but not for Śiva. Satī's eyes came to rest on the empty place. Then, with horror, they saw she was walking over to Dakṣa, who was still unaware of her arrival, absorbed in the sacrificial ritual. But for the first time in his life, Dakṣa broke off from the sacrifice. They saw him turn slowly toward his daughter. It was as if he had been expecting her. Satī began to speak in a quiet, tense voice, a whisper that could only just be heard. "You and only you may dare be the censor of that which is. Thus do you condemn me, whom once you called Satī, 'She-who-is.' You and only you may list the offenses of he of whom the world is but a breath. You chase off fullness like some disreputable vagabond. You believe the world is made up of your rites. You believe these motions contain the whole. You have excluded wholeness from your invitation list. You offer sacrifice to all, but not to sacrifice itself. The flowers of your rituals are rain falling from Śiva's feet. When the blue-necked god dallies with me and calls me 'Dakṣa's daughter,' I am overcome by shame. For this body of mine is juice of your body, all I can do is expel it, spew it out like a vile food. You cannot live without performing sacrifice, but I am the sacrifice."

Dakṣa listened, rigid and pale. He whispered a few words only Satī could hear: "Where shall I find you again?" Never had his voice been so soft and helpless. Satī replied in an almost identical whisper that only Dakṣa could hear: "You will find me everywhere, in every time, in every place, in every being. There is no thing in the world where I shall not be." Then she crouched down to one side of the altar. She looked north, wrapped in her yellow robe. She wet her fingertips in a bowl of water and drank a sip or two. She closed her eyes. She remembered *tapas,* how she had first practiced it here as a child, evoking Śiva, the invisible lover. Now it was enough to evoke his feet. A heat rose from the depths of her body. Satī saw no one, though they were all staring at her. Her arms, her face turned thin mother-of-pearl over a shadow flickering behind. It was the flame that burst from within and consumed her, leaving her standing erect, a statue of ash.

The officiants, her sisters, her mother, the servants, the gods, the Genies, the children, Dakṣa: they all stared at what was left of Satī. When the thin crackling of hidden flame ceased, the silence settled heavily. Not a breath of wind. Far away across the plain to the north, a black clot formed in the air, a tiny flaw in the enameled brilliance of the sky. It grew slowly, spiraling. "Where does this dust come from?" the women whispered. "It's the god who shreds the constellations," said one of Dakṣa's wives, as an evil wind lifted her robes. The place of sacrifice, which had been a dazzle of light, was filled with a gloom of dust. All became shadow churning shadow. Right around the enclosure, red and brown figures suddenly stood out stark like scarecrows, menacing sentinels, but turned inward rather than outward. Each one held an unsheathed blade. They were the Gaṇas, Śiva's soldiery. Behind them snarled packs of dogs. In the center of the clearing, amid the whirl of dust, a huge shadow could just be seen, braid upon wheeling braid. "Who is it?" everybody asked. They couldn't have known, because this monster had only just been born. When Satī burned, Śiva, watching from Kailāsa, had torn off one of his coiling plaits. As soon as the hairs fell on the rock, there was a roar and Vīrabhadra was formed. Mild and devout within, his appearance struck terror in them all. He moved toward Dakṣa's sacrifice. Tall as a mountain, he was a flailing multitude of heads, arms, feet, swords. Laden with jewels, dripping with blood, decked out with snakes, tiger skins, and wreaths of flowers, he set about killing every creature he came across with indiscriminate ferocity. But there were those he was looking for in particular. He was looking for Sarasvatī, Brahmā's wife, and he pulled off her nose, so that she looked like a slave. He was looking for Pūṣan, who had laughed while Dakṣa was railing against Śiva, and he broke his teeth. He was looking for Agni, to cut off his hands. As for Bhaga, he left it to Nandin the bull to gouge out the eyes that had narrowed in agreement at Dakṣa's words. Kicked about by the Gaṇas, the gods rolled on the ground like sacks. No one bothered to touch the brahmans: a hail of stones smashed in their breastbones. There was not one ceremonial object that the Gana did not crush to pieces. They urinated in the hollows that should have held the fires. They splattered the colorful foods, now soggy, on the open wounds of the dying.

The sacrifice contemplated the massacre. Then it took the shape of an antelope and flew off into the sky. But an arrow from Vīrabhadra sheared off its delicate head. Now Vīrabhadra was looking for someone else. He went to the altar. Pressed against the bricks, Dakṣa huddled there, trembling. One of Vīrabhadra's many hands gripped him by the back of the neck and dragged him through the dust to the sacrificial pit. A soiled head stuck out from the shapeless bundle of the body. Vīrabhadra cut it off. Dakṣa's head was seen to disappear in the fire. Then Vīrabhadra laughed. A rain of flowers fell from the sky through an air now suddenly clear again. They settled on the broken bodies, drifted in pools of blood.

The destruction of Dakṣa's sacrifice, the most radical criticism of sacrifice, came from within sacrifice itself: it showed how irresistibly sacrifice is transformed into massacre, and thus looked forward to the whole course of a history no longer yoked to sacrifice.

The premise was a simple breach of etiquette, of terrifying eloquence. If Śiva was not invited, sacrifice could no longer bring together the totality of the real. Thus he who was excluded took revenge. And the form of revenge he chose was once again the sacrifice. But this time a funereal sacrifice. The victim honored that day was sacrifice itself, the ceremony.

Since Satī had burnt from within, her body was left standing, calcinated, on the sacrificial clearing. It was light, but it did not disintegrate when Śiva lifted it up and began to make the steps of the Tāṇḍava, repeating the dance that follows every destruction of the world. Always alarmed by the excesses of others, the gods looked down on the scene. The earth shook. Then, for safety's sake, Viṣṇu took his sharp disk and set about mutilating Satī's body as it turned on Śiva's fingers. Down fell the arms, the breasts, the feet, breaking up in ashes as they settled on the ground. Śiva didn't notice, rapt in the dance. But when Satī's vulva fell on Kāmarūpa, the dance stopped. And they saw that the vulva had come to rest on the tip of a smooth column of rock. There it remained, like a rug.

Śiva went back to Kailāsa. Crouched in his cave, he realized that for the first time he was alone. No more Nandin with his powerful breath. No more snakes. No more Gaṇas. No bustling procession around him. All had withdrawn from the presence of the Lord of the Animals. A sinister wind was whistling, and the air was too clear, abrasive. On a shelf, he looked at Satī's few remaining belongings. Some tiny makeup boxes. Her robes folded in one corner, a soft, lifeless heap. Satī had never grown used to not having a home. More than once, when the monsoon raged, she had asked Śiva if they were always to live as vagabonds beneath the sky. He had never answered.

Now Śiva looked around and saw how the moonlight had set apart an array of powder puffs and makeup brushes with mother-of-pearl handles, and beside them something of a yellowish white: the begging bowl, the top of Brahmā's skull. His gaze rested long on these objects. They resisted him. It was they that oppressed him. The fierce pangs for the loss of Satī. The dull throb of guilt: not only had he decapitated the Creator, not only had he mocked and mutilated the father of all beings. But worst of all: he had wounded a brahman. That was the most heinous thing anyone could ever do. He who strikes a brahman swallows a tormenting hook, lives scorched by a firebrand in the throat. Śiva took the bowl of bone in his hand. It stuck to his palm like a sucker. He tried to hurl it away. He couldn't. Someone was watching, a shadow lurking in the cave. He knew who it was, that silent and abhorred companion. A girl with red eyes, dressed in black and noble rags: Brahmahatyā, the Fury of the Brahmānicide. Of that woman alone might Satī have been jealous. She alone jolted his mind without truce, like a bat beating against the walls of a cave. Śiva watched pain and guilt slowly fusing together, as like substances will. They came rushing from the ends of the earth: they were all the pain and all the guilt, compressed and sealed within him. He remembered the stories of tortured lovers. Of the lost and the suicides. Of those whose name no one knows. They came like fine dust. Sparks flew and fell back in the brazier. He recognized every one of them. They greeted him, like his own faithful. A blink of Śiva's eyelids was their response. Each had a name. All lapsed back into him.

. . .

It was never clear for what reason and to what end, if end there was, Śiva left Kailāsa. Motionless, he was accustomed to entertaining everything within his mind. But now, ever alternating, merging, just two images afflicted him: the bone and the ashes. Brahmā and Satī. Was it this persecution that goaded him to set off on his travels, like the commonest of wretches who seeks to lose himself along the highways and byways of the world? Clad in rags, surly, his eyes fiery and dark, the vagabond Śiva flitted across village and valley like a shade. His bowl never filled with water when he held it under a fountain. That was the most painful moment of all. He looked at that modest piece of bone and was bound to admit that it was bottomless: no liquid, be it blood or water, would ever fill it. No one recognized him. Śiva begged before Śiva's temples. Sometimes the devout would trample him as they thronged to worship. Sometimes he would writhe and yearn like a madman lost among other madmen. He was the nameless, he who has no country, no caste, he was the lover forever bereaved, the murderer who cannot be pardoned, the missing person who is missed by no one. He got no more attention than a charred log. It was a breath of warm and quivering air that brought him back to himself. He felt a sudden tremor in the ground, the distant thunder of spring. And all at once his wanderings found a destination: the Forest of Cedars.

As he was approaching the Forest of Cedars, his light, feverish steps obedient to an inflexible determination, Śiva was aware of being inhabited by three passions, all living together within him and each exasperated by the presence of the others, even though each was exclusive and ought to have repelled all others. The first, the most remote, was the guilt for his brahmanicide. It seemed to Śiva he had been born with that guilt, even though he well remembered how many millennia had passed before his left thumbnail had sliced off Brahmā's fifth head like a ripened fruit. But that seemed no more than a belated consequence. A consequence of what? Perhaps of the existence of the world.

The second passion was his mourning for Satī. And again, although this was recent, a still open wound that cut through his fiber from one end to the other, nevertheless it seemed it had always been part of him. Every lover loves, first and foremost, an absentee. Absence precedes presence, in the hierarchical order of things. Presence is just a special case in the category of absence. Presence is a hallucination protracted for a certain period. But this in no way diminishes our pain. Looking into the future, Śiva could see certain presumptuous and ingenuous natives of the distant West, who would one day believe they were the only ones to suffer, sectarians of the irreversible. Seeing them, Śiva felt sympathetic and, murmuring words they would never hear, addressed them as follows: "Whether the world be a hallucination or the mind be a hallucination, whether all return or all appear but once, the suffering is just the same. For he who suffers is part of the hallucination, of whatever kind that may be. What then is the difference? This: whether in the sufferer there is—or is not—he who watches him who suffers." More than that, for the moment, he would not say.

Then there was a third passion, something that the first trembling of the air had awakened within him and that now grew, swelled in a wave that thrust him forward along the most rugged of paths, invaded by a euphoria, an insolence, a rashness that he hadn't felt for a long time. What was it? The premonition of many women as yet unknown, the remote agency of bodies he had never seen but sensed he could already glimpse, ready as he was to overwhelm them. But who were they? Stern women, the purest of women, princesses careless of principality, charioteers of the mind, flushes of celestial heat that had settled on the earth, conserving within themselves the substance of the stars.

Śiva toiled on, climbing toward the Forest of Cedars. Only rarely did he find traces of travelers who had gone before. Nature greeted him, hurrying on his awakening. To anyone passing by, he would have looked like a pilgrim or beggar, lost on his way to a sanctuary. Or, if ever he had lifted his eyes from his feet, like a bandit gone to ground in the mountains. He was seeking the one place that is sufficient unto itself, which is within the world but ignores the world. Sometimes an antelope would come out of the undergrowth and rear up on its hind legs, pushing its muzzle into Śiva's hand, to feed on the leaves he offered. Their eyes met, and there would be a flash of recognition. At that moment, they were the only creatures who would have known how to find him.

In the Forest of Cedars life was quiet, almost static. There, in society, lived those who had chosen to sever all ties with society. Rude huts of twigs were scattered among bushes and tall trunks, set apart but within sight of each other. One constant sound: running water—which sometimes merged with the mighty rustling of the wind. Here lived the *ṛṣis* and their wives. There was no market, no carts, no soldiers: none of those things that make up a community. Yet the inhabitants shared every rule of thought and deed. Such was their unspoken accord that the place was like a hard, transparent stone. Solitary women, magnificent and proud, walked the forest ways. They went to fetch water, or to bathe, or to see friends. It was pointless to ask what the *ṛṣis* did: they practiced *tapas*. Was this fullness? Was it emptiness? Was it tedium? Was it freedom? Was it memory? Was it renunciation? Was it happiness? No one ever established that with any certainty. Another dweller in that stasis was doubt.

Why did Śiva want to upset the life of the *ṛṣis* in the Forest of Cedars? Wasn't it as close as any could be to the life he himself had lived for so long on Kailāsa? Wasn't that perennial practice of *tapas*, that pure abandonment to mind and sex, as like the breath of Śiva as anything to be found in all the world? Then to live alone with one's partner, in solitude and withdrawal, with a *tapasvinī*, mightn't that even have seemed like an imitation of the happy time when Śiva had met no other gaze but Satī's? Or was that exactly what provoked Śiva's malice?

In a clearing in the Forest of Cedars a group of women were gathering flowers and firewood. It was early morning. They saw a man they didn't know come out of a bush. He was half naked, his body gray with ashes, but here and there the skin showed through in streaks of gold. His hair was thick, black, plaited. He held a bowl in his hand and said not a word. All the women turned to look at him. In the silence the man bared his teeth, which were terrifying. Then he began to laugh, with a sound they had never heard before. The women went toward him, as though to shut him inside a circle. But Śiva paid no attention and walked through them. He went on toward the village. The women fell into line behind. They began very slightly to sway their thighs. Now it was Śiva who was silent, while laughter slithered along the snakelike procession behind. At the same time, the *ṛṣis'* women who had stayed in the village to do the housework stopped, forgetting whatever they had been doing. Something drew them to the windows, the doors. Some stepped out, still in their nightclothes. Others left hearth or makeup table. Bracelets fell from their wrists and were left where they lay. Soon the women were walking one behind another along the road, without so much as a word. Their feet made small dance steps, hips swaying ever so slightly. Having reached the last huts, they saw the Stranger coming toward them, followed by his procession. They tagged along, falling into step with the others.

Shortly before reaching the Forest of Cedars, Śiva had evoked Viṣṇu and entreated him to assume the shape of Mohinī, the marvelous celestial courtesan to whose exploits the gods owed a great deal. That day Mohinī appeared, her body laden with jewels and ribbons. Śiva's hand, dry with ash, squeezed Mohinī's, moist with sandalwood oil. Thus they walked along for a while, like brother and sister, then took diverging paths.

The *ṛṣis* were uneasy. Nature's awakening came as a disturbance to them. In the morning mist their heads steamed. They thought with annoyance that once again they were to be subjected to the cycle of the seasons. But if they really were liberated-in-life, why this annoyance? Then there was an unusual silence all around. The monotonous, reassuring accompaniment of domestic clatter was missing. Perhaps it was time to go and bathe, they all thought at once. And on the way to the river, they met Mohinī. Those powerful men, so solemn and severe, followed her, with avid eyes. Under long white robes, phalluses grew erect. They wanted to sit beside the river and talk to that beautiful Stranger, who doubtless knew every world there was and was cloaked in the breath of taverns, palaces, bedrooms, ports, ships, horses, cut roses. Could she be an Apsaras, come down from the heavens once again to mock them? No, there was something in this woman, her hips just slightly swaying before them, that far surpassed any previous pleasure. The *ṛṣis* hadn't said so much as good morning to one another. Each followed Mohinī as if alone. Suddenly, out of the forest, came a muddled sound, of laughter and shouting, of bells and cymbals and tambourines. The swaying procession of the *ṛṣis* ran into another swaying procession. They recognized their wives: they were following a man whom no one knew, but who was obviously up to no good. But there was no time to size him up, for already the two processions were mingling. In an instant the *ṛṣis* changed expression. They began to scold their wives. They had come out of the village to look for their women—they said—and now they found them disheveled, improperly dressed, trooping about after a filthy beggar. Well, they were going to punish him, that was for sure. But where was he? They looked around—and they were looking for Mohinī too. There was no trace of either of them. Angry and confused, the *ṛṣis* ordered their wives back home, like prisoners under armed and surly guard.

The *ṛṣis* hadn't recognized Śiva, but Śiva had recognized some of them as his noble brothers-in-law. Vasiśṭha, Atri, Pulastya, Aṅgiras, Pulaha, Kratu, Marīci: they were the names a loathsomely smug Dakṣa had rattled off to Satī to heap shame on her repugnant, ash-smeared groom. They were the right men, who did the right things and thought the right thoughts. Some of them Śiva had seen before, not on the earth but in the sky, long watched them in the tremulous light of the Bear. In the heavens those lights looked nostalgically through billowing shadows toward their distant loved ones, the Pleiades. On earth they lived like aging husbands, inured to repetition, shut away in the bubble of air that separated them from the world's impurity. Wasn't it precisely these lofty sages, after all, who had been responsible for Satī's ending up in a heap of ash? Ash. Of course. That was what the *ṛṣis* didn't understand, what they shunned, what haunted them. Everything mingles and merges, everything is leveled in ash. There is no illumination without ash. There is no illumination until all are understood to be so many animals. Animals communicate in ash. Only ash can make the propitious fragrant. That was why the *ṛṣis*'s women had followed Śiva so frenetically.

The *ṛṣis*' wives shut themselves up, each in her own home. The *ṛṣis* got together and were grim. They'd have to hunt down that Stranger, they said. Kill him, said a voice. Castrate him, said another. As Gotama had done with Indra. No one mentioned Mohinī, as if she had never appeared. Meanwhile, their anger consumed the immense *tapas* they had stored up. Exchanging glances, they might have been the commonest of men, so many roughnecks out for revenge. Splitting up to search the forest, they were fooled by laughter, braying, howls, roars. The Lord of the Animals mocked them and vanished. But in the end they found him in a clearing, sitting on a log. They surrounded him. "If you want to castrate me, I'll do it myself," said Śiva, calmly. Grasping a reddish phallus and scrotum with one hand, he tossed them into the deep grass.

Where Śiva's phallus had fallen, the astonished *ṛṣis* saw a serpent of light snake away. There was a smell of burned grass. Slowly, silently, the *ṛṣis* set off after the light. They thought: "It isn't like any other light." They didn't even realize that Śiva had disappeared. The penetrating light slithered down to the lake. The *ṛṣis* stood on the bank, to watch. The light wriggled on, deep below the water. They saw it reach the other bank. Then it rose into the air. The sun had set, and shadows were creeping across the lake. In the center, water and sky fused in a single dazzling furrow. You couldn't tell where it began or ended.

Leaving the Forest of Cedars behind, Śiva wandered from place to place, his bowl of bone still stuck to his hand. Just a couple of paces behind, the ragged Brahmahatyā followed in silence. Nobody took any notice. They were just a pair of beggars like so many others. They would stop in the marketplace, by a palace, a harbor. Śiva's eyes were vacant. Nobody spoke to them. Around a fire beside the road, they heard other beggars saying they were going to Kāśī, for that is the place where it is well to die. Śiva longed for death. But not the repeated death, *punarmṛtyu*, he had introduced into the cosmos to save it from perishing once and for all in the conflagration provoked by Brahmā's fury. No, he was looking for something rarer and sweeter: the one, definitive death, the irreversible dissolution of that atrocious contact with the bowl of bone. But was the world able to set free he who had brought it into being?

Brahmahatyā was leading the way for once, when they saw the town in the distance. It looked like any other big town. But there was something different in the air, countless grains of the finest dust, a subtle smell, at once sweet and sour. From beyond the warehouses and workshops, the cattle sheds and markets, palaces and parks, came the sound of a river in full flow, a river like the sea, its further shore lost in the mist. There, they whispered, was release, on the further shore of the Gaṅga.

Before going into the town, Siva and his companion tried to approach a clearing where a lavish sacrifice was going on. But this time they were chased off. Someone noticed the bowl of bone hanging unnaturally from the beggar's hand. They stopped him. Using a long stick, laughing, they tried to tear it off him. The bowl fell, but immediately another grew out of his hand. Nobody was laughing now. They stared in horror. Śiva and Brahmahatyā went away, unfed.

It was the eighth day of Mārgaśīrsa, the Head of the Antelope. Śiva hurried on toward the town as if eager to revisit a place he already knew. He was walking swiftly, and Brahmahatyā saw how his steps were turning into a dance. Śiva was heading not toward the lights and the bustle of the travelers but toward a dark, smoking expanse, dotted with pyres. Then Brahmahatyā felt her feet sinking in a soggy mush: ashes, blood, charred flesh. You couldn't see the jackals and vultures, but you could hear them. Ambiguous shadows flickered by the fires. It was a huge cremation ground, called Avimukta. As he walked ahead of Brahmahatyā, Śiva's steps were delicate and precise. From time to time a pyre would flare up; others sank into embers. Śiva sat down, motionless. Brahmahatyā stood and watched. She had never spoken so much as a word to him, but now she felt a tremendous urge to use his name, as if they were lovers and that cremation ground their bed. She couldn't do it. In a dark light of moon and pyres, she saw Śiva's open palm offering its bowl to the night. The skull was crumbling away. She saw Śiva's lean hand, free at last. Beneath her feet the ground grew softer. It gave way and sucked her in. Without a sound she plunged down into a yawning crack.

VI

Hardly anything ever happened in the city of Himavat. Sometimes a *ṛṣi* would stop by—and soon set off again. No wars, no uprisings. The roads had an unnatural shine to them. Parrots, cranes, and swans were painted on countless palace walls. With all the fountains and canals, the sound of gurgling water was everywhere. The city spread out like a quilt over a plateau of the Himālaya. The gods gazed down covetously, as they always had. They knew that in its bowels, beneath cellars full of spices, was hidden, lined with rock, the greatest store of gems in all the universe: the heart of the mountain. A halo of that dazzling, concealed light seemed to seep upward to the surface. It provided a soft backdrop welded to the sharp outlines that dominated the landscape, indifferent to the slow decay of everything that is. It was here that Pārvatī grew up, she had seen nothing else of the world: this nature at once too sharply etched and too clear, metallic almost, was the only nature she had known.

The first time Pārvatī heard Śiva's name, it was from her playmates. The little girls would stifle their laughter, and sometimes they blushed, when they chanted rhymes about him. "Lord of ashes and oil," they would say. But what did the words mean? Or they would say: "Snake among snakes, goad of the bull." Pārvatī loved it when she didn't understand. What attracted her most was obscurity. Otherwise the world that surrounded her would have been too transparent.

Her old father, Himavat, old as the mountain itself, was made of rock, as she was, and they understood each other without speaking. Her mother, Menā, seemed to have lived her whole life between palace and gardens. Her worries and anxieties seemed futile to the small, severe Pārvatī. Only very occasionally would Mēna loosen up a little and mention a voyage of long ago, to a "white island," where, like a princess on a world tour, she had gone with her two sisters, Dhanyā and Kalāvatī. Something had happened there, a serious offense, a lapse on the part of those cheeky princesses. But at whose expense? There was always some *ṛṣi* or other who was upset. But Pārvatī never managed to get to the bottom of it, however stubbornly she questioned her mother. It was as if that story belonged to another, unmentionable life. Even Himavat sometimes seemed to be talking nonsense, spoke of himself as the "Guardian" and came out with incoherent remarks about a time when everything was still "closed" and only he, Himavat, had known what "fullness" was and had protected it. But whatever her parents' past may or may not have been—thought Pārvatī—they certainly led a childish life now; they didn't suffer, they had no knowledge—and she, the little Pārvatī, eager as she was for change, already felt older than they, who perhaps had lived thousands of years.

Tāraka shook the world. He had already stolen the gods' wives. He rode on a lion, strangled his enemies with ten thousand hands. He was an Asura. A powerful ascetic, on a par with so many other demons before him. But this time, faced with the havoc he was wreaking, Brahmā let slip an unprecedented admission: only Śiva's son would be able to kill him. But how could Śiva have a son? The gods felt impotent as never before: Indra's thunderbolt, Varuṇa's noose, Viṣṇu's discus lay scattered about like forgotten toys.

Tāraka plundered the gem reserves of sea and sky. He broke into the celestial homes of the Apsaras. Out tramped long lines of girls, their eyes on the ground, like prisoners of war.

The gods fled: but Tāraka came at them from every side. At their wits' end, they turned once again to Brahmā. The god smiled. "It is my will that Tāraka flourish. It is hardly likely that I will destroy him. He can only be killed," the gods had to hear for the second time, "by the son of Śiva." "But Śiva has no time for us, or for the world," said the gods, gloomily. "He's always wrapped up in himself." Brahmā answered: "Śiva's seed rises and goes around in his body. No one has ever seen it. No one has ever received it. But now a woman has been born capable of making that seed squirt. Seek out Pārvatī, daughter of Himavat."

"To seduce Śiva," thought Indra. "Who can help us? Only Kāma." He went to see the old friend who had goaded him on so often in his adulterous exploits. Kāma's welcome was both gentle and proud. "We're about to be overthrown," said Indra. "The time has come to show that you're my friend. Only you, Desire, have the weapon that will do it." Kāma didn't bat an eyelid. "I can overthrow gods and demons with the sidelong glance of a woman. Brahmā too, and Viṣṇu. The others aren't even worth mentioning." Then he fell silent a moment and added, solemnly: "I could even overthrow Śiva." "That's what I came to ask of you," said Indra.

Kāma stroked his bow and his five flower-arrows. Just brushing that bowstring was enough to fill the air with a hum of bees. "First of all," he thought, "we need spring." He looked at Rati, his beloved, who followed him everywhere, the way Pleasure will follow Desire, and sent her a nod full of complicity.

That spring came out of season. It surrounded and invaded the mountain where Śiva was sitting, motionless.

It crept into the Forest of Cedars, where the *ṛṣis* were practicing *tapas.* They had the sensation of an acute and unbearable torment. They felt their resolution crumble. Stubbornly, they stuck at it, but secretly they were floundering. Beside Śiva, Nandin, the white bull, lifted his head just a little. And the Gaṇas, the Genies who surrounded him as though in a gypsy camp, sniffed the air, intrigued.

Out of the thick foliage came Pārvatī, with two of her maids. Little girls, adolescents, women? Who could say? Kāma crouched down behind a bush. He was studying Śiva's chest, solid and upright as a column, looking for some point his arrow might pierce. Pārvatī had some flowers in her hand. As she was placing them at Śiva's feet, her tunic came open a glance. Śiva lowered his eyes and fastened them on Pārvatī. Then he spoke to her, in a whisper: "Lotus, moon, Kāma's bow, water drop, cuckoo, flax, corolla: all is within you. Upon your hips is laid the sacrificial offering." Śiva stretched out an arm toward Pārvatī. He was stroking her clothes, and already a hand slipped inside. Pārvatī blushed, stepped back. "Just looking at you is such an immense pleasure," thought Śiva. "What on earth will embracing you be like?" And immediately he plunged back into his *tapas.*

Then Kāma went into action. He loosed an arrow that would have transfixed anybody else. But it did nothing to Śiva, who knew desire too well. With the three petrified girls watching, Śiva sent out a blaze that enveloped Kāma. His ashes whirled in an eddy with the dust, then settled. Stepping backwards in silence, a pale Pārvatī retreated into the forest with her two maids, vaguely aware of Rati's sobs as she madly tried to recover some crumbs of ash from the grass, desperate for a relic of her vanished lover. Shoulders bent, she stumbled off, clutching a knotted rag of gaudy cloth, packed with ash. Flowers, bees, mangoes, cuckoos: it was into you that Desire dispersed when Śiva's blaze consumed him. Henceforth a humming or a birdcall, a flavor or a scent, would open a wound in those far from their loved ones. And many were wounded, if it is true that "upon seeing things of great beauty or hearing sweet sounds even a happy man may be seized by a fierce nostalgia."

On returning to the palace, Pārvatī felt she was a new person, born again. She said not a word. But the maids told the tale, dissolving at last into tears of terror. Old Himavat, Lord of the Mountain, took his daughter on his knee. He realized that Pārvatī was crying, but not in the way she had cried as a child. She took no notice of her father. She was crying because she was away from Śiva. Even in the days that followed, she still said nothing. Her eyes were gloomy and vacant. Sometimes the maids would catch her whispering the same name over and over: "Śiva, Śiva, Śiva."

A guest came to stay in the palace, Nārada, the *ṛṣi* who loved to meddle in others' affairs. Pārvatī hid in her rooms. But Nārada wanted to see her alone. He was the first to address her as an adult, without embarrassment. "Pārvatī, I know what you're feeling. You love Śiva, but you aren't ready yet. You must transform yourself by practicing *tapas*. Otherwise you'll never be able to get close to him: he would just burn you up. His fire must shoot up in rapture with the flame you learn to unleash. Not to worry: to look at, you won't be any different from any young girl with rounded thighs. Now let me teach you something: repeat these five syllables after me." Thus, tense and attentive, fever in her eyes, Pārvatī heard Śiva's *mantra* for the first time. "There's no other way. But I'm telling you that Śiva will be your husband." They were the last words Nārada spoke to her. Then he left like a man in a hurry.

Now Pārvatī was radiant. She immediately spoke to Jayā and Vijayā, her maids. She told them they were about to part company. Then she told her father that she was going to the forest to practice *tapas*. Himavat gave his assent. Nārada had spoken to him. Then Menā arrived, alarmed, breathing hard. "If you want to practice *tapas*, do it at home. We've got altars to all the gods in every corner of the palace. We've got temples. There are images and to spare. Who ever heard of a little girl going off into the forest to practice *tapas*? Don't be so pigheaded." Then, running out of breath, she stopped, and sighed: "Oh, no!" (*u mā*). Thenceforth Pārvatī, who already boasted many names, would have another: Umā.

But nothing could change Pārvatī's mind. Carefully, she removed all her princess's clothes, chose an antelope skin and a grass girdle, cut out a bodice for herself from a fabric made of tree bark. Once alone in the forest, she went straight to the place where Śiva had burned up Kāma. She found an empty clearing rustled by a breath of wind. There was no trace of either Śiva or his entourage. Looking down at the ground, Pārvatī tried to find some trace of ash. Then she followed Nārada's instructions. She chose a point in the middle of the softly wafting breeze, crossed her legs, and immersed herself in the heat of her mind. From a distance, she might have looked like the stump of a tree.

Pārvatī knew almost nothing of *tapas*, but she discovered it without even realizing. Soon she had eliminated father, mother, maids, garden, and palace from her mind. Eliminating her elder sister, Gaṅgā, was not so easy. Her image continued to flit around Pārvatī for a long time. She decided she hated her.

Meanwhile Pārvatī was seeing Śiva, exploring him unceasingly, as if climbing a mountain in comparison to which the mountain whose daughter she was, and which dominated all others, looked like a mere hillock far away in the plain. Time was a slow succession of scorching waves that flooded over her, then retreated. It was as though she were doing something she had always done, something she was more familiar with than her dolls. She felt Śiva's sharp edges. She rolled and unrolled the carpets of the mind.

. . .

Pārvatī's *tapas* grew so much that the gods began to notice. The ground under Indra's feet was scorching, the seats where he sat boiled. He realized it was the work of Pārvatī. So he went to talk it over with the other gods. They decided to go and see Śiva.

When Śiva heard the story of Tāraka and the young Pārvatī, of how she was practicing *tapas*, he smiled that mocking smile the gods had always feared: "I thought you'd be grateful I'd burned up Kāma, spared you all the idiocies you'd have gone on committing every time he lifted a finger . . . I thought you'd be pleased finally to be able to meditate without having to defend yourselves from the snares of Desire. Not that it took much to distract you. And instead you come here in a procession, to petition me, it seems. You want to offer me, who know no bonds, the one bond that is stronger than any metal: a woman. All the Vedic masters could have told you: there is nothing in this world so greatly to be feared." Śiva went on smiling while the gods were already losing hope. But then, almost without stopping, he began to take a completely different line, as though talking to himself. "In the end I can do anything. I am well-known for having kept the rules and broken the rules just as I like. In the end I love my devotees more than anything else. If they are so forward—or so desperate—as to ask me to do something that doesn't suit me, like marry, why not?" Then he looked at the anxious gods: "As for you, didn't I swallow the ocean's poison to save you? Young Pārvatī will be my *soma*."

Oppressed by the memory of Satī's death, Śiva wandered about aimlessly. The Gaṇas went with him, but they were unusually quiet. Śiva thought he should start ignoring the world again. He looked for a place that was undefiled, while making a mental note of the existence of a girl child, born in a palace amid the mountains. For a long time he walked toward the source of the Gaṅgā, along the back of the Himālaya. Then he stopped. The Gaṇas spread out to stand a melancholy guard around him. Nandin crouched on the ground, looking ahead with mild and vacant eyes.

In the palace of Himavat they got word that Śiva was coming. Someone had run into his silent retinue. Himavat went to Menā and said: "Menā, you know how old I am, older almost than the world. You know that we have lived for years like leisurely sovereigns of a kingdom where nothing happens, if only because one day something must happen on which everything depends. Do you remember the night our daughter Pārvatī was conceived? That was a long, long night. Do you remember how you looked at me in fright? You said I was delirious, though I was performing the same loving motions you knew of old. You said your body seemed to enter mine, drawn by some powerful undertow. And at the same time you felt that I was far away, terribly far away, so that it almost seemed you had a stranger in your bed. The truth is that that night Devī, the Goddess who lives in Śiva, bound herself to my mind. I whispered to her—and spoke to you as you shone in the light of the Goddess. For once, that night, I felt invincible again, invincible as the fire in the forest. Just as I did in my past life, when I was guardian of the rock that hid the light of heaven. You almost wanted to escape from me, because what was happening escaped you. In the end, you fell asleep exhausted. I lay awake, still clinging to your body. And I saw Night come. She had a small box in her hand, like the ones you women use for your makeup. Without so much as a word, she crept into your moist womb. Then I saw that very delicately she was touching the embryo of the child who was to be our daughter Pārvatī, with a tiny brush she was painting a dark, glossy dye on her. Then she was gone. I fell asleep myself. It all got muddled in my mind, like something extravagant I couldn't be sure was real, but then it all came back with compelling clarity, when Pārvatī was born. I was euphoric at the news—so much so, do you remember, that on impulse I gave my ivory-handled sunshade to our dear steward—and then I saw the tiny body of my daughter for the first time, that wonderfully burnished skin she has. Now Pārvatī has grown up, now the moment our lives were planned for is at hand. Once again you must obey me and follow me. Nothing of what is about to happen must upset you."

Pārvatī was stubborn and wild, but that didn't mean she had given up on being a princess, or that she didn't want everything to happen to her just as it should happen to a princess. If Śiva really meant to be her husband, the first thing he would have to do was ask—or have somebody else ask—her father, Himavat, for her hand. And as far as the wedding was concerned, Pārvatī left no one in any doubt that she expected a magnificent ceremony, scrupulously faithful to the most ancient customs. Mildly smiling, a patient Śiva called together the Saptarṣis at the Mahākośī waterfall. They would be his ambassadors. They went down to Oṣadhiprastha, where Himavat received them at once in the presence of Menā and Pārvatī. While Aṅgiras launched into a speech of great and characteristic eloquence, solemn images spouting from his lips like drops of crystal, Pārvatī concentrated on counting the petals of a lotus flower, like a little girl playing in a corner and pretending not to listen to what her parents are talking about. Menā couldn't conceal her anxiety. Himavat looked at her to ask for her consent. Menā's nod turned into a prolonged shiver.

When Śiva's retinue passed through the second gate of Oṣadhiprastha and the procession behind found themselves up to their ankles in flowers, wind ruffling their standards of Chinese silk, there was a sudden, unanimous movement, like a beating of wings, among the women hidden away in the palaces. One dropped a garland she had been fixing in her hair; another took her henna-wet foot from her maid's hands and ran to the window, leaving red prints on the floor; another rushed over with one eye made up and the other not; another broke off in the middle of tying her robe and, pressing her forehead against the grating, had a bracelet cutting into her navel as she tried to cover her bare belly with her hand; another had been lacing a girdle of pearls and suddenly let go, leaving the pearls to fall and scatter. The procession pressed on through the empty streets, while behind a thousand embroidered screens bright splashes of light trembled like lotus flowers besieged by swarms of bees.

The city disappeared. The villages disappeared, likewise the travelers. The noisy escort disappeared. Nature thickened, withdrew into itself. Piece by piece, Pārvatī felt the world she had known fall away from her. She had scarcely left her parents' house and already she had no idea who she was. A little girl? The Goddess? Both followed the footsteps of the man with the wiry legs as he walked ahead along the path that climbed slowly up Kailāsa, and never turned back to look at her. Behind them, they could hear the warm breath of Nandin the bull, carrying their few belongings, only witness to the scene.

Then they had fallen asleep, welded together like two metals, and Śiva had begun to move in Pārvatī's dreams, then they had fought like two swords, then stopped, suspended in the air, then laughed, bit into fruit, drunk, blindly, oafishly, then left their supine bodies, looked at themselves from above, motionless while their bodies stirred ever so slightly, Pārvatī had begun to wander off, already she could see the lights being lit in her temples, except that the temples were inside her, they rose up everywhere Śiva's phallus, like a quiet, inquisitive traveler, prodded and explored her, at which Pārvatī saw a name impress itself on the vast landscape around her—Yājñavalkya—and couldn't remember who it might be, then she heard Śiva pronouncing those same syllables, as he recited the texts of the *ṛṣis,* and beside the name were some words she hadn't understood at the time and had marked for later attention, because she sensed that one day they would be useful, and she had forgotten them, but now they came back like obviousness itself, the obviousness of the Self, of the *ātman*, which, according to that *ṛṣi* of whom she knew nothing aside from his name, causes us to feel like the man who embraces the woman he loves, the man who "no longer knows anything of without and within." "No longer knows anything of without and within," Pārvatī said to herself, muttering a knowledge that surpassed even her pleasure, which in turn surpassed everything else, and at the same time her eyes moved cautiously around those temples at once remote and intimate, but it was then that she caught a sense of something suspicious, insidious, something that disturbed her, and she found the eye of Kālidāsa, the poet, crouched on the steps of one of those temples, as if trying to blend in with stones—and instead he was watching her and writing. "This must not be," murmured Pārvatī, assuming the terrifying shape she often played with. "A curse on you if you proceed, by so much as a syllable, with your description of Pārvatī's pleasure." But Kālidāsa had already melted away, crept back into the gloom of time.

Pārvatī said to Śiva: "Please explain. Pleasure leaves no memory. I mean: during the twenty-five years of our first embrace, when I had just left my father's house, I often thought, as though making a long journey: I must remember what happened just now, exactly how this moment was, how we got there and how we left it behind. I was quite determined—and everything seemed quite clear and sharp, but the way dreams seem clear and sharp while we are dreaming them, we decide to remember them and fasten on every detail—and the idea that we might forget something seems so ridiculous we almost smile, because it is all too real, but then when we wake up that thing evaporates along with all the rest. Try to understand: everything that happened is there inside me, just below the flux of my mind. But I can't recall the sequence of it all, I could remember far better the sequence of something quite unimportant to me: how I dressed one day, what makeup I put on, how I went down into the palace gardens, how I walked along a particular path and how I mounted my dappled horse, my two maids behind me, and how the maids were dressed, and the first words we spoke to each other. Yet Kāma, Desire, is also called Smara, Memory. Indeed, it's as if that were his real name. Or at least that's the name I always use for him. And I saved his life, remember? For days I sat motionless before you, at a respectful distance, immersed in *tapas*. We didn't know each other then, and I was just a girl. You kept your eyes closed all the time. When you opened them and saw me, you spoke, without even looking at me: "What's happening?" you said, "Kāma is here." Kāma barely managed to get to his feet—he was behind a bush—and to draw his bow with one of the five flower-arrows, before your eye had shriveled him up. Then you looked at me, as though this was the first time you'd really seen me, and invited me to ask a boon of you. I said: "Now that Kāma is dead, there are no more boons to ask. Without Desire there can be no more emotion. Without emotion men and women may as well ignore each other." So you granted me this boon, that Kāma might go on living, but invisibly. When I was a little girl and used to invoke him, looking at the miniatures I'd painted of you, though I'd never seen you then, all I would say was "Smara, Smara . . ."

It wasn't unusual for Pārvatī to fall asleep while Śiva recited the Vedas to her. The hymns made her impatient or drowsy. But she would soon rouse herself again, as if driven by a goad. There were only two things she never tired of discussing: theology and women, the latter insofar as they were—or had been—Śiva's women. Pārvatī sat up in bed, bare-breasted, her skin moist and glistening. She gazed steadily ahead of her and spoke to Śiva, who was lying by her side: "*Prakṛti, māyā, śakti:* you see how, when we set off along the path that leads back to the beginning, we always come across this element that flaunts its feminine noun. Never existing alone, but always such that nothing else can exist without it. Nature, illusion, power: these are the words your ingenuous Western devotees will pronounce one day, though generally without realizing how each is the shell of the other. There is no nature without illusion, there is no illusion without power, there is no power without nature. As for *māyā*, rather than 'illusion' it would be more apt to call it 'magic,' that strange thing that those supposedly of sober mind are convinced does not exist, while actually it would be far more sober to say that nothing in existence can exist without it. But even that would not be enough, and this is what I want to talk about, that's why I'm here next to you waiting for you to lay me down on that tiger skin, get rid of your Gaṇas and launch your *liṅga* on the vessel of my thighs, so that the *māyā* in me may cloak it in a liquid veil."

Pārvatī said: "Your mouth comes to me like the unmanifest that rejoices in qualities. Then I feel I am flowing in you. But sometimes you look at me like a man who sees loose women going into an empty house and doesn't so much as touch them. No less secret, at such moments, is our own contact. When we don't touch, it's as if I were putting my fingers in my ears. Then I hear the sound that dwells in the space within the heart: like a river, like a bell, like a chariot wheel, like the croak of a frog, like the rain, like the word spoken in a cozy corner."

One day they went down to the sea, which Pārvatī had never seen before. On a beach not far from Kāñcī, Umā played with Śiva's phallus, which was a column of sand. She didn't notice the sea swelling up. Soon the waves came crashing down on her. Umā clutched the *liṅga* in her arms, like a doll, to protect it. When the waves withdrew, the column of sand was etched with the scars left by Umā's bracelets and nipples.

. . .

They spun out the game of pleasure, *ratilīlā,* made it digressive, circular, rambling. At their feet, Nandin the bull slept, occasionally shaking his big head. White with ash, Śiva's chest was crossed by two dark stripes: a cobra and Pārvatī's arm. Śiva whispered to her: "Kālī, you Black One." It was a name Pārvatī didn't want to hear. She had always wished, stonily, for her dark skin to grow pale, to be like the skin of those princesses who lived beyond the mountains, whose miniatures people had sometimes shown her. She slipped out from Śiva's grasp and hissed: "You are the Great Black One." An argument began. Ever since they'd been alone, this had been their life: sex, dice, *bhaṅgā,* arguing, *tapas.* And erratic conversation. Each phase enhanced the others and came around again quite regularly. Śiva said: "You're hard as a spike of the rock you were born from. There's nowhere one can get hold of you, you're like the sheet of ice around your father. You're tortuous and twisting as a mountain path." Then Pārvatī sat before Śiva, hugging her knees tight, shut up in herself, staring at him with furious eyes. "And the only thing you like is ash, you smear it over yourself the way my maids rubbed themselves with sandalwood oil. You're only happy when there are corpses burning all around you. Your earrings are snakes. Why did you drag me away from my palace, from my family, if my body isn't enough for you? Why do you make me live like a tramp, wandering about aimlessly? Why do you prevent me from having a child like any ordinary woman would? I'm only black because I'm part of you. If you see me as a snake, I must be the only snake you haven't loved." Pārvatī jumped to her feet, choking with rage, and went out. Nandin followed her, imploring her to stay. "Go away," said Pārvatī. "The only thing you should worry about is making sure no other women come here. Your Master thinks of nothing else. Don't forget to keep your eye on him through the keyhole. When I get back, my skin will be a golden apple, its down soft and light as the dawn. I'll dazzle him. My *tapas* is strong enough to do that and more." And the proud Pārvatī went off, her hand clutching Gaṇeśa, who, full of dark thoughts, lowered his big elephant's head.

. . . .

Nandin stood guard, never moved. But he was half asleep one night when a snake slithered up. It was Āḍi, the demon, who had long been waiting for a chance to get even with Śiva, who had killed his father. Sliding along in the dark of the pavilion, Āḍi assumed the likeness of Pārvatī. Motionless, Śiva watched her approach. He felt happy. He had always counted on her sudden changes of mood. And this time she had been away too long. Through the window casing, the moonlight fell on a magnificent, shy girl, with dark skin. "So nothing's changed," Śiva thought. The false Pārvatī was walking around him. It was a habit they had, before touching each other. Śiva began to undress her, slowly. He lifted her hair to find a tiny blemish she had, the shape of a lotus flower, on the nape of her neck, to the left. He couldn't find it. He realized he was being tricked. The false Pārvatī had stretched out on the ground, arms raised in an arch above her head, fingers twining. From Śiva's phallus sprouted the *vajra,* the three-pronged thunderbolt, flashing a moment before burying itself in the false Pārvatī. The vulva it penetrated concealed an adamantine tooth, ready to shred Śiva's phallus. For a while the scene resembled a convulsive coitus. The two bodies arched. Then the false Pārvatī shuddered and stiffened, heat blazing from within. Then she fell back on the floor.

Just then Vāyu, Wind, went to the real Pārvatī, who was sitting on a mountaintop deep in *tapas,* and whispered in her ear that a woman was lying dead beside Śiva's bed. Pārvatī smiled and didn't move. She spoke to Night: "I know very well that when I was conceived you slipped into my mother's womb and colored my embryo with a dark liquid. Even then I turned against you. Though I know that you meant it as a gift, because I partake of the Black. The gods wanted me to be born to seduce Śiva and with his seed produce a son the color of gold. That son is not yet born—and never will be from my womb. But the gold is mine by right. I can't bear for Śiva to lose interest in me, as he did with Satī and with my sister, Gaṅgā, and all the others.

Take back my veil of flesh. Make me pale as a foreigner." Even as the bold Pārvatī spoke, her dark skin fell from her body to lie in folds on the ground like a rag of cast-off muslin.

Nandin was curled up, all too aware of his shortcomings, when a radiant being with familiar features appeared before him. Pārvatī paid no attention to the guardian bull. She was longing for Śiva to see her. She sat before him in the same position as when she had last seen him. Śiva was silent as his eye took in the golden down of her arms shining from her white robe. Without a word he drew her into himself.

"As many as are the aeons, so many shall be the ways in which Gaṇesā's story is told." Many the aeons, many the stories. Only one thing is certain: Gaṇesā was born of Pārvatī "without husband," *vinā nayākena.* Which is why they call him Vināyaka. He was often to be seen lying awake beside Pārvatī's bed. He was her mild and thoughtful guardian, trunk curled up on his round belly and one tusk broken. To his right he kept a stylus and inkpot. Pārvatī couldn't help stroking him whenever she passed by. "You are my son. You're mine. I can't say that of anyone else." She remembered so clearly the day she had lain exhausted on her bed, every pore of her body drenched in sweat, Śiva's and her own, and begun to fantasize quite furiously. Would she never have a child? Śiva was evasive when she beset him with her questions. Once he had said: "How could I have a child? There is no death in me." The words were a dagger. "Then I'll have a child to spite you," Pārvatī thought. With slow strokes she spread a scented oil over her body, mixed it with her sweat, with the flakes of spent skin. The palms of her hands rubbed angrily over her belly, her legs, her breasts. She was almost scratching herself, so as not to miss the smallest speck. She gathered a lump of something, and Gaṇesā was born from that. He didn't have his elephant's head at first. He was a beautiful little boy who never left his mother's side. Śiva pretended to be pleased, but actually he was annoyed. Expert as she was in jealousy, Pārvatī rejoiced to see Śiva suffering the torments she knew so well.

One day, after a fight, Gaṇesā went so far as to bar Śiva from Pārvatī's room. Śiva hacked off his head. And immediately, with Pārvatī dumbstruck before him, a huge wave of affection for that lifeless body rose within him. He told Nandin to tear off Airāvata's head, Airāvata being Indra's elephant. In times past, when Indra was the indisputed sovereign of the gods, the idea would have seemed absurd. But the Devas were a spent force now. One day Nandin returned carrying Airāvata's noble head on his back. One tusk had been broken in their ferocious duel. With a craftsman's skill, Śiva fixed the elephant's head on Gaṇeśa's neck. Pārvatī looked on, eyes full of tenderness. She saw how deftly Śiva was performing the delicate operation. And at once it crossed her mind that only now would her son be truly himself. From that day on she was no longer afraid of being alone. When Śiva set off on a journey and she had no way of knowing whether he meant to practice *tapas* on his own, or to seduce an Apsaras or a common woman, or to destroy or give life to some part of the world—whatever the reason his absence irritated her—Pārvatī would stretch out on her bed among heaps of cushions and dictate one long story after another. Stories of the world she had never seen. Curled up at her feet, Gaṇesā wrote them down. He was a fast and tireless scribe. As soon as she had finished, Pārvatī stroked the broken tusk and kissed his broad and wrinkled forehead.

Nothing attracted Pārvatī so much as that huge blue stain that shone through Śiva's neck, even from beneath the ashes. When she was a child, they had told her the story of how Vāsuki the snake had vomited poison into the ocean and how Śiva had swallowed it up. It had gathered like a lake in his throat. On the surface, the color made one think of sapphire, or the ringed eye spots of a peacock feather. It looked like the mark a bite leaves, many, many love bites, and an ornament too. Pārvatī's hands circled the stain like a noose. "Why do you like pyres and jackals and bones and vultures and ghosts so much? And when you move around, why are you followed by a procession of disfigured and terrifying creatures, why do you treat them like your oldest friends? In the palace where I grew up, I never saw such things. Yet I always loved to invent songs full of words that made me shudder, because I was told you partook of such things, and my friends looked at me as if I were daring them to do the same. Horror and pleasure must have been born together. That's how it was for me. I know they live one inside the other. That's how it has to be. Otherwise they would be dull. But now that we're alone, and will go on being alone, with only the whines and wiles of the gods to bother us from time to time, tell me: why do I always suspect that you get more pleasure from your ashes than from my body?" Stubbornly, brazenly, Pārvatī went on and on asking these same questions. Then Śiva would smile, would laugh, would say nothing, change the subject, shift his grip on Pārvatī's body, turn her this way and that in his hands. But one day he looked Pārvatī straight in the eyes and said: "Daughter of the Mountain, since you reproach me with my love of ashes, I shall tell you a story, the story you have always wanted me to tell you. You know that when I met you I was a widower. I would still rave wildly from time to time thinking of her death, of Satī, of She-who-is. Before Satī was born, reality was less real . . ."

Even when he retires to remote mountain peaks, when he is rapt—in thought? in *tapas?* or in something that is both thought and *tapas?*—Śiva is never alone. From his long hair, so black it is almost blue, drips the Goddess, now Gaṅgā. They rarely speak to each other. But Gaṅgā is witness to everything Śiva does. She is present at his embraces that have no end. Yet she is never jealous. She flows—that's all. But it's enough to drive Pārvatī wild. Majestically, she sits beside Śiva on Kailāsa. All creatures bow before her, none sure of attracting her attention. Sometimes Pārvatī looks anxious: she casts a sidelong glance above Śiva's ear, at his temple.

"Who is that damn woman hiding in your hair?" said Pārvatī. Once again she couldn't stop herself. "The sickle moon," said Śiva, as though thinking of something else. "Oh, so that's what she's called, is it?" said Pārvatī, in a tone that would one day be the model for all female sarcasm.

"Of course, you know that perfectly well," said Śiva, more absentminded than ever.

"I'm not speaking about the moon, I'm speaking about your girlfriend," said Pārvatī, snarling.

"You want to talk to your friend? But your friend Vijayā's just gone out, hasn't she?" said Śiva. Pārvatī went off, white with rage.

Śiva and Gaṅgā met as two excesses. Śiva allowed the celestial river to break over his head before touching the earth, which otherwise could not have survived the impact. And in ever bathing the motionless Śiva's head, ever flowing in streams down his face, Gaṅgā stopped the scorching god from withering up the whole world. This beneficial and ever-renewed equilibrium was also a secret love affair. Of no other woman was Pārvatī so jealous as of Gaṅgā. No sooner did she come close to him than she saw her sister in the quivering drops on Śiva's face. Even his saliva smacked of Gaṅgā.

A stream crosses the sky: a stream of souls, of waters, of the dead, of subtle substance. It is the Milky Way. It runs from one end of the sky to the other, then flows on upon the earth. Earth and sky are the two banks of one great river, and it would be hard indeed to find the place where that river passes from the celestial to the terrestial bank. Where is the meeting point? Where do the celestial waters plunge down to earth, with their tremendous mass, where do they carve out their bed? Such is the disparity of force, between heaven and earth, that it is perilous, rash, to pass directly from one to the other. The flow of the Milky Way headed down to where a mighty corrugation lifted earth to sky. It was the Himālaya. Thus, flowing down from the mountaintops, the Milky Way became Gaṅgā, Śiva's lover, and daughter of the king-mountain Himavat. But if left to themselves, those waters would have flooded the earth. To avoid overwhelming life irremediably, the celestial stream came down on Śiva's head where he sat motionless, deep in *tapas.* The impact shattered the mass of water, which then came on down to earth in a thousand small streams. That was Gaṅgā's body, forever twisting around her lover's head, streaming over his lips, pouring from his jet black tresses. When Śiva wore his turban, the waters hid among the folds, bridesmaids to their amorous play, then spilled over. Life on earth is possible because Gaṅgā's body breaks unceasingly over Śiva's. Śiva can be "Propitious," as his name would have it, only so long as Gaṅgā's cataract plunges constantly down upon his head, only so long as his secret, ever-exposed lover dribbles down his thin tresses, the way water drips down on the stone *liṅga* from a jug hanging above. The dry sign of algebraic equivalence must ever be drenched in the tongue's lymph, just as coitus means swimming toward the recognition of those waters from which Word, Vāc, emerged.

Śiva and Gaṅgā were the first example of a perennial love, renewed at every instant by a stream that knows no end. But the beginning was rather different, closer to hate and war. Looking down from the height of what would one day be called the Milky Way at the bluish mass of Śiva's head, where she had been told she would have to shatter herself before touching ground, Gaṅgā thought: "I'll sweep him away like a straw." In the end, what did a god mean to her?

Amid her waves the gods surfaced, then hid again. It was true of Agni, true of Soma. And likewise of Sūrya, Sun, every single night. They were a dazzle, a heat made manifest in her from time to time. But without her waters they would never have existed. That motionless figure on the ground, that taciturn god who was perhaps trying to look like a tree trunk, would be just one among many.

Gaṅgā plunged with a crash onto Śiva's head. She was impatient to touch the ground, to taste this new flavor. She wouldn't even see Śiva's face, she thought, unless already swept off on billowing waters, far away. But no sooner had she brushed against that head than Gaṅgā felt lost. Śiva's hair was a forest. And what was a forest? Her waters were constantly being diverted, divided, humiliated in tiny streams. They settled in huge lakes, surrounded by a thick darkness that was no longer the darkness of the sky. Huge, angry waves kept beating down on Śiva. And Śiva had gathered himself in one spot. From there, like silk from a spider, his *māyā* spun out, the sticky enchantment of his mind. Śiva held back the waters, wound around she who winds around all, multiplied the meanders that would soak her up. Like a spoiled princess used to having her every whim obeyed, Gaṅgā pounded down upon him, loathed him. "I'll never see the earth if I go on wandering about in this stupid, frightening forest," she thought. Gaṅgā didn't know it, but her fury enhanced her splendor. Streaming down Śiva's hair, she saw a corner of the god's mouth lift, in a hint of a smile. That made her even madder. As she renewed her attack, boiling in obscure little ditches, a few drops of foam spurted out beyond the forest. For a moment they found themselves suspended in the void, astonished. Finally they tasted a sharp, dry flavor. It was the earth. Those drops formed Lake Bindusaras, the Lake of Drops. From there they flowed into a bed that seemed to have been made for them. Men called that river Gaṅgā.

For thousands of days Śiva was united to Pārvatī, and that contact transmitted a tremor to the earth. Their bodies were twined together, but all at once Śiva noticed that Pārvatī was cold, as if she were rejecting *tapas*. Her fire concentrated in a single point: her eyes, which were no longer staring into Śiva's eyes, but at his tresses. In the dripping dampness of his hair, she had recognized her elder sister, Gaṅgā, still clinging to Śiva's body. Every drop bespoke the delicate swaying of her generous hips. And the corners of her mouth upturned in a constant complicity of pleasure and mockery. Pārvatī thought: "So all the time Śiva has had me wrapped in his serpentine embraces, he was still carrying Gaṅgā on his head, still dripping with her body. How will I ever be able to show forth Devī, the Goddess who belongs to Śiva's body, who is his body, how will I ever be able to immerse myself in pleasure if I'm forever meeting Gaṅgā's eyes, as when we played together as children, if Gaṅgā's eyes are forever telling me that she is immersed in a pleasure perhaps even greater than my own? So, while for years on end Śiva's body has been glued to mine, at the same time I have been witnessing another of Śiva's loves, which began before mine and is still going on, wrinkling his forehead and pouring down his tresses. How naive I was to think those signs were due to the heights of our pleasure . . ." Pārvatī was shot through by an overwhelming jealousy and anger. What did it mean, now, to have practiced *tapas* so long, for no other reason than to attract the god? What did it mean to have schemed with her father to distract the god's mind and have it wander all over her body? What did it mean, if the truth was that Śiva's head was still streaming with her sister, the loathsome Gaṅgā? Pārvatī turned her eyes on Śiva and said in icy rage: "You play with my body, but your head is still playing with Gaṅgā." With a sudden animal move that made the mountain quake, Pārvatī wrenched herself free from Śiva's embrace. Then she turned to the river Gaṅgā and cursed it: "May your waters be forever impure." The god gazed at Pārvatī and thought that he had never seen her look so beautiful, as when they played dice and Pārvatī cheated. Then she would laugh, with a trill that concealed a similar and opposite fury.

. . .

When Śiva wiped out the world, all combinations of existence would flow within him, without needing to exist. The mind and the outside were not separate entities—perhaps not even entities at all. Penetrating each other, they lost all their shyness. The stream was one. The dreadful and the delicate surfaced together, in pairs, indifferent to each other, like distant relatives. Then they bid each other goodbye. Immediately something else took their place. An incessant migration. All forms, all forces: they were Śiva's herd. That's why they called him Paśupati, Lord of the Herds.

"For Śiva excess is the norm. An everlasting turbulence. None of his states can guarantee the earth peace and quiet," thought the thirty-three gods, perplexed. If Śiva practices *tapas* and ignores the world, then creation grows dull, loses its fragrance, like a woman dressing up for a lover who doesn't notice. If, together with the Goddess, or with a woman, he indulges in the game of pleasure, then it goes on for months and years, until the constant, exasperated contact between their bodies, its never-ending friction, infects the world like a fever and threatens to burn it all up. So the gods came to the conclusion that, however Śiva manifested himself, at some point or other he should be diverted, disturbed, interrupted, so that life might run its course, mediocre though that might be. They knew that Śiva was he who brings imbalance—and that even though it could never vibrate without him, the world could absorb only a tiny fraction of his turmoil. The only conceivable balance would be a sum of imbalances, all of them originating in Śiva.

When the Snake and the Turtle that the earth rests upon began to tremble, the gods got together again, aggrieved and grim. "Those two think of nothing but dice and sex. Tāraka could make slaves of us all, and they wouldn't turn a hair. The world will have crumbled away beneath our feet before we know it," said one of the Thirty-three. "We'll go and ask Viṣṇu's advice again," they agreed. This time Viṣṇu didn't try to reassure them. "Śiva might perfectly well wait another whole aeon before releasing his seed," he said pensively. He acted as their guide on the road to Mount Kailāsa. The gods walked along the path up the valley like a caravan of ants, until finally they sniffed the breeze of the *locus amoenus* where Śiva dwelled. They didn't deign to give its delights so much as a glance. Coming out of the forest, they suddenly found themselves among Śiva's Gaṇas. Some were asleep, some playing dice. "Where's Śiva? You must tell us, our distress is crushing us." "There's not much to tell. One day, a long time ago now, Śiva withdrew into Pārvatī's rooms. He still hasn't come out. We don't know what he's up to. We've been left here yawning ever since," said one of the Gaṇas. Cautiously, the gods pressed on, until they reached what Nandin the bull referred to as the Nocturnal Pavilion: an enchanting, childishly embellished, polygonal structure that stood on thin columns and boasted a terrace where Śiva and Pārvatī gave themselves up to astronomy and pleasure. Viṣṇu had taken charge. It was he who dared to knock on the pavilion door, he who spoke, in a voice too shrill and tense: "Our supreme Lord, what are you doing in there? We have all come to seek refuge with you, oppressed as we are by Tāraka. Grant us your assistance." From behind Viṣṇu's voice came a buzz of praise and celebration. Each of the gods was murmuring something.

That knocking on the door, the babble of voices, Viṣṇu's shrill words: it all slid into Śiva's mind like a splinter of some mineral whose composition he knew only too well. "The world again," he thought, impatiently, slowly shifting the angle at which he was penetrating Pārvatī. Their coitus had been going on for some dozens of years. Initially it had been violent (they had just argued because Pārvatī was cheating at dice), then it had been like a liquid flow, then it had all dissolved like ashes in water, then it was all water, and the water trembled ever so slightly, as if it were feverish—and all at once Śiva had remembered how one day Pārvatī, the little-girl theologian, had appeared before him, self-possessed and resplendent, impeccably decked out in tree bark pulled tight with a belt of leaves at the waist, and announced in what was almost a rage: "How dare you presume to ignore the *prakṛti* you're entwined to? How could your mind breathe if it didn't devour your substance, myself?" Śiva had laughed. Then they had tried to touch each other using nothing but their teeth. For years Śiva had drenched himself in that substance, invading it, invaded by it, burning. But now, he felt, he was returning to a state not very different from the time he had stood fast in a motionless column deep in the waters, and shut the world out from himself. Yet from time to time he would feel nostalgic for that world. To go back to watching the sky and shooting his arrows or wandering around the forest with his animals, or going to the markets as a juggler or dancer, lost in the crowd. When would he be doing that again? It was the sign that Śiva was about to detach himself. He was only holding off because Pārvatī was still absorbed in her pleasure. And now this gaggle of gods. Śiva immediately crushed the profound irritation that had pricked him a moment before. He got up from his bed, opened the door, saw the gods' faces, masks of fear and curiosity, their eyes not daring to meet his and at the same time taking advantage of the situation to sneak glances behind him, where they hoped to get a glimpse of Pārvatī in the half-light. Distracted by this ludicrous sight, forgetting himself for one tiny fraction of time, Śiva realized that his phallus was squirting out its seed. Quick as lightning, Agni darted forward and opened his mouth wide to take it. Regaining his composure, and likewise his mocking smile, Śiva said: "Isn't that what you wanted?" Behind him a door opened, slowly. And as the gods crowded around like a bevy of dim-witted schoolchildren, Pārvatī appeared, her moist skin cloaked only in a thin and crumpled robe. The Mother of the Universe glared from furious eyes. She said: "I hate you and curse you all. It is you and the fear that consumes you that have stolen from me, from the Mother of the Universe, the happiness of giving birth like a normal woman. I shall be sterile, but likewise sterile shall be the wives that the demon Tāraka took from you and whom I hope he defiles, so that they may learn from him the pleasure that you were unable to give them. If they are sterile, then all the gods will be sterile. The era of these pusillanimous celestial families is over. There are too many of you, you are old and the world is impatient to be rid of you. Up there, where you live, there will be nothing but emptiness, and that emptiness will enchant men even more than you have enchanted them. Only Śiva shall be motionless, pervasive, intact, as he ever has been. I despise you." Pārvatī shut the door. Without a word, the gods stepped contritely backwards and withdrew. Later they could be seen climbing down the mountain. On a litter, they carried a writhing Agni, his throat scorched by Śiva's seed.

Śaravaṇodbhava, Born-in-a-reed-marsh: that was one of the names they gave Skanda, Squirt, the boy who was to save the world. Fire burned by fire, Agni spat out Śiva's seed into a meander of the Gaṅgā. Still water, under moonlight. The Pleiades, the Kṛttikās who watch over from above, saw the scene. Then a glow in the water drew them irresistibly. Having conversed so often with sailors and helped them find their way, they were eager to know the earth. Only the ever punctilious Arundhatī stayed where she was, reluctant to touch the world. Six girls descended in line from the night sky. They hid among the reeds, as though behind screens. Śiva's seed penetrated the pores of their pulsing bodies. They lay there, feeding it, six guardians of a single womb. Then the white torsos of the entwined sisters rose from the waters as they all gave birth together. There was a profound silence, but that was not to say no one was watching. Hidden behind bushes on the riverbank, impatient for a sight of the boy who meant survival for them, the gods gazed hard at that glowing swamp.

The reeds rustled in a first breeze. They saw six pairs of hands lift and caress a child above the surface of the water. Pārvatī was far away, alone, shut up in the shadows, melancholy, despondent. Quite suddenly she felt the milk flow in her breasts. And at the same time a spasm more painful than any birth, because it meant that she would never give birth. The milk was a mockery. But it did confirm that Skanda was her child, even if he hadn't been born from her womb. "Your flesh is made of my *tapas* and my pleasure. You exist because Śiva touched me," murmured Pārvatī to her distant son. And already Skanda was laughing amid reeds and mud. Six women offered him their breasts. They looked more like playmates than mothers. The divine infant's six mouths stretched out to suck the milk of the Pleiades.

The world was never so peaceful as during Skanda and Gaṇeśa's childhood. The boy with the elephant's head and the boy with six heads played unceasingly around Śiva and Pārvatī, who no longer bothered with their lovemaking, rarely spoke, sat for hours on a smooth rock surrounded by pastel-colored drapes. Nandin the bull squatted down and gazed into the void. Gaṇeśa played at wrapping snakes around Śiva's chest. With the same movements she had once made to string pearls in her palace, Pārvatī was engrossed in lacing little skulls onto Śiva's garland. Skanda helped by holding one end of the string. The other animals around them—a peacock, a mouse, a lion—kept quiet and slept. For once almost nothing was happening in the world. No tremor from the coitus of Śiva and Pārvatī. No threat of Tāraka rocking the earth from its foundations. Skanda had chased him off like an insect in no time at all. Even the gods were finally at rest.

VII

Driven into the year like a wedge, the three last days of the *aśvamedha*, the "sacrifice of the horse," came as the climax of what was the king of all sacrifices, the sacrifice that allows he who celebrates it to become king of all kings, to obtain everything he desires. Three days of ceremonies, but the whole year converged on that short segment of time. All year one sensed a hidden tension, all year something was going on in preparation for those days, as if the ultimate purpose of the year was to home in on those three days. After which another year and other ceremonies would follow, as though to attenuate the consequences.

To be sovereign of the whole earth, one need do no more than think of oneself as sovereign of the whole earth, one need do no more than celebrate the rite of him who is sovereign of the whole earth: the sacrifice of the horse. What is real in effect (actual sovereignty over the whole earth) is secondary and derivative with respect to what is of the mind, and to the rite that is its consequence.

The place of sacrifice was an even, well-trodden stretch of land, flat but sloping gently toward the east. Beyond its eastern edge, there was to be no sign of another, similar space that might itself become a place of sacrifice. Rather, there had to be water to the east, water all year round. Usually a pond. Above all the place was an empty space, a clearing. Something entirely normal and nondescript. The only thing that mattered was that there be no other place, at once equally normal and nondescript, in the immediate vicinity. Because there a rival's shadow might one day loom. It was also important that one be aware of the presence of water.

Before the sacrifice of the horse, there is an empty clearing. After the sacrifice of the horse, there is an empty clearing, with a few remaining ashes and a melee of foot and hoof prints. Some of the items necessary for the sacrifice, like the *mahāvīra* pot, were made during the sacrifice itself. Making these things was part of the sacrifice. And they were then destroyed at the end of the sacrifice. Again this destruction was part of the sacrifice. You might say that the main concern of those officiating was to start from zero and return to zero. To make everything themselves, accepting nothing ready-made, nothing already in existence. Then to destroy everything, leaving no trace, as if what was being worked out within the sacrifice was of the same stuff as time, which looms over all but is palpable to no one.

Everything begins, and ends, with the eye, within the eye. In the beginning, Prajāpati saw the sacrifice of the horse. He saw it as one sees an animal passing by. But what was the horse? Prajāpati's eye.

This happened: Prajāpati was watching and desiring, in the void. His left eye began to swell (*aśvayat*). His left eye fell to the ground. Prajāpati looked at his swollen, now detached eye, lying in the dust, and saw that it was the horse (*aśva*). Upon which he thought that more than anything else he would like to be whole again, to recover his eye. Then that very moment he saw the sacrifice, saw the white horse with the black patches galloping by, its mane blowing in the wind. He knew he would kill it, knew he would cut into the horse's flesh on its left flank so that his left eye might return to its socket as before. But now there would be the almost imperceptible mark of a suture. That scar would be the sign of sacrifice, of life passing by.

Agni, the firstborn, had just fled. The other gods were crowding around Prajāpati: "Follow him! You've got to get him back! Agni won't show himself to anyone but his father!" they said. So Prajāpati turned into a white horse. For a long time he wandered around at random, tried every direction. While drinking from a pond, he saw a lotus leaf with a blaze of light flickering over it. He raised his muzzle to look. His mouth was seared by fire. And his eyes too were affronted by the blaze. Agni realized he had hurt the Father. As he burned beneath the horse's noble and solemn muzzle, he said: "Father, I shall grant you one boon. Ask . . ." Prajāpati said: "That whoever goes in search of you in the form of a white horse shall find you." From that day on white horses have red mouths, as if seared, and delicate eyes. They are the marks left by that wound we call knowledge.

Preparations for the sacrifice of the horse were long. The craftsmen had to make the wherewithal. They cut down twenty-one trees to make as many poles, to which the victims would be tied. Thirty-six long-handled spoons were required. Four four-wheeled chariots. Four silver-buttoned headdresses were prepared for the brides of the sacrificer-king. They baked the bricks for the altar of fire. They forged two hundred and forty-two knives. Three hundred and thirty-three gold needles, the same number of silver, the same number of bronze. Then a pot to cook the horse's blood in. Three cushions were embroidered with gold. Hundreds of animals were rounded up, from every village. "The tame animals they keep in the villages; the animals of the forest in a forest; the animals of the mountain on a mountain; the animals of the rivers in the rivers; the birds in cages; the reptiles in pots."

. . .

Thus it was at the time of the Veda: scores of shabby, worn-out things; a huge clearing, most of it empty; a tension that galvanized the space from end to end, with invisible threads vibrating from one fire to another, one hut to another.

Thus it was long afterward, on the threshold of the *kaliyuga*, when Yudhiṣṭhira, near the end of the bloody war against his cousins, the story of which is told in the *Mahābhārata*, chose to celebrate the sacrifice of the horse to expiate his guilt: the elements were the same, in accordance with the ancient canons. But the twenty-one poles to which the victims were tied were all golden now. Around the place of sacrifice a huge city had hurriedly been built, to host the kings who would attend, each with his retinue; to house the animals, some of every species; to offer shelter to the ascetics who had come down from the mountains to be present at the ceremony. "The whole island of the Jambū, with all its many and diverse peoples, assembled together for the king's sacrifice." It was the biggest bazaar anyone had ever seen. Never had so much jewelry and so much crockery been gathered together in such a space. "No one there was sad, no one was poor, no one was hungry, no one was unhappy, no one was rude."

It was easy to miss the moment the sacrifice began. You would see four priests crouching down. One, the *adhvaryu*, prepared a cake of boiled rice and shared it with the others. A commonplace, everyday thing to do. Yet it was the beginning proper. That white cake was the seed. That seed was desire. For something to begin, desire must take shape like a substance that expands, that radiates outward. That white rice cake—or again the four glittering gold pieces that the sacrificing king handed out to the priests while they ate from their bowl. "Because rice cake is seed and gold is seed."

. . .

The *adhvaryu,* priest of countless ritual gestures, he who enjoyed such close contact with the sacrifice that he came out scorched at the end, would look the sacrificer-king in the eye and say: "Hold thy voice." Why? "Because the sacrifice is voice (*vāc*)." That is what was meant. And that was the signal that one was entering into the sacrifice.

In the evening, in the hut of fires, they celebrated the *agnihotra;* they poured fresh milk, mixed with water, onto the fire. They heated the milk on the fire named *gārhapatya,* they poured it out on the fire named *āhavanīya.* Those two fires were the poles of every ritual tension. Everything that happened was a passage from one to the other.

The procession of women arrived from the south. Silent and absorbed, they advanced in four lines. Leading them were the four wives of the sacrificer-king, their thick hair and complicated headdresses studded with silver buttons. The *mahiṣī,* the first bride, the consecrated; the *vāvātā,* the favorite; the *parivṛktā,* the neglected; the *pālāgalī,* of inferior caste. Each was attended by one hundred maidens: a hundred princesses for the *mahiṣī;* a hundred of noble birth for the *vāvātā;* a hundred courtiers' daughters for the *parivṛktā;* a hundred stewards' daughters for the *pālāgalī.*

In the shadow of the hut, a zigzag barrier of women. After pouring out the milk, the sacrificer-king lay down, naked, between the thighs of the favorite, likewise naked. There he would stay, all night, without moving. With the constant contact he would desire her, but without possessing her. He would let *tapas* grow within him; he knew he would be needing that austere ardor for a long time, a whole year, the duration of the sacrifice. Behind them, in order, the other women were stretched out on the ground.

. . .

Why that night, at once erotic and motionless? It was "a form of the state of wakefulness." Wakefulness was essential. That for the whole first night of the rite the sacrificer-king should stay awake. Friends were with him to keep him from sleeping. But above all: wakefulness meant that constant contact with the body of the favorite.

When the sun rose, and the sun was the horse, they were ready to greet it with twenty-one formulas: the first six had to do with sight ("Homage to he who contemplates attentively"), two with hearing, six with being and nonbeing, then one with sight, one with hearing, and finally five with the mind ("Homage to the *brahman*! Homage to *tapas*! Homage to the stillness!" were the last). Each homage was a phrase, a musical articulation. Behind every composition lies the sequence of those formulas.

Before the sacrifice of the horse begins, the sacrificer-king entrusts his power to a priest, the *adhvaryu*. "The *adhvaryu* is king for the duration of the sacrifice." But the sacrifice lasts a year. And the year is everything. Thus the king stands aside from his kingly offices for the whole period during which he celebrates the sacrifice that makes him a king. Which, again, is all the time there is. Thanks to the *aśvamedha* one can acquire sovereignty; but, if one doesn't possess sovereignty, one is "swept away" by the sacrifice of the horse. Such is sovereignty's vicious circle. There is no sovereignty that is not founded on that vicious circle.

At this point the *adhvaryu* would pass a rope around the horse's neck. This was the beginning of the sacrificial act. What had come before was training, purification, making oneself fit, preparing oneself, baking the mind. Now came the moment for action pure and simple. It is action that binds. The first act was a rope passed around the horse's neck, while the *adhvaryu* said to the animal: "You are he who encircles, you are the world; you are a guide, a protector." But how could that mere rope go around that which goes around everything, encircles the world? Yet that is what it did.

The most brutal part came soon enough. With a rope around its neck, the horse and a black dog ("with four eyes," they said: but it was just a black dog with two white patches above its eyes), were pushed toward the pond near the sacrificial clearing. Preceded and followed by relatives of the sacrificer-king, by the son of a prostitute, by a priest. The dog stepped into the water. The horse stepped into the water. When the dog was out of its depth and began to flounder, the *adhvaryu* said: "Kill"—and the son of the prostitute attacked the animal with a wooden club. Usually it was *sidhraka* wood, but the important thing was that it be a wood whose name included the syllable *ka*. Briefly, the dog would try to lift its head above the water again. Again it was clubbed. Then the priest would push its already inert body between the horse's hooves, saying: "Away with the mortal! Away with the dog!" But why did the banishment of what is mortal have to be so cruel, one wondered, as already the dead dog slid away southward on the surface of the water? A whole year, a cycle of noble deeds and lofty formulas was set in motion by that cowardly act.

The most cowardly act was now followed by the most noble. For a while the rope had been tied around the horse's neck. Now it was untied. And they let the horse free to wander around at will. But before letting it free, the *adhvaryu* and the sacrificer-king stood beside the horse and murmured a number of formulas. They told the horse who he was and what they were asking him to do. "Follow the path of the Ādityas"—the path of the sky—was what they chiefly urged. Meanwhile the four hundred armed guardians who would escort the horse wherever it chose to go had already gathered around. They would defend it, even if it meant killing whoever might get in its way; they would watch over it to see that it did not mount a mare or plunge into water. Thus they pressed on for almost a year. The horse must never turn back. As with the sun, had it turned back, "everything would have been destroyed." The animal's wanderings, ever free and ever further away from the place of sacrifice, must never stop. Thus "continuity" (*saṃtati*) was not broken. And, as the horse trod ever new lands and the path it took became an ever longer and more tangled thread, so each day at the place of sacrifice the *adhvaryu* would repeat the formulas that state the "forms" (*rūpas*) of the horse, while his thoughts, and those of the other priests, remained fixed on the invisible and wandering animal—and what the *adhvaryu* did then, this incessant repetition of formulas, protected the continuity of that thread that bound them together.

Any lands the horse trod in its wanderings became the property of the sacrificer-king. Anyone who saw the horse knew that from that day on he had a new king. It is not through war that one conquers, since conquest is the unbridled running of the horse. War occurs only if a prince attempts to stop the horse. Then the sacrificer-king must break off the sacrifice and declare war on that prince. War is an incident that interrupts a rite.

Freedom is the wandering of the horse. Everything else is obligation and precept. Freedom is manifest only within the frame of the bond. At the beginning the horse has two ropes around its neck. Then it is untied. Not the opposite.

As long as it continues to wander, the sacrificial horse is like the young Siddhārtha in the park of his father's palace. He too is escorted, he too is secretly led in order that he not see anything: the horse in order that he not encounter mares or water; the Buddha in order that he not encounter old age, illness, or death. But both will encounter what they should not: the horse on his return to the place of sacrifice; Siddhārtha, by chance, in a corner of the park. The Buddha is Tathāgata, "He-who-came-thus." The horse is "he who has been led" (meaning: to the sacrificial pole). In those two verbs ("came," "led") lies the difference between the two. One emerges from thick forest, like a common pilgrim: thus does the Buddha reappear to his companions—and risks not being recognized. The horse too reappears from thick forest, to find himself once again in the place of sacrifice from whence he set out, as if he had come back by chance, but behind him, imperceptibly, his escort has been guiding his wanderings. Blessed are the footsteps of both the one and the other, the Buddha and the horse.

Every time they met a brahman, as they wandered through forest, villages, and meadows, they would ask him: "Brahman, what do you know about the sacrifice of the horse?" If the brahman couldn't answer at once, they robbed him. Indeed, "he who, being a brahman, knows nothing of the sacrifice of the horse, knows nothing about anything, and so is not a brahman and as such is liable to be robbed." Of all those they met they would ask: "What happens during the sacrifice of the horse?" If they couldn't answer, all their belongings were plundered and seized. The victim of robbery is he who does not know. Thus they set out to base conquest on knowledge. For all the peoples who lived around them, all who came after them, the opposite was true: they set out to base knowledge on conquest.

While the horse was wandering through lands unknown, the sacrificer-king and the priests sat around the altar on gold-embroidered cushions. Then the *hotṛ* began to tell stories. They were stories of ancient kings, exemplary stories, which the new sacrificer-king would revive. They were cyclical stories, starting over and over, the whole year long. Thirty-six times, in cycles of ten days. Hence their name: *pāriplava*, the story that keeps beginning again (*pariplavate*).

We can try to imagine what the *pāriplavas* were like, those stories of the deeds of gods and kings, endlessly recited throughout the long twelve-month wait for the horse's return. We may even plausibly suppose that they were the earliest models for what would one day become the *Mahābhārata*. None of them has survived. We know of them through other channels: through the hymns of the Ṛg Veda, which offer allusions, enigmas, dazzling glimpses; through the speculations of ritualists, who refer only to fragments of the stories, particular details useful for expounding some line of thought they are developing—and otherwise consider them as common property. Yet those stories don't give the impression of being lost to us, rather of occupying a space within a frame, a space at once empty and clearly delineated. And in this case it is the frame that is the real center of the picture. The frame is the story of the stories: the Romance of the Horse that no one told, but that every deed showed forth, that every deed helped to bring about throughout the arc of a year. That forever untold romance not only contains all the other stories, which can spring forth only within its intervals, but also is their secret articulation, as if all the doings of the gods and the first kings were above all a consequence of that story-frame, that no one ever tells, but that all, from the sacrificer-king to the priests to the most humble of bystanders, help to evoke, to have happen within the sacrificial clearing.

Narrative emerged during the wait, the long wait for the horse's return. And it was a way of preventing the relationship with the wandering horse from being broken. The narrative wandered around like the horse. The secret thought of the narrative is the horse. The secret thought of the horse is the narrative. And what did the *pāriplava* recount, every ten days of the horse's absence? "This cyclical legend recounts all realms, all regions, all the Vedas, all the gods, every being."

There were two lives running parallel. There was that of the wandering horse, followed by his escort of four hundred warriors, an unpredictable, uproarious horde, who crossed villages like a whirlwind, leaving travelers bewildered. They would see a cloud of dust and say: "It's the sacrificial horse."

And there was the life of the priests and the sacrificer-king. Their thoughts were always on the horse. Their greatest fear: that the horse would get lost. Whatever they did, their ritual gestures—which were innumerable—was done in order to tense the thread that linked them to the horse. Sometimes you would see them pouring oblations into the hoof marks the horse had left in the dust.

And one day the horse would reappear. With great familiarity, as if it had never been away, the priests welcomed it into the hut they had built for it out of *aśvattha* wood on the sacrificial clearing. It would be shut up there for seven days while the priests and the sacrificer-king busied themselves with oblations all around. As the *soma* was being filtered, the sacrificer-king would murmur: "From nonbeing lead me to being; from darkness lead me to light; from death lead me to immortality."

It was time for the bloody part of the sacrifice. The priests opened the door of the horse's hut and got it to come out. The horse led the way. The *adhvaryu* held it by the tail. The priests followed in single file, each holding a flap of the robe of the one in front. Why did the priests follow the horse? Because the horse knows "the path of the sky." It also knows some chants better than the priests. Thus the *udgātṛ*, the chanter, let the horse take his place. The horse approached the enclosure where the mares were hidden. The enclosure was opened. At the sight of the mares, the horse neighed, high-pitched, in the silence. "The horse goes *hiṅ*, and that shriek is the *udgītha*." The *udgītha* is the chant that the *udgātṛ* must make. It is the chant the *udgātṛ* would now imitate from the horse.

There is a privilege bestowed on whatever takes place in the intervals, the chinks, the gaps. It is a memory of the continuous. Thus in addition to the twenty-one equidistant poles to which sacrificial victims were tied, there were also victims tied in the intervals between the poles: all wild animals. Thirteen for every interval. Including three sparrows (for the Summer); three frogs (for Parjanya); three crocodiles (for Varuṇa); three peacocks (for the Aśvins); three eagles (for the Year); three moles (for Bhūmi); three deer (for the Rudras); three buffalo (for Varuṇa); three elephants (for Prajāpati); three midges (for Sight); a tawny gazelle (for the Apsaras); a porcupine (for Hrī, Modesty); a black snake (for Mṛtyu); an owl (for Nirṛti, Dissolution); a boar (for Indra); and a pied gazelle (for the Viśve Devas, the All-gods).

The wild animals were a noisy, colorful lot. Hard to keep them quiet. Inevitably they would get mixed up with the other three hundred and forty-nine victims, all tame animals, tied to the twenty-one poles. It was a circus and a slaughterhouse. Anyone would have thought they all awaited the same fate. But that wasn't so. Or at least, not from a certain point on. All the victims, wild animals or tame, were anointed, using different sticks and knives depending on their kind. For the horse, the knife was encrusted with gold; for the victims tied to the horse, it was decorated with copper (the horse was tied to the central pole, but twelve lesser victims were tied to his body and hampered his movements); for the other victims it was decorated with iron. It seemed, then, that all the animals were being prepared for the sacrificial slaughter. And you could feel sure of this when the *agnīdh* began his circumambulation around the victims, waving a firebrand. A circle of fire was traced out around each victim. But just when you expected that the two hundred and sixty wild animals were about to be strangled (and already perhaps people were wondering how the priests would manage with the midges), to your amazement you would see that one by one the wild animals were being untied and set free. Why? To answer that question is to have the answer to everything—and since "the *aśvamedha* is everything," it also includes the answer to this question.

What would have happened if the wild animals had been sacrificed? "If they were sacrificed, they would soon drag the sacrificer dead into the forest, because wild animals partake of the forest." So the sacrificer-king spared the wild animals in self-defense. At the same time, the sacrificer-king remembered that when Prajāpati wished to reach the world of the gods, he did so by taking possession of the wild animals: "With the tame animals he took possession of this world, with the wild animals he took possession of that world [the world of the gods]." So what was to be done? To sacrifice wild animals meant to kill oneself. Not to sacrifice them meant not to reach the world of the gods. Of course, one would still possess "this world," something one could do by sacrificing the tame animals. But how important was *this* world in the end? Man is born into untruth, "this world" is precisely that, the world of untruth. The sacrifice is precisely that which allows us to go beyond this world, to gain access to the truth. Thus, if one forgoes the sacrifice of wild animals, one commits a "violation of the sacrifice." Yet if they are sacrificed, you know that you, as sacrificer, will be swallowed up in the forest, dead together with the beasts sacrificed. Here loomed the invisible crag of contradiction. Here one was banging one's head against the hardest of walls. What was to be done? The ritualists, those who thought out the *aśvamedha* exactly the way Prajāpati had evoked it, were experts in logic and metaphysics. They knew that contradiction is close, as close as can be, to the untrembling heart of thought. They also knew that thought would not overcome contradiction. Yet there was something that might at least get around contradiction, that might allow something prodigious to come into being: *a* and *b*, its opposite, simultaneously. And what was that? Gesture. If the wild animals are arranged in the intervals between the twenty-one poles to which the tame animals are tied, if they are anointed, if they feel the coldness of the blade, if, finally, the *agnīdh* circles around them with a burning brand in his hand: well then, at that point *in a certain sense* those victims have indeed been sacrificed. But at the same time, these are the very victims who are not sacrificed, because shortly afterward another priest will untie their bonds and set them free. Thus the sacrificer does not lose himself, is not swallowed up in the forest, and yet no "violation of the sacrifice," something that could have even more serious consequences, has been committed. When one gets to the bottom of the bottom, one encounters that strange particle much loved of the ritualists: *iva*, "in a certain sense." One encounters those strange figures that "are neither something offered in sacrifice nor something not offered in sacrifice." Is it any surprise, then, if ultimate knowledge can only become manifest through enigma? And if enigmas are more than anything else the pretext for generating further enigmas? Enigmas are what issues from *brahman*. They are what the priests of the *brahmodya* exchanged between themselves, the dialogue they conducted while seated on opposite sides of the central pole, from which fanned out, symmetrical and equidistant, the other twenty poles, to which the other three hundred and thirty-six tame victims of the sacrifice were tied. That dialogue was de rigueur as one approached the irreducible, insuppressible nucleus of the ceremony, of the story of the horse: the killing.

The *brahmodya*, the dialogue by enigmas between the two priests seated one to the south the other to the north of the sacrificial pole, began shortly before the horse was slaughtered. "What was the first thought?" was the first question that the *hotṛ* asked the brahman. Then: "Who is the great bird? Who was the tawny one? Who was the fat one?" Unhesitating, the brahman replied: "The sky was the first thought. The horse was the great bird. The night was the tawny one. The sheep was the fat one." But the *hotṛ* pressed on with other questions. Insistently, he challenged the brahman: "I ask you what is the extreme point of the earth. I ask you what is the navel of the world. I ask you what is the seed of the stallion. I ask you what is the supreme home of the word." Again unhesitating, the brahman replied: "It is the altar (*vedi*) that is called the extreme point of the earth. It is the sacrifice that is called the navel of the world. It is the *soma* that is called the seed of the stallion. It is the *brahman* that is the supreme home of the word." What had happened? The *hotṛ* had put forward enigmas. The brahman had solved them. But what were his solutions? Enigmas of a higher order. This alone was enough to suggest that they were the right answers.

They were constantly thinking of residues, of completeness, the possibility that something would be lost. They saw the sacrificial horse, in all his splendor, anointed, decked out for the ceremony, grass in his mouth, a bridle around his neck, going toward the gods, toward his death. And they wondered: the things we gave him—the bridle, the drape, the grass—will they too go with him to the gods? But what will become of the meat that the flies get? Of the shreds that stick to the ax? Of the meat caught beneath the fingernails that tear it apart? This too, all of this, should go to the gods, this too will need an invocation to help it on its way to the gods. So they dedicated an invocation to the flies.

The most distressing moment for the horse was not when, glossily decked out, he led the procession toward the sacrificial pole. Nor when the *adhvaryu* and the sacrificer-king murmured in his ear that he would be done no violence, that he would not suffer, while the horse knew very well that he was about to be done violence and that he would suffer. Rather it was when, having tied him to the sacrificial pole, they then tied a further twelve victims, goats for the most part, black and white, to various parts of his body, and the goats would writhe around and tug at him, because they sensed that they were about to die. Hence the horse could no longer have his customary freedom of movement. To know that liturgical speculation considered these animals who were tormenting him as his subjects could be of little interest to the horse. He would have preferred to be alone and untrammeled for the brief time that lay between him and his death.

"Thou who, kindled, adorn the granary of prayer": such were the words with which the *hotṛ* began the "stanzas of approval," that part of the liturgy that led to the killing of the horse. Never had the priest's voice been so soft and thick with emotion. He spoke of the "happy gates," tall, wide, gleaming, as if they were there before his eyes. But there were no gates to be seen, only animals pushing and shoving in their panic, legs tangled in ropes. Patiently, the horse endured it all. In generous flourishes, enumerating the gods, bringing in the sky and the flies, the *hotṛ*'s words circled closer and closer to the horse, grew more intimate, more familiar. Finally he whispered: "May your dear life spare you from suffering, as you go on your way. May the ax cause no lasting pain to your body. May no clumsy, impatient quarterer fumble with your joints, mutilate your limbs. You do not die thus. You are not hurt. On easy paths you go to the Gods." They were the last words the horse would hear, before setting off in another procession. But this time he would not lead the way. Before him he would see a priest with a firebrand in his hand. Then he would have to stop: they made him lie on a cloth. Soon his neck would feel the butter-drenched linen drape they would strangle him with, while his eyes could follow the priests, who had moved away now, sitting in silence around the fire *āhavanīya.*

The last procession moved northward, because the path of the sky is to the north. At its head was the *agnīdh,* the firebrand in his hand indicating that the sacrifice was moving into its fiery, irremediable phase. The horse followed. Behind, in single file, the other priests. The first brushed the horse's flanks with two spits. At the rear came the sacrificer-king. Having reached the place where the horse would be killed, the *agnīdh* placed two blades of grass he had been carrying on the ground. Then he stretched a drape over the blades of grass, then a blanket and a gold plaque. It was a bed. They made the horse crouch down there, then strangled him with the linen drape. The other animals—hundreds of them—were strangled with cords. The word they used was *saṃjñāpayanti,* "they make it acquiesce." The texts explain: "When they make a victim acquiesce, they kill it."

As soon as the horse had breathed his last, as soon as the other victims had breathed their last, the four brides of the sacrificer-king would step forward together with a young girl, led by the priest assigned to them, the *neṣṭṛ.* In their hands they would be holding jugs. Behind them, at an appropriate distance, came the four hundred ladies of the retinue. The wives took up their positions around the dead horse. They lifted the hair on the right sides of their heads. A slow, conscious movement. Then they let their hair down on the left. Then they clapped their right thighs while circling the horse and calling it "my lord" and fanning it with the flaps of their long robes. Sometimes the *mahiṣī* would use a golden fan as well. The fanning was intended to make the horse more comfortable in his deep sleep. Or did they want to wake their lover? In any event, the texts remark that, through this gesture, the women "perform an act of contrition" toward the horse. They moved slowly, like dancers, circling the horse nine times.

The wives sprinkled the dead horse with water from their jugs. They said it would purify his life breath. The fresh drops fell on the animal's every orifice, and the wives recited: "May your mind be magnified! May your voice be magnified! May your breath be magnified! May your sight be magnified! May your hearing be magnified! May all that has suffered in you, all that has been hurt in you be magnified and settle! May it be purified!"

Lying on its drape, dripping with water, the strangled horse awaited the *mahiṣī*, the first wife. It was a motionless white mass, its hooves side by side. It bore no signs of violence. Only the shudder of its breathing was missing. Finally alone, the regal wife came close. She lay down and pressed her thighs against the thighs of the dead horse. At the same time she spoke to it, urged the horse to tighten its hooves around her thighs. The priests watched. When the horse and the *mahiṣī* were glued together, distinguishable only by the color of their skins—the *mahiṣī*'s light brown, the horse's a bright white—then the *adhvaryu* would cover them with a blanket and say: "Wrap yourselves together in the sky." Just before the blanket was laid over the two lovers, the *mahiṣī* was seen to take the horse's phallus and introduce it between her thighs. It wasn't easy. So the sacrificer-king would step forward and encourage the horse to penetrate his wife, thus: "Place, O male, that which anoints, great joy of womankind, within the vulva of the one who spreads her thighs, and enter her." None of the priests uttered so much as a word. Why not? So as not to appear to be in competition with the sacrificer-king.

. . .

When the *mahiṣī* lay beside the horse, she immediately pulled up her robe showing her vulva. The *adhvaryu* covered them with the linen drape that shortly before had been used to strangle the horse. At the same time the *mahiṣī* would be using her hand to place the horse's member between her thighs. All eyes were concentrated on her. But the *mahiṣī* showed no sign of being aware of it. She went on with her gentle constant complaint. She spoke to the horse, and kept on speaking. "Mother, little mother, dear little mother. There is no one to show me the way. Little horsey is asleep." Now the king's other wives, who stood in a circle around the two lovers, began to speak too: innuendos, obscenities. But they got no reply, for the *mahiṣī* went on with her quavering lament: "Mother, little mother . . ."

Tight together under the blanket, the dead horse and the queen were joined in coitus. Around them, in a semicircle, stood the priests, the sacrificer-king, the girl, the king's other wives, and their serving maids, four hundred of them. The coitus went on, silent and invisible, while a weave of innuendos shuttled back and forth between priests and women. The priests spoke of a fist disappearing into a crack, of a bird wriggling around, of a couple who climb a tree and play together on top. The women came back sharply with biting disrespect: "Hey, lassie!" "Hey, *adhvaryu*!" came their voices. "Hey, brahman, your mother and father play around on the treetops. They wriggle around like your mouth when you try to speak. Hey, brahman, don't mumble!" At any other time it would have been inconceivable to show such insolence to a brahman. That buzz of obscenities hid something solemn and arcane, evoked it through its opposite. Then the chatter stopped. The queen's first handmaids approached the blanket, from which the horse's head and the woman's were poking out. They helped the *mahiṣī* to climb decently to her feet. Meanwhile they were thinking: "May we prove able, with all kinds of words, to obtain for ourselves our every desire."

The *mahiṣī* was standing up now. With a tuft of grass she dried herself where she had touched the horse's member. Then she looked hard at the girl, whose role had so far remained unclear, and, tossing the tuft of grass at her, spoke these words: "I transfix you with the ardor of coitus." From that moment on the girl was called *sāhā* and was allowed to enter the *sabhā*, the room where the men gathered. Her body would be available to anyone who used the room. To one side the priests were reciting: "I have sung of Dadhikrāvan, the victorious horse, the fiery horse. May he bring a sweet smell to our mouths! May he prolong our lives!" They were aware of feeling tainted and extremely tired, for "life and gods will depart from those who at the sacrifice use impure speech." But the ceremony still had other phases to go through. First the mouth must regain its sweet smell. Meanwhile the four hundred and five women walked away, "just as they had come."

Soon the women reappeared. This time they had needles in their hands. Gold, silver, and bronze. Gold, the *mahiṣī*'s, silver the *vāvātā*'s, bronze the *parivṛktā*'s. Many, many needles, as many as the pearls that the same women had earlier threaded to the horse's mane and tail. When the wives threaded the pearls to the horse's hairs, other women from their procession would hang seashells on the hairs too, to keep the pearls from falling. Nothing of what was offered could be lost. Each had a hundred and one needles. They went up to the horse and delicately marked out lines on its body: they were drawing "the paths of the knife." As they did so they never stopped repeating the appropriate formulas. You would hear: "May the human wives prove able to divide your hide with wisdom"; "The needles weave and weave on the hide of the fiery horse." Like land surveyors, like surgeons, the women traced out geometric shapes on the lifeless body of the animal who only shortly before had been, at least for one of them—and she represented all the others—a lover. The onlookers saw no more than three women intent on their work around the horse, as though around a loom. They weren't in a position to follow the lines the needles made. But they knew that the three wives would divide the skin into thirty-six parts, like a *chandas,* a meter. That great hunk of dead flesh was to be broken up like a line of poetry.

The horse's hide had now been etched out, if not actually cut open. But inevitably there comes a point when blood must be drawn. The *adhvaryu* stepped forward with a blade of grass and a knife with a golden hilt. He placed the stalk on the horse's belly, then severed the animal's skin immediately beneath the blade of grass. But who was the agent of this action that was irreversibility itself? *Who?*—the *adhvaryu* asked himself, as the knife began to probe the entrails. And the answer was: *Ka.* Which means: *Who?* The answer to the question was another question. And everybody knew that that indefinite subject, forever undefinable—*who?*—was the secret name of the one person whose existence was in no doubt: Prajāpati. If Prajāpati was Ka, all the more so was the anonymous priest at the moment he buried his knife in the horse. Action, at its source, has an unknown subject. Looking at the horse, the *adhvaryu* would murmur: "Who is slicing into you? Who is cutting you to pieces? Who is your wise quarterer? It is Ka who is slicing into you. It is Ka who is cutting you to pieces. It is Ka who is your wise quarterer." But where is Ka to be found? He was never among the other gods, as he was never among men. He was so discreet, so elusive that many thought they could do without him. But then everything would break down. Neither gods nor men can live without recourse to Ka. To be precise: they may survive, but they cannot understand. But how to understand Ka? He's as obscure and elusive as his name is commonplace. There was another word that was at once obscure, elusive, and commonplace: *ātman,* "Self." Another pronoun, this time a reflexive pronoun. Were they the same perhaps? The knife was raised. All gods, all men, all meters, all powers: everything in that moment, the moment of the irremediable gesture, dissolved before that one syllable, Ka, that evocation of an ever unknown subject, who with great ease gathered every name, every other being who could claim to be a subject, within himself. The rest was butchery.

When Prajāpati "saw" all his desires and everything he would like to achieve, he also saw the *aśvamedha.* "By sacrificing therewith, he obtained all his desires and attained all attainments." Perhaps this is why the fulfillment of all desires has been looked on with such suspicion ever since. For that fulfillment implies a death. Or rather: a killing. What is most obscure here, what was always obscure and will ever remain so, lies in the answer to the question: what happened exactly when Prajāpati "saw" the *aśvamedha* and "sacrificed with the *aśvamedha*"? Prajāpati was, among other things, a white horse. And likewise "the first sacrificer." But on this occasion was he horse or sacrificer? Was he the horse who was sacrificed or the sacrificer who killed the horse? Never did active and passive come so close to each other, to the point that they were superimposed one over the other, confused one with the other. It was not out of a desire to conceal things that this question remained obscure. Its very nature was obscurity, whatever one might try to make of it. "Being active or passive," thought Prajāpati, "doesn't make that much difference. Or, at least, it doesn't make the enormous difference men will see there. Every active is someone else's passive. But this is a truth that, in the normal way of things, would confuse men's minds rather than illuminate them. If they accepted it, everything would become hopelessly tangled. And this is the reason why a part of the teaching must remain secret: to prevent the course of world events from being paralyzed by knowledge; to create a situation where the only people who can gain access to knowledge are those who, even when imbued with it, will allow the world to pursue its course."

. . .

Ahiṃsā, Gandhi's nonviolence, was already there in the writings of the ritualists, some three thousand years before him. Literally, it means "not to wound," from the root *hiṃs-*, "to wound." "Like the-one-who-does-not-wound, *ahiṃsantaḥ,* he takes apart the limbs"; these words referred to the person who cut into the flesh of the sacrificed animal, and hence, here, of the horse. *Ahiṃsā* doesn't mean to refrain from violence. But to exercise violence—which is there in any event and involves everyone—*in a certain way,* without wounding. To wound is more serious than to kill. Violence cannot be eliminated, because it is part of life's pulse. But wounding . . . A wound can be inflicted in a thousand different ways. There may even be cases where it is not perceived to be a wound. The knife blade separates the joints with such delicacy and precision, it's as if it were dividing up Prajāpati's body to be scattered through the world before being reassembled in the altar of fire. That the greatest importance was attributed to this particular doctrine of the ritualists is demonstrated by the fact that the word *ahiṃsā* appears in the Laws of Manu, as in Baudhāyana's *Dharmasūtra* and again in the *Chāndogya Upaniṣad;* alongside the word *satya,* "truth"—and in each case immediately before it. The obligation not to wound the living (and everything is living), the obligation toward the truth: the two were pronounced together, and *ahiṃsā* came before *satya,* as if getting to the bottom of the one word one discovered the other.

The first man to have his head cut off was a young fellow, a squire's son, who had been given the job of cutting up the body of the sacrificed horse. Many lost their heads in this way, for generation after generation. Set upon a chariot, they were led to the horse, "dressed up and weeping, like those who go to their deaths." When they had completed their task, when they had cut into the body of the horse, their heads were cut off. But one day Dīrghatamas Māmateya woke with a start and said: "Who's that crying?

What's all this noise about?" They told him what was happening. Then Dīrghatamas Māmateya went up to the young man who had been chosen to plunge his knife into the horse and said: "Listen, I'm going to tell you how you can cut up the horse without getting yourself beheaded. Follow the paths of the knife across his body, and as you do so say: 'Who is it slicing into you? Who is it cutting you to pieces?' Then, seeing you talking to yourself, someone will come up to you and say: 'Young man, what are you doing? This is how you cut up the horse.' Then he will take the knife from your hand and cut into the horse. And his head will be cut off."

In the person of Dīrghatamas Māmateya, a new figure had arrived on the scene: knowledge. Knowledge is the question of the identity of the agent. Between the young man given the task of plunging his knife into the dead horse and Arjuna on his war chariot there is a relationship of direct descent. They are the same person. Just as Dīrghatamas Māmateya is Kṛṣṇa, the charioteer.

Knowledge is not an answer but a defiant question: Ka? Who? Knowledge is the last ruse, which allows us to escape being killed, to obtain a—provisional—stay of execution. Which was another reason why one celebrated the sacrifice of the horse.

There is a horse's head rolling along the surface of the sky: it is the sun.

There is a horse's head rolling across the earth: it is the receptacle of sweetness.

There is a man's head rolling across the earth: it is the person who hasn't solved the enigma of the horse's severed head.

• • •

Like everything, the *aśvamedha,* which is everything, began and ended with water. There was a bath at the beginning. There was a bath at the end. After the final bath (*avabhṛtha*), "those who do good and those who do evil return to their village together, hand in hand."

VIII

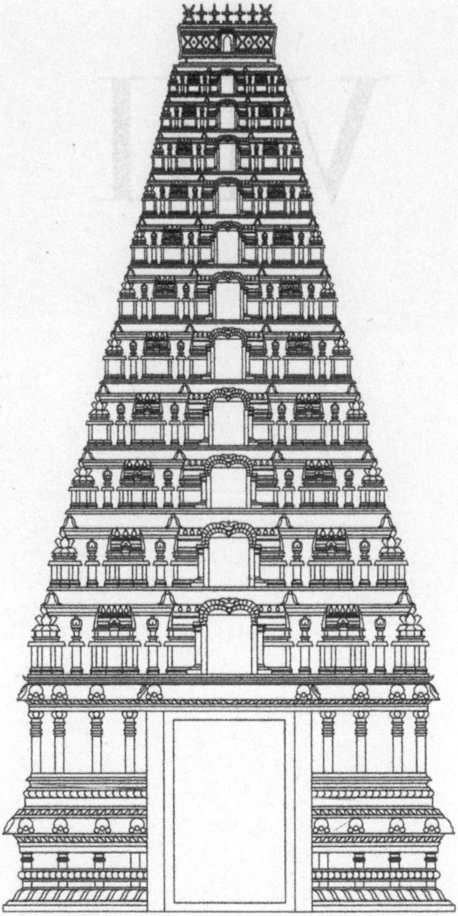

The *sabhā* is a hall: a place for meetings, royal audiences, games. Something happens there, something is made manifest: it is the place of initiation. In the beginning, it was a place where dice was played, where a cow was killed. In the beginning is always something that later gets hidden. The *sabhā* was already there, we discover, before the world—what we call "the world"—began. It was in the middle of the palace—subterranean, invisible, watery, celestial—of Varuṇa. And it was still there at the end, when India was invaded by the Islamic swarms. It stood in the middle of the palaces of the Mughal princes. It was in a *sabhā* that the Pāṇḍavas and the Kauravas, cousins and enemies, tossed dice to decide their destinies.

There are two indispensable elements in any *sabhā*: doors and columns. Everything else is optional. Lots of doors, lots of columns. Varuṇa's palace has a thousand columns and a hundred doors. And this place that belonged first and foremost to the dead became the model for every other *sabhā*. It is to this that the rule which establishes that a *sabhā* must be erected toward the south, in the direction of the dead, discreetly alludes.

Varuṇa had invited the more eminent *ṛṣis* to his *sabhā* together with a number of foreigners and theologians. Welcoming them, he said: "The time of cruel disputes about enigmas, the time of the *brahmodyas* that ended with someone getting his head broken or cut off, is over. Maybe it's to do with the aeon coming to an end, I don't know, but it's getting hard to find anyone who realizes that when you think you risk losing your head. All the same, we're still responsible for the task of keeping thoughts moving and turning. More and more things are tending to unfold in the form of intertwining monologues. I'd be the last to oppose this new style. I just wanted my *sabhā* to host some travelers from the far West. Hybridization is de rigueur these days."

When you went into the *sabhā,* the columns generated a sense of vertigo, as though you were in a geometric forest, or an alcove walled with mirrors. It must have been the same in the *telestērion* in Eleusis: the candidate for initiation came in and couldn't understand the purpose of this parallelepiped of air measured out by columns standing at the same distance from each other in every direction. Then, in the huge hall, something would be moving. Shadows between the columns. They were the Cows, at once silent and docile. They wandered about as though in a field. A dull clatter of hooves on stone flags. But the Cows were also the Dawns. They filed by like heavily made-up dancers in a hurry to get onstage. And they were Words too. Whispered syllables. Lifting your eyes between the columns, you would suddenly see a golden swing. Everything else was doors and columns. Something was about to happen. But where was the center? Everywhere seemed central, each point protected by columns equally innumerable. Would the prodigy appear? They called it "the sun in the rock." It was the vision that Varuṇa granted to Vasiṣṭha, born of the seed he had squirted in the air: the vision that brings clairvoyance, that made Vasiṣṭha a *ṛṣi.*

Varuṇa, the god hidden in the place of the *ṛta,* in the waters that are Truth and Order, never confided in men. Nor in the *ṛṣis* either. Everybody, every second of the day, felt the eyes of his spies upon them. And every second of the day they feared the bite of Varuna's nooses tightening around them. They all knew that at least one of those cords, whether long or short, thick or thin, was ever wound around them: the noose that keeps everyone tied to the *yūpa,* the pole from which the *paśus,* the domestic animals, the herds (*pecus*) destined for sacrifice, can never move too far away. Men are counted among the *paśus.*

But Varuṇa did strike up a friendship with one of the *ṛṣis,* a friendship that later went sour: with Vasiṣṭha. As a result, the other *ṛṣis* treated Vasiṣṭha with a respect that was mixed with envy and fear, tacitly recognizing him as superior to themselves, because he had knowledge that had been granted to him alone. People spoke of Varuṇa and Vasiṣṭha as having made a mysterious voyage together on the sea. They sailed across the ocean. A ship appeared and disappeared amid the cresting waves. With no sailors, no helmsman, no weight. Two motionless figures trod the deck and gazed at each other. The taciturn Varuṇa chose this watery waste to reveal secrets no one else ever heard.

Vasiṣṭha also claimed to have sat on the gold-and-silver swing that hangs from the sky. As if he were an Apsaras. Was he to be believed? After all Vasiṣṭha was in some way related to the first of the Apsaras, Urvaśī.

They were celebrating a *soma* ceremony. Solemn, already intoxicated, the gods stood in their ranks. Then Urvaśī crossed the sacrificial clearing. The gods looked up, some thrilled, some obtuse. They had never seen such beauty, nor such a bold, easy manner, that paid them no attention. The Apsaras didn't exist as yet. But the gods sensed that with Urvaśī a new kind of being had made its appearance. A kind they would always be chasing after. Urvaśī crossed the clearing with a swift, light step, her feet barely showing under a long robe fastened tight beneath the breast. But immediately her presence filled the entire space. As she passed, Mitra and Varuṇa simultaneously squirted off their seed. It fell into a large bowl, standing among the liturgical accessories. It was from that bowl that Vasiṣṭha together with Agastya, was born. That's why people called him the Kumbhayoni, "He-whose-womb-was-a-jar." He grew up feeling he was the child of Varuṇa and Urvaśī. They said he was "born from the mind of Urvaśī"—and not just from the seed of Varuṇa and Mitra.

Perhaps this is why Vasiṣṭha always lived in the greatest intimacy with Urvaśī, even if he never so much as touched her body. As for Varuṇa, being his son is a dangerous business. Often Varuṇa will generate in order to kill. Vasiṣṭha knew that, but he was proud of it too. He would always remember the time he had been alone with Varuṇa in the midst of the ocean. Once, at night, he entered his father's palace by one of its hundred doors. He ran along ever-identical corridors, as though in a mirror. He knew that no living creature had ever set foot here. He wasn't looking for anything. He just wanted to be able to say: "I've been in my father's house." But while he ran he felt the terror of the cattle rustler upon him; his throat was dry. And when the cord of a snare tugged at his ankle, he was brought down like a cattle rustler. He didn't even see his father. He found himself outside, propped against a wall like a bloated, worn-out goatskin, an old man suffering from dropsy. His father's waters again. Everybody hurried past on the road to the market, the way one does hurry past the disfigured and useless, while his damp and flabby lips still whispered the words of ciphered hymns.

Viśvāmitra, Jamadagni, Bharadvāja, Gotama, Atri, Vasiṣṭha, Kaśyapa: who were they? The first *ṛṣis*, the Saptarṣis, the Seven Wise Ones crouched on the seven stars of the Great Bear, the Progenitors, sons born-of-the-mind of Brahmā. Or again, in another aeon, those who composed the body of Prajāpati, which preceded Brahmā. The *ṛṣis* didn't write the Vedas, they saw them. Which is why they were sometimes called the "Vedic seers." To Viśvāmitra tradition ascribes many hymns of the third and fourth *maṇḍala* of the Ṛg Veda; to Vasiṣṭha, Ṛg Veda 7.2 and other hymns of the seventh *maṇḍala;* to Bharadvāja, hymns 6, 17, 18, 22, and 30 of the sixth *maṇḍala.* Jamadagni is said to have seen hymn 10.128 while arguing with Vasiṣṭha. The *virāj* meter is also ascribed to him.

The *ṛṣis* were sometimes called *vipras,* a word that suggests vibration, throbbing, trembling. Motionless, shut up in the cage of the mind, they vibrated. They fed *tapas* within themselves. This was their only conceivable activity. When they sacrificed, around the sacrificial pole, around the strangled victim, around their gestures, their oblations, around the flame, a burning canopy would form, separate from the world. And they would stay under that canopy a long time, days perhaps, perhaps weeks—then later it moved inside them when they were on their own. But can one speak of before or after? The sacrificial fire lights up because the heat of *tapas* is already there—and the heat of *tapas* grows because the sacrificial fire is already there. Here, as sometimes happens between gods, generation is reciprocal.

The word *ṛṣi* indicates an effort, a friction that unleashes heat. And what is the matter that one acts upon in immobility and that produces at once both light and heat? The mind. One operates on the mind with the mind. What else is there, after all? The world, nature, is a rare occurrence, a variation of the mind. So thought the Saptarṣis, born-of-the-mind of Brahmā. They had never dwelled in a womb, they didn't know what it meant to be born from a woman's belly. To live, for them, meant to ply the mind, the same smooth way they plied the skies back and forth between earthly valleys and the pinpoints of the Great Bear.

The Vedic hymns are not of human origin; they are *apauruṣeya,* "not from man," not attributable to anyone who might have composed them. Or, alternatively—and this is the doctrine the Sāṃkhya later espoused—there was a person behind them: the primordial Puruṣa. But even he didn't compose them. The hymns emanated from him like exhaled breath.

Sitting immersed in *tapas*, the *ṛṣis* saw the hymns. Syllable by syllable, they appeared, then faded. At first, the hymns were disseminated everywhere, like plants. Much later, at the dawning of a new age that would no longer want hymns but stories, someone split them up into groups and collected them. *Ṛg Veda Saṃhitā,* "Collection of the Knowledge Made of Hymns": such is the title under which they have come down to us. Each of the central books, from the second to the seventh, associated with a *ṛṣi:* Gṛtsamada, Viśvāmitra, Gotama, Atri, Bharadvāja, Vasiṣṭha. To them, or to other *ṛṣis* descended from them. That's why they are called the "family books." It was Vyāsa who arranged them in this way. He gave his life to this work of devotion and philology before embarking on the *Mahābhārata,* which he dictated to Gaṇeśa, who crouched in a corner, with his soft, young man's arms and wrinkly elephant's head with a broken tusk, like some toy left over from an earlier generation of children.

Atri said: "Our eyes, the eyes of the Saptarṣis, which now flicker from the stars of the Great Bear, were ever wakeful over all that happens. That something merely happens is pointless. But that something happens and a watching eye gathers it into itself is everything. Thus we came before the gods. Thus do we keep our watch after the gods. The gaze came before the scene. The world didn't exist then. But it didn't not exist either. It was the mind, if anybody knows what that might be. It was our mind. We seven, already old, yet unique and first among beings, watched each other. We were eyes watching other eyes. There was nothing else to let itself be watched. And we knew: we haven't the strength, alone, we beings who are entirely mind, to bring into existence, to make existence exist, unless we compose something that goes beyond he who watches. It was time for vision to split away from the seer. We watched each other and said: 'This way we will never exist. This is not existence. What's required is for someone to be composed of us.' Then, in the silence, we began to burn. The mind concentrated on a fire—and we were the substance that that fire consumed. That's why we were called *ṛṣis*: because we consumed ourselves: *riṣ-*. Whom did we want to compose? A person, the Person: Puruṣa. Who was he? An eagle with wings outspread. Two of us squeezed ourselves in above the navel, two below the navel, one was a wing, one the other wing, one the claws. All the flavor of life we had within us we brought together above, in the bird's head. That Person, that Purusa, became the Progenitor, the Father, Prajāpati, became this altar of fire, which we are bound at every moment to construct."

Kaśyapa said: " 'In what are you experts?' they asked us. In the sensation of being alive. We are wakeful—or, if you like, we vegetate. *Vajra,* the lightning flower, the ultimate weapon of the gods, is connected with *vegeo,* 'to be wakeful, vigilant,' from which we have *wacker, wach,* and *wake,* 'awake.' The lightning is the lightning flash of wakefulness. 'Vegetation' and 'wakefulness' share the same root. That which every instant implies, which every instant conceals, as the mind's mill grinds out its images, that was our place, our *sabhā* where we meet and clash, where we recount our terrestial incursions, without ever having to leave our post between these columns."

Seen from afar, the *ṛṣis* looked very like Plato's Guardians. But it wasn't a State they were guarding. A State would have been too small, too circumscribed for a gaze such as theirs, bending down from the stars. They watched over the world, or rather the worlds, each linked to the next like vertebrae in a spine. They were wakeful. Throughout their immensely long lives they knew adventure, intrigue, duels, passions, furies, idylls. But such stories were only minute and sporadic blossoms along the unbending branch of their longevity. When the stories came to an end, it looked as though the *ṛṣis* had disappeared. Whereas in fact they merely returned to their normal state. They were wakeful, and that was all. The worlds' existence, submerged in and reemerging from the *pralaya*, from dissolution, could claim some continuity, claim to be the same existence, ever composing, decomposing, recomposing itself, only insofar as its every phase was gathered up in the pupil of the *ṛṣis*, the cavern where everything echoes and re-echoes.

When there was only the inexistent, *asat*, the *ṛṣis* were already there, since "doubtless the *ṛṣis* were the inexistent." We don't know whether they gave birth to the gods or were born of the gods—or both. The texts tell us that it was one and the other. In any event there was one priority, one privilege, the *ṛṣis* claimed over both men and gods. They and only they had been there, hidden in the nonexistent, before existence existed. And what was there in the nonexistent? Before the object there was an image. A breath before there was flesh to animate. Desire before there was a body. The *ṛṣis* were the sovereignty of the mind over every other reality. They were consciousness, that unique manifestation that needs nothing but itself. They were the gaze that burns. Already wizened before anything dawned. Thus it was that, despite their immense strength, they immediately appeared as venerable ancients, whetted and honed with exercise.

As the *ṛṣis* saw it, the secret of existence was implicit in just a few actions common to all: waking, breathing, sleeping, coitus. They saw the metaphysical in the physiological, whereas the first Westerners who wrote commentaries on their hymns imagined them as mainly concerned with clouds and storms.

Masters of the goaded, greased, hard-brushed, well-honed word, the *ṛṣis* were dazzled by one revelation: the elementary fact of being conscious. There was no need to drink *soma* or develop techniques or be inspired. The bare fact of being conscious was enough in itself. Everything else was a supplementary hallucination superimposed over the primary hallucination: that of living inside a mind. Beset by nature's profusion, they shriveled it with a glance. For nothing, in nature, led to the mind. While nature itself might turn out to be but a brief experiment, a mise-en-scène of the mind. Wasn't that how it had been in the beginning, before the gods?

What does the world look like? It's an upturned cup. What's it made of? Bone. Looking up we see filaments of light filtering through cracks and scratches on the vault of that old bone: the stars. On the edge of the cup you can see seven figures, silently crouching, wrapped in their cloaks. They're the Saptarṣis, who keep watch. The twins—Gotama and Bharadvāja, Viśvāmitra and Jamadagni, Vasiṣṭha and Kaśyapa—are arranged in parallel, gazing at each other. Below, where Atri shines, the cup has a narrow spout. What is it that hangs suspended in that upturned cup, that dark and empty hemisphere? The "glory of all forms," they said. A brain saturated in *soma*: the mind.

The Saptarṣis stood guard at the seven gates of the fortress: the ears, the nostrils, the eyes, the mouth, which Atri watched over. Each controlled a breath, inside and outside the cup. The world, which imagined it existed alone, reproducing itself like a reflection in so many tiny, upturned cups of bone, became aware that it lived within an immense cup of bone, which yet was cramped, for only beyond it, as one might glimpse through a thousand tiny chinks, lay the realm of light that floods in.

To his foreign guests, Vasiṣṭha said: "You have entered a place where amazement is vain. Everything is normal here. There are fathers who are sons of their sons or sons who are fathers of their fathers and their sisters, who are their lovers and wives too. Here the latter-day priest is also among the first of the gods. Here the monster is an ascetic and the ascetics fight the monsters."

Nārada was the only one of the *ṛṣis* who wandered around among the columns. Coming alongside a group, he would whisper something, then move on. Restless, his eyes hinted and winked. He listened long, then couldn't help butting in: "If we wish to respect the laws of hospitality, we must remember that we *ṛṣis* are remote indeed from those strangers who have come here, far more than mere geography might suggest. We must remember that they are attached to habits quite different from our own. Of any and every event they want to know when it happened, by which they mean in what year, forgetting to ask in what aeon. They bow down before a word we hardly recognize, 'history,' a word that for us exists only in a plural form. At most we might speak of stories. Just as they speak of "water" and we prefer to speak of "waters." Doubtless, misunderstanding makes life more flavorsome. But allow me to tell you something about those who have long celebrated and meditated upon our words . . ." He wasn't able to. For Atri had interrupted, brusquely. Turning his eyes to the silent strangers in the *sabhā,* he said: "Let us remember our children, your ancestors: those who called themselves the Āryas, the Noble Ones, those whom you call the Indo-Aryans. They stormed down from highland wastes, bleak mountains, they burst forth with their horses and chariots; brandishing torches they set fire to the forests. They looked down from above on the boundless plain and filled it with scars. They killed or enslaved the dark-skinned, noseless, mean, and minute beings they found in their path. But where did their path lead? Toward the sun, toward the place of Indra, yet they never reached that place and the earth stretched on and on, ever flatter, ever more vast before them. They stopped on the banks of a huge river, amazed. Nature's unceasing hum surrounded them on every side. Perhaps there would be no more people on the other side of the river. Just that hum beginning again, under trees that looked the same—or perhaps were the same, shifted there by magic, as though in a mirror. This happened over and over again, because everything happens over again.

"One day, or a thousand days, they halted their advance. Accustomed to tumult, they realized it was going on within them. But where? Where was that tumult? Things they had burned to ashes rose up again, but a sharp eye could shrivel them once more. The eye was more powerful than fire. And slowly a second eye split off from the first, and gazed at it. Motionless, humming with insects, all was exactly as before. Yet all had changed. Everything was covered in a shiny film. They sensed that within the box of their consciousness a sovereign was observing them. He watched them, but they couldn't see him. Him, they decided, they would obey."

Then Gotama said: "For many peoples, things began with a series of kings. For the Greeks it was a series of women. For the Āryas, a series of seers, of *ṛṣis.* The kings conquered, the women united themselves with a god. And the seers? Motionless, they vibrate within the *brahman.* From this origin, more elusive and improbable than others, since everyone knows what war is, or coitus, but few know what *brahman* is, and even less what it might mean to vibrate within it, proceeds the irreducible uniqueness of what was to happen, what did happen, what still happens, in that land that would one day be called India. Here, the further back one goes, the more something that elsewhere emerges only as a final, circumscribed, and explicit result is to be taken as understood, implicit, all-embracing. The Spirit of the World, which Hegel saw on horseback in the streets of Jena, and which even then was no more than a conqueror, was, for the Āryas, a horse's head that, in the beginning, revealed the doctrine of honey, whose drops still trickle to this day."

. . .

Unique among the ancients, they made themselves known exclusively through their language and their cult. Words and gods. They left nothing else. Nor wished to perhaps. They built no stone temples, no palaces. They left no chronicles of their achievements, made no lists of their possessions, created no images that survived the course of time. Perhaps they felt such things would be a mistake—or in any event unworthy of mention. But the invocation of a divine name, variations of an enigmatic formula, hints at matters celestial, these they never tired of repeating. Right from the word—*veda*—which would one day be used to describe them, they were devotees, perhaps fanatics of "knowledge." There had been men who saw knowledge and passed on in "what may be heard" (*śruti*), hence through words, that consciousness whose origin was "not from man" (*apauruṣeya*). These men were the *ṛṣis*, the "seers." Their dealings with the gods were complex. Sometimes they were superior to the gods (definitely so when it came to knowledge), sometimes they even generated the gods, sometimes it was the intensity of their *tapas*, the heat that blazed in their minds and could well have damaged even the mansions of heaven, that led them to flee the gods. The ultimate game in the cosmic match, the most subtle and occult of them all, was that played out between gods and *ṛṣis*, while the manifest game was fought between the Devas and the Asuras, between those gods and antigods who never ceased to confront each other. As for men, they might host "portions," splinters, fragments of this or that contender, offering a further battleground where their deeds could unfold in new and more complex variations. But did men exist, on their own? Men who did not host within themselves parts of that other world which we are unable to see? Of course they did, but as accidents of nature that blossom and fade without further significance.

Cows were important, indeed vital, to the Āryas, just as they were to the Dinkas along the Nile and to many other tribes of nomadic herdsmen. But it was only among the Āryas that cows became, like the unknown quantity in algebra, an abstract agent that could be applied to everything, transform everything. When they said "the cows," the Āryas hinted at a secret that was an operation of the mind. The cows were water, coinage, word, woman, dawn. They were the unit of exchange, the lingua franca of existence. The Āryas had the revelation that it is not only the element on which one operates that may be secret but likewise the operation itself. Anyone who does not know this is excluded. He does not know "the secret name of the cows." Actually, the cows have twenty-one secret names. The uninitiated would hear the Āryas pronouncing them and imagine they were raving in some obsession. In fact they were experimenting with speech raised to a higher power, an abstraction hitherto unknown that now entirely reshuffled the pack of appearances. Before each word, they were seized by panic in the face of overwhelming allusiveness, a devastating expansion of meanings. But at the same time they were enchanted when the scattered elements of the world came together like a herd within the receptacle of consciousness, which vibrated as it named, evoked, invoked. Thus did the Vedic hymns make themselves manifest.

No artifacts have come down to us from the Vedic era. Nothing that those who intoned the hymns of the Ṛg Veda touched with their hands has survived. Not merely because wood rots faster in a tropical climate. Not merely because they chose not to build in stone. Not merely because they decided not to have temples. The hymns speak of palaces with a hundred gates. They speak of well-crafted jewels. Of bronze palisades. They list the paraphernalia of ritual. They speak of arms and chariots. It is as if everything had been pure mental reality that allows the object to appear, then reabsorbs it. What remained were the forests, scarred here and there where the fire had burned. And the hymns, the meters, the names. They preserved words and fire. What else did one need?

. . .

For hundreds and hundreds of years, before the Āryas came, there were cities on the hills above the Indus valley. They had cobbled roads, huge baths, canals, engraved seals, defensive walls, granaries. None of this is mentioned in the Vedas. Yet the hymns do speak of Indra demolishing a hundred *púr* in his warrior charge. Some have understood *púr* to mean "walls"—and think the passage alludes to the walls around Mohenjo-daro and Harappa being demolished by the invading Āryas. But the more plausible meaning of *púr* is "livestock corral." Thus the Vedic lines might refer merely to cattle rustling or sheep stealing. No remains give conclusive support to the notion that the towns of the Indus valley were destroyed by the Āryas. Though there is nothing to say they were not. It may well be that there was a gap of around two hundred years between the destruction of these towns and the arrival of the Āryas. But aside from chronological inconsistencies, clearly a great blank separates the Āryas, who left nothing tangible at all, from the inhabitants of the Indus valley, whose seals traveled as far away as Mesopotamia.

The further they pushed on into the vast Sindhu plain, the more the Āryas turned their backs on the *soma,* the inebriating plant that grew only in the mountains. It was *soma* that had given them their strength and vision, and with the impetus generated by that strength and vision they were now conquering something that would deny them access to *soma,* except through memory. A different landscape lived on in their minds. A northern homeland of long, long nights, prodigious dawns. That was the territory where truth was manifest. Each new conquest was but a temporary camp set up further and further from the place of meaning, useful only insofar as it refreshed the memory. Already living in places where the length of the days hardly varied, they cherished and nourished that memory most stubbornly in word and gesture. To their eyes, every image of beauty, of seduction, of splendor, emanated from a dawn long faded beyond the mountains, to the north.

Ever more difficult to reach and to grasp on its high mountaintops, from the moment the Āryas settled down in the torrid plain, *soma* began to take on the nature of a simulacrum. Or was it perhaps the origin of all simulacra? Already, the simplest of the liturgies that referred to it was "fearfully complicated." The substance at the center of everything was quickly becoming the void at the center of everything. And the web of liturgical prescriptions grew thicker and tighter, as if those devotional gestures were partly intended to conceal an absence, where the twofold power of a divine body and its cast still lingered.

The life of the Āryas revolved around but a few elements, a few objects. Always the same, ever repeated. Nor was there any attempt to add others. But the variations on those elements, those objects, were such as to make the head spin. Every morning they confronted the same simple liturgical articles, and every morning, once the mind was yoked up, a stream of thoughts would begin. Grasses, wooden cups, a wooden sword, sour milk, butter, wooden spoons, two carts, water, a gold ring, two wooden boards, five stones, an antelope hide, an antelope horn, a red ox hide. That was what they carried around with them: the wherewithal for the simplest of sacrifices. A temple was unacceptable, because that would have meant using something ready-made, once and for all, whereas what you had to do was start from scratch, every day, transforming whatever clearing you found, scattered bushes and all, into a place of sacrifice, choosing one by one the positions for the fires and the altar, measuring out the distances, evoking the whole from an amorphous, mute, inert scene, until the moment when the gods would come down and sit themselves on the thin grass mats that had been carefully unrolled for them.

They lived without the comfort of crafted images. Not

because they didn't trust them. On the contrary. A mental spring of images bubbled up unceasingly. But there was no need to copy them in stone. Rather they must be channeled by ritual. Bridled with hymns. Made to travel with the hymns, which are chariots. Every gesture unleashed more of them, like shadows. And if you tried to find where they came from, you arrived at something that "burns without wood in the waters."

They thought so much about sovereignty that they no longer dared to exercise it. Their history was one of progressive abdication. Having consumed its every variation, from the most avid to the most austere, in the heat of their minds, they chose to refrain from dominion, and let the first invaders seize it from them. They would put up with anything, so long as they could think. And, if possible, think what the ancients, what the *ṛṣis* had thought before them.

They were more interested in grammar than in glory. Their inquiries reached their supreme expression in Pāṇini's treatise, a generative grammar, as two thousand, four hundred years later those who were convinced they had invented generative grammar were bound to recognize. Pāṇini's construction was so perfect it eclipsed the numerous others that had come before it. In four thousand aphorisms, or *sūtras,* it analyzed the phonology and morphology of Sanskrit, that language "through which the light passes."

Between the conquering Āryas and the Buddha: a thousand years and not a single object. Not a stone, not a seal, not a city wall. Wood: burned, rotted, decayed. Yet the texts speak of paintings and jewels. Immensely complex metrics—and the void. One thousand and twenty-eight hymns collected in the Ṛg Veda. Not a trace of a dwelling. Rites described in the most meticulous detail. Not a single ritual object that has survived. Those who glorified the leftover left nothing over themselves, except what was filtered through the word. A highly articulated language, fine-wrought as a palace. But no palace remains. Had the texts been lost, the India of the Āryas, the India of the Vedas, might never have been. Then, finally, in the reliefs of Bhārhut and Sāñcī, one touches stone. And already it is crowded. Genies, dancers, tradesmen, that nameless crowd so useful for filling the void. But a void is ever present: protected by a parasol, where the Buddha was.

Then Atri spoke again: "Just as some claim that every true philosopher thinks but one thought, the same can be said of a civilization: from the beginning the Āryas thought, and India has ever continued to think, the thought that dazzled us *ṛṣis:* the simple fact of being conscious. There is not a shape, not an event, not an individual in its history that cannot, in a certain number of steps, be taken back to that thought, just as Yājñavalkya demonstrated that the three thousand, three hundred and six gods could all be taken back to a single word: *brahman.* And what is *brahman?* That, *tyád.*

"Thus far, everything is extremely clear. But it becomes less so when some of you, drawing on your lexical resources, seek to define that void to which everything leads back. There are those who speak of 'absolute,' as if the absolute were something self-evident. That may be so, but the term is hardly congenial. At the opposite extreme, there are those who speak of an 'enigmatic formula,' as if the whole cosmos could be reduced to a linguistic trick. Back and forth between these two extremes, other definitions abound. All lofty in tone. For scholars are convinced that something solemn, something aulic must connect with that word, in the absence of any other specific fact. Something elevated anyway. Whereas we find the *brahman* at every level of life, high or low. This much we know: that if one seeks to define almost everything—or rather: everything except a single point—that point must remain undefined. As in geometry, one cannot do without an axiom. And an axiom is not proved. An axiom is declared. Now, there is a form of declaration that does not come through words. There is something self-evident that is comparable with what happens in our minds when we read a word. What does happen? Something that can hardly be identified with that black mark on a piece of paper, nor yet with any of its meanings as given in a dictionary—which after all would be just more black marks. Yet something does happen. And it's something that changes every time we read that word. How can we, then, find a definition for something that is ever-changing and what's more has no boundaries? Where does it end, for example, within our minds, that word 'black' we just read? At what point can we claim that we are no longer subject to the reverberation of that word 'black'? That reading, which took but an instant, may have infiltrated all the other words, all the other silent waves that dwell within us. Perhaps we will never be able to disentangle it again. It's as if it had been lost in foreign territory. But what is this land one speaks of as unknown, yet locked away within us? Indeed, it might just as well be outside us, given that we shall never set foot there. We can describe it in any number of ways—and all, once again, will confer a certain coloring, as if we were eager to grant the place a meaning even before knowing whether it has a meaning or not. For the territory where meanings arise and lie hidden might well turn out to be meaningless. A notion that frightens and embarrasses us all, but that we ought to cherish, because—down there where definitions cannot hold—everything is, above all else, uncertain. Indeed, it's salutary that it should be perceived as such. But let's try to see what happens when we are obliged to recognize (and not to define) the existence of *that*. When does this happen? When we wake up. Awakening: it is the only physiological phenomenon that has to do with *that*. I will add but one further remark: try to think of a *second awakening*: of an awakening that happens within our being awake, that is not simply added to that wakefulness but multiplies it, by a quantity *n*, whose value we shall never be able to establish. I don't know if that's how it was for you. But such, for us, was thought. Such is thought."

· ·

As if continuing where Atri had left off, Vasiṣṭha said: "The neutral divine, *brahman,* comes before the gods. 'In the beginning *brahman* alone existed.' The gods, 'as they gradually woke up to it, became it.' This is the decisive step: awakening. Something invisible that happens within thought. Something that adds a new quality to thought: consciousness. To become aware that one is thinking: this is to enter into *brahman.* The gods entered there, the *ṛṣis* likewise, and finally men too. 'He who knows thus,' *ya evaṃ veda,* the ever-repeated formula that divides men into those who know and those who don't, refers to this knowledge. The gods would like to banish 'he who knows thus' from that state, but 'they cannot prevent it.' And why is it that the gods don't invite man to enter into *brahman,* why do they try rather, and with treacherous insistence, to lead him astray? Because without that knowledge man is no more than a 'herding beast' to the gods. And herds of men are useful to the gods, in just the way that herds of beasts are useful to men. They constitute wealth. 'That an animal be stolen is regrettable; but how much more regrettable if a large number of animals be stolen. Hence it is irritating for the gods that men should know this.' Where 'this' means *brahman.* Thus began and thus goes on the taciturn hostility between gods and men."

Viśvāmitra said: "What we thought has been thought many times and in many places—and each of these thoughts, successive and coincident, is linked together in a single chain. But there is one thought that was our thought, insofar as it had never before been pursued so stubbornly, nor would be ever again, had never before achieved such sharpness, nor would ever after. One thought that was the arrow that buried itself within us—and that penetrated deeper and deeper into our brains and into every gesture we made. Until ultimately it became our only thought, ultimately would almost dull the minds it had too brightly illuminated. How to describe it? The recognition that the existence of the universe is a secondary and derivative fact with respect to the existence of the mind. Perhaps no more than its efflorescence. That's how we speak of it today, but time ago we would never have used these words. Indeed, we wouldn't even have understood them. Or we would have despised them. But that's not the point . . . Let's go back to where we were: for those brushed by the wing of that thought, the world was the same as before, nothing was the same as before. Nothing would ever go back to being as it had been before. Yet it is not a spontaneous, natural thought. A creeping oafishness is natural. And even we would sometimes have to struggle to rediscover that thought. Far easier to think of oneself as a ghost imprisoned in a box of skin and bone, surrounded by objects as stable as they are solid. But for anyone who opens his eyes on that other thought, all this falls apart and can never be restored.

"It was strange, how it happened. We forfeited history for that thought. As though, the moment it took shape, a saber had swept down from the sky and cut off our hands. We were paralyzed in whatever action it was we had been involved in. Often they were violent actions, the actions of conquerors come down from the highlands and drought-stricken mountains into a plain too vast, too densely grown and torrid, that we were invading—and that would soon invade us. It was this thought that stopped us, nothing else. We went no further, or only sporadically, discovering new rivers and new forests, threatened by dark creatures lying in ambush in scrub and brushwood they knew so much better than we did. All of a sudden the impetus was gone. Something had distracted our attention, forever. Something that made everything else hollow. That didn't mean we settled down to build palaces and temples, canals, gardens, cities with walls. Everything remained much as it was: a camp of nomad warriors who seemed suddenly to have forgotten their old habits, the fury of conquest."

. . .

Then Jamadagni said: "What is the characteristic that sets us apart from every other being? And what is the knowledge that could only come from the Saptarṣis? For us the mind, the pure fact of being conscious, imposed itself with a conviction far greater than any other. Nature, in comparison, was an opinion. Or rather: nature was a flickering backdrop or momentary flowering or in any event something to treat with the same condescension that, in more recent times, would be reserved for hallucinations. The underlying implication was this: that everything, among the gods and before the gods, as likewise, in the end, among men, happened within the mind. Hence the first substance the world was made of must have been none other than that element from which the mind emerged. But what was that? A subtle heat, a hidden simmering, a burning beneath the surface, which sometimes flares up, with images, words, and emotions clutching at its seething crest, but above all: there blossomed the naked sensation of consciousness, like an incandescent point. All this we called *tapas*, 'heat.' Every story arises from *tapas* and is reabsorbed in it. The normal means of generation, at that time, was not sexual union. One used to say of countless beings that they were 'born-of-the-mind.' When the mind concentrated on a figure, *tapas* would feed it and its profile would emerge, perfectly formed: that was generation. Beings would arise from the *tapas*, grow in the *tapas*, multiform, impudent, airborne multitudes, rigid ascetics, celestial Nymphs. They came pouring forth on the scene as though in a market or at a fair. Then we grew tired. And another story began.

"Nothing is so subtly undermining for *tapas* as sex, because nothing has a greater affinity with it. In eros a body acts upon another body, and is acted upon by another body, in the same way that in *tapas* the mind acts upon the mind and is acted upon by the mind. Sexual union, this whole made up of elements that are each both active and passive, is the activity that most closely resembles the activity of the mind. What they have in common is *tejas*, the flourishing energy, of desire and knowledge. Two fires, which may from time to time become one. We lived suspended between the two. They alternated within us. Neither could go on forever. As Sāyaṇa observed, sex and asceticism were the 'two ways' (*ubhau varṇau,* 'the two colors,' but *varṇa* also means 'caste') that the *ṛṣi* Agastya 'cultivated.' "

When the *ṛṣis* turned their attention to the world, they would often display anger and lust. The immense *tapas* they had accumulated would boil over in all its turbulence. They could not have been less like those images people have of pious, pale, and passionless men. Rather you recognized them for their volcanic ferocity, a darting fury, blazing eyes. One common error was to imagine that they would also display the other passions to excess. Not at all: anger and lust, these and only these were their banners and their torturers. Why? The substance that burns in anger and lust is purest *tapas,* the substance the *ṛṣis* were made of. Giving way to anger and lust, they consumed themselves. Yet, were they not born-of-the-mind of Brahmā precisely so that they might be the first finally to penetrate a woman and generate those beings who would then inhabit the world? And what is the power that, like some cosmic police force, guarantees the order of the world against any and every violation, if not the anger of the *ṛṣis,* the ever-present threat of a curse that devastates and destroys like a gust of fire? Thus the *ṛṣis'* lapses into those passions that destroyed their hoard of *tapas* amounted, perhaps, to nothing other than the continual renewal of the two supreme functions—creation and destruction—to fulfill which they had been called forth by Brahmā, the god they had previously called forth themselves.

It wasn't only the gods who feared the anger of the *ṛṣis.* The rivers were afraid too. Once, Viśvāmitra and Vasiṣṭha had been quarreling from opposite banks of the Sarasvatī. The majestic flow of the waters was wounded by their shrill voices, lost in nature. Each was claiming that his own *tapas* was superior to the other's. Vasiṣṭha's smile was fierce: how could this impudent fellow, who wasn't even a brahman, imagine he possessed a kind of *tapas* greater than his own? Didn't he know—everybody knew—that Vasiṣṭha's *tapas* was so strong it made it impossible for him to kill himself? Vasiṣṭha well remembered the day he had succeeded in scaling the summit of Mount Meru and, confident and eager as for an amorous encounter, at once leapt from the rock into the void. He longed for death as for the most exotic, the most unavailable of women, he would cling to her as he plunged through that immense expanse of air before his body, with supreme pleasure, crashed down upon the ground. But it was not to be. He fell on his back and found it caressed by the soft petals of lotus flowers, beneath which blossomed more lotus flowers, which rested on yet more lotus flowers. They formed a pillow that went deep into the earth. Ever more exasperated, he had tried to kill himself on a number of other occasions. He had thrown himself into the river Vipāśā, as a shapeless sack wrapped with ropes. But he emerged from the waters unharmed, unbound.

Thinking about this, Vasiṣṭha became extremely gloomy. What had driven him so determinedly to seek his own death if not his desperation at the death of his hundred children? And who had brought about that slaughter if not the horrendous Viśvāmitra, now glaring at him from that small white patch on the opposite bank of the river?

Suddenly Viśvāmitra broke off shouting insults and ordered the river to snatch Vasiṣṭha in her waves and hand him over. Terrified, Sarasvatī obeyed. She tossed up Vasiṣṭha on Viśvāmitra's bank, while the latter hurried off to his *āśrama*. He was looking for a knife to cut his rival's throat. Then Sarasvatī once again snatched Vasiṣṭha up in her waves, for she was afraid the *ṛṣi* might curse her. The river was seen to leave her banks behind and swallow up trees and meadows like a freakish snake. Then suddenly she went back to her bed, flowing coolly by, while the two *ṛṣis* once more crouched down on opposite banks and obstinately went on insulting each other. Vasiṣṭha shouted to Viśvāmitra that he would never be able get beyond his dumb warrior mentality. True, it had served to terrify the gods. But it wasn't enough to terrify Vasiṣṭha. He was not so ingenuous as the gods.

Indra was handsome, strong, and not without a dose of cowardice. The pressure of the missions assigned to him was making him uneasy. A hundred horses to sacrifice—and any number of monsters to slay. All over his skin, a thousand vulvas surfaced in delicate tattoos, each opening just a fraction, like a sleepy eyelid. They were a sign of servitude, the indelible signature of a priestly sarcasm's response to his adulterous crimes. Those vulvas—or butterflies?—would ever remind him of a disastrous adventure.

One day, Indra began to buzz around the ancient hermitage of the *ṛṣi* Gotama. The sage had gone down to the river for his morning ablutions. His gloriously beautiful wife Ahalyā was sitting in a flowery clearing, rapt in thought, playing with some twigs. Disguising himself as Gotama, Indra went up to her. Mimicking the ascetic's voice, he said: "Woman of admirable calm and slender waist, I wish to unite myself with you, for the pure pleasure of it." Ahalyā looked up and immediately saw through the clumsy disguise, in which, rather than the solid build of Gotama, a bull among his fellow seers, Indra's slimmer, adolescent body was all too evident. Bored with her life in the forest, she consented to the false husband's proposal, but in such a way that the god would appreciate that she had immediately recognized whom she was dealing with and meant to be possessed by him, not her husband. She headed for the hut. Looking up at the sun, she worked out how long they had before Gotama came back, then concentrated on her pleasure. It was an angry, exhilarating coitus. The climax was scarcely over when, with one eye steadily measuring the progress of the sun, Ahalyā coldly pushed Indra away from her and steered him toward the door with her foot. "Go, my lord," she said. "Protect me—and yourself." Hair still tousled, Indra rushed out of the twig hut. But coming toward him with calm and heavy step was

Gotama. He was shaking the water of his sacred bath from his polished skin, a bunch of herbs in his hand, and his penetrating eye quickly took in the god's nervous gesturing. "O evil being," said Gotama, shaking with anger, "this gross disguise deserves a solemn punishment." Indra was petrified. Accustomed though he was to fighting monsters, cutting off their numerous heads and hurling lightning at their scaly backs, he felt lost before this massive man with his deep voice, weaponless and fearless, transfixing him with piercing eyes. Gotama walked up to Indra. One hand went down between the god's thighs, closed around his testicles, tore them off, and tossed them on the grass. "Henceforth you shall eat the wind and sleep on ashes," said Gotama. Then he turned to Ahalyā, who was watching, motionless. "Many an epic cycle shall pass before someone comes one day to free you," he told her. Then Gotama went off alone, in search of a peak no woman had ever trod.

Indra writhed in pain on the ground and told himself that never had any god been so humiliated. His confused mind boiled with rancor against the other gods: "As always, I undertook this adventure on their behalf. And, as always, I alone must suffer the consequences. The gods are snoops, always scanning the earth, anxious and apprehensive, tormented by their one fear that some *ṛṣi*'s *tapas* will grow stronger than their own. Then they always resort to the cheap trick of ruining the seer with the help of some Apsaras or courtesan. Or they get a god to seduce his wife. And who better than I, Indra, the woman thief? I was acting on behalf of the gods—and all the evil has befallen me alone. Meanwhile the anger I aroused in Gotama has destroyed his reserves of *tapas*. So the gods are safe again. But they won't remember me."

When the thirty-three gods heard these words, they decided they had better get together and see to the matter. Agni spoke first. His right hand rested on the neck of a large ram. "Look here," he said. "This ram has got testicles. Indra, who is king of the gods, has lost his. I propose that we give Indra the ram's testicles." Solemnly, the other gods agreed. Gripping the ram's neck with one hand, Agni tore off his testicles with the other. Then he went down to Indra, still on his back by Gotama's abandoned hut, and attached those dark testicles to the god's bright body.

"Ascetic" ("he who exercises himself" is the Greek sense of the word) offers us a sober definition of those wise men, the *ṛṣis*, who spent their lives kindling *tapas*, expanding a nucleus of heat. Were the ascetics to succeed in absorbing the world into themselves, nothing would ever happen. Nature would gradually spread its leaves and weeds over the many scattered rocks that nurse incandescence in their depths. Not only would there be no history, but there would be no stories either. Or at least no visible stories. The landscape would be swept bare and refashioned by the wind. But that is not the case. The ascetic—be it Śiva himself, greatest of all ascetics—cannot stop the world's existing and flourishing. Deep down, he wants the world to exist and flourish. How do we know that? Beside the ascetic there is always a woman. It might be the beautiful Anasūyā, wife of Atri, devourer of meditation, who is busying herself with the housework when all of a sudden the three supreme beings—Brahmā, Viṣṇu, and Śiva—turn up like a bunch of rogues and grab hold of her. Or it might be the wives of the *ṛṣis* in the Forest of Cedars, who one day see a stranger approaching, his clothes ragged, his eyes feverish, his body smeared with ashes, and suddenly they are following him, swaying their hips as if to the sound of cymbals. Or it might be the magnificent courtesan whom the ascetic Ṛśyaśṛṅga meets in the forest and mistakes for a young man, an aspirant to spiritual ascent with whom he can exercise his *tapas*. Or the celestial Nymphs, the Apsaras, to whom any malevolent god may entrust the task of leading another ascetic astray. Wherever we find the ascetic, there is also the most beautiful of women, at once tempted and tempting, moving in circles around him. This figure is the first concretion of *tapas*, a ghost who weaves herself a body, which is then used to protect her origin—the ascetic—or recklessly to attack and destroy it. The ascetic becomes the only lover she ever knows; or alternatively he will be ridiculed and humiliated by this woman, will spill his seed without touching her; or he may ignore the Nymph. But a female figure will ever revolve around him, in her circle of fire.

Yājñavalkya said: "Thinking is dangerous. And it was never more so than the day Janaka of Videha invited me for a sacrifice, and likewise invited the brahmans of the Kuru-Pañcālas. On arrival, I found myself walking through a huge fair. Behind a stockade, a thousand cows were lowing, coins tinkling around their colored horns. Those cows were the prize Janaka was offering to whoever proved best able to answer questions about *brahman.* The Kuru brahmans all looked at me with suspicion, and some with resentment. I was seeing many of them for the first time, but we all knew something about each other. I was renowned for my brusque manners and didn't want to disappoint. The meeting began: it was made up of two white stripes, the brahmans and the cows, between which milled a colorful crowd of women (some of them, I noticed, supremely beautiful), merchants, warriors, and craftsmen, in short people who keep quiet and bear witness. Then I turned to Sāmaśravas, the young disciple who followed in my footsteps: 'Sāmaśravas, my boy, go ahead and get the cows.' I had spoken softly, but it seemed everybody had heard. There was a buzz of noise, with everybody speaking in everybody else's ear.

"Aśvala, the *hotṛ* of Janaka, who was master of ceremonies on that occasion, stood up and asked me: 'So, Yājñavalkya, you really are the best, are you?' His voice was calm, his mind seething with rage. 'I'm ready for anything,' I said, 'but I want those cows.' The contest began at once. Gazing along the line of brahmans, I had the impression that every eye had narrowed to a slit: each mind was looking for the sharpest question. They wanted my head to burst. The first question was Aśvala's by right: 'Yājñavalkya,' he said, 'everything that exists is tainted by death. How can he who sacrifices not be tainted by death?' There was a strong wind that day, bright sunshine, tents and banners hummed like sails. The wind bared my head. Everybody was looking at it. They wanted to see if the bones would shatter. The questions went on and on. With the concentric circling of the hawk they were homing in on *brahman.* But my head was not bursting.

"Then Gārgī stood up. She was the most beautiful of all women theologians, and the most to be feared. Few were the brahmans who dared compete with her. Yet, rather than at the woman herself, I found myself looking at her robe. I hadn't known that a fabric could be so splendid, hugging her body as if it were itself a body and eluding any definition of its color. She must have woven it herself, was my first thought, since I knew that Gārgī did some weaving as a pastime. She was famous for her fabrics, though one never saw them. Then I thought, 'Perhaps the excellence of Gārgī's thinking was a pastime when compared with her art as a weaver.' As this thought came to an end in my mind, so did Gārgī's first question. Playing the coquette, the woman who will speak of nothing but women's matters, she was asking me a question about fabrics. 'Yājñavalkya,' she said, 'if the waters are the weft on which all things are woven, on what weft are woven the waters?' An easy question, or so it seemed. But watching her facing me, I sensed that Gārgī was determined to beat me. The deceptive modesty of this opening was just a way of leading me into a trap. Ten times she asked me on what weft had been woven the world that was the weft of the preceding world. And I answered without hesitation, as though repeating a liturgy. After the tenth question, she looked up at me with blazing eyes: 'And the worlds of *brahman,* what weft were they woven on?' Then I felt fury well up within me against that insolent woman, temptress of the mind. 'She believes that what her hand weaves is everything, that everything is there in her loom, beneath her fingers. Quite probably no man has ever dared contradict her. And she's too proud and mad about her body ever to have invited a man to her bed,'

I thought. Then I found a new vibrancy in my voice, it was harsh and tense as I heard it pronounce these words: 'Do not ask too much, Gārgī. Take care, lest your head should burst. You ask about a divinity beyond which there is nothing more to ask. Do not ask too much, Gārgī.' And Gārgī fell silent.

"But it wasn't over. Gārgī was holding back her last attack. She let the other brahmans ask their questions one by one. Then she came forward again, but her manner was different this time. She was no longer the impressive painted statue. Now the warrior came to the fore. First she looked at the brahmans and said: 'If he answers these two questions, none of you will beat him.' Then she turned to me, legs braced like a man: 'Yājñavalkya, I stand here in front of you like a warrior from the country of Kāśī or Videha. I have strung my bow. I hold two arrows tight in my hands, ready to transfix you. They are two questions. Try to answer.' I'd been preparing myself for an attack from a different quarter. But once again Gārgī displayed supreme elegance. Again she spoke about weaving. She asked me what time was woven on. I knew that she knew that I had already answered this question. But I decided to answer softly, calmly, intimately, as if speaking only to her. I told her that time was woven on the indestructible. I said that it was woven on he who neither eats nor is eaten. On he who knows the one who knows. I said this looking straight at Gārgī, knowing perfectly well that I wasn't telling her anything new. It wasn't this she wanted to hear. So I added something else as a gift, a gesture of homage to lay at her feet. I said: 'In this world, Gārgī, he who makes offerings, celebrates sacrifices, practices *tapas*, but does not know the indestructible, his virtues will come to an end, be it only a thousand years hence; in truth, Gārgī, he who leaves this world without having known the indestructible is a wretch, but he who does not leave this world unless he has first known the indestructible, he, Gārgī, is a brahman.' I saw Gārgī's eyes flash when I said the word 'wretch.' That was the word that right from the start she had wanted to hear spoken at this gathering, in front of those tight-lipped brahmans, wretched every one quite probably. She had wanted to hear a word that would speak contempt for virtuous deeds. At the same time I sensed an unspoken complicity between myself and Gārgī that nothing could undermine, a complicity that, were we never to speak to each other again, would be with us forever. Then Gārgī turned around and said: 'Brahmans all, rejoice, for you can never escape this man except by rendering him your homage. None of you will ever beat him in theology.' "

Yājñavalkya was renowned for his bluntness. He never stooped to the polite commonplace. The words that came from his mouth were as unpredictable as his natural authority was immense. Everybody remembered the time when a group of brahmans had plunged into the most dazing speculations vis-à-vis meat eating—and it was clear that many of them were only speaking in the hope that Yājñavalkya would notice how clever they were and perhaps drop a compliment. So giddily high-flown was the dispute, you would have thought that none of the brahmans had ever eaten meat in his life. Yājñavalkya listened, eyes staring at the ground, face inscrutable. Everybody went on behaving as if he wasn't there, but everybody knew that the outcome of the discussion depended on what, if anything, he would say. They were exhausted—and still Yājñavalkya hadn't spoken. Then he looked up from half-closed eyes. All he said was: "When I eat meat, I like it tender and juicy." Nobody dared add so much as a word. Later, when they cast their minds back on that day, it was with a feeling of terror.

On other occasions, however, Yājñavalkya would use the most obscure and unfamiliar words as if they were perfectly common. And some would immediately be convinced of the poverty of their learning, since it didn't include the meaning of these words. Nothing dumbfounded his listeners so much as the formula they heard him come out with one day, speaking in a whisper, as if trying to hide what he was saying. The subtle Śākalya had been asking him how many gods there were. Patiently—and this in itself was surprising—Yājñavalkya had brought the number down from three thousand, three hundred and six to one. But Śākalya still pressed him. So Yājñavalkya said: "There is a divinity that lies beyond all questioning." Then in a fierce hiss he added that one day pillagers would steal Śākalya's bones by mistake and scatter them in contempt. Which came to pass. But it wasn't this that so impressed itself on the minds of those present so much as the words "There is a divinity that lies beyond all questioning." They had never heard anything like this before. What were the gods, if not the object of their questioning? Now it seemed that something gave way, went deeper. But how much deeper? Though nobody could claim to understand them, the words passed from mouth to mouth, like a proverb.

Yājñavalkya was also famous for certain irreverent remarks about women. About certain women in particular, but also about women in general. Yet none of Yājñavalkya's disputes was so intense, almost unbearably so, as the one he had with a woman, the proud Gārgī. Never had he answered another brahman with such ferocity. Those listening felt they were being annihilated. Every scrap of air had been appropriated by those two overwhelmingly sovereign beings. They battled together—and perhaps something else was going on between them too, something no one could follow, at once evident and ciphered. Somebody recalled, on that occasion, another of Yājñavalkya's enigmatic remarks, about man being composed of himself and a void. "Hence that void is filled by woman," he had said. Now it seemed—and it was almost a hallucination—that Gārgī's shape was superimposed over that void, and that she was making herself at home there, taking on the outline defined by its boundaries, as the dispute went on, sharp and cutting.

Yājñavalkya had two wives, Maitreyī and Kātyāyanī. No one had ever seen them quarrel. And this alone would have been enough to unsettle people, since it ran contrary to everybody's experience. They rarely appeared in public together. And when they did so, they treated each other with affectionate circumspection. Kātyāyanī had a soft, inexhaustible beauty. Even in lands far-flung, people would say that no beauty could rival Kātyāyanī's. Few could claim to have heard the sound of her laughter, but they said it was a wonder, like the sudden flowering of the *udumbara.* Maitreyī on the other hand was often present at the brahmans' disputes. Indeed, the brahmans were afraid of her, knowing that she was capable of spotting where their doctrine was weak. And they envied her, because they also knew that Yājñavalkya spoke to her about *brahman.* Nothing worked so fiercely on their imaginations as the thought of those conversations, of which they would never know so much as a syllable.

Yājñavalkya had no children. He traveled from place to place with his two wives and a considerable retinue, like a tribe. There were those who waited years for him to visit. Generally they would prepare a list of questions. One day Yājñavalkya said the same words, at two different moments, to his two wives: "I shall shortly be leaving this stage of life. Make haste, I want to settle your affairs first." Maitreyī and Kātyāyanī immediately understood what these words meant: they were never to see him again, he was going into the forest. Kātyāyanī said nothing and stroked his hand. Maitreyī asked a question she had asked him many times before, as if this were a day like any other: "Master, if I possessed the earth and all its riches, would that make me immortal?" Yājñavalkya smiled, in memory of their talks together. He gave an answer Maitreyī already knew: "You would simply lead the life of the rich." As though following a liturgy, Maitreyī replied: "What can something matter to me, if it does not give me immortality?" Yājñavalkya looked at her, holding her hands on his shoulders. "You are dear to me and say things that are dear to me. Now sit down and I shall teach you. But you must give me all your attention." After a moment, he said: "The bride does not desire her husband because he is dear to her, but for love of self." This was a new formula. How was it to be understood? Everything turned on one word: "self," *ātman.* Was "for love of self" to be taken as meaning "for love of one's own person"—something with a name—or as "for love of Self," of the *ātman,* for love of something that stands above the ego and absorbs it into itself? Was it another of those fearfully harsh and true observations Yājñavalkya would use to crush the claims of the sentiments—and above all the noble sentiments? Or was it the last word on things as they are? Maitreyī was of two minds, she hesitated. Yājñavalkya watched her with a sweetness no one was to witness. He went on talking about the *ātman,* he told her secrets he had never told before. But already he knew that Maitreyī could no longer hear him, for a veil of tears was falling on her heart. Pulling herself together, Maitreyī caught only the last two things Yājñavalkya said by way of farewell: "How to know the one who knows? . . . That is the secret of immortality." Maitreyī caught the cadence of the words but not their import. More than immortality, what mattered to her was that voice, which she would never hear again.

Kaśyapa said: "You are continually finding the word 'sacrifice' in the texts and you ask yourselves: why this word, this obscure act, and why so soon? Why does it come before all others? Why doesn't it appear, if appear it must, after the completion of the more basic actions? To know the answer, you must first remember. See the beginning. 'With the eye that is mind, in thought I see those who were the first to offer this sacrifice.' So say the texts. Who were the first to offer the sacrifice? What was there to see?

"The sky was empty. On the earth but two groups of beings, gods and *ṛṣis*—those gods and those *ṛṣis* who were called Ādityas and Aṅgiras. Watching the sky, they wandered around the earth, and desired. They desired the sky. Each group knew the other harbored the same desire. They watched each other from a distance. Each wanted to make their move before the other. Canny and deceitful, the gods managed to sacrifice first. No sooner had they conquered the sky than they asked themselves: 'How may this celestial region be made unattainable by men?" Immediately a thought came to them: 'Wipe out the trail.' They sucked the essence from the sacrifice until it was quite dry. Then they decided to hide the essence, the way bees hide honey. Down below, on earth, they could still see the sacrificial clearing: ashes, sticks, heaps of stones, grass, logs. It looked like an abandoned bonfire. But you could sense that something had happened there. So the gods took the sacrificial pole, the *yūpa* to which the victim was tied, and used it like a broom to smooth over the earth, cover up and confuse. That's why the pole is called *yūpa,* because the gods used it to wipe something out, *ayopayan.* Soon enough the Aṅgiras turned up. They suspected a trick, because the gods had slid off. They looked around, in that speechless clearing. They sang and kindled their inner fires. They said: 'There must be some telltale sign, something must be peeping out in this clearing.' All they could hear was a rustle of ferns. The Aṅgiras prowled around, cautiously, silently, taking care where they put their feet. A turtle popped up out of the grass. The Aṅgiras exchanged glances. 'It must be this, then, the sacrifice . . . ,' they said. 'Let's stop it.' As it turned out, the turtle was indeed the sacrificial cake. They surrounded it. They invoked the names of many gods, to stop it. The turtle paid no attention and went right on walking. They pronounced the name of Agni. At that the turtle stopped. It drew in its legs. They picked it up, heaped together some wood, lit the fire. They wrapped the turtle in Agni. It was their offering to the gods. Thus the Aṅgiras too conquered the sky. From that day on they have plied back and forth between earth and sky.

"I was that turtle."

Atri said: "Since we watched everything from above, from the light of the Bear, we were the model of those who observe, those who watch over: the brahmans. Only one thing distinguished us from them, our not performing a certain gesture: we were not obliged to eat the *prāśitra,* the 'first portion,' that piece of wounded flesh, torn by Rudra's arrow and no larger than a grain of barley, which a brahman on the contrary has to eat. If the brahman doesn't open his mouth to take the *prāśitra,* the sacrifice will not be able to heal. The brahman eats the guilt, he assimilates it into his circulation. Thus he 'restores what was torn asunder.' The tearing is within the ceremony—and the ceremony itself serves to heal it. Everything is within the sacrifice. With the sacrifice one heals the sacrifice. I say this so that you might not imagine it easy to escape from sacrifice. In every sacrifice there is the uncertainty of a journey toward an unknown destination. 'When exactly did the journey begin?' two priests asked themselves. 'Did it go to the home of the gods?' 'Did it really go?' 'It went!' 'I ask the gods that they may listen!' 'That they may acknowledge it!' The sacrificer must make himself heard, must make himself seen. What was the vehicle of sacrifice? A chariot, made up of meters. The *gāyatrī* and *jagatī* meters are the sides of the chariot. If the word doesn't scan, the chariot won't travel. And *vāc,* 'word,' is Vāc, the divine maiden who steers the mind toward the sky, who supports it on its journey, nourishes it, helps it."

Jamadagni said: "We are here to speak because struck down—quite for how long we do not know, though the first signs came early—by the disease of the ritual. The building was still majestic, the joints meticulously executed, there were no cracks. Or rather, only the prescribed cracks, the three bricks with the holes, heralds of the immense that remained outside our construction. But would it be enough? Mightn't a murderous wind blow up one day, to destroy it all? Mightn't the tension slacken one day, the frail ship of the ceremonial word go down in a storm? And above all: hadn't our presumptuous idea of building been of its very nature vain, since building inevitably implies a series of gestures, and thus falls within the category of action? *Action:* a mysterious, terrible word. Yājñavalkya and Ārtabhāga withdrew to discuss the matter. Not all were to hear. Not all would be able to bear that truth. Can action,

action of whatever kind, free us? Or is action perhaps the main thing, indeed the only thing, from which we must free ourselves?"

Atri said: "Even before breathing, men desired. But what is desire? Before our eyes, there is nothing; behind our eyes something lights up: an image, a few words that return obsessively, or just one word. The world is a desert: where can we find the expedient that would turn that presence behind the eyes into something before the eyes? There was action, the gesture that changes things. But do action and gesture belong to he who accomplishes them? If they do, to accomplish an action once implies accomplishing it always. If not, every action that seeks to evoke the object of desire is aleatory. The object might appear, but only the way an animal might cross one's path in the forest. And this was exactly our experience. At which point we began to suspect that actions do not belong to he who acts. But in that case, what does belong to such a person? Where does the action begin? It was important to know that to understand where what belongs to he who acts ends. There was the danger that everything might come apart, that even the desiring mind might start to doubt whether it really belonged to itself: for isn't a desire similar to an action? Isn't it, like an action, something that appears, complete with its own shape, its momentum and direction? But, if the two resembled each other, perhaps we might pass from one to the other—and from the latter, once again through resemblance, to the object desired. And what was the nature of the object desired? A place, a being, a state, a substance: something unique, not to be mistaken for anything else. Something irreversible. Something that, once it appears, must ever belong to what is. But where to find an action that has these characteristics? Whoever drinks water will always repeat the same gesture of drinking water. The action has nothing unique or irreversible about it. It can be repeated as often as one comes across running water. Unless there happens to be a radical difference between one example of running water and another. But no one ever claimed as much. Rather we asked ourselves what action might be of its nature both unique and irreversible. And linked to something's appearing. Perhaps it was this latter consideration, the most important aspect of all, which pointed the way. To cause something to appear was beyond us. But to cause something to disappear? Things can resemble each other by contrast too. So we posed ourselves a question that sounded like a riddle: what is that action that is unique and irreversible—and can evoke the unique and irreversible? One day someone came up with the answer: Causing something to disappear. But we were bound to recognize that, at least as far as men are concerned, causing to disappear is another way of saying 'killing.' Perhaps this partly explains why a delicate halo of mourning surrounds every desire achieved. In the vain, formless, undefined realm of gesture we had succeeded in finding one, and only one, this one, whose characteristics corresponded to those of the object of desire. So we placed our quiet trust, *śraddhā,* in this: that that object might prove to be the last link in the chain of that particular action. The link where to that which disappears there corresponds, in another part of the chain, something that appears: the fruit. That was sacrifice. But at the beginning, between ourselves, we called it 'the wheel of desires.' That wheel is also the punishment to which desire is ever tied."

Vasiṣṭha said: "This was our axiom: that what was not manifest took precedence over what was manifest, that the manifest was subject to the unmanifest. And since the manifest, insofar as it depended on the unmanifest, was merely a consequence of it, and a consequence, what's more, that had not been clearly and unambiguously desired, as the events of Brahmā's early life bear witness, the manifest could be considered as a *residue,* a leftover, a remnant, the place where whatever was superfluous, and could not be reabsorbed in the realm from which it originated, had gathered.

"Rather than for the thing itself, the substance, which is ever beyond our grasp and in any event overwhelming, we fought for the leftovers, the residues. And fought among residues. That is our territory, the only territory where the presence (memory?) of another territory might flash across our minds. Never forget that even the most noble gods, the Twelve, the Ādityas, took their form when Tvaṣṭṛ, the Craftsman, cut the Sun down to size, because its light was flooding the world. Shut up in his workshop, Tvaṣṭṛ clipped it, pruned it, pushed it back and forth on his grindstone. As though from a blacksmith's bench, shavings of bright sunshine fell to the ground. The Ādityas were born of those shavings. And if they were scraps, how much more so is the earth and those who inhabit it . . ."

Atri said: "What's the first thing we notice, when we bend our gaze down upon the plains of earth? Fires. We recognize them as people. They are the toughest of living beings. Our vast memory recognizes, in a certain mud hut in the forest, down near Kāñcī, the same fire we once saw dart from the hands of an ancestor as he strained to climb the ridges of the Hindukush or gazed through mist at the immense folds of lands still to explore, toward the east. We alone know that that fire has been ever the same, fed and renewed for hundreds of years by kinsmen who know nothing of each other, terrestial model of the fragile, unfailing life that no man ever manages sufficiently to imitate."

Viśvāmitra said: "You see that Agni means fire—and you are satisfied. You think that such a precious and dangerous element deserves a great many honors. But you are wrong. Agni's secret name, the name the gods use when they speak of him—and it is also a common word in our language—is *agre,* 'forward.' Before he is fire, Agni is everything that goes beyond us, the dazzling light that darts ahead of us wherever we are. When we go forward, we are merely following Agni. Man's conquests are the scars Agni leaves behind in his progress across the earth."

Jamadagni said: "Where does fire come from? From the mouth. From the vagina. From a smooth, moist cavity. From the burning lake. There is a fire beneath the waters. It is the Submarine Mare. Her name is Vaḍavā. Hot blasts issue from her mouth. One day, when the oceans can no longer hide her, when all the waters have been devoured, then the Mare's head will surface once more. It will be the end of a world."

Bharadvāja said: "The mind is ever treacherous, even when it is but one component of the innumerable tiny beings who populate the earth. Even in that fragmented, occulted, clouded state it preserves its nature, the same that caused it to rise as desire from within the *asat*, the boundless which is not, and yet desires. But how can that which is not lie at the origin of that which is? It almost seems as if there were two states of being, each of which seeks to deny the other. Yet the poets, the *kavis*, having long searched their hearts, discovered that there was a connection, a *bandhu*, suspended between the two states, a rope that ended by hiding itself (knotting itself) in the *asat*. In the void? In the fullness? This they didn't say—and doubted whether anyone could. 'The one who looks down on it, in the highest heaven, only he knows—or perhaps he does not know.' But why should the mind have this privilege? Why should the mind be before and after every other thing? Because it can never be found in the world. You can open up any body, any element, with the finest of metal points, you can turn everything inside out and expose all that has been hidden, until matter becomes a whirr of dragonflies. To no end: you will never find so much as a trace, not even the tiniest, of the mind. The banner of its sovereignty is precisely this: its not being there. No one can ever claim to have grasped it. It is like a dazzle on water: you can follow it, but however far you go toward it, it will always move the same distance away."

The impatient Nārada was the only one who felt the need to offer explanations. He took advantage of a period of silence to take up the discussion again, turning toward their foreign guests: "It has come to my attention that in your land a person who writes a work read by generation after generation is said to be 'immortal.' And the work too is said to be 'immortal.' This seems to me an improper use of the word 'immortal.' It would be enough to say that this man is evoked, through his work, in the minds of many. That he is a frequent guest of the memory. But no more. Immortality is not so simple as the passing on of memory. But it does have a relationship with the word. In the beginning, the gods were afraid of death, not unlike yourselves. They felt exposed, like animals grazing who know they are being followed by the predator's eye. To keep death at a distance they decided to hide. But where? In the Vedas. They wrapped themselves in the meters as though in robes. The metres are called *chandas* because the gods wrapped themselves in them, *acchādayan.* But death saw them there too. 'The way you see a fish in water,' say the texts. The meters certainly have something to do with escaping death, but they are not enough. They are transparent water, a fleeting protection, as our clothes for us. So, to hide, the gods went beyond that. Leaving meters behind, they moved on to the syllable. And here one would have to consider whether the syllable can escape death. But we will talk about that some other evening. In any event we shall be far indeed from fame, a word unduly close in your minds to the word 'immortality.' "

Vasiṣṭha said: "To attribute infinite duration to the gods, or infinite knowledge, or infinite strength, is groveling and superstitious. The gods are simply those who have come closest to *brahman.* It's true that, vain and fatuous as they were, they claimed to be responsible for their victory, claimed to originate their own actions. Men do the same, to imitate them. But it is pure boastfulness. The only knowledge is the getting closer—and the recognition of what you are getting closer to. Agni, Vāyu, and Indra tried as much. There was a mocking Yakṣa who belittled their power. And they couldn't work out who he was. Then, while trekking up through the woods, Indra had a stroke of luck: he met Umā, that is Pārvatī, the Mountain Girl. It was she who explained to him, in that brusque way women have: 'You are still glorying in a victory that isn't yours. That Yakṣa was *brahman.* He was responsible for your victory.' So Indra was able to recognize *brahman* in a Yakṣa who never showed his face again. He had gone a step further than the others. Something similar happened among us *ṛṣis.* One day I met Indra face-to-face. And this is still a difference between myself and the other *ṛṣis.* But then Indra was lost to my sight too."

Bharadvāja said: "What you foreigners recently called the coincidence of opposites, what you developed as a thesis, was, for us, a state. A formless, tremulous, borderless extension, moving of its own accord—and within it a glow and a warmth, which at first glance look like a will-o'-the-wisp. But then they expand, they radiate outward in the waters from a red-hot bar. The first of all states, the one to which, after each event, one returns as to a final barrier, behind which we shall always meet the same barrier and so on and on for all time, is the birth of fire from the waters. Of Agni from Soma. The liquid fire.

"For this reason, and only for this reason, *tapas*—the heat—came before the word, the number, reasoning, deduction. This is why the first image thought chose for itself was that of a submerged, pervasive brazier, a glow in the water. It was the only way to lead us back to that state that preceded all others, when the waters issued forth from the mind and the mind from the waters. Who could say which came first?"

Jamadagni said: "There are many worlds—and never fewer than two: this and that. This is the world of men, that is the world of the gods. Look at the animals and you will see what I mean: tame animals are the world of men; wild animals, the world of the gods."

Yājñavalkya said: "To gain access to that world, to move toward it, one must yoke together mind and word. No other chariot will carry us there. But one must watch carefully to see that the yoke is balanced. For the word is smaller than the mind. So, beneath the main bar of the yoke, on the side of the word, it is well to slip another wooden plank, so that the bar stays flat. Such are the precautions upon which the course of our lives depends."

Atri said: "Many have asked and will ask themselves: why does something happen, if it must then be submerged? What is the point of an intact *dharma* among corpses? What is the difference between one era and another, if all are swallowed up? I was asked this question many times. I asked it myself every time I was left with only the billowing waters beneath me. In the midst of that indigo or sometimes of that interminable grayness, there was but one black speck, a wandering bed. On it lay a sleepy Viṣṇu, glued like a lover to the coils of Śeṣa and protected by the canopy of his heads: a delicate toy no child could ever play with. Śeṣa was a lump, a leftover, the residue of what had been. Not all had been hallucination, so long as that lump still drifted around. It was here that deeds undone, fruits uneaten, gathered and clotted. Waiting to measure out the days of the new era.

" 'But then does nothing new exist?' they asked me. 'One

should be thankful that anything exists at all, why ask for it to be new as well?' I answered with a brahman's impatience. Yet I knew that, however tiny, the new does exist. While all expands and all is reabsorbed, ever in the background a faint hiss tells us the arrow is heading toward its target. The feather ruffled by the arrow is the new."

Viśvāmitra said: "I remember. It was nearly time to press the *soma*—the midday pressing. It was winter, almost at the solstice, like today. We were celebrating the *mahāvrata*, the 'great vow.' I had just finished intoning the thousand verses of the hymn called the *mahaduktha.* All at once I realized that Indra was sitting next to me. I thought it was an illusion. I went on with the verses, looking straight ahead of me. Then, furtively, I risked another glance. Indra was still there. So I said: 'I am honored to see you here in my home, but my wish would be to join you in your own beloved home, in the sky.' Meanwhile the ceremony continued. The verses echoed around like a swarm of hornets. Indra said: 'Follow me.' When we were in the sky, I said to him: 'I would like to get to know you.' Indra answered: 'I shall grant you this favor.' Then he fell silent. For a long time we sat opposite each other. Then Indra said: 'I am *prāṇa*, breath. You are breath. All beings are breath. Breath is what burns below. Thus do I penetrate all spaces. The *mahaduktha* you were reciting is also breath. It is light too. It is food.' Indra then explained that there are seven breaths—and each goes in a different direction. As he was describing them, I recognized them: they were none other than ourselves: the Saptarṣis. Now I understood why, during the *mahaduktha,* the hundred harp strings were brushed in seven different ways, using an *udumbara* twig. Now I understood why the *hotṛ* had pushed the seat of the swing, with immense care, in seven different directions. That day Indra revealed to me why we must celebrate the rite we were already celebrating. On my return, I told everyone of my vision. So today we know why we celebrate the *mahāvrata.* This is the right sequence of events. The vision comes *afterward.* First one must arrange the gestures. But without knowing exactly what they mean. The vision throws light on how and why things must happen as they already do. Since everything already happens. But how did it happen?

"The *mahāvrata* was an ancient ceremony—like all the ceremonies founded by the *vrātyas.* People no longer speak of the *vrātyas,* but they are the shadow that accompanies our every gesture. And if one does not know the shadow, one knows nothing. So I will speak of them. With black turbans and black sandals complete 'with ears' (as they used to say), wrapped in robes with red and black fringes, antelope skins on their shoulders, a metal-pointed stick and small loose-strung bow in their hands, grouped around a rickety cart, open-topped, that lurched askew, off the beaten track, drawn by a horse and a mule, driven by a man with long, loose hair and a silver collar, stiff as a corpse: thus did the *vrātyas* wend their way. They were always followed by a whore and a man from the Magadha. Although, according to the precepts, they were a 'non-whore called whore' and a 'man-not-from-the-Magadha called man-from-the-Magadha,' *apuṃścalu puṃścalūvākyā* and *amāgadho māgadhavākyaḥ.* I know this may sound strange. But consider: anyone taking part in a rite is *not* what he is. He is something else . . . And the life of the *vrātyas* was nothing but a rite, throughout their ceaseless wanderings. The *vrātyas* traveled, made music, bullied, stole, danced, spied, plundered, cursed. But they were also the butt of curses, outcastes, emissaries of the unnameable, all that you would like to leave behind but that always comes back, like the past. They were a 'pack,' *vrāta,* a band, a fraternity bound by a 'vow,' *vrata,* which imposed a certain 'way of life,' *vratá.* They were the eternal ambush. When the people who lived in the *grāma*—the communities, likewise nomadic, though they moved more slowly, with their herds—chose to evoke an image of terror, they didn't think of the beasts of the forest, nor of the enemies they met on their wanderings and would have to fight, enemies who had no horses and did not speak the 'perfect language,' Sanskrit. They thought of the *vrātyas.* Occasionally some of the young people in the community, particularly the younger sons, would disappear, and it was rumored that they had joined the *vrātyas.* Everybody knew there was another community in the forest, a parallel, tighter community, whose contrasting gestures, behavior, language, and dress formed a counterpoint to the life of the *grāma,* sometimes invading it, with brash ferocity, striking as suddenly and unexpectedly as Rudra's arrow. Thus they thought of them as of Rudra's wandering bands. They were the esoteric itself, precipitous, rapacious, self-contained. They congratulated themselves on being indistinguishable from each other, like two-legged wolves. They referred to themselves as 'dogs.' They would have no truck with the exoteric, which alone allows a community to exist. The brahmans, on the other hand, who were the guardians of the esoteric, also wished to be guardians of the community, of normal life, life without upheavals or excesses of knowledge. Knowledge they would take care of themselves, in silence. All everybody else had to do was to live. But the *vrātyas* were not like that. Often they were announced by a great din. Harps, drums, rattles, flutes. To their minds, even the earth was first and foremost a sound. They dug a deep hole. They laid out the skin of a sacrificed animal. They beat on it with its tail. It was the earth drum. Like a strip of sound they slithered around the encampments of community life—and this in itself sufficed to alert those who lived there, in transient settlements, with their carts and herds, that an *other* life was always open, always flitting outside and beyond; that the community was not everything. Thus, for a long time the *vrātyas* were the sensible presence of the esoteric. But what is the esoteric? The esoteric is the forest. To grasp the ultimate significance of what happens in the society of men, one must go outside that society. There are traces of servitude and blindness in everything formulated within that society. He who goes out of it breathes for the first time. For the first time he is alone. He feels terror—and provokes terror. The forest is the roaring of wild packs, two-legged wolves—and it is the silence of the renouncers. The young predators and the solitary thinker, still as a log, communicate through their knowledge, remote now, beyond the grasp almost of the knowledge of the householder who observes the rites of the hearth and home. What is the esoteric? The thought closest to the vision things have of themselves.

"This is why I found myself on that occasion among the celebrants of a *vrātya* rite. This is why I inclined toward them, unlike the brahmans, who secretly detested them and were only waiting for the chance to eliminate them from the canonical course of events altogether. And they almost succeeded. I was always an anomaly among the *ṛṣis,* because I am a warrior, a *kṣatriya.* I had a kingdom to rule too, in my life, not just an *āśrama.* I am also the only one who ever managed to upset my companions, the *ṛṣis* of the Great Bear, the time when, out of sheer spite, since they refused to welcome my favorite Triśaṅku into the sky, I caused seven other *ṛṣis*—identical to them—to appear in the southern sky. They saw those other *ṛṣis* take shape in the starry depths and recognized themselves, as though in a terrifying mirror. And they imagined that, at the other end of the universe, seven pairs of eyes must be looking at them with the same terror. Who was who? But the *ṛṣis* got to the bottom of that uncertainty, like all the others . . . What has never ended, on the other hand, is the quarrel between myself and Vasiṣṭha. Even when I was a heron and he a marsh bird, we pecked each other with our sharp beaks. They said of us that we were 'always entangled in love and hate, always impatient in anger.' I don't deny it. Nor will I renounce it. All this by way of making clear that, if ever a *ṛṣi* were destined to celebrate a rite with the *vrātyas,* with those who were outcasts because they knew too much, it was I.

"But now let's speak of the rite itself. It was a *sattra,* something different from all other rites. *Sattra* means 'sitting': one sits, perhaps for a very long time, sometimes as long as sixty-one nights. Other rites were celebrated in an open space, often on a riverbank, the *sattra* in a thicket. To other ceremonies one walks, to a *sattra* one creeps. You see the sacrificers moving in a line, bent double, circumspect, each holding a corner of the robe of the person in front. Thus one arrives at the place of sacrifice: creeping. Why? The sacrifice is like an antelope, it mustn't be frightened. Otherwise it runs off.

"In other rites there is a patron, and there are officiants. In a *sattra* all are patrons, all are officiants. Hence there are no ritual fees, no *dakṣiṇā.* What does one sacrifice, then, in a *sattra*? Oneself. At the center of the *mahāvrata* there is a swing. It is the sun. Then they mark out something like a track, for a chariot race. And they set up a target, in this case a cowhide. Then the water dance begins. Nine girls, six in front, three behind, move from left to right, tapping one foot lightly on the ground, each with a full jug of water on her head. 'Here is the sweet,' they said, over and over. At the end of the dance, they poured out the water on the ground. I didn't know why until I met Indra, but that dance enchanted me. I had never seen anything more graceful in my life. Then the *hotṛ* approached the swing, but without climbing onto it. He touched the seat with his elbows, with his hands, then with his chin. He looked like a snake, testing the ground. Then, as though the angle were the result of long calculation, he would slowly push the seat toward the east, then upward, downward, sideways. It was the ceremony of the breaths. When the *hotṛ* finally climbed on the swing, the hymns burst out. All desires were made word. The drums sounded, the flutes and harps played. The officiants sang till they were out of breath. There were many other phases, including the chariot race and the coitus, behind a quivering curtain, of the 'non-whore called whore' with the 'man-not-from-the-Magadha called man-from-the-Magadha.'

"All this is very far off. The brahmans concerned themselves not only with thinking but also with covering their tracks. The *vrātyas* were cast out among those best left unmentioned. They lived on as ghosts. Which in a sense they had always been. The herds of the dead. And yet the breaths, we Saptarṣis that is, whom every renouncer knows as his last companions when he withdraws into the forest and speaks with them alone, the breaths without which thought could not mingle with existence, since the one mingles with the other only by virtue of breathing—yet the breaths, I say, were first revealed to the *vrātyas,* who arranged the right gestures, through the revelation Indra gave to me, that day I am now remembering."

Vasiṣṭha said: "What is knowledge composed of? If it wishes to know the world in its very fiber, knowledge must achieve the highest level of affinity with that state from which the world arose. That state is knowledge. Every other descends from it. One is what one knows: 'One becomes what one thinks: this is the eternal enigma,' say the texts. He who knows, transforms himself. Whatever does not make one become like the thought that has been thought is not full knowledge. Which is another reason why thinking is dangerous. If whoever thinks horror becomes horror too, his thinking will have to be vast indeed if the horror that gathers there is not to suffocate all around it, as has happened, and still happens to many a wretched mind not lacking in perception."

Yājñavalkya said: "I know that for many of you the real torment is that you must abandon your dear bodies. You imagine, not unreasonably, that the happiness of a disembodied spirit has something dreary about it. But that is not the case. After death, you will find yourself wandering through a haze, shouting without being heard, but all at once it will be you who hear. You will become aware that someone is following you, like an animal in the forest, only now in the darkness of the heavens. The person following you is your oblation, the being composed of the offering you made in your life. In a whisper, he will say to you: 'Come here, come here, it is I, your Self.' And in the end you will follow him."

IX

Sukanyā was beautiful and curious. She had left her friends behind and was wandering alone in the forest, when she came across a huge anthill. She went closer to take a look, and felt looked at herself. Behind the ceaseless motion of the laboring ants, she sensed that there was something still. Two reddish points of light glowed in the labyrinth. Two imprisoned fireflies perhaps? Sukanyā took a thorn and pricked them. There came a low moan. Sukanyā walked on lighthearted, thinking nothing of it.

Śaryāti soon noticed that his kingdom had been struck by a scourge: people were unable to void their bowels. Along with everybody else, he tried to find out if some evil deed had been done. One of those he summoned was his daughter Sukanyā. "Do you remember doing anything wrong?" "Nothing," answered Sukanyā. Her smile was at once sweet and tinged with mockery. "Think carefully," said her father. "I pricked two firelies with a thorn." "Where?" "In an anthill." Śaryāti lowered his eyes and turned pale. Nothing could be more dangerous and delicate than an anthill. It is the earth's ear. It is the place where the leftovers of sacrifices are left. It is the home of the snake. It is the threshold of the world below the earth. There are temples in whose cells the *liṅga* rises from an anthill. Śaryāti fell silent. Sukanyā said: "I remember exactly where it was. I'll take you there, if you want." "Let's go," said the king.

. . .

Cyavana was "decrepit and ghostlike" says the *Śatapatha Brāhmaṇa,* when, having raised the power of their rituals by every possible means, the Bhṛgus finally felt ready to set sail for the sky on the ship of sacrifice. They were impatient to be off—and at the same time knew that it would be a disgrace to leave their old father behind. But Cyavana had seen their embarrassment. Ironic and allusive, he watched them through the narrow slits in his ruined face: "Please go ahead. Don't worry about me. By all means leave me here with the leftovers. I have the formula of the Lord of the Residues. Perhaps I'll manage something more uplifting than going to heaven." He laughed, though nothing but a dry rustle came from his throat. His sons looked at him and hesitated. Then they laid him down like a bundle of bones wrapped in a rag near a tree trunk where the leftovers of their sacrifices had been heaped. Soon he was covered by ants. For years they climbed all over his body.

Śaryāti appeared humbly before the anthill. He saw clots of blood where Cyavana's eyes had shone their light up toward Sukanyā. Śaryāti said: "My daughter Sukanyā is careless, but she means no harm. Relent, we pray you." "Sukanyā . . . ," came a distant voice from the anthill. There followed a few short words: "What can I do but curse her—and all of you with her? Or, alternatively, marry her." "I shall have to get advice," said Śaryāti.

They talked it over for a long time. Sukanyā was so desirable that her family had for years been dreaming up plans for gaining the greatest possible advantage from her marriage. Alliances, land, palaces . . . "Sukanyā would certainly bring us a treasure or two," said one counselor abruptly. "But the brahman's curse means losing everything. We have no choice." So Cyavana's proposal was accepted.

. . .

Sukanyā saw father, friends, dogs, and elephants head off in a huge cloud of dust and chatter. Perhaps she was never to see them again. Cyavana, her husband, had crept out of the anthill and appeared in all his ancientness like a sheath of smooth bone. That night Sukanyā tried to run away. But she hadn't gone a pace or two before she found a shiny black snake in her path. Sliding out of the anthill, it arched up to glue itself to her body. Sukanyā stepped back, her face suddenly mature, and fell silent for long time. Beside her the motionless Cyavana did not even raise his eyes.

Her life with Cyavana was one of unyielding monotony. Having once let her rancor and nausea overflow, Sukanyā was surprised to find herself taking a secret pleasure in looking after her decrepit husband. "Since my father has consigned me to this man, I must do it," she said to herself at the beginning, gloomily determined. Then she was forced to admit that she wouldn't give up dressing and undressing, feeding and washing that old man for anything in the world. They spoke only rarely, but Sukanyā felt Cyavana's eyes on her at every instant of the day. It was as if his gaze gushed up from a glowing well. Even when she indulged in her favorite pastime—that of imagining furious and exhausting lovemaking with splendidly handsome men, whom she had never known, going from one to the next in her fantasies—she knew that Cyavana never left her; on the contrary, it was when Sukanyā pictured the most violent and subtle erotic gestures that he slipped into her mind. And it was not a persecution. Her pleasure was kindled by the presence of that eye, the tightening of that imperceptible cord that held them together.

As she was walking in the forest, gathering what scanty food there was, Sukanyā thought: "Cyavana and I: the people we most resemble are Agastya and Lopāmudrā. Time and again, and for such a long time too, I keep thinking of the words to that hymn I heard as a child: 'For many autumns I've done my best, night and day, for many mornings, that make us older. Age chases beauty from the body. Must men never go to their women?' But when Lopāmudrā said those words, she could already feel her beauty, her great beauty, fading—and I have only just grown to be a woman. Then Agastya was still a vigorous *ṛṣi,* while Cyavana is a poor heap of bones. Lopāmudrā could look back on her life as a caravan laden with emotions. I can recall but a few syllables of the hymns I heard people singing in distant rooms. My life begins beside someone who has already seen too much of it—and denies me the intemperance I crave. If anyone were able to watch us here in our solitude, they would say that Cyavana burns his entire self in *tapas,* and I in my desire for a lover. And that we shall never be able to meet. Yet I feel it is not so. When I touch him undressing him or when Cyavana leans on me, I know that we are lovers. In the web of his wrinkles, I meet his eye and something gives in the middle of my breast. Then I think of the other words of that hymn, words I didn't understand at all, or frankly even care about, where it says that 'the powerful *ṛṣi* had cultivated the two colors.' Perhaps Agastya knew to attend not just to his own fierce exercises but to Lopāmudrā's fierce desires too? Was there a way of emerging victorious from the 'battle of the hundred stratagems' that desire casts us into—or rather, desires, since 'the mortal has many desires'? Is it possible to comply with the desire that rises 'from here, from there, from everywhere,' without losing oneself? And is it true that the earliest ancients, who spoke of the truth with heavenly beings, never got to the bottom of—the truth? Cyavana and I have never spoken about such things, as if they didn't exist, as if he were nothing more than a worn-out ascetic and I a restless girl, homesick for her friends' chatter. Yet I'm constantly speaking about them inside my head, and it's his voice that answers me. One day I even remembered two lines of the hymn they used to whisper behind my back, because I was still a little girl. But I won a bet with one of my sisters who was already a woman, and as a prize

I forced her to tell me what they said. 'Lopāmudrā makes her man melt, the foolish woman drains the groaning sage dry.' When I remembered those lines, I thought that I would like to be as foolish as Lopāmudrā myself. And, while I was thinking that, Cyavana, who was sitting in his usual position, smiled at me like a man of the world and asked me for a bowl of water."

One day Cyavana said to Sukanyā: "What do you think I was doing, while I was under the anthill? I was waiting for you. Not just because I desire you, but because I need you. And you still don't know why." The last words were spoken as though to himself. Then he went on: "When you appeared in front of the anthill, I called you, but you didn't hear me. My voice was too faint, and your mind was elsewhere. But you couldn't help noticing my glittering eyes, and you tortured them with those thorns. The ants got drunk on my blood. Never had the world sent me such a painful sign. And it was the necessary first step to reaching you. If I hadn't stared at you from the anthill, you would never have noticed my existence. If you hadn't wounded me, I wouldn't have been able to unleash the curse that is the only power I have. If I hadn't cursed your family, I wouldn't have had anything to offer in exchange for you. If you did not now belong to me, I couldn't offer you for . . . ," Cyavana stopped. Sukanyā didn't want him to finish the sentence.

As on every other day, Sukanyā went down to bathe in a quiet, delightful bend in the Sarasvatī. While she was in the water, she had the habit of running through variations of her imaginary love affairs, which, by now, were as numerous as they were tangled. It was a private ritual. She celebrated it with the same devotion and diligence she would any other ritual, but with the added pleasure of caprice and mental waywardness. She looked up from the water toward the bank and the familiar screen of trees. That day, for the first time, there was something new. She saw two young men sitting in the same position on two boulders, each the same distance from herself. Both men had one leg slightly raised, one the right leg, the other the left. They formed two points in a perfect triangle. The third point, Sukanyā realized, lay within her own eyes. She immediately noticed that the two strangers were of fearful beauty. But another thought unnerved her: could it be that the visible world had become a double mirror, which she was now looking into? What she saw to her right was the exact inversion of what she saw to her left. Could the world, this place of disorder, be thus—or was the scene before her nothing more than the projection of the story her mind was inventing as she swam? Alarmed, amazed, she didn't realize that she was climbing out of the water. At which she saw something that left her paralyzed. At the same moment, curling the same corner of two mouths, the young men smiled. And Sukanyā heard these words: "Woman of the lovely thighs, who are you? Who do you belong to? What are you doing in the forest? Speak, we want to know." Sukanyā blushed, her whole dripping body turned red. She hurried to pick up her clothes, a strip of muslin she never changed. Eyes on the ground, she said in a barely audible voice: "I am the daughter of Śaryāti. I belong to Cyavana." She felt angry then, because the young men responded with a shrill laugh. "Why on earth did your father give you to a man who's already a wreck? Even among the gods there's no one so beautiful as you. You were made to be adorned in the most precious robes, not these rags. Leave Cyavana, he's not complete, whole, perfect, as you are. There'll always be something missing in your life, almost everything in fact. Choose one of us. These are your best years. Don't toss them on a rubbish heap . . ." Sukanyā no longer felt either amazement or desire, just a cold fury. She didn't even answer and walked away toward the place she considered her home, a flimsy cane shelter near the anthill.

She found Cyavana motionless as ever, with his sharp bones and knowing eyes. She told him what had happened, without sparing a single detail. Her voice trembled. Cyavana gazed at her with immense sweetness and a shrewd, almost mocking gleam. He said: "They were the Aśvins, the divine twins. They wander around the earth, helping people here and there, healing them. What they told you is true, but not the whole truth. Tomorrow they'll be there again, perhaps in the same place, and they'll say the same thing. They won't give up. Then you must say: 'It's you who are not whole, because you are not allowed to drink the *soma.*' You'll see how they'll change their tune at that. They'll ask you who could take them to the *soma.* You'll say: 'My husband. He drinks the *soma.*' They'll follow you like two tame dogs, you'll see. Bring them here to me."

All went as Cyavana had foreseen. The twins and the old Cyavana fell to talking with some familiarity. But now the Aśvins' voices were anxious and urgent. Sukanyā didn't know if she was supposed to be listening. They were whispering. Then Cyavana's sharp voice rang out very clearly: "Agreed. This is the deal. I help you get to the *soma.* All you have to do is find a priest called Dadhyañc. In return, you give me youth. And Sukanyā will choose whichever of us she most desires."

Taking advantage of a moment when the Aśvins were confabulating together, Cyavana came to Sukanyā and muttered: "We're going now. When we come back, you won't be able to tell me from them. The moment I arrive, I'll lift my hand to my right eye, where you pricked me. That way you'll know who I am."

Then he set off toward the Sarasvatī. Standing by the door of their hut, Sukanyā watched the magnificent backs of the Aśvins and, between them, the shrunken, skinny Cyavana. They reached the water and jumped in. When Cyavana reemerged and looked around, the Aśvins were beside him. Deft as devoted servants, they stripped "the skin off his body, like a cloak." Cyavana felt a sudden exuberance flood in. Without a word they climbed out of the water. They were three prodigiously beautiful young men, with sparkling earrings, all naked and identical. Sukanyā left the bushes where she had been hiding and went to meet them. "Choose which of us you desire," said a single voice. Sukanyā lowered her eyes, but not so far as not to see one of the three young men rub an eyebrow. She nodded in his direction. As soon as the Aśvins were gone, Sukanyā abandoned herself to the exploration of Cyavana's body. Thus began their unending embraces, "like those of the gods."

"How are we to find Dadhyañc?" the Aśvins asked themselves. "How are we to recognize him?" They wandered anxiously around. They had hoped to set off with a resplendent bride on their chariot, as though a new Sūryā, Daughter of the Sun, were traveling with them on the earth. But all they had gotten was a name. They repeated it to themselves as if it were a password: "Dadhyañc, Dadhyañc . . ."

Still, they were all three quite sure of themselves when they met in the crowd that milled as though at a market in the field of the Kurus, where in times past the gods used to sacrifice. Each knew the other at once. Before being men or gods, they were horses. They recognized each other's stride and rhythm.

Dadhyañc was used to being alone. He knew his knowledge could not, must not be communicated. Why? Honey cannot flow into the world without turning it upside down. So Dadhyañc was a seer like so many others, he kept himself to himself.

The Aśvins looked him straight in the eye and said: "We want to be your disciples." Dadhyañc had never seen creatures of such beauty. It was as though they were transparent receptacles for doctrine. But most of all he felt an affinity with them, and this disturbed him. It happened the moment they shook out their hair. He realized he wanted to neigh with them.

"You're asking me to teach you what the head of the sacrifice is. I'd be glad to. But one day Indra came to tell me that, if ever I revealed it, he would cut off my head. Indra is sovereign among the gods, and he would sense it at once. Nothing escapes him. I must live alone."

The Aśvins didn't give up. They looked at Dadhyañc and said: "There is a way. Let us cut off your head." They waited. "Then we'll put a horse's head in its place. With that new head you can teach us the doctrine of the honey." Dadhyañc was already smiling. "Of course Indra will find you out one day and cut off your head. But he'll be cutting off the horse's head. Then we pull out your human head from a safe place. And we stick it back on your neck. We can do that kind of thing. We're doctors. What we don't know about is the doctrine of the honey."

Dadhyañc had big, trembling nostrils, which stood out in his long, pale face. "They look like ours," said the Aśvins. Observing this person who had accepted them as disciples, they shared a feeling of inexplicable familiarity. They had come to the aid of the blind and the crippled, of widows, aging spinsters, imprisoned seers. They had always had a goddess beside them, whether visible or invisible, third wheel to their cart. But they had never known their father. And they couldn't ask their mother about him, for she had abandoned them. People said she was the immortal woman the gods would not let mortals see. There were all kinds of stories about their birth, none of them entirely convincing. The gods claimed to have cut them off from the *soma* because they helped men too much and traveled too much around the earth. But the Aśvins were convinced that this was a pretext. "Perhaps it's our past we need . . . ," said one of the Aśvins. "Perhaps it has to do with the doctrine of the honey . . . ," said the other.

The Aśvins sat next to Dadhyañc. He still had a pinkish scar around the top of his neck, where a new white head had been attached, topped by a glossy mane. Dadhyañc spoke as if he had finally found his own voice and his own face.

He said: "Before ending up as a papier-mâché sign over the door of some *boucherie chevaline*, I know I have to speak to you. The doctrine you want from me is not human, that's why it is I who reveal it to you. And you too are more horses than gods. Your mother, Saraṇyū, was a mare who practiced *tapas.* She saw a stallion approaching her and chose at first to move away, thinking it was one of the many who wanted to mount her and disturb her spiritual exercises. Then she saw that the stallion was still coming toward her, and was dazzling. She decided to go to him. The important thing was to cover her back from attack. Thus their muzzles met, and rubbed together. The stallion was Vivasvat, the Brilliant One, or rather the sun, or rather the amorphous, white-hot husband who had always desired her but whom Saraṇyū had quickly abandoned. That desire was a burning well within the stallion: his seed streamed out from warm nostrils. And it was immediately sucked into the mare's nostrils; it was the only way she could touch her partner's body now. That is how you two were conceived."

Another day Dadhyañc said to the Aśvins: "Here's something else you ought to know: Viṣṇu was standing still, deep in thought—half asleep perhaps?—his chin resting on the tip of his bow. Strewn around him were a pink shell, a sharp discus, a hammer. On his bare chest glittered the Kaustubha gem. The gods crouched in a circle around him, and were hostile. Watching Viṣṇu and seeing his enigmatic, self-sufficient repose, they had the suspicion that he had something in him that was about to escape all of them, something that they would never know. Viṣṇu had seized the splendor that shines out at the end of the sacrifice, and he wanted to keep it to himself. The gods had tried to overpower him, but in vain. Alone, Viṣṇu kept them at a distance. Indeed, and this was the ultimate insult, he smiled. That smile spread out across the surrounding grass. But it is dangerous to smile like that. The bright force is frittered away. That is why an initiate must cover his mouth when he smiles, to preserve the bright force, say the texts.

"What were they to do? A deal with the ants. They promised the ants that they would always find water wherever they dug. A line of white ants set off toward the bottom of Viṣṇu's bow, where it was thrust into the ground. They worked in silence. Viṣṇu was still on his feet, motionless and radiant. The ants began to gnaw at the bowstring. How long did it take? There were Viṣṇu's half-closed eyes—and there were the gods' greedy eyes, staring at the ants. The sun was setting, the days came and went. The white ants never ceased their gnawing. One team took over from another. The silence was full of menace. Then there was a hiss, a new sound: *grn.* The bowstring had been bitten through. Springing open, the bow whipped off Viṣṇu's head. Lymph poured down on the grass. The gods leapt at it like dogs. But Indra threw himself on Viṣṇu's acephalous body. He placed his own hands, torso, legs, and feet over Viṣṇu's. He wanted to cover his whole body, to be what Viṣṇu had been. Then they resumed the sacrifice. It was a dull, demanding, useful sacrifice, but they did not conquer the celestial world, because it was a sacrifice without a head."

Dadhyañc went on speaking: "The world was sad then, but it did work. Indra took care of the wheel of sacrifice, kept it perennially turning, like the year, like the rains. He was a reliable administrator. No one thought any more about conquering the sky.

"One day, Indra appeared before me. Even before speaking, he knew. He'd felt my eyes go right through him. 'You know the doctrine of the honey . . . ,' said Indra, looking around, to make sure no one was listening. 'Yes,' I told him. 'If you reveal it to anyone, I'll cut off your head,' said Indra, his voice full of hate."

. . .

Dadhyañc added: "The world is a broken pot. Sacrifice tries to put it back together, slowly, piece by piece. But some parts have crumbled away. And even when the pot is put back together, it's pitted with scars. There are those who say this makes it more beautiful. To know the head of the sacrifice also means to know the sacrifice that happens in the head, that cannot be seen, that has no need of gestures, implements, calendars, liturgies, victims—or even words."

The Aśvins spoke some more with Dadhyañc. They told him that, despite bringing relief to the world, they themselves felt orphaned and alienated. The gods would not accept them in their circle, said they had no dignity because they were forever moving around. And even accused them of connivance with men. The woman they had most desired had preferred her decrepit husband. Now, at last, they knew something of their birth. But what had happened before that mare and stallion rubbed their muzzles together? The brighter they appeared, the greater the haze that stretched behind them.

Sitting between the Aśvins, Dadhyañc lightly inclined his long nose and again began to speak: "I know what you are feeling. You have always loved horses—and now you discover that your mother was a mare. You have always yearned for the *soma*—and now I am about to tell you that the lord of the *soma* was your grandfather Tvaṣṭṛ, the Craftsman, father of your mother, Saraṇyū. It is with him that the endless chain of twins began. Saraṇyū was herself a twin. Of Triśiras, the insolent Tricephalous, whom Indra decapitated. This too, perhaps, will be useful for you to know," added Dadhyañc, mildly smiling. "It's not clear why there began to be twins. Perhaps because the moon reflects the sun. Perhaps because reeds are reflected in the water they grow in. Perhaps because the Craftsman's mind reflected a shape as yet unmanifest. Perhaps because the cup the Craftsman forged reflected the cup that resides in his mind. But perhaps for another reason too: in order to breathe, to branch out, life needed the help of beings in whom sameness and diversity were simultaneous and inseparable, to the point, almost, of being exactly superimposed, one over the other. Otherwise we wouldn't know how to know. Every apparition would leave us overwhelmed and speechless. Whereas sameness and diversity allow us to travel far, very far—as you travel on your cart. And men follow in your tracks.

"But let's get back to your complicated family: Saraṇyū herself was born as a reflection. Tvaṣṭṛ couldn't break away from her. They slept in the same bed." Dadhyañc's voice dropped. "I can't rule out the possibility that one of you may be his son." Dadhyañc resumed: "Tvaṣṭṛ knew that he ought to break off with his daughter. But his choice of a husband for her was governed by malice. Tvaṣṭṛ possessed all the forms there are (indeed they called him Viśvarūpa, the Omniform One), and so as his daughter's husband he chose he who has no form, the shapeless solar globe, whom they now call Vivasvat, the Brilliant One. It's time you knew this as well: the Sun, at first, was a Dead Egg, Mārtāṇḍa. And that's what they called him. He was stillborn from Aditi's womb. Never trust nature. It's never simple. It's never natural. But back to Tvaṣṭṛ. Was his choice a punishment? A bad joke? No doubt there was jealousy. Physical contact with her husband must be a torture, for thus Saraṇyū would yearn only for her first lover, her father. Embracing her, Vivasvat scorched Saraṇyū's tender, opalescent skin. But all the same she gave him two children. Yama and Yamī. Twins again. In the bed where she had given birth, Saraṇyū felt she would never be able to bear her husband's embraces again. Her mind formed a simulacrum, identical to herself, called Chāyā, Shadow. If her father was the master of forms, it was she who would evoke copies. And we've been beset by them, enchanted by them, ever since. Saraṇyū told Chāyā what to do: she must take her place, look after the little ones, sleep with her husband. 'You can do it,' she told her, 'because you are a shadow. Not even he can burn you. You can survive anything.' Then Saraṇyū left. 'They hid the immortal from mortals,' the hymns say. When men lose their heart for a beloved, it's Saraṇyū they are seeking, but they embrace a copy. Vivasvat didn't realize that he was dealing with an identical copy, not with Saraṇyū. He was merely amazed to find her so accommodating. Foolishly, he imagined that motherhood had calmed her down. At last their life seemed to be running smoothly.

"That's how Manu, first among men, was procreated. That's why men always go after simulacra. They are born of a simulacrum. That's why they are never sure if they really exist. And never will be. Meanwhile Saraṇyū wandered around and meditated. She had taken the form of a mare. One day Vivasvat opened a door and caught Chāyā scolding the little Yama quite bitterly. It was as though she were a servant taking advantage of her mistress's absence. 'She can't be his mother.' The thought forced itself upon Vivasvat's mind. He ran outside, overcome by rage. As he was running, he heard the drumming of hooves. He was a stallion. In the distance, in the middle of a meadow, he saw a mare, motionless, immersed in *tapas.* As soon as she caught sight of the stallion, she became nervous. She fled. She did everything not to turn her back to him. You already know the end of the story."

"But now let's go back a bit," said Dadhyañc. "No sooner had the gods been born than a cloud of dust arose. Within it: a shuffling sound. On the ground: the first footprints, which immediately became mixed up. Seven beings were dancing. They felt they had been freed, because born to Aditi, to the one whose name is She-who-loosens. But Aditi had given birth to eight children. Seven were dancing, one was an amorphous fetus, a piece of flesh as broad as it was long. The mother had pushed it away, with a kick. The dust of the gods, who had already gone, sifted down onto Mārtāṇḍa, the abortion. Then the dead egg rolled slowly in the waters. Nature swelled with lymph. Surrounded it. The gods remembered their brother, and they said to themselves: 'We mustn't waste him.' They pulled him out of the water and tried to give him a form. So Mārtāṇḍa became Vivasvat, the Sun. But they couldn't rid him of Death, who dwells within him and in every descendant of his son, Manu: in men."

Dadhyañc went on: "It's not so surprising that Death dwells within the Sun. What is surprising, when you think of how he first appeared, kicked away as trash by his mother, is that the Sun is alive. It was his brothers, born before him and all well-formed, who saved him. They didn't want him to be lost. So they gave Vivasvat his shape. One day he would generate the line of those who procreate and die.

"Left alone, abandoned by Saraṇyū and aware now that he had been tricked by her simulacrum, Chāyā, Vivasvat thought back to the day of his birth. He suspected Saraṇyū might have returned to her father's house, out of nostalgia for her real lover. He would look for her there. Tvaṣṭṛ greeted him calmly. He said that yes, it was true, Saraṇyū had come back, but they hadn't let her stay, on the contrary, they had chided her for this rash decision. Then Tvaṣṭṛ looked up at Vivasvat and said: 'You'll never find her again, the way you are now. Saraṇyū lived in terror when she was with you, ever afraid of your touch. If you'll let me, I could try to make you more suitable, more tolerable to living beings.' Even as he was speaking, he had started to clear a big bench strewn with tools. He invited Vivasvat to lie down on it. Then he set to work with a grinding wheel. First he used a liquid to grease down Vivasvat's limbs, then he went over them with that strange tool. Vivasvat found it a relief to suffer. Bright shreds fell away from him to roll into the corners of the workshop, where they continued to shine on their own. Losing light came as a relief, gave him an uplifting thrill. And at the same time he felt the agony of those parts of his body that left him. Tvaṣṭṛ worked away like a craftsman absorbed in his task. He'd begun with the shoulders and trunk. Now he was grinding down his thighs. When he touched a knee, Vivasvat felt he had to do something. With one hand he grabbed Tvaṣṭṛ's wrist and said: 'No further that way. It doesn't matter if my feet stay shapeless. No one will know what they're like when I'm standing on my chariot. There will always be a charioteer to hide me. I'll wear boots when I have to walk. But no one will have to see my feet. The formless is part of me. I can't abandon it. You all feed on the formless. Even you wouldn't exist if it weren't for my formless feet, which you vainly sought to grind down. The world is held together by something left over beyond it, that overwhelms it. But if that something weren't there, there wouldn't be anything. Now leave me be. And thank you. I'll be on my way once more to find my only bride.' "

The Aśvins listened, their eyes on the ground. They were discovering the many branches of their family, after having long wandered the world as orphans. But above all they wanted to know more about one of their stepbrothers: Mṛtyu, Death. Dadhyañc realized even before they asked. He went on: "The more thoughtful, loving, and delicate her husband was with her, the more terrified Saraṇyū felt. A hem of the robe he took off coming to bed could set fire to a continent. Yet it wasn't that that frightened Saraṇyū. It was the freezing cold. She didn't want to be inside Vivasvat because she felt an enormous, silent cavity open up within him, echoless, empty of all vibration. She felt that in getting to the bottom of Vivasvat she would come across an invasive guest, who refused to leave the house, or perhaps was its master. She didn't want to meet him. But she couldn't help reproducing him. When she gave birth to twins—everything for her came in couples or copies—she recognized Death's features in the male child, Yama. It was as if that son had come from the last receptacle of Vivasvat's substance and then, in his mother's womb, met his copy, his twin sister, Yamī. Now at last he would agree to go down into the world and have a history like so many other gods. He would no longer be merely the black shadow that forms behind all that dazzles. But he couldn't have become manifest unless together with Yamī. There was a pact, so it seemed, between death and duplication." Here Dadhyañc fell silent. Then he went on: "Before becoming Yama, Death didn't have a proper name, as if he were a thing rather than a person. Yet the most terrifying thing about Death was his appearance as a person. A figure with indistinct features, who would not let himself pass incognito. You recognized him in the pupil of anyone who came to meet you, be it lover or enemy. Or you glimpsed him behind the burning screen of the Sun, like a black silhouette that penetrated the eye of anyone who saw it, and for a long time refused to go away, an intrusive guest.

"Death sank up to his thighs in the substance of the Sun. His torso emerged from the red-hot mass and looked downward. If you raised your eyes from the earth, behind the barrier of light you could sometimes glimpse a dark outline, as though of someone greeting you from afar. No one was eager to answer that greeting. They said they didn't want to look at the Sun so as not to be blinded. The truth is they didn't want to acknowledge the greeting of that silent, unknown being, to whom, in whispers, they would sometimes allude, in the name 'black sun.'

"Death is sunk up to his thighs in the Sun and in the heart, as in a soft and burning pastry. From afar people would see his shadow fording the Sun as if it were a ditch. All of a sudden the shadow seemed to reach a shallow spot, because more and more of it appeared. You could see the thighs, the knees. When you could see Death's feet someone would say: 'He's been cut off'—and at that moment someone else would die.

"Death is that person half buried in the Sun, who slowly devours it. Just as the 'person,' *puruṣa,* who can be seen at the center of the pupil—and it is the one, barely perceptible sign the mind allows us of its existence—slowly devours the body in which it has been set. Death is to be found wherever some substance is consuming itself. Death is the act of eating. Thus we are a debt owed to Death. We pay that debt every passing moment, cunningly stretching it out and breaking it up with the strength Death itself gives us, stingily conceding, moment by moment, to the Person in the Eye a particle of ourselves to devour.

"The Person in the Eye is not born alone, cannot exist alone. The first couple were the two Persons in the Eye. In the right eye was Death. In the left eye his companion. Or again: in the right eye was Indra. In the left eye his partner Indrāṇī. It was for these two that the gods made that division between the eyes: the nose. Behind the barrier of the nose two lovers hide, as though separated by a mountain. To meet, to touch, they must go down together into the cavity that opens up in the heart. That is their bedroom. There they twine in coitus. Seen from outside, the eyes of the sleepers are hidden by the eyelids as though by a curtain around a bed. Meanwhile, in the heart's cavity, Indra and Indrāṇī are one inside the other. This is the supreme beatitude. That's why you mustn't wake a sleeper suddenly, so as not to disturb Indra and Indrāṇī's lovemaking. That's why whoever is woken finds his mouth sticky, because those two divinities are emptying their seed, while in the sleeper's mouth the liquids of Indra and Indrāṇī mingle.

"Death and duplication go together. Never the one without the other. The science of reflection and scission, the unleashing of doubles, systematic substitution, simultaneous glances, both inward and outward: all these are the works of duplication. Only he who encourages them can gain access to knowledge. But duplication comes together with Death. And only knowledge can defeat Death. This is the circle."

They were sitting on three stools. Dadhyañc had a view of the Aśvins' almost identical profiles as they focused their attention elsewhere. One of them said: "When we were still children, we were given certain words that were attributed to Prajāpati and that none of the Devas or Asuras claimed to have understood, though they had committed them to memory. These were the words: 'The *ātman*, the Self, released from every evil, subject neither to age, nor death, nor suffering, nor hunger, nor thirst, whose desires and whose thoughts are reality, this one must seek, this one must strive to know. He who achieves that *ātman*, that Self, and knows it, shall possess all worlds and all desires.' " Then the other Aśvin said, as though taking over from where his twin had left off: "Could it be that the sovereign of all words is this *ātman*, a reflexive pronoun that declines like a masculine noun, a word we've used every day without thinking, without sensing that this was the secret, that it was to this we must come?" The more baffled they felt, the more they wanted to learn—they told Dadhyañc. He looked them in the eye and said: "The *ātman* comes before the *aham*. The Self comes before the I: the reflexive pronoun comes before the personal pronoun: why? The most basic thing is not that a being says 'I': all animals say 'I' from the first moment they emit a sound. Between Self and I there is but one difference: the Self watches the I, the I does not watch the Self. The I eats the world. The Self watches the I eating the world. They are two birds, they sit on opposite branches of the same tree, at the same height, at the same distance from the trunk. To anyone watching them, they are almost the same. Like yourselves. No one can separate them. The first words the Self said were: 'I am.' Nothing existed as yet when the Self said: 'I am.' The I owes its existence solely to the fact that it was pronounced by the Self. From the start the two had the shape of a person, *puruṣa*. Even though the whole world would later appear from the Self and the Self would sink into it right to the tips of his fingernails, still the Self and the I too preserved the form of a person. Which is why we speak to them and they to us."

Dadhyañc went on explaining the doctrine of the honey to the Aśvins. His speech spread through them from pores to marrow. The world was the same as before. Nothing was the same as before. One day Dadhyañc said: "Śaryāti wants to celebrate a *soma* sacrifice with both gods and men. Do you know who he is? He is the father of Sukanyā, the girl who rejected you. And he is the son of Manu. Thus Sukanyā is your niece, through the simulacrum, Saṃjñā. But at this point you would hardly be surprised by any relationship . . . You must come to the sacrifice too. This is the last time you shall see me with my horse's head. Now, go . . ."

The Aśvins wept. Although they hadn't yet savored the *soma*, they knew that the best part of their lives was coming to an end.

Given that the Aśvins were born of a mare, given that they always traveled by land and sea—and even in the sky—on a chariot drawn by white horses, given that they learned the doctrine of the honey from a being who had a horse's head, it would seem obvious that their name should derive from *aśva*, "horse." But the etymologists of ancient times did not restrict themselves to such obvious reflections. The name also derived, they said, from *aś-* "to gain." Why? Because they were the first to gain the Daughter of the Sun, Sūryā, when they won her in a contest; because they "gained everything." How so? "One with wetness, the other with light," says the etymologist.

Sons, lovers, husbands, brothers, friends, paranymphs, conquerors, chosen ones: such, simultaneously, were the Aśvin for the woman they traveled with, or who traveled with them. It might be Uṣas—or Sūryā. And they would have liked it to be Sukanyā. They were the "Lords of Ornament," Śubháspátīs—and there was no other god who could boast that name. Which is why women were drawn to their chariot, as if to a jar full of honey. The two of them were never alone, even though they were to fill the world with duplication. There was always a third, as their chariot had three wheels, a girl between them, often invisible. In her they communed.

. . .

The "honey whip," *káśā mádhumatī,* darted from the Aśvins' hands and cracked down on the earth. Who can be sure what it was made of? What is sure is that people wanted nothing better than to feel its edge. A goatskin bursting with honey poked out from the Aśvins' three-wheeled chariot. They would dip their whip in it before cracking its dripping sweetness all around them. Where did the whip come from? From the mother of all mothers, from Aditi, the Unlimited One, from the one who has no need of a husband to bring forth fruit. The supreme moments of the Aśvins' lives always had to do with a female figure: when they awoke—and all they saw was Uṣas's tawny hair bowed over them; when Aditi silently placed that whip in their hands; when, at the end of a wild chariot race—the time their fourth wheel was lost forever—Sūryā stood waiting for them on a rostrum beside the finish line and climbed onto their chariot, "for such was her wish," she said. Only a mortal, Sukanyā, whom they had seen rise from the waters like a goddess, rejected them. And that rejection—they thought—had been their salvation, because it had led them to Dadhyañc. Thus they had gained what had always been lacking, the one element that is ever the thing we lack: knowledge. From the honey to the doctrine of the honey. Isn't this the only step we can ever make? All others depend on it—or are illusory. They smiled into emptiness and set off on their way again.

A great crowd had gathered. In a circle, in the middle, were the gods, mingling with the *ṛṣis.* The Aśvins kept to one side, like travelers who have happened upon a scene by chance. The ceremony began, very slowly. The Aśvins watched the celebrants. There was a familiar face among the *ṛṣis.* But who was it? He resembled themselves, with a more solemn expression. "Cyavana . . . ," they both whispered. The rite went on. They saw Cyavana lift a cup. They heard his clear voice: "This is for the Aśvins . . ." There was a sudden whirlwind. Indra was on his feet, furiously tearing the cup from Cyavana's hands: "I do not recognize this cup . . . ," he said. Clouds of dust made it impossible to see what was going on. "Who dares to wrench the cup of *soma* from a *ṛṣi?*" boomed a voice. The Maruts shook their spears. In the uproar, Agni went to Indra and said: "It's not in our interests to provoke the *ṛṣis.* In the end, they are better than we are. We were born of them. Swallow your anger." But even had they wanted to, there wasn't much the gods could do. Summoned up by the *ṛṣis,* Mada, the demon, was intoxicating them. Nothing was clear anymore, in sky or on earth. Eyes lowered, Indra stood still. The whirlwind settled. The Aśvins found themselves beside Cyavana, who had the cup in his hand again. Thus the Aśvins at last brought the *soma* to their lips. Then they looked around: the gods had slunk off. "That was the last time that men and gods drank the *soma* together." And one day someone would add the gloss "In ancient times they drank together visibly, now they do so in the invisible."

X

The *soma* has been identified with many plants over the course of time. One thing is clear: the sap of the *soma* was inebriating. That substance was sensation: the one quantity that was quality. Everything depended on its being won or lost. There had been a time when even the gods didn't have the *soma*. And they called it by another name: *amṛta*, the "immortal." But they had yet to find it, to discover it, to touch the substance that was free from death, and that freed from death. All children of Prajāpati, though divided into the opposing ranks of the Devas and the Asuras, they agreed that for this once they could join forces, for this one undertaking, from which all others descend: the churning of the ocean.

The ocean seethed. The waves foamed like madmen in all directions as a vast pendulum plowed the waters. Torn from its roots, bristling with trees and sharp rocks, Mount Mandara thrashed the liquid mass like the beater in a churn. All the juices, the resins, the lymph of the plants flowed into the water along with liquid gold and cataracts of gems. All essences streamed together into the marine desert. Meanwhile the huge carcasses of deep-sea creatures hitherto unseen by any eye were driven up from the depths by the ceaseless motion of Mandara, who braced himself on the back of the giant turtle Akūpāra, the only creature to have remained impassive in the tumult. Looking closely, you could see a sash slithering around the lush grass of

Mandara's flanks. Or was it a thick rope? It was a snake, Vāsuki. With the Devas gripping its tail and the Asuras its head, it was being tugged back and forth to keep Mount Mandara churning beneath the waters, while from its mouth rose fumes that swirled around the Asuras and muddled their minds. But then it was they themselves, proud firstborn that they were, who had insisted on holding Vāsuki's head, because the head is always the noblest part of anything.

"All this," thought the Devas, "recalls the beginnings of *tapas,* that first friction in the mind from which every marvel is born." But what was to appear this time? Or would anything appear? The Devas were exhausted. Like slaves at their oars, they held on to Vāsuki's scales, just able to see in a steamy distance the grimaces of their eternal enemies, the Asuras, whom for this one undertaking they had accepted as allies. "When the stakes are high, one must be ready to make allies of one's enemies, like the snake with the mouse," Viṣṇu had exhorted. One must risk the ultimate, if one wants to gain the *amṛta,* the "immortal."

At that time the Devas and Asuras were still too alike. Coarse, greedy, hot-tempered, their main ambition was to destroy each other. And to escape death. But death struck them down just the same. After each gory encounter with the Asuras, the Devas would count their corpses. They thought: "One day there'll be none of us left to do the counting." Then they were plunged into melancholy. And roused themselves in fury when their spies came to tell them what they had seen in the camp of the Asuras. There too the dead, many of them disfigured, were piled high under the vultures' gaze. But then Kāvya Uśanas, chief priest of the Asuras, would come down and with a calm wave of the hand resurrect them one by one. To him, and to him alone, Rudra had one day imparted the *saṃjīvanī vidyā*, the "science of resurrection." Thus the place teemed with Asuras. You couldn't say they didn't know death, because they were often killed and spent some time in death's kingdom, suffering like anybody else, but then they came back to life, with no memory, no knowledge. They were merely shot through by a long and invisible wound: the enduring sensation of having already been killed. They suffered from that—but then they would laugh wildly when they looked toward the camp of the Devas, where the dead would never stand up and walk again. All the same, even the Asuras, who never died a final death, were eager to keep death at bay. Hence, and for just this once, they agreed to ally themselves with the Devas. Like their enemies, the Asuras were eager to conquer the *amṛta*.

But here came the crucial uncertainty: would immortality become substance? The Devas and Asuras knew that they were involved in the first *opus alchymicum*. But what if their material were to remain opaque? What if the ocean did not yield up the "sweet wave"? Haggard and exhausted, they raised their eyes to find a splash of opalescence spreading out between Mount Mandara and the ocean. Suspended in the glow, like idols without pedestals, like actors who come forward one after another to greet the public, like bright rings in a bracelet, like painted figures on the breeze, like amulets strung across the torso of the cosmos, appeared the *ratnas*, the "gems," sovereignty's procession. First came Sun, then Moon—and then you could see the shadow of Śiva's outstretched arm and hand encircling the white sickle like a slim girl and gathering it into his plaited hair, where it remains to this day, a shining clip. Next came the Apsaras, the waters, modeling the eddies in enchanting bodies dripping with shimmers of jewels. Both Devas and Asuras were equally avid for them, but they made no move: they knew that the Apsaras are living coinage, they pass through every hand. Not suitable as brides. Then came Uccaiḥśravas, the White Horse, swift as thought, who dazzled them with a toss of his mane. And there were more gems forming in the light. In white robes, fragrant and still, Śrī appeared majestic, then sank down on Viṣṇu's breast.

But still the *amṛta* hadn't appeared. The Devas and Asuras hung on, at the ready. "Perhaps," they thought, "the world isn't able, we aren't able to distill that supreme essence." Then a dark mass stood out against the glow, rolling like an ocean across the ocean. It was Kālakūṭa, the poison of the world. Viṣṇu spoke once more, his voice calm, and again his irony escaped those listening, as before when he had advised the Devas to join up with the Asuras, their all too kindred enemies. He said: "Śiva, supreme above all, yours is the beginning, yours the first fruit of everything. Only you can drink Kālakūṭa, the poison of the world, the first thing the world offers to us. Only he who can destroy the world can assimilate its poison. Only he who assimilates the poison of the world will have the strength of compassion." Śiva answered: "My wish is to please you."

Śiva bent down at the ocean shore, as the black mass began to lap around his feet. The Devas and Asuras watched, amazed, as though he were about to let himself be swallowed up by that unknown liquid. "This poison is born of the desire for immortality," said a voice among them. Then they fell silent. Śiva plunged his left hand into Kālakūṭa, then raised it to his mouth, his face set in the expression of someone expecting delectable refreshment. He drank, swallowed, took the poison into his body, let it seep down and course through him like a secret river. The Devas and Asuras watched him, ever more amazed. An efflorescence formed on Śiva's neck, like a tattoo, of a deep blue, whose brightness was reminiscent of a peacock feather or a sapphire. Śiva went on drinking, and the stain spread over his neck. Nor would it ever go away. They called him Nilakaṇṭha, the Blue-Necked One. One day a blushing Pārvatī would confess that the first time she saw him—when she was still a solemn child—and Śiva turned toward her, so that she saw his neck, all her desire had concentrated on the tip of her tongue, which longed to lick that blue stain, even if it meant splitting in two, as the snake's tongue did.

Like tarot figures upturned, the gems stood out against the column of light. The White Horse, the Precious Stone, the Nymph, the Elephant, the Physician, the Moon, the Cow of Desires. People still argue over how many there were and in what order they appeared. But one thing is certain: the *amṛta* could only appear within the procession of gems, within the sequence woven over the epiphanic veil. Nothing that appeared there was new or unheard of. Everything that emerged from the depths had emerged before. And yet everyone was amazed: because now existence was being formed, composed. With the churning of the ocean, the gems that have ever sparkled along the seams of existence were once again brought into being as second nature, elaborated, fixed, separate substance. The gods toiled like slaves in a smoke-filled workshop to have these emblems, seals of perennial existence, shine forth anew. "Elaborate the emblems and existence will follow," such was their motto, and so it was. Then they left men to their own devices in the tangle of the existent world.

Last among the *ratnas*, the "immortal" liquid finally appeared. Gathering it in a cup, the gods' Physician, Dhanvantari, offered it to the void. Among the Devas and Asuras, wonder soon gave way to apprehension, apprehension to avarice. Who was going to get it? Allies became enemies again. Petulant, childish voices were raised: "It's mine, it's mine . . ." Viṣṇu looked on, unsurprised. To head off another bloody battle between Devas and Asuras, perhaps even total reciprocal destruction—something that must not happen, since both the gods and their enemies are necessary to keep the world in equilibrium—Viṣṇu chose to resort to what had proved the most effective trick in his repertoire: turning himself into a woman. He became Mohinī: the Enchantress. Like a princess, like a courtesan, like a simple girl walking thoughtlessly by, Mohinī paraded before the Asuras, distracting them from whatever else was in their minds. Thus the Devas were able to grab the *amṛta* and take a quick drink before hurling themselves into the fray. Now they would slaughter each other as they always had. But soon they would be back in line again, invulnerable marionettes. The *amṛta* had made its entry on the world stage. The wiser of the Devas, however, felt it would be sensible if Viṣṇu took it under his care. Thus it disappeared once again, into the sky.

The stories of the *soma* tell of repeated conquest, repeated loss. Nothing is constant in its being but the *soma* itself. This applies to the gods too. Many have said that the gods are immortal and live in the sky. Not true. "Soma was in the sky and the gods here on earth." The gods didn't possess immortality. They thought of ways of getting it. They wanted to snatch the *soma* from the sky. Where was it hidden? In two golden cups, one upturned on the other, their sharp rims snapping shut at every blink of an eye. Flying across the skies came an eagle, Vāc, Word, sent by the gods. She tore the two cups apart with her beak, then sank her claws in the soft *soma*. But a Gandharva, Viśvāvasu, intercepted the eagle. Once again Soma eluded the gods. "We'll never have eternal life without Soma." "Soma was ours, all we have to do is buy it back," they said. Vāc spoke up: "The Gandharvas are crazy about women. Give me to them in exchange for the *soma*." The gods looked at her and said: "No, we could never live without you." "It cost us dearly to win you from the Asuras. How could we live if we lost you again?" Calmly, Vāc answered: "Afterward, you could always buy me back again." The gods fell silent. Then they nodded their agreement. Thus the gods assigned Vāc a second mission. She must seduce the Gandharvas, get them to forget the *soma*. But this time she wouldn't need to be an eagle. All she had to do was to put on some makeup and the prettiest clothes she had.

The gods took Vāc to the borders of Gandharva country, like a group of suitors dating a dancing girl. They were in a daze from her perfume. But they thought: "The Gandharvas will be in even more of a daze than we are." And others thought: "Perhaps it's the last time we'll ever see Vāc. We'll be reduced to the same wretched creatures we were before. Why live at all, without Vāc and without Soma?"

Days went by. Then a delegation of Gandharvas suddenly turned up to speak to the gods. Normally carefree, cheeky, happy creatures, they seemed awkward, tormented. Almost unrecognizable. They began to speak with a solemn, uncertain tone: "You know that Vāc is among us." Pause. "She has enchanted us all. With due respect we would like to ask if we might keep her." The gods pretended a half smile of incredulity. "And what would we get in exchange? What could equal the worth of the most beautiful and enchanted of women, she whose bed lies in the waters, who bends Rudra's bow, who pervades both earth and sky?" The Gandharvas lowered their eyes. Then one of them said softly: "Soma." Apparently unimpressed, the gods accepted. "With her as a great naked one they bought Soma the King," say the texts.

The Gandharvas were already walking away when one of the gods stopped them: "But what will you tell Vāc about this? You're not planning to force her against her will . . . Vac has to be courted. At least let it be hers to decide who she wants to be with. Let's invite her to a party . . ." The Gandharvas accepted. They thought they knew Vāc now. They prepared themselves with great determination, studying the Vedas. They would sing her the most sublime and difficult hymns in impeccable voices. And so they did, at the party. The splendidly handsome Gandharvas looked like austere brahmans. Their singing was pure and exact. Then it was the gods' turn. They had used their time to invent the lute. They danced, they played, they sang, with a lightness and impudence no one had ever seen in them before. When they had finished, Vāc turned to them and smiled. She went back to the gods. The texts say: "That is why even today women are nothing but frivolity."

Vāc: Voice, Word. Although eminent scholars hardly noticed her existence, Vāc was a power at the world's beginning. Her place is in the waters, which she herself fashioned. An elegant woman, decked in gold, celestial buffalo, queen of the thousand syllables, fatal bride, mother of emotions and perfumes. Of the men she singles out Vāc says: "He whom I love, whoever it may be, I give him strength, I make him a brahman, a *ṛṣi*, a wise man." There is no merit or virtue of any value in one whom Vāc has not singled out. He will forever be someone who looks without seeing. Since Vāc "knows all, but does not move all." Guardian of inequality, she descends from above and touches only her chosen ones. Her help brings salvation. It was she who suggested she be bartered as a prostitute so that the gods could get back the *soma.* Quick to take offense, every intonation vibrant, her anger, should someone neglect her or prefer another, is terrible. Then she leaves the gods' camp behind, but without going back to the Asuras. She wanders around the no-man's-land between the two armies. Life dries up, things lose their shine. The word becomes treacherous to touch, to articulate. No one wants to speak. There's a shadow in the undergrowth. No longer the painted woman with her gleaming jewels whom everyone desired, she approaches like a lean lioness, ready to tear her victims apart: that's Vāc, now.

On the seventh day of the moonlit fortnight of March they met together where the Sarasvatī silts up in desert sands. They were setting off to celebrate a rite that was also a journey from which one might not return—from which some did not want to return. They headed east, against the flow of the Sarasvatī, because "the sky is against the flow." And the place they hoped to reach was none other than the "bright world," the *svargaloka*, the sky that once the gods had conquered. The light of that world opened out in a place called Plakṣa Prāsravaṇa, where the Sarasvatī came down to earth after her celestial journey, spreading out in ponds and meanders. Before setting off, they consecrated themselves to Vāc, to the Word, because "Sarasvatī is the Word and the Word is the way of the gods." Traveling toward the source of the river, they would be traveling toward the source of the Word, whence it vibrates. "They go even to Plakṣa Prāsravaṇa; Plakṣa Prāsravaṇa is the furthest border of the Word; at the furthest border of the Word, there is the bright world." They said to themselves: "The Word, Vāc, is the only way to reach the bright world. Vāc is Sarasvatī, this running river that silts up here, in our world, and loses itself. Setting out from this point, from the sands of our world, we must follow the river upstream. It is a long, hard undertaking, that goes against the way of things, which know only how to go down. The Word, and these waters, are the one help we have. We shall follow the Word, so as to be able to leave it behind. A mere span to the north of Plakṣa Prāsravaṇa, the Word is no more. Only something that shines. The center of the world."

The *gṛhapati*, first among the celebrants and leader of the expedition, took a cart chock and hurled it as far away as he could. As he hurled it, he yelled, and the others yelled with him. They yelled and beat the ground, because "yell and blow are shows of strength"—and strength was something they needed. A herd of cows came after them, patient and silent. There might be ten, there might be a hundred. Where the chock fell they kindled the fire called *gārhapatya*. Then thirty-six paces to the east they prepared the fire *āhavanīya*. Thus for forty-eight days they walked along the banks of the Sarasvatī, sacrificing according to the phases of the moon, tossing the chock toward the east and stopping where it fell, yelling. That was their life: walking, yelling, "*tribu prophétique aux prunelles ardentes.*" Each time they stopped to sacrifice, they would take some of the sand left on the altar and carry it to the next place. A traveler who came across them without knowing anything of their ways would have thought them mad.

Walking upstream along the Sarasvatī was not without its dangers. Once, the daunting huntresses of the Śālvas attacked a group of celebrants and killed their *gṛhapati*, whose name was Sthūra. The others mourned him. But one of the celebrants saw their dead friend ascending to the sky along the line of their sacrificial fires. Another said: "Don't weep for Sthūra. Whoever dies along this path ascends directly to the heavens. Don't mourn these deaths. Once we were wretched, now the heavens await us."

If they got as far as Plakṣa Prāsravaṇa, they would find a tree. At its feet rose the water that descends from the Milky Way, that is the Milky Way. The nearer one gets to that place, the more one feels the Word wear thin. "The breeze passes through the fabric," thought the celebrants. The Word stretched thinner and thinner, to the limit. The more they sensed it, the closer they knew they were to the "bright world." And, immediately beyond the point where the Word ended, they had reached their goal. But there were other ways the rite might be accomplished. One day they realized they had lost all they had. They woke—and the cows were gone. Stolen? Run off? Or the *gṛhapati* might die along the way. Perhaps he was killed in an enemy ambush. Or perhaps he just died on his feet. Even in these cases the rite had been accomplished. Or they might discover, one day, that the ten cows they had set out with were now a hundred. And again this might mean that the rite was accomplished. But whatever happened, when it was over, before returning to their lives so as not to go mad—"If he did not descend again to this world, he would either depart to a region which lies beyond all human beings, or he would go mad," warned the *Pāncavimśa Brāhmana*—they bathed in a delightful bend of the Sarasvatī, in Kārapacava, just as Cyavana had immersed himself with the Aśvins in another meander of the Sarasvatī, rediscovering his youth.

. . .

Whether directly or indirectly, Indra's adventures always had to do with the *soma.* God of entrenchment, of all that exists because made, mind muddied from his effort to fix the flux, Indra reigns, yes, but in the perennial fear that some force beyond might unsettle him, might take the cosmos back to the blessed and terrifying oscillation to which he put an end when he clipped the mountains' wings.

It is thanks to Indra that the waters subsided, that the world doesn't quake, isn't forever swinging from side to side but supported by a prop that allows things to be distinct and have identity. He was the crudest and most ignorant of the gods, the only one who constructed himself, using the *sva-*, the prefix that signifies whatever is self-made. Indra had no science, no splendor. Only thrust, energy. He was often afraid when confronted by powers older than his own; he found them elusive. In his duel with Vṛtra, which was the ultimate purpose of his life, as well as the undertaking that would one day make it possible for all of us to live, he only won because when Vṛtra's father, Tvaṣṭṛ, the Craftsman, had created that footless creature who slithered along stuffed with the *soma* he was born from, he, Tvaṣṭṛ, made a mistake pronouncing a word, got the stress wrong. Otherwise Indra would have been swallowed up. And the world would never have drawn breath. Who would have noticed? No one. Only when heady with *soma* did Indra display some virtue—or at least strength. But in the beginning it was Indra himself who had been denied the *soma.* He gazed with hatred at the three heads of Viśvarūpa, the Omniform One, son of the Craftsman, pampered firstborn of the cosmos, who drank the *soma* with one of his small heads while reading the Veda with another. Indra wasn't particularly worried about not knowing the Vedas. But why did he have to be denied a liquid that might be exquisite? For a long time he studied the priestly hauteur of the Omniform One. Then he suddenly sliced off his heads.

No sooner was the ill deed done than Indra felt the urge to go further. For the first time he crossed the threshold of Tvaṣṭṛ's palace. Empty rooms, fine-wrought. Indra had never seen what form can become when imposed by a knowing hand. He was intimidated, overwhelmed. But this wasn't what he was looking for. In the half dark of a room sliced across by blades of light gleaming from tall windows, he found a golden basin brimful of some whitish liquid. At last, the *soma.* Like a weary soldier at the end of a long march, Indra drank it greedily, making no concessions to ceremony. He drank and crashed to the ground. The high ceilings, all fine stone tracery, began to expand. Indra crept into the vegetable pleats of the stone, like an insect. He rocked from side to side, no longer able to distinguish between what he was thinking and what he was seeing. He wasn't afraid of being caught now. Murderer and thief: how pointless! The porosity of the stone called to him in a way that was far more urgent. Slowly Indra discovered that many worlds were folded away in that empty room, worlds of which he knew nothing. His huge body lay abandoned on the floor, arms and legs outspread. From ears, nose, sphincter, and phallus a liquid dribbled down. It formed a puddle all around him. Only the mouth stayed tight shut and dry. Indra passed out. He lay motionless for hours, moonlight shining down on his powerful, defenseless body.

It would be misleading to think of the slaying of Vṛtra as of a duel between a big, clumsy dragon on the one hand and a blond hero, Indra, on the other, bursting with courage as he sought out a weak point where he might bury his sword. It was all much more complicated. To start with, Vṛtra was a brahman. True, he slithered across the ground like a shapeless lump, yet his voice rang clear and sharp, the voice of a priest, of one who knows. This was hardly surprising: Vṛtra kept the Vedas hidden in his belly, handing them over to Indra only shortly before being slain by him.

But the most delicate question was something else altogether: from time to time, from Vṛtra's mouth, one could hear the whispering of Agni and Soma, for they too were hidden in his belly. It was with them that Indra would be obliged to negotiate long and hard. "What are you doing inside that brute?" he said to them one day. "You belong to another world, to my world, why are you being so stubborn?" "This brute was born from us, when Tvaṣṭṛ threw me in the fire, or at least what you left of me when you drank me up, greedy and impetuous as ever," said Soma. "This brute is our child, even if he did devour us afterward. What will you give us if we come over to your side?" added Agni. "You're used to betraying and running away," said Indra, who had recognized Agni's voice. "And you are travelers. My part is the part of sacrifice. The sacrifice is a journey. It's true that if you stay in Vṛtra's belly, you will be able to recite the Vedas, but you will feel oppressed, glutted with monotony. Whereas with me there will always be something that gets poured away, from sky to earth. Something that flows, that travels, that appears and disappears. Think about it." That night, as Vṛtra slept openmouthed, Agni and Soma slithered out on his saliva, stealthy and swift, and went over to the side of the gods.

In the beginning all the gods were shut away in a transparent membrane. They peered through at an outside as yet undistinguishable, an outside which, to be exact, didn't exist. They were brimming with power, but obliged to hold back. In the darkness they knocked against each other. Father Asura, who had stuffed them all in the cavity in his body, in the warmth of that which prefers not to exist, felt that this was the only appropriate way of doing things. Or rather, he didn't know what doubt was. He thought of existence as something eccentric and deceitful. In any event, reprehensible.

From that indistinctness beyond the membrane they heard Indra's whisper, calling to them. Unlike the others, Indra had refused to be born from the vagina. It was "an ugly passage," he said. He managed to get himself born sideways, from his mother's flank. And he murmured that one day he would do something that no one else had done. But who was Indra? A solitary calf. The gods followed him silently with their eyes as he wandered around the fullness. But would they be able to maintain that powerful inertia forever? The first one Indra called to was Agni. "Come here, guest," he said. "Leave your dark house and strangers will welcome you." Agni was the first to emerge. Then Varuṇa slithered out. Last of all came Soma. What was it that drew them? It was this changing of tribe, cautiously, while yet remaining tied to each other, like a band of renegades. It was this passing on to another life, while still having someone with whom to remember the previous life. Then there was the mystery of that new word—*yajña*, "sacrifice"—which Indra was constantly flaunting and whose meaning they hadn't really understood as yet (why, for example, must it have five ways, three layers, and seven threads?), but which seemed set to alter every equilibrium. Then Indra had hinted that it was connected with immortality. Better to achieve immortality than already to have it, they thought with divine logic. Shut up in their father Asura, they were immortal, of course, but deep down they were afraid of suffocating in that fullness. Like thieves in the night, they slipped out of the membrane. Silence and desolation lay all around. Yet that was the moment when the balance swung and a new regime was established. They still hadn't grown used to an ever more diffuse and penetrating brightness, when they saw the waters burst in—the waters, the cows, the syllables, the chants, like the chatter of a gaggle of girls—and in the midst of the waves' billow they saw a white patch, a swan, that would suddenly beat its wings and thrust its beak into the water in answer to the voices all around. They exchanged glances, then Agni said: "That must be Indra."

Soon after the flight of Agni and Soma, Indra struck. Crushed and creased up in his agony like an empty wineskin, Vṛtra looked at his killer and whispered: "Now you are what I was." The *translatio imperii* was complete, and the shapeless, shoulderless creature chose to seal it with his own words. But what was to become of that gasping carcass that had until so recently contained the supreme powers? "Nothing is dissolved, everything passes on," thought Indra. "Split me in two," groaned Vṛtra. So Indra split him into two parts, which went on swelling and contracting, the way a lizard's severed tail will go on flicking from side to side. Still dripping with *soma,* one part moved toward the sky: that was the moon. The other became the bellies of men. They have never ceased to expand and contract since.

Agni was the last of four brothers. Three died before him, were lost. They all suffered the anguish of being "yoked." Fire is ever in mourning for those brothers.

In the beginning, Agni was more like a spy than anything else. Hidden away, he watched the *ṛṣis'* brides about their baths: they shone like altars of gold, like white slivers of moon, like crests of flame. Agni thought: "I shouldn't get excited and desire them. When I am in the hearth at home, I can gaze at them for as long as I want and lick their feet too." In the evening, the women stretched out by the smoldering logs and bared their feet. Agni loitered with them alone, studied them, desired them. He knew the soles of their feet, the folds of their robes. He slowed his flame down to be able to watch them as long as possible. His desire intensified.

The gods had gathered around Agni. They seemed friendly enough, but they were surrounding him. "We'd like you to be our *hotṛ,*" one began. "I don't feel I'm a priest, I'm not up to it. Three of my brothers have already died that way. I don't want to be useful to anyone. I just want to burn. They ran like madmen between earth and sky. Then one by one, they disappeared. I am no better or worse than they. So why try again? I cannot bear to have a yoke around my neck. Even if it is studded with emeralds. I don't want to be obliged to follow just one path," said Agni—and he fled. He wanted to hide, but where? Varuṇa is present, even when two strangers are plotting together. There's nowhere safe to hide in this world. So Agni decided to hide himself in himself. For fire, hiding in oneself means in the waters. That was where he had once appeared from. Agni looked for a pond, for rushes rustling in the wind. He slipped into a bamboo cane. Finally he sensed that there was nothing above him. All was silent, no sound of messengers. In the pond a sleepy frog felt the water burn his soft, white belly. He looked around, nervously. Who could be disturbing this stillness? Was Agni back? Hopping slowly along, the frog went to find the gods. "Looking for Agni, by any chance? Check the canes in my pond," he said. Once again Agni was surrounded. But this time they grabbed him like a wretched runaway. Yet still the gods spoke sweetly to him, reassuring him: "We won't do you any harm, we won't hurt you." Agni bowed his head: "I accept, but don't forget my brothers, let a part of the offering go to them." "Don't torment yourself, Agni," said the gods. "Your brothers will always be near you. They will be the three sticks that mark out the fireplace. Something will fall on them too . . ." "If that's how things stand . . . ," said Agni, sadly.

The mind was confined in a compound, like the Cows, like the Dawns. Whatever happened, happened inside a fence, inside the walls of a palace, inside a cave sealed by a great stone. Outside foamed the immense ocean of the world, barely audible beyond a thick wall of rock. Inside, in the compound, was another liquid, a "pond," which, however small, was nevertheless equivalent to the ocean without. The ocean was outside the mountain but inside the mountain too. By splitting the rock, Indra allowed the inside ocean, "the ocean of the heart," *hṛdyá samudrá*, to communicate with the outside ocean, the palpable ocean of the world. It was a moment that opened up a new way of knowing. For the *ṛṣis* it was knowledge itself, the only knowledge they wished to cultivate. Not the mind shut away in its airy cage reconstructing a conventional image that corresponded point by point to the vast cage of the cosmos. But, quite the contrary: the waters of the mind flowing into those of the world and the waters of the world flowing into those of the mind to the point where they become indistinguishable one from the other. The ultimate difference between the knowledge passed on by the *ṛṣis* and every other knowledge consists in this: for the *ṛṣis* and all their descendants, knowledge begins when the Cows flee from the compound, when the Dawns awake, when the Waters flow through the cleft in the rock, when the doors of the mind are thrown open and it becomes impossible to say which waters are flowing in and which flowing out, what is substance and what is the substance of the mind. And everybody else? They live in ignorance of the compound, the rock, the Cows, the Dawns, the Waters. It's hardly surprising if misunderstandings abound.

How often Indra was greeted as he who had opened the rock of Vala, who had freed the Cows, who had let the Dawns loose in the sky. But Indra knew it wasn't true. And he knew that others knew too: the watchful eyes of Bṛhaspati and the Aṅgiras were ever on him. He couldn't pretend with them. For it had been Indra, the hero, who had fallen into line behind them, the priests—and not vice versa. It was from them that he learned to transform his harmless babble into a whisper that worked, that changed things.

So Indra preferred to tell the story of how he had slain Vṛtra. Here too he had been helped—and helped a great deal. But the story could be presented as a duel between two champions. And when handed down by word of mouth, that was all that would be left: a monster and a hero, a handsome hero with a blond beard that dripped with *soma.* Yet nobody ever took Indra completely seriously. Alone, downcast, gazing at the stagnant water of a pond, he would say to himself: "You can make the whole world—and still it's not enough. They'll always look down on you with their arrogant, unblinking eyes." They, the brahmans.

Indra wasn't an intellectual god—and the *ṛṣis* often treated him with disdain for his hotheaded adulteries, his tawdry adventures. But at bottom Indra existed to accomplish a single deed: the splitting of the cosmic mountain. Without that enterprise there would have been no knowledge. Especially not the knowledge the *ṛṣis* cultivated. All this we owe to that vigorous, impure god on whose body the *ṛṣis* mockingly tattooed scores upon scores of vulvas. It wouldn't be right to say that Indra gave an order to nature and made it possible for the world to exist. There was already an order—even with that mountain looming between earth and sky and keeping its treasures prisoner. What was missing was the flow within the order. That was what Indra made possible.

Indra is needed because without him there are things that can't be done. But then he is left to one side, a cumbersome relic. A Western cousin of his, Apollo, loosed his arrow at Python, coiled up like Vṛtra on the mountain at Delphi. Indra too could claim to have slain the monster. But when Apollo had conquered Delphi, he made it the place of possession, which is composed of divination and syllogism. Indra wasn't in a position to aim so high. With *ṛta* in the sense of "order," he still had much to do, when he settled the world down, clipped the wings of horse and mountain, or scooped out the beds of the celestial rivers. In his role as cosmic engineer he was respected and even loved. But what did he know of *ṛta* in the sense of "truth"? In only one of the seventy-seven times it speaks of him does the Ṛg Veda grant Indra the epithet *ṛtā́van,* "endowed with truth." The realm of the true word, the realm to which nature answers, was closed to Indra. Others had claimed it before him, severe and secretive figures who shunned him as a parvenu. Hounded by guilt and derision, ultimately ousted by a child god, Skanda, after having so often been mocked himself for being new and self-made, Indra ended up wandering around like a melancholy king beset by ungrateful subjects who look the other way when he passes by.

. . .

For a long time they walked through the shadows, following the tracks of the she-dog Saramā. Leading the way, face ever set in the same expression, Bṛhaspati cleared their path. Then came the Aṅgiras, all moving with the same rhythm, like a single person. Indra, with heavier step, brought up the rear. Having reached the horizon, they pressed on without a moment's hesitation. They trod the back of the sky. Thus for days they marched while beneath them the deserts stretched out like vast carpets and the forests shrank to dark stains. From time to time they would be caught by gusts of opalescent stardust. Beneath them, far away, the earth. Above, close by, the stars, like ships in the night. They looked neither behind nor below. Without turning, Bṛhaspati raised his hand. Indra looked up and saw an immense wall of smooth gray rock. "Why does it seem so earthly? We've left the earth behind," thought Indra. Above them the rock seemed to stretch away forever. It had the nobility, the coldness, of something that does not wish to exist. It ignored them, as it had always ignored everything. "Here it is," said Bṛhaspati. They stared in silence. A long time passed before the Aṅgiras began their murmuring. In the indistinct stream of sound, occasional syllables flared and faded. Bṛhaspati was rapt in thought. Then he joined in with his sharp, almost shrill voice. Indra was the most uncertain, then followed the others' example, with clear tones. They fell silent again. There was a distant shuffling. "They're in their stall," said Bṛhaspati. "The secret names of the Cows number one and twenty. We must find them all," he added. There was a faint light and an immense solitude. For a long time they stood motionless. Perhaps for years. There were no witnesses, unless hidden behind the glow of the Bear. All of a sudden, a few sharp, silvery syllables sheared off from the dull, monotone murmur. Chained together they pealed out. They became meters, recognizable as contours. They stood out in the air. From behind the rock a distant lowing answered, and swelled. From the darkness, the Cows. Slowly, like a fabric torn away thread by thread, a cleft began to open up in the rock. They gazed long on that thin line, etched in the grayness by some invisible hand. Ceaselessly they uttered the syllables. They composed names. A stream of light and dust, a clatter of hooves, a dazzling herd. The Cows emerged from the cave of Vala. The light was made of waters, which filled the sky. On the crest of the waves came the Dawns. Like songsters on a merry-go-round, clutching papier-mâché carriages, they rode the foaming billows, pink breasts leaning into an empty sky. Behind them, like a sovereign and a shepherd with his crook, who comes after his flock, appeared the Sun. Saramā barked. No one paid her any attention. Bṛhaspati, the Aṅgiras, and Indra looked on with glazed and happy eyes.

XI

King Soma—they called him. He was a king and a substance. Of whatever deeds he did, little has come down to us. But he was the object of others' deeds. Abducted, ambushed, retaken, sold. Then pressed, filtered, slain. These are the things one hears tell of Soma. Rather than a king, Soma is what makes someone king. He is sovereignty itself. He is what all who ever wished to be king have sought. He is a brightness buried in the waters. He is guarded by a Nymph-Snake. Then there was a Nymph and a Snake. Or just a Snake, or just a Nymph. No one who aspires to sovereignty can achieve his goal except by means of the Snake and the Nymph. The Nymph can bite into that substance, chew it, and then with a kiss slip it into the mouth of whichever hero, god, or man turns up.

Soma was brought to earth in the beak of an eagle. Then, they said, "The thinkers have found the form that gives joy, when the eagle brings the juice from afar." Later, in the words of the hymns, he ascended from earth to sky on the "vessels of truth." Like Agni an indefatigable messenger, he would sometimes sit awhile on the back of the sky and watch the two tribes he was constantly traveling between: the gods in their celestial palaces, the men on the earth. He yearned for horses, flocks, men, waters. Above all, waters. And the Ten Sisters. He knew it was dangerous to let them, the fingers, touch him. But it was immensely pleasurable too. So Soma sat motionless, head veiled, between the ten shrewd and silent girls who brushed him throughout the sacrifice. So much for what took place on earth. In the sky, on the other hand, beyond the rocky vault, he would find the Seven Sisters who glide among the fringed branches of the Milky Way. More slender fingers thrust deep in the shadows. Islands, ponds, river meanders, a delta arching over everything. "How many games with numbers . . . ," he once thought, smiling to himself. But he wasn't confused. Those seven rivers that divided up the sky were mothers, sisters, lovers, subjects. He entered them like sun in water.

The *soma* was placed on two wooden boards carefully lined up over two holes dug out in the ground to amplify the sound. An ox skin was stretched over the boards. Five stones were placed on the skin in the shape of a quincunx. The stone in the middle was the biggest.

Soma arrived like a lover ten girls were waiting for: the fingers, the Ten Sisters. They would caress him, handle him, squeeze, kill—but only and always indirectly, through the stones. Because those ten girls were in league with the five stones. The lovers' tryst was an ambush. Soma, King Soma, would arrive wrapped in a cloth, his robe. They would undo the knot, the turban, revealing a bundle of stalks. Then a celebrant would pick up the cloth and wrap it around the head of the *grāvastut*, "praiser of the stones." The cloth would fall on his eyes, so that he couldn't see. He would be a blind singer. The *grāvastut* would speak with his face turned to the stones and the *soma*, would celebrate them while the liturgical motions were performed, while the stones murmured their part, rubbing against each other, crushing the *soma*, but he wouldn't actually witness the murderous deed acted out before him, until the inebriating white sap hidden in the *soma* stalks began to flow.

What the Devas and the Asuras called *amṛta* (and they claimed to be its children too) men called *soma*, perhaps out of discretion, not wanting to insist too much on that nondeath that the *soma* did win for them, but never sufficiently, so that it was always having to be won all over again. Without the *soma,* nothing in the world could shine, nothing shone in the mind, nothing emanated sense. Around that substance—as likewise around the memory of it, indeed mostly around the memory of it—were composed gestures, deeds, hymns, adventures. Looking around themselves at everything in existence, men saw it was all made up of variations of just two elements: fire and this clear liquid. Agni and Soma, the Devourer and the Devoured. "Everything down here without exception is devouring or devoured." Likewise themselves, moment after moment after moment, devoured, devouring.

As the *ṛṣis* saw it, creation, the tangible state of the world, was a secondary phenomenon, recent and modern. The first thing to understand was what made perception of creation possible. They saw a flux, the waters. In the waters an eye surfaced: the *soma.* This was what they meant when they sang, "The rivers that do not deceive, that have made the eye great." *Soma* is, "among the gods, he who is awake." By this we know him: that he is a god who is also an edible substance, and hence the most material; that he is perfect wakefulness, and hence the most immaterial, the nearest to the elusive flow of consciousness.

The firmament is a tent that shelters the world. We see the inside of that tent. But what would we see if we were stretched out on the other side? We would be on the back of the world, which Agni treads when he carries messages to the gods. Filled with a surge of dazzling light, we would see the *rocaná,* the "space of light" that has no end. A pole props up the tent of the sky and what opens out beyond the firmament. A pole, a trunk, a mountain. What is so amazing is not so much the existence that lies below the tent—the matter, the world—nor what is outside the tent—a mass of light—but how there can be a passage from one to the other: how it happens that shabby and perishable substances are ever being renewed by something that one can only suppose is inexhaustible and that settles on things below like a translucent film. This was what the *ṛṣis* wanted to concentrate on, this was the prime object of their thought. Creation, nothingness, freedom, on the other hand, these were preposterous questions doomed to remain forever deferred, unresolvable.

To approach the *soma* is to approach exchange. First and foremost Soma is something that passes, that flows, from one place to another, one hand to another. From the Asuras, the mountain, the sky: to the Devas, the plain, the earth. Or, again, in the opposite direction. There is always something violent involved in its passage, which comes as a result of war, or theft, or sale. The Asuras lie heaped in blood. An arrow plucks a feather from Garuḍa as he flies off with the *soma* in his beak. No sooner has he made his sale than the *soma* merchant is beaten up. Why? What did he do wrong? It is as if the *soma*, the substance that is the essence of all substance, that fills mind and veins, that is the ultimate guardian of the world's existence, could only be obtained thanks to some crime, some act of violence: an excess of giving or taking, a theft, an act of prostitution, as when Vāc offered her body as a trade-off with the Gandharvas. Substitution, which is the wound of exchange, chose to assert itself in the most secret place of substance, there where matter becomes consciousness. If it were not so, everything would remain static, there would be no stories, the world would not even try, albeit in vain, to recompose itself—and perhaps the *soma* would not allow us to reach the absent, the sovereign, the dazzling flow, that lies on the other side of the world's back: *rocaná*, the "space of light."

Soma isn't just taste, sense, lymph—all that causes life to live and makes it understandable. Soma is something that circulates. And since the world is a single being, but broken up into myriads of bodies and entities, insofar as Soma circulates, it is something that must be exchanged. The moment when something is exchanged—and hence goes out of itself, crosses a border—is the critical moment, the moment that forces us to recognize that the world is not a continuum. Substitution, sale, theft, prostitution: at such moments a brief convulsion occurs, soon to be effaced. But such moments remind us that every being is suspended in the void. Crossing that void provokes violence. A head rolls, a merchant is clubbed, a queen gives her body to a dead horse, tightens her thighs around his legs. This too must take place if the *madhuvidyā*, the "doctrine of the honey," is to trickle down.

Exchange is based on the circulation between the body and the world outside. We are alive only insofar as one element—oxygen—is continually entering and leaving our bodies. Only because we take and give with every passing moment. The only area where the Devas showed that they enjoyed a supremacy over the Asuras, a supremacy that wasn't just a question of brute force, was this: the Asuras sacrificed inside their mouths, while the Devas realized that they would have to sacrifice outside. "The Asuras, in their arrogance, thinking, 'Why sacrifice to anyone else?' sacrificed in their mouths . . . But the Devas went on making offerings one to another." The existence of an outside, the recognition of the presence of something without, was all that would distinguish, forever, the Devas from the Asuras.

For an instant, and it was the moment when the merchant sold his stalks, substance and substitution converged to the point of coinciding in the *soma*. Substance (source of every quality, and hence of every likeness and analogy) is that which exists unto itself, needing no other. It is the primordial autism. Substitution is something that exists only insofar as it takes the place of something else. Garuḍa stole

Soma from the sky to ransom his mother, Vinatā. It was the first ransom. And the first exchange was payment of a ransom. It was as if exchange could only be conceived insofar as it freed from servitude or guilt. But the liberation involved another crime, another guilt: the theft, then the killing of the *soma,* prelude to its consumption. With the *soma* the object of desire appears on the scene for the first time. And since any desire is immediately shared by someone else, or imitated by someone else (and shared because imitated), its object can be exchanged. Or rather: it is that which gives rise to exchange. "Since the king [Soma] has been sold, everything down here is for sale."

The surface of the wakeful mind trembles without cease, like the surface of the waters. And like the waters, it assumes the shapes of those forces that press upon it. The creatures closest in both nature and name to the "waters," *āpaḥ,* were the Apsaras, Nymphs, seductive creatures, sometimes benevolent, always capricious. They could lead you to madness. They came out of the waves like "the first seed of mind": desire. And this, like everything else, was eager to open out into its own plural. Were the Apsaras so called because they "flowed," *sara,* in the "waters," *āpaḥ,* or because they were "without shame," *a-psaras?* Philologists still dispute the question, solemnly. The Apsaras see them at it—and laugh.

The first pact between mind and matter was sealed upon the waters. Even the gods of Olympus were terrified of breaking an oath made on the waters of the Styx. There is a perennial bond between the waters and the truth. But why should what is fluid, elusive, and mutable coincide with the unshakable precision of the word that enounces things as they are? This is the mystery, the ultimate obscurity of Varuṇa, and it is what makes him more remote than any other god. Between the word and the waters another element slips in, an element in which water and word flow together and mingle: consciousness, the raw sensation of whoever is awake and knows himself alive. This sensation is more amazing than any marvel the eye will ever see. In this regard the *ṛṣis* were not so far away from Wittgenstein: *that* the world exists is far more amazing than any *how* the world exists.

The water flows and reflects. On the one side: time. On the other: the image, the simulacrum, the mental phantom. These opposing *liṅgas*, "tokens" of conscious life, are already announced in the waters. And only in the waters. If time is sovereign, and almost the model of every sovereignty, the waters of consciousness are the first subjects capable of recognizing the fact. Even that plural—the way right from the very beginning one never speaks of the water but of the "waters," a multiplicity of feminine creatures—is a token of consciousness: its ceaseless branching out, sprouting new leaves. Drifting around the celestial waters, wandering aimless among his lovers, Soma was the "only seer" amid the waves: the eye that watches the multiple expanse of the wakefulness in which it is immersed.

The "waters" to which the Vedic texts endlessly refer resemble nothing more closely than the *jeunes filles* of Proust's *Recherche*. Did Andrée exist in herself, did Albertine? a suddenly dazed Marcel asks himself in the *Prisonnière*. Likewise the waters. It's not for nothing that from their first appearance the *jeunes filles* are confused against the backdrop of the sea, in an air heavy with the salty, blue spray of the front at Balbec. Then, with imperious self-assurance, Marcel decides that they "embodied the frenzy of pleasure." And from that moment on, their existence becomes the vertigo of a ceaseless mutability, punctuated by names, scarves, dresses, episodes, golden drops ever different from each other yet no more individual than a succession of lights sparkling on waves. Like a lover, like a *ṛṣi*, Marcel watches Albertine as she sleeps. In her mute abandon to merest breathing, he sees her as a plant, a stalk. The natural realms mingle together, finding themselves in the same element. They flood silently through the watchful mind, and through prose. The obsessive detail is a bud in the pond. The waters are plurality itself, fringes swinging back and forth, the slight trembling of wakefulness that precedes the word. Immersing itself in them, the mind follows the royal way toward revelation of itself to itself, in its shifting lunar essence. But this is not their ultimate mystery, which only emerges when they appear as messengers in an outside scenario, in the blind structure of matter, eyes closed like Albertine's, emissaries of a self-sufficient and remote existence, which one can pierce but never grasp.

It happened to many gods, to Mitra, Varuṇa, Brahmā (frequently!), to Viṣṇu and Agni: they would be celebrating a rite, concentrating on what they were doing, on observing the prescribed ritual, when suddenly a female creature—an Apsaras, a goddess, a woman—would enter their field of vision. They would desire her. The fact that she appeared at that particular moment, during the ceremony, surrounded only by sacred objects, would make her all the more irresistible. She was other, the invincible other, the substance forever expelled by the autism of ritual, but who now came back there, triumphant and uplifting. And at the same time: since the rite centered on the *soma*, this substance they were ever and tirelessly filtering, crushing, pressing, and since that substance then filtered into their minds, or rather filtered their minds, when they drank it, transforming the mind into a luminous cloud, it would now seem that that cloud had flowed outside them again to appear dressed in a white robe, splitting itself in two, to beguile them, and imposing itself with the certainty of an equation: it is the *soma* it is the mind it is that female creature.

First among the Apsaras, Urvaśī appeared with her swanlike elegance in the place of sacrifice. There was a jug there that was used for keeping the "overnight" waters, *vasatīvarī*. Mitra and Varuṇa just managed to grab it in time to shoot their sperm into it. From that jug, that sperm, two of the greatest *ṛṣis* were born: Vasiṣṭha and Agastya. Then Mitra and Varuṇa pulled themselves together with a shiver and raised their eyes. They saw Urvaśī looking at them, watchful, proud, motionless in her long, white robe. They thought they caught a hint of a smile lifting a corner of her mouth. As if she knew everything they knew and something more too. Then they glared at her with resentful eyes and said: "A curse upon you . . . You shall go down to the earth, doomed to satisfy the pleasure of the descendants of Manu."

So it was that Urvaśī would one day discover what it means to fall in love with a man. He was a prince, of course, indeed the first among princes, and a seer. His name was Purūravas—and Urvaśī claimed to hear in that name his "roaring" (*ruvan*) progress through the clouds. She found him far more attractive, dark, and unpredictable than the gods. And she wasn't averse to upsetting the Gandharvas, who had been her companions in love until now but who had one shortcoming: they were all too similar to one another—and to her. Whereas a man, the earth: that was adventure, that—she suspected—would mean suffering too, given that Mitra and Varuṇa had seemed so pleased with themselves when they threw her down into these forests.

When Urvaśī's passion settled on Purūravas, the Apsaras thought: "What shall I do? Must I show myself to him? So that my beauty overwhelms and terrifies him? So that what always happens between men and women may happen immediately? No, there is something better than that . . . I want this state to last for a long time, as long as possible, this swooning feeling I get when I'm looking at him . . ." So Urvaśī decided to transform herself into Purūravas's charioteer. He was young and very handsome, but Purūravas hardly seemed to notice. He spoke to him as one speaks to an animal about the house—and Urvaśī bubbled with pleasure. They got smothered in dust together, racing across desert lands, as far as the horizon. Sometimes they had to get down from the chariot, ford marshes, force their way along impassable valleys, reconnoitering. Then Purūravas would take the lead and Urvaśī would follow him, gazing happily at his back, his neck. The longer Purūravas said nothing, the greater the pleasure Urvaśī felt. She didn't want Purūravas to think of her as the only person around to talk to, but as something more. She wanted to blend in with his shadow, to become the crumpled cloth of his robe.

They rode through the bush. The charioteer up front, firm hand on the reins. Looking down, Purūravas saw a split in the side, a hole getting bigger. He could see the earth through it, racing away. The chariot was about to break up. Brusquely, Purūravas shouted an order and jumped down to the ground. He looked at the chariot, frowning, while the charioteer tried hard not to show emotion. The chariot seemed to be intact. There was no sign of anything coming apart anywhere. Purūravas climbed up again. The hole reappeared, like a vortex set to swallow him up. Again Purūravas got down from the chariot. Again the chariot seemed to be intact. Purūravas thought he must be going mad. "Charioteer, can you see anything?" he asked tensely. "I can see you, my lord," said the charioteer. Purūravas looked down again, gloomily. "You're not mad, it's me making that hole appear," said a female voice. He looked up. It was the charioteer, except that now she was the most beautiful woman he had ever seen. She filled the air, and already Purūravas felt he was immersed in her. He realized he would have to start negotiating at once. "Who are you?" he asked. "I am Urvaśī, an Apsaras. I have been following you around for a year, out of love. Take me with you." "It's difficult to deal with a divine being," said Purūravas. "What do you require?" "A hundred ceremonies of homage. And a hundred jugs of cream a day." "All right," said Purūravas. "There's something else: I must never see you naked," said Urvaśī. "The other things you ask are easy," said Purūravas. "But how can we manage this?" "You must always have a cloth wrapped around your loins." "So be it," said Purūravas. Urvaśī had also specified: "You can penetrate me three times a day with your rod, you can have me even when I don't want you." (Whence the dispute between Vedic scholars, accustomed to arguing over every syllable: most of them understood Urvaśī as meaning "you cannot possess me when I don't want you," but Hoffmann, in his study on the injunctive tense, came to the conclusion that she had meant the opposite: "you can possess me even when I don't want you"; relationships between men and women have been marooned in this ambiguity ever since.) So long as Purūravas always kept that white cloth around his loins. Soon they thought no more about it. They were rarely apart. And then they were sleeping, but even in their sleep their minds continued to mingle. The only impression they had of what was happening outside them was of a succession of blades of light, pointing in different directions. All Urvaśī knew was that when she thought of Purūravas the same words would always come into her head: "Sovereign of my body."

Urvaśī and Purūravas's room was always in shadow. But with two bright patches that sometimes melted together: two white lambs, tied to the sides of the bed. "They are my children," Urvaśī had said. Purūravas had asked nothing more. They treated them with love, and fed them, but never let them loose. The bed, the lambs, Urvaśī's and Purūravas's bodies made a single pearly mass.

They slept. The lambs had curled up by the bed. There was a tearing sound, a feeble bleating. Then another tear, another feeble bleat. The lambs had gone. Without them the room seemed no more than a dreary shelter. Urvaśī sat upright, cold and angry, careless of her marvelously slanting breasts. "They're taking away my loved ones . . . And there's no man here to defend me." Purūravas was deep in a sleep that was carrying him far, far away. Urvaśī's voice came like a needle in his heart. With a shudder he leapt from the bed. He would rush off anywhere in his rage. There was a dazzling flash. For one long moment Purūravas's body stood out in sharp silhouette against the air, completely naked. Thinking back on that moment—and he was to think back on it his whole life—Purūravas always experienced the same strange sensation: while he was suspended in the air, his entire body tense as an athlete's, he was also fighting an elusive woman, very like Urvaśī, but hateful and mocking, who was grabbing his thighs and pulling off the white cloth he was never without. In that dazzling light, Purūravas felt someone, some creature he didn't know, touching him, handling him, humiliating him. Then all was suddenly dark again. Purūravas rushed out. He came back with the lambs. "I've got them," he said. But Urvaśī was gone.

This was the first time two lovers had ever been separated. For Purūravas it felt as though every sweetness had gone out of the world. He began to wander around. The earth at that time was a mass of vegetable decay. Ferns, riotous grasses, huge trunks fallen flat, plants growing on plants. What was missing was that liberating element: emptiness. Nothing was ever reduced to ashes, because fire was as yet unheard of. Purūravas found that nothing is so important as absence. He tried to get himself killed. He called for the help of some wild beast. Otherwise he would hang himself. Meanwhile he walked on, in no particular direction, ever further from anything he had known.

For some time he'd had no idea of his whereabouts when he found himself by a pond full of lotus flowers. Anyataḥplakṣā, in Kurukṣetra. It was majestically beautiful, but the only thing it offered him was a place to drown himself. Far away across the water, seven swans took shape. Purūravas paid no attention. As they approached the bank, Urvaśī said to her companions: "See that tattered man, with the feverish eyes . . . I lived with him for some years." The other swans stretched out their necks, curious and incredulous. "Let's make ourselves beautiful . . . ," said Urvaśī. Then they began to preen their feathers with great concentration. At the same time they were getting nearer and nearer the bank. When they touched the ground, they became Urvaśī and the six Apsaras who escorted her everywhere. But now they left her alone.

Acting quite naturally, Urvaśī sat down without a word on the grass next to Purūravas. Her lover lifted his empty eyes and recognized her. "Don't disappear this time," he said at once, as if afraid that Urvaśī were a vision. "You are cruel and dangerous, but we have some secrets we must tell each other. Otherwise, in times to come, we won't have the joy that comes from having said them, at least once, in days gone by." The stern Urvaśī raised her high cheekbones a fraction. In her contralto voice she said: "What's the point of talking about it? I slipped away like the first of the Dawns. I'm like the wind, you can't hold me. Go back home . . ." Purūravas gazed at her, her hard, elusive beauty: he remembered their first days together, when Urvaśī had begged him to keep her with him and it had been he who wasn't interested. He had agreed to live with her out of curiosity, and for the vanity of having a divine being beside him, but always thinking of her as a stranger, who could be ditched the morning after. "All right," he said. "Your friend will be off on his way. I am a companion of death, and I shall know where to find her. There must be some wolf willing to tear me to shreds. If not, I can hang myself." The trap worked. Urvaśī's expression was changing. A look of suffering rippled across her features. "Purūravas, don't die. Don't get yourself killed. But don't believe in friendship with women: they have the hearts of hyenas. Go back home." Purūravas was exultant, because he could see that Urvaśī was giving in. And at the same time he was still afraid she might disappear from one moment to the next. But Urvaśī went on speaking, albeit as though in trance, and to herself more than to him. She recalled the years they had lived together. Pervaded by her presence,

Purūravas wasn't even listening. All he heard were her last words: "I still remember those drops of cream you offered me every day. I can still smell them. It gives me joy to remember them . . ." Urvaśī had yielded. But immediately she recovered that lucid, determined expression Purūravas had noticed when they'd made their first pact. "All right, from now on we will meet for one night every year. We will have a son. It will be up to you to come to me this time, in the golden palace of the Gandharvas." Speaking these words, Urvaśī was almost sad, as though thinking: "Of course, it won't be so fine as before, when we had the two lambs tied to the sides of the bed. But it is all we are allowed . . ." Then she added: "Tomorrow the Gandharvas will grant you a favor. They are my lovers, they are jealous, it was they who stole me from you. But they will grant you the favor of becoming one of them, one among many. Accept. What matters, for you, is not so much to become a Gandharva, but what you will have to do to become a Gandharva."

The following day, as solicitous as they were diffident, the Gandharvas explained to Purūravas what he and indeed all men and the earth were lacking: fire. "As a companion of death," they said, "and you are all companions of death," they insisted, "you can never gain access to the sky without fire." That was why the earth was heavy and dull. It knew nothing but growth and decay. Now it would finally be able to destroy, and to destroy itself.

Purūravas went back to earth holding the hand of his son, Āyus, born of Urvaśī. In the forest, not far from his old home, he left the fire and the pitcher the Gandharvas had given him. Before performing what he knew would be a fatal act, he wanted to see the house he had left. He showed it to his son, who thus far had known only the sky and its palaces. A squeaky door opened onto a huge, empty room, full of dust. Against the far wall, a big bed. On the sides at the bottom, Purūravas recognized two hooks and two broken ropes. He said nothing, weeping inside. He went back to the forest with his son. The fire was gone. In its place he saw a tall fig tree, an *aśvattha* stretching its branches toward him. He broke two twigs off, like a sleepwalker. He rubbed them together, sensing that something was rising along each piece of wood, as when he used to go to Urvaśī's body and brush himself against her. A light spurted, and it was fire, forever. From that day on those two twigs—and all other pieces of wood later used to make fire—were called Purūravas and Urvaśī.

to the forest with his son. The fire was gone. In its place he saw a tall fig tree, an aśvattha, stretching its limbs toward him. He broke two twigs off, like a [illegible]. He rubbed them together, sensing that something was rising along each piece of wood, as when he used to go to Urvaśī's body and brush himself against her. A light sparked, and it was fire forever. From that day on those two twigs—and all other pieces of wood later used to make fire—were called Purūravas and Urvaśī.

XII

Nothing was ever more cheerful than Kṛṣṇa's childhood. He was the ragged, cheeky kid everybody knew in the clay huts of Gokula, the fields around Mathurā, the courtyards of the rich—the kid whose endless mischief they always forgave. Wherever he went, he would always be carrying a cowherd's goad. His first, perhaps only, rule was that nothing is so sweet as sweets that are stolen. Wherever he passed by, cream would disappear. He began his adventures by splashing in all the muddy puddles around the village. The experience would remain in his mind as the measure of all happiness. A band of little boys followed him everywhere—and he hid among them. Apart from these companions in adventure, the only creatures he ever had dealings with were of the other sex. The mothers would look up from their embroidery, craning their necks, and laugh to see the boys returning smothered in dust, and feel suddenly young again themselves, ready to leap off like antelopes along the Yamunā. And then the enchanting *gopīs*, the cow girls. Like children in another school you could climb a wall and signal to. There was a never-ending game between them: teasing, stifled laughter, races, practical jokes, gifts. And then the cows, those slow, solemn creatures who were the coinage of the countryside, and everywhere in circulation.

Trying to keep a straight face, Yaśodā, Kṛṣṇa's mother, would often listen to the complaints of other mothers who had become the butt of the urchin band's adventures. It was a comedy everybody felt bound to act out. Soon they forgot about it and talked about something else. Only once was Yaśodā alarmed. Some little boys had been spying for her: "Kṛṣṇa is grubbing around and eating filth like a pig." Yaśodā rushed out and found the boy on all fours. She yelled and scolded but then was shocked to see a terrifying flash light up his eyes. "Mother, it's all lies. If you don't believe me, look in my mouth." "Open up," said Yaśodā.

The mother watched those small lips, whose every crack she knew so well, come apart. Yaśodā bent down to study her son's palate and found a vast, starry vault that sucked her in. Already Yaśodā was traveling, flying. Where the back of his throat should have been rose Mount Meru, strewn with endless forests. To one side were islands, which perhaps were continents, and lakes, which perhaps were oceans. Yaśodā breathed with a new calm, as if she had walked into the open air for the first time in her son's mouth. The vision that most enchanted her was the wheel of the Zodiac: it girded the world obliquely, like a many-colored sash. But Yaśodā went further. She saw the mind's back-and-forth, its lunar inconstancy, its monkey leaps from branch to branch of the universe. She saw the three threads all substances are made of twist together in balls, which produced other balls. And behind it all she saw the village of Gokula, recognized its narrow streets, the patterns of its stonework, the carts, the springs, the wilting flowers. Until finally she saw herself, in a street, looking into a little boy's mouth.

For years the lives of the two bands, the little cowherd boys and the *gopīs*, ran parallel. They were like a single body split into two patrols, divided into two wings, moving on opposite sides of a low hill, shouting insults and gesturing defiantly at each other from the two banks of a stream. But it was hard to tell who was speaking and who was answering. They were a twin flock, milling in the air. There wasn't a ripple in the one that didn't find its dimple in the other.

But the *gopīs* were growing up too. One icy dawn in the

first month of winter, they met to celebrate a rite in honor of the goddess Kātyāyanī. They were proud and very aware of doing something new. This time the band of boys would not be on the other bank of the Yamunā. They were callow, probably asleep. The *gopīs* felt more adult. Only they, they thought, could go through this ceremony, only they could gain intimacy with the Goddess.

It had barely begun to grow light when they reached the Yamunā and took off all their clothes on the bank. They pretended it was a normal thing to do, but they were trembling with excitement on seeing each other's naked bodies for the first time. They walked off, apparently deep in thought, leaving their robes, all embroidered at the hems, in soft little piles behind. Then they went down into the water till it was halfway up their thighs, which were quickly turning to columns of ice.

They had to make a statue of the Goddess out of sand. They worked like skilled craftsmen. They adorned it with garlands, poured sandalwood oil over it, lit little flames around it, laid it on a bed of leaves, fruit, and rice. They worked of one accord and in silence, and as they did so each one was praying in the silence of her mind, frightened almost by the words she was hearing there, words which for the first time were hers and only hers. They would never have wanted to say those words to any of their companions. They blushed at the mere thought that such a thing might happen. At the very same time, in the mind of each *gopī*, the same words were being pronounced: "O Kātyāyanī, sovereign of the mind and of deceptions, let Kṛṣṇa, son of the herdsman Nanda, become my husband. I bow down before you." Not one of them was more eloquent, not one spoke a word more. They had but one desire, but one name to name it. Each felt at that moment that she was the protagonist of a story none of the others could possibly know. Each felt separate from the whole for the first time, and inebriated with being so, ready to endure that corrosive, melting sensation she now discovered in the pit of her stomach.

But they soon passed from praying to playing, in the water. And all at once these lovesick girls went back to being children who tussle together and laugh. Kṛṣṇa slipped out of their minds. But Kṛṣṇa was watching them. Perched on the forked branch of a huge *nīpa* tree that bent over the river, the bright eyes of his companions darting among the leaves all around, Kṛṣṇa watched the *gopīs* at play in the water as he raised the clothes they had left behind to his lips, breathing in their perfume one after the other. For the first time he saw the *gopīs'* breasts, and found they were like the domed temples of elephants. For the first time he saw the curve of their hips, which he had long glimpsed in the hidden movements beneath their clothes. For the first time he saw those bellies tight as drums converging on that dripping hair that appeared and disappeared amid the waters of the Yamunā. For the first time he saw the agile thighs, thrashing through the waves as they played. One by one he raised their robes to his mouth, whispering the name of the *gopī* they belonged to. Each time it seemed Kṛṣṇa had found the ultimate name, the name that cancels out all others, the name he would go on repeating forever. But then immediately afterward, he was pronouncing a new name, in a slightly different whisper. This went on for a long time, until one by one, after each had been brushed by Kṛṣṇa's lips, the *gopīs'* clothes passed from the right fork to the left of the branch of the *nīpa* tree.

All of a sudden one of the *gopīs* lost interest in their game. She looked toward the bank, turned her head this way and that. The little heaps of clothes were gone. She screamed. She didn't need to explain anything. The others turned their heads and joined in. It was a solid, penetrating scream, raised in a freezing, empty dawn. Then, wary and sidelong, the *gopīs* slowly lifted their eyes to the leaves of the *nīpa* tree. And then they heard Kṛṣṇa's voice. It was the voice of the tormentor who played tricks on all of them together, and the voice of the lover sending a coded message to each in her separateness from the others. Kṛṣṇa said: "Girls, don't be afraid, your clothes are all here. You of the slender waists, come one by one to get them back." He was finding it hard to keep a straight face: the *gopīs* had all sunk down into the waters of the river, last veil for their nudity, so that all you could see was arched brows over bright eyes staring at the tree. Only their hair floated free, like tendrils of aquatic plants. But the longer the *gopīs* stayed down in the water, the more an icy cold clutched at their throats. Then they spoke: "Kṛṣṇa, this is the meanest trick you've ever played. You are our beloved, but you also know the rules of law and custom. If you don't give us our clothes back, we will have to tell your father." Kṛṣṇa answered in what was now unequivocally a lover's voice: "If you really are my slaves and want nothing better than to obey me, then you will come up here to get your clothes back, you of the lovely hips." So one by one, shivering with cold, and for the first time making that gesture of covering their dripping bellies with their hands, the *gopīs* came out of the water and approached Kṛṣṇa. For a moment each imagined that Kṛṣṇa would take her by the hand and run off, with her alone. But Kṛṣṇa did nothing more than give each girl her clothes back, taking care that their fingers didn't meet.

Before they covered themselves up again, Kṛṣṇa wanted to gaze at them once more, to see those bodies he had stared at, dreamed of, completely naked, out of the water. So, finding a solemn voice, he said: "By bathing naked in the Yamunā, you have sinned against Varuṇa, you have exposed yourselves to him without shame. Now you must seek his forgiveness. Before dressing, raise your arms above your heads, press the palms of your hands together, then bow down. May the god forgive you." The *gopīs* obeyed. Kṛṣṇa watched them, putting on a stern face, while making mental notes: that one had breasts that pointed away from each other, a sort of felicitous squinting; this one had buttocks that arched over two dimples, like hills rising from tiny lakes; that one's knees were small, round shields; this one's eyes couldn't concentrate on the invisible Varuṇa but were shifting sideways to follow Kṛṣṇa, as though tied to him by a thin thread. The ceremony went on a long time, a ceremony that in no way resembled the one the *gopīs* had come down to the river for. Kṛṣṇa was eager that it be as solemn as possible. Everything proceeded in silence. In the end, Kṛṣṇa said: "My beloved ones, I know you want nothing better than to adore me. Your desire has made me glad, and deserves to be fulfilled. When this desire has been satisfied, no other desire will replace it. It is a flower that hides no seed. You may touch my feet with your hands. Then go back to Gokula." Immediately afterwards, one by one, the *gopīs* were to hear the words that would stay with them all their lives. They heard Kṛṣṇa say their names and then: "I will be with you every night." Then, bowing their heads, reluctantly, the *gopīs* walked off in single file and without looking back returned to the village.

While spying on the *gopīs,* hidden in the leaves of the *nīpa* tree, Kṛṣṇa was discovering a higher form of theft, which was his vocation and delight: the theft you commit with your eyes. But was he the inventor of that theft? Or was this gesture the reflection of another? The *gopīs* had shown him the way, before their dripping bodies became the way itself. One day—Kṛṣṇa was five years old—Yaśodā was holding him in her lap, feeding him something white and creamy. They called it "butter," but it was curdled milk, the common milk that came from the cows of Vraja. Kṛṣṇa was having his breakfast. The god's face had the round brightness of the moon, and wore an expression of total absorption, as if the butter dripping on his dark chest were everything there was. In the kitchen, hidden in the shadows, two *gopīs* were watching the scene. It was a "vision," *darśana,* and if by vision we mean the surrender of the one who looks to that which he sees, then this was the first of all. The substance of the world and the substance of the god mixed together, rising and falling, like the wave of the first beginnings, where all was dissolved and latent. The *gopīs* felt they were immersed in the god, as one day they would be immersed up to their eyebrows in the Yamunā to escape his gaze.

. . .

Another day Kṛṣṇa had climbed on a stool and plunged his hands into a terra-cotta jar full of butter. Motionless in the shadows, two *gopīs* watched that black creature whose glossy skin overlay the gloom of the dark. Did they glimpse two small, flailing arms? Or were there four? As they watched Kṛṣṇa in the deep silence of the kitchen, they felt liquid and warm, and each in her mind spoke the same words: "Oh, come and steal from me, come and steal me."

And there was another time when the *gopīs* got together to watch Kṛṣṇa. Exasperated by the complaints of all those Kṛṣṇa had stolen from, Yaśodā had bound him to the mortar, exposing him to the public gaze. This time the *gopīs* came openly, and in numbers. The show of morality gave the scene its erotic spicing. Could anyone imagine anything more exciting? To be asked to watch a punishment that offered the witnesses material for pure pleasure: to gaze on the body of a helpless Kṛṣṇa? The *gopīs* tried to look as stern as they could. Their eyes were greedier than ever: for the first time they saw a Kṛṣṇa who was forced to stay still, not that flashing, darting creature they were used to. Then Kṛṣṇa cried, tied up as he was, and the teardrops that fell on his chest sparkled together with his earrings like golden crocodiles. Yaśodā played prison guard. The *gopīs'* eyes were directed at Kṛṣṇa, but it was Yaśodā they pierced. Never had they felt so jealous of her, handling Kṛṣṇa and bossing him around as if he were a little animal.

The *gopīs*, about sixteen thousand of them, suffered jealousy for Kṛṣṇa, a jealousy galvanized by three rivals: Yaśodā, the mother; Rādhā, the favorite lover; Muralī, the flute.

What we call "history," right up to its blazing conclusion, appears between the seventh and tenth "descents," *avatāras,* of Viṣṇu. From that moment on, the key players are no longer prodigious animals, like the turtle, Kūrma, and the boar, Varāha, but two men, in succession: Kṛṣṇa and the Buddha. Since then the white horse that will be the harbinger of the end has never appeared, but in the meantime life has swung back and forth between the consequences of Kṛṣṇa and Buddha, the eighth and ninth descents of Viṣṇu. We mull over the deeds of these two as if they were characters in a novel, sharing with them an intimacy we cannot have with the primordial beasts.

It is to Kṛṣṇa that the world owes the extinction of the heroes—and of himself, when he took part in the massacre of Kurukṣetra, the "field of the Kurus," as counselor and ally of the sons of Pāṇḍu. But in his infancy and adolescence, when he wandered around Vraja like a cowherd surrounded by cow girls, he had already made us a gift that was to be the most precious viaticum for the age of conflict, then about to begin and as yet still with us: the gift of "devotion," *bhakti.* In this dark and faltering age, one cannot practice knowledge without oiling it with devotion, without subjecting it to that impetus of the heart which the *gopīs* unearthed once and for all. At once superior and inferior to every distinct form of knowledge founded in itself, devotion is an ambiguous gift, yet not so ambiguous as that offered by the next *avatāra.* For the knowledge the Buddha brought has a corrosive quality, which can lead to a dissolution of devotion or to its exaltation in a sparer and more abstract form, of a kind the *gopīs* hadn't yet achieved, and perhaps never wanted to.

Kṛṣṇa came down into the world when many possibilities had already been exhausted. Wars no longer took place between gods but between potentates. There were no more *ṛṣis,* powerful as the wild beasts of the forest, threatening the heavens with the stillness of their minds. Instead there were shabby, shaggy ascetics. The Apsaras no longer sallied forth from their celestial palaces in embroidered robes and sparkling sandals to meet together by wood or riverbank.

Instead there were wild-eyed, barefooted girls gathering herbs, quick to theft and flight.

The *gopīs* knew no discipline. Their days were not arranged around ritual duties. They obeyed only their emotions. They were the first quietists. It was not that they weren't familiar with the ceremonies or didn't respect them, just that as soon as they got the chance they ran off to tend the cows. They neither imagined nor desired that their lives should have direction. They thought of the city as a foreign place that you might visit for the market, or to sell butter and buy small trinkets. Every *gopī* was obedient to a secret vow. They welcomed new arrivals as though into a sorority. But there was no need to explain a doctrine, just as one doesn't explain what water is. Some didn't stay the course. They would go back to the village and wander from room to room for a while with gloomy faces. Then they forgot—or pretended to forget. They became part of the family again. Whereas the *gopīs* belonged to no one, answered to no one.

The *gopīs* were good-looking cow girls with thin, nervous legs, gypsylike, as violent in play as in their feelings. While they were tending their cows, the oranges, violets, blues, yellows, ochers, greens, and reds of the clothes they wrapped so carefully around their bodies would stand out against grass and sky. Walking along the road, balancing jars of butter on their heads, they were as conspicuous as colored ribbons fluttering in the breeze. Sometimes, if they had been playing with Kṛṣṇa and the other herdboys, rolling around on the muddy ground, they would be grimy with dust, bristling, tousled. But for long periods they wandered around alone. Then they would get together in a circle, whisper, conspire. There was one thing their minds came endlessly back to: how to explain Kṛṣṇa's managing to steal some *gopīs'* sugared butter every single night without ever getting caught? They told each other how they would tie him up with a long scarf of red silk. They thought of all the insults they would make up to heap on him. They knew no school but the meadows, woods, and canebrakes. They knew no music but that which issued from Muralī, Kṛṣṇa's flute. They were jealous of it, because Muralī is a feminine creature, and she would abandon herself to Kṛṣṇa's mouth before their eyes. They never yearned for another life. When they walked in single file toward Mathurā, there was only one excitement they were hoping for: the game of the butter tax. Kṛṣṇa and the other boys might sneak out of the bushes. Wearing crude masks, they would claim to be the king's guards and demand that butter duty be paid. The *gopīs* would resist. But already Kṛṣṇa and the other boys would be grabbing the pitchers and mussing up their clothes. Then they ran off with the loot, brash and cocky as bandits.

Closer to Fénelon than to the Vedas, untempted by any articulated form of knowledge, the *gopīs* would only ever know an alternation of the presence that melts, the privation that paralyzes. All possibilities between, the things that make up ordinary life, were of no interest to them. Precisely, painstakingly, but like so many sleepwalkers, they got on with their daily duties, milked the cows, looked after the children, drew water, fed the fire. Agreeable, obliging, but absent. Across their bright, empty eyes slid a shadow, the only time you might have suspected the inklings of a thought was when they sat down to put on their makeup. Then they conversed with the mirror as though the two images of their face were two flimsy fabrics that clung to the air between, flittingly haunted by Kṛṣṇa's phantom.

Rasa, "juice," "sap," also means "emotion," "taste," "flavor." Kṛṣṇa is the determined thief of a barely curdled liquid because he himself is liquid. Kṛṣṇa is forever stealing from himself. It is the emotion that steals the heart. Kṛṣṇa is he who opens the liquid path toward the bazaar of love.

Going there is as dangerous as diving into waters from which one may never emerge.

When the first full moon of autumn approaches and the jasmine is in bloom, the shrill, soft sound of the flute penetrates the rooms. It is Kṛṣṇa calling. Whatever they are doing, the *gopīs* are roused. One gets up from the half-empty pail where she was milking a cow. One gets up from the flickering twigs where she was lighting the fire. One gets up from the bed where her husband was about to embrace her. One gets up from the toys she was playing with on the floor. One knocks over the bottles she was using to perfume herself. They are little girls, adolescents, wives who suddenly and furtively set off toward the forest. All you would hear then was a tinkling of bangles and ankle bracelets through the dark. Slipping out from the trees, each believing she was alone, they found Kṛṣṇa in a moonlit clearing. He looked at them, as they stood still, panting from haste, smiled and said: "Women of good fortune, what can I do for you? The night is full of frightening creatures. Sons, husbands, and parents are waiting for you in the village. I know you have come here for me. This is happiness. But you mustn't let people stay up worrying on your account. Celebrate my name in silence, from afar." Then one of the *gopīs* spoke up on behalf of all the others: "Nothing we have left behind is as urgent and important to us as adoring the soles of your feet. No one is closer to us than you are. Why is it that learned men can find refuge in you, and we cannot? We grovel in the dust of your footsteps. Place your hand on our breasts and our heads." Kṛṣṇa smiled again and began to walk, playing Muralī, the flute. From behind a curtain of leaves came the sound of the Yamunā flowing by. One by one, in order, the *gopīs* came up to Kṛṣṇa and, shaking breasts damp with sweat and sandalwood oil, brushed against his blue chest. Whenever Kṛṣṇa laid his mouth on a new hole of his musical rod, his lips wet a different part of the *gopīs'* bodies. In the milky light you could just see the pink marks his nails left. Dancing ever so slowly, the circle of the *gopīs* closed around Kṛṣṇa as he went on playing Muralī. Each felt seized, abandoned, seized again, as if by a wave. Then all at once each noticed that her eyes had met those of the *gopīs* on the opposite side of the circle, while the center was suddenly empty. Yet again, Kṛṣṇa had disappeared. Then they scattered. Some mimed Kṛṣṇa's deeds, like actresses. One was Pūtanā, the evil wet nurse who tried to poison Kṛṣṇa with her milk; another gripped her breast, sucking it violently as Kṛṣṇa once had. Another copied the slight sway of Kṛṣṇa's gait. Another put her foot on a companion's head and said: "I am here to punish the wicked." But others were quiet and stared at the ground. They were trying to find footprints. Not just Kṛṣṇa's but the light step of another *gopī*, Rādhā, the favorite. Doubtless Kṛṣṇa had left them to hide away alone with her. There were those who to their dismay could remember seeing Kṛṣṇa lie down like a riverbed between the columns of Rādhā's legs and speak words that made them blush: "Adorn my head with the sublime bud of your feet." The *gopīs'* eyes glittered with anger as they hunted. Another clearing opened up, and in the middle, arms clutched around her knees, hair loose, shut up in herself like a bundle of colored rags, they found Rādhā. When she raised her face, it was furrowed with tears. Kṛṣṇa had just left her.

The *rāsalīlā*, "the dance game," the circular dance that is echoed in every other dance, couldn't get started. Each of the *gopīs* wanted to be nearest to Kṛṣṇa. They were all trying to get close enough to color his skin with the saffron paste smeared on their breasts. That way they would have managed, even if only for a few seconds, to have left a trace of themselves on him. A cluster of shawls, bodices, and slender, glistening chests closed him in on every side. Then in order to get the dance going, Kṛṣṇa decided to multiply himself. He resorted to his knowledge of mirrors and reflection. In the circle, between each *gopī* and the next, another Kṛṣṇa appeared, holding them by the hand and looking alternately at one, then the other, as though following the steps of the dance, though each *gopī* was convinced that he was there for her alone. The yellow cloth wrapped around his loins was always the same, but the color of the skin varied, from dark blue to hyacinth. These were the many Kṛṣṇa, while the one Kṛṣṇa remained in the center of the circle, where the *gopīs* could see nothing at all.

Is the love of Kṛṣṇa and Rādhā, or of Kṛṣṇa and the *gopīs* for that matter, *svakīyā* (legitimate, conjugal) or *parakīyā* (illegitimate, adulterous)? It's a theological question which cleaves the centuries like a flaming sword and over which scholars have argued vehemently and rancorously. In 1717 they hastened in their scores to the court of Nawāb Ja'far Khān to confute the positions of their enemies. They came from all over Bengal and Orissa, but likewise from Vārāṇasī and Vikrampur. They debated the matter for six months, to the point of total exhaustion. Pale and haggard, they argued over the greater or lesser intensity of Kṛṣṇa's erotic games with Rādhā, and their celestial consequences: if the *līlā* that briefly occurs at Vṛndāvana is no more than a feeble replica of the one perennially performed in the celestial Vṛndāvana, does that then mean that adulterous love is sovereign in the sky as on earth and offers itself as a model even to the gods? And must what is a model for the gods by that very token be one for men too?

Then there were other questions, less lofty perhaps, but just as thorny. If the sixteen thousand *gopīs* were all married, what went on in their homes at night while they were dancing the *rāsalīlā* with Kṛṣṇa? How was it that those sixteen thousand husbands never complained—perhaps never even noticed their wives' absence? Would one have to subscribe to the theory according to which sixteen thousand *gopī* simulacra stayed calm and quiet in their legitimate beds while the bodies of the real *gopīs* wrapped themselves like parasites around Kṛṣṇa.

The controversy was violent in the extreme, and over those months of debate at least six centuries of war were echoed. In the end the disciples who upheld *svakīyā* conceded defeat. They underwrote a document in which they accepted as correct the doctrine they had always abhorred. But what were the decisive arguments that sealed the triumphant sovereignty of the illegitimate? *Parakīyā* is that which brings the metaphysical element in love to the point of incandescence. And what is that element? Separation. Never is the "flavor" (*rasa*) of "separation" (*viraha*) so intense as in illegitimate passion. Furthermore: whatever is *parakīyā* is denied the permanence of possession. It is a state in which one can only occasionally be possessed. This corresponds to the essence of every relationship with Kṛṣṇa. Finally: the woman who abandons herself to a love that is *parakīyā* risks more than other women. To violate the rules of conjugal order is to deny this world's bonds and abandon oneself to what calls to us from beyond the world. Such love does not seek to bear fruit, and it never will. Whatever seeks to bear fruit will consume itself in that fruit. While that which disregards every fruit is inexhaustible. This is pure *preman*, liquid, diffuse "love," unsatisfied by the obsessive arrow of *kāma*, "desire," but absorbing it into itself and keeping it circulating there, the way Kṛṣṇa's seed continues to circulate in his body without ever bursting forth. He who follows *kāma* wants nothing better than for the arrow to strike its one target, pleasure. But he who follows a love that is *parakīyā* must always take his pleasure mingled with fear, indeed with a twofold fear: the fear of separation and the fear of punishment. Both weigh on him, constantly, surrounding every sensual delight with a livid and thrilling aura. Yet it is only that twofold fear which gains us entry to the "sweetness" (*mādhurya*) which is Kṛṣṇa's ultimate nature, the trait revealed when a lover's being has, little by little and ever so slowly, been stripped of all its clothes. She who reaches that point will feel Kṛṣṇa's hand grip her wrist, as though to help her place her foot on the stones of a stream before launching herself into him on the other bank. Thus did the theologians and ascetics set off on their ways, once more having accepted a doctrine whose very name boasted a flagrant and glorious contradiction: the *parakīyādharma*, the "law of the illegitimate."

"Heart thief and butter thief," Kṛṣṇa was called. Or again, "thief of the heart's butter." But when his favorite, Rādhā, doubts him and demands to hear every one of his names, she doubts each of them, for they could each refer to someone else, except one, that is "butter thief." It is the only epithet that identifies Kṛṣṇa beyond all doubt. Even when he was exploring Yaśodā's kitchen on all fours, the little boy was drawn to those terra-cotta jars and their inebriating, creamy contents. Soon Yaśodā decided to keep the jars hanging in the air so that Kṛṣṇa couldn't get them. But nothing was beyond his reach. He climbed on beams and windows. Sometimes Yaśodā would catch him with his hands in the butter. "I'm chasing off the ants," Kṛṣṇa would say at once. Butter was the element through which he communicated with other creatures, with all women, with his mother, with Rādhā, with the *gopīs*.

Kṛṣṇa means "Black," "Obscure." The first creature the word was used to refer to was the antelope, who was also the first among creatures. It was in the black pelt of a skinned antelope that the loins of the sacrificer were wrapped. And sacrifice is the perennial second act, the act that extracts an essence from the first, an articulation that then allows us, through the third act—ordinary life—to move on to every other.

As a lover Kṛṣṇa did not look black but blue, purplish, or sometimes even lighter: mauve. Often his skin resembled the big bluish stain on Śiva's neck where the ocean's poison had concentrated, the stain his partners loved to lick. When he fought and cut off heads, Kṛṣṇa might go back to being black again. Then a yellow fabric would arch up from behind his shoulders and, like the whites of his eyes, gleam out against the dark.

One night when the moon was full, in the month of Kārttika, the gods got together in a circle to watch the dance of the perfect lovers, Kṛṣṇa and Rādhā. This time Śiva sang an accompaniment in a voice that was rarely heard. Gazing at the two twining bodies, the brilliant colors mingling together, the gods fell into a gentle swoon. When they awoke, the lovers had melted to become a spring that flowed silently into the Gaṅgā.

Kṛṣṇa left the forest and meadows of Vṛndāvana for the city of Dvārakā, where he was united in wedlock to eight queens. The *gopīs* now roamed in silence. Accustomed to the emotion of stolen love, when they were alone they would sometimes say the words "you thief" over and over, but without getting any response. Life went on as though Kṛṣṇa had never been with them. Separation, emptiness, absence: this was the new emotion, and the only one.

Shut away in his palace, his eight worthy, pompous queens orbiting around him with implacable precision, Kṛṣṇa was getting bored. Occasional relief came in the form of conversations with the old Nārada. Born from the neck of Brahmā, condemned by Brahmā to wander forever without respite, Nārada had been through so many stories, seen so many places. Old now and cunning, curious, part pander, part court counselor, a great musician, a great teller of tales, deceitful, voyeur, flatterer, intelligent, malevolent—who better than he to distract one from melancholy? thought Kṛṣṇa. They spent the nights playing chess and talking. Then Nārada would play the *vīṇā*, as masterfully as ever. Kṛṣṇa enjoyed teasing him too. Once he said: "Now tell me about the life when you were a worm and tried to avoid the chariot of that king." "Of course, we are always attached to our bodies, even when we're worms . . . ," said Nārada. He smiled, but somewhat nervously. The stories Kṛṣṇa liked most were the ones about the two lives when Nārada had been transformed into a woman. "Even though you have lived as a woman and borne dozens of children, before climbing over their corpses that time to pick a

mango, you never understood anything about women . . ."
"You might be right," said Nārada. "For example, I don't understand how you manage with all these queens . . ."
"But these are not *women*," said Kṛṣṇa, suddenly gloomy, and he went back to staring at the chessboard.

One evening Nārada realized that Kṛṣṇa was shivering, his eyes glazed. "What is the matter, my Lord?" he asked. "I've got a fever," said Kṛṣṇa. The next day, Kṛṣṇa didn't get out of bed. "He's delirious," whispered the serving girls. Days went by, and the fever was as fierce as ever. Nārada sat alone in his rooms, already thinking of setting off on his travels again, but worried. A doctor knocked on the door. "Lord Kṛṣṇa is still delirious," he said. "He has but one wish. He says he will only get better if someone brings him the dust stuck to the feet of certain women. We were wondering if the wise Nārada, who knows the world better than anyone else, might be able to help," the doctor finished, embarrassed. "Of course," said Nārada. He had never refused an assignment that whetted his curiosity. And he was curious about everything. "I'll do what I can," he added.

His first move was to ask for an audience with the eight queens. He spoke with his subtle, supple eloquence, as though advancing a noble and solemn request. The queens looked at each other for a moment. Then the first spoke for all: "How could we? Our feet are perfumed with jasmine. We spend our time making sure that every inch of our bodies is pure. We couldn't offer our Lord Kṛṣṇa anything that wasn't perfect. We've even forgotten what dust is." Nārada was taken aback. Kṛṣṇa was still delirious. Nārada went to the most noble ladies of Dvārakā and repeated his request, at once urgent and uneasy. Nobody would agree to it. To do something the queens had refused to do would doubtless be an unforgivable indiscretion. They didn't say as much, but they feared for their heads.

The despondent Nārada went back to the palace, where he found a message from a doctor: "Lord Kṛṣṇa asks whether Nārada, who seeks far and wide, has also sought in Vṛndāvana." No, Nārada said, he hadn't been to Vṛndāvana. He set off. Leaving the city behind, he came across some huts and animals. The countryside was ever more lonely and enchanting. In a meadow surrounded by tall, dark trees, near the waters of the Yamunā, he saw a patch of dazzling colors. A herd of cows were grazing. It was silent. Getting closer, he saw that the patch was made up of a number of crouching figures, who now started toward him. "You are Nārada, you have seen Kṛṣṇa," said a sharp-eyed little girl as the others gathered around. Nārada was looking at the ground. He saw all those small, bare, dirty feet. "Lord Kṛṣṇa is ill," he murmured. "He needs the dust stuck to certain women's feet." The *gopīs* didn't even answer. One took off a blue rag, and all of them shook the dust from their feet into it. They even scraped dust off with their nails. Then the first gave the rag to Nārada. "Here. Give it to our playmate. If this is a crime, we will face the punishment. We are ready. We are always ready. Kṛṣṇa is everything to us." Nārada said not a word. He put the rag full of dust on his shoulders, like a bundle, and set off again toward Dvārakā. He walked deep in thought, head bent. He looked like a pilgrim now, or a beggar. All at once he stopped and caught himself saying out loud: "Kṛṣṇa, you were right. Now I understand."

XIII

Memories of his time with the *gopīs* would well up in Kṛṣṇa's heart like a spring of clear water, hidden beneath rushes. Now he was surrounded by people who knew nothing of his herdboy's adolescence, who thought of him only as a shrewd, mature king, his body still powerful, his face furrowed with fine wrinkles. Kṛṣṇa hardly ever spoke about himself.

One day he was visiting Indraprastha, where his sister Subhadrā had married Arjuna and borne him a son. Kṛṣṇa celebrated his nephew's birth rites. The hot weather was setting in. Arjuna said: "I'd like to leave the city and bathe in the Yamunā with our girls." Kṛṣṇa added: "I'd like to play with our girls in the Yamunā too." Preparations were made. At first light, a colorful procession set out from the city gate. Servant women, maids, and ladies clustered around carts laden with fragrant food baskets.

Hidden among the sunshades, Arjuna's two wives, the majestic Draupadī and the enchanting Subhadrā, talked together. It looked like an exodus of young maidens. Among them, toward the end of the procession, came just two men, Kṛṣṇa and Arjuna. They too were talking together.

The sun was still low when they reached the banks of the Yamunā. The provisions were unloaded in a chatter of trilling voices. The girls spread white and embroidered cloths on the grass. Like skilled craftsmen they erected delicate pavilions. The water was already sparkling. Behind them the grassy clearing was surrounded by the dark presence of the Forest of Khāṇḍava, the Sugar Candy Forest. The air rang with the highest spirits. Already you could hear flutes, *vīṇās*, tambourines. Some of the girls had dived in the water, others had gathered in the pavilions, others were laying out the food. There was laughter, weeping, the whispering of secrets. Draupadī and Subhadrā were seen taking off their jewels and fastening them around the necks, wrists, and ankles of the first girls they came across.

Kṛṣṇa and Arjuna were not much in evidence. They had asked to be away from the group and were sitting on two inlaid chairs at the edge of the forest. Left alone, they said nothing, suddenly solemn expressions set on their faces. All at once Kṛṣṇa turned to the women in the distance: all he could see there was a swarm of colored points, milling madly. Voices and sounds came faintly through the air, a quivering in the background. He would never see anything so delightful again in all his life. Indeed he would hardly see anything delightful at all in the time that remained. Arjuna didn't know that, couldn't know it, but he was beginning to feel it. There was no need to speak to him. In the silence he was preparing himself for an immense catastrophe, albeit without knowing exactly what would happen.

Then they saw a tall figure emerge from the dense forest, upright, emaciated, with a red beard and skin of molten gold glimmering beneath a black robe. A brahman. He seemed exhausted and irate. He said: "I know who you are. I am a voracious brahman. Give me food I can eat." Kṛṣṇa asked him what food would satisfy him. "I'm Agni," said the brahman. "Only this whole forest can satisfy me. I can't burn it because I haven't the strength and Indra protects the place." Kṛṣṇa looked up: he saw heavy clouds gathering darkly. They would have to fight together against Arjuna's father, king of the gods. Secretly, Kṛṣṇa was pleased. "How can it be that Agni is unable to burn?" he asked. "I could, but only if you help me. It's a sad story. A mad sacrifice. A rash and arrogant king fed me on melted butter for twelve years. He hoped his sacrifice would help him scale the sky. He wore me out with that butter. Now I want plants and meat. My mouth is sick of butter. Now I want nothing but wild food. I look at this forest, and I can't make any impression on it. Seven times I've set it alight, and seven times elephants and Nāga have put it out. Indra poured down cataracts from the clouds. But I can offer you weapons that are invincible. And you'll soon be needing them," Agni finished with a chuckle. The bow called Gāṇḍīva was surrendered to the grip of Arjuna's hands. The disk and the mace appeared in Kṛṣṇa's.

Then the brahman turned back to fire again, creeping through the grass toward the forest. Suddenly there was a huge blaze, a whirlwind and a crash. Arjuna and Kṛṣṇa took up positions at either end of the clearing and stood motionless. Together with the crackle of fire came the piercing shrieks of wild beasts. The animals swarmed toward the clearing with desperation in their eyes. Elephants, antelopes, monkeys, buffalo, butterflies, tigers, moles, demons, goats, snakes, squirrels, colored birds. Arjuna brought them down one by one, the fiercest and the most harmless, the gigantic and the tiny, pulling out arrows from his two inexhaustible quivers. As every arrow whistled off, he felt at once and with equal intensity both the pointlessness and the necessity of what he was doing. How many more times would he have to kill? And at bottom every other killing, even the most justifiable and irreproachable, would be like the massacre of those beasts fleeing from one death to another. The pointlessness was glaring, the necessity just a thread, but the toughest thread of all, the one that tied him to Kṛṣṇa, that friend in whom he so deeply confided that it sometimes seemed Kṛṣṇa was at work inside him, ensconced there in a cell that just occasionally would open. Even now, as he drew out his arrows, Arjuna's hand was a glove with the steady hand of Kṛṣṇa flexing inside. Meanwhile, from the opposite side of the clearing, Kṛṣṇa hit out incessantly like some automaton. Few were the animals who escaped the razor disk that flew from his hand and then immediately returned. And even those fled in vain: the mace brought them down at once. Toward the forest, nothing but devouring flame.

Amazed, the gods gathered in the sky to watch. "Why is

Agni burning these creatures? Is it a sign that the world is about to end? Is the Submarine Mare raising her head?" they wondered, turning to Indra. "And why must Arjuna of all people, your son, help the world to consume itself? Why are you letting them destroy this forest you have always protected?" Indra didn't answer. Without a word, he unleashed the waters. They fell in dense, liquid sheets. But as they approached the flames, they evaporated. Arjuna's arrows darkened the sky and wounded the drops. By now the clearing was covered in a carpet of festering corpses. Here and there they were heaped in mounds. They were the sweetmeats in Agni's diet, the red-hot candy he loved so much. The forest went on burning for six days. The sounds of unseen death throes went on and on. Fewer and fewer animals or Dānavas made it to the clearing. Then the shrieking gradually died down. There was still the occasional thudding sound, in the distance—and the hissing whirlwind of the flames.

Agni reappeared before Arjuna, glossy and replete, having bolted down oceans of fat and bone marrow. He thanked his two accomplices and bade them farewell: "Go where you please." There was a moment's sudden silence, immediately broken by a light flutter. Kṛṣṇa, Arjuna, and Agni looked up. They saw four birds flying into the sky. The only surviving creatures. They were the four Vedas.

Arjuna and Kṛṣṇa looked down again, impassive, at the charred forest. Behind them, the ground stretched dull and gray as far as the banks of the Yamunā. Standing in a line, the maidens and ladies who had come with them were watching. Together they made a ribbon, a film of ash on every face and robe. The pavilions were gone, swept away by the wind.

Thus was the war between the five Pāṇḍavas and their cousins, the Kauravas, announced. Kṛṣṇa and Arjuna lingered on the banks of the Yamunā, alone, watching the water flow by. Then they wandered back to Indraprastha like two vagrants, without so much as a word.

While the Forest of Khāṇḍava was burning, Arjuna had remembered the crackling of another pyre, not long ago, where, had his Kaurava cousins had their way, he himself would have died along with his four brothers. This was the burning of the lacquer house, an elegant, flimsy, deathtrap building where they had been staying for a long festive period, in Vāraṇāvata. There too there had been melted butter. The cloying, penetrating smell mingled with the smells of hemp, cork, and cane in the four great halls. Even the narrow columns had been smeared with butter, the better to catch fire.

Hinting, enigmatic, Uncle Vidura had given the game away. The Pāṇḍavas dug themselves a mole's burrow. At night they would sneak down into their hiding place, with their weapons, and keep watch. For months they waited for a chance to escape, while letting the others think they had died in the fire. One night, five drunken, unsuspecting Niṣādas sprawled on their cushions with their mother. They didn't even hear the flames roaring. Their charred forms convinced the Kauravas that those execrable cousins, the Pāṇḍavas, would be in their way no more.

Together with their mother, Kuntī, the Pāṇḍavas ran through the night like hunted beasts. Slipping out of their burrow, they dashed for the forest, the glow of the fire fading behind them. The trees were shaken by angry gusts. The tension of a year of forced and harassed wakefulness was melting away. But they didn't dare assume they were free yet. Only Bhīma, in the midst of the group, cut down every obstacle. Trunks crashed to the ground as he passed. He saw the others gasping. So he gently lifted Kuntī onto his back. He grabbed the twins, Nakula and Sahadeva, then Arjuna and Yudhiṣṭhira, holding them tight under his arms. Then he pressed on, like an animated mountain. He was the stormy gale that beat down the plants, cutting a path through darkness.

. . .

Ever since they were born, the five Pāṇḍava brothers, who were Pāṇḍu's sons in name only, each of them boasting a "portion," *aṃśa*, of a particular god, in that they had been fathered in Kuntī's (and Mādrī's) wombs by different gods—Yudhiṣṭhira by Dharma, Bhīma by Vāyu, Arjuna by Indra, the twins Nakula and Sahadeva by the Aśvin twins—ever since they were born, the Pāṇḍavas had been aware of a malignant tension between themselves and their Kaurava cousins. When they played games together, it was as if they were fighting to the death. So tangled was their common ancestry that there was no way of being certain which of them would one day be the legitimate king of Hastināpura. The theories offered to establish legitimacy were too contradictory, though each could claim to be reasonable up to a point.

When the Kauravas, set up the lacquer house trap, hoping their cousins would be burned alive there, the Pāṇḍavas were not surprised. "And now," thought Arjuna as the Forest of Khāṇḍava was burning, "another fire. To kill hundreds of desperate animals, I've had to fight against my father, Indra. In return for a deed that many will think dishonorable, I have been given Gāṇḍīva, the bow I always desired. To create a desert of ash, I have for the first time done something together with my lifelong friend Kṛṣṇa. If all that seems senseless, it must be because it makes too much sense."

Seen from afar, the imminent war between the Pāṇḍavas and the Kauravas might have looked very like the massacre of those animals fleeing the Forest of Khāṇḍava. It would overwhelm rank and rancor in flight and death. Kāla, Time, was in a hurry to put an end to an aeon. The war was mainly a pretext to make things easier for him. Not so much that day, as he tirelessly drew his bow before a forest of flame, but later, years later, Arjuna would be constantly asking himself why that slaughter had come about. And in what sense it had come about "for the good of the worlds." In the end, killing one's relatives was much easier to justify.

But those animals fleeing the burning forest? Why? Arjuna never got an answer. Time and again he would see Kṛṣṇa, ruthlessly wielding his lethal disk and mace. Then he would remember how Indra, his father, had appeared, humiliated by his son's arrows, and magnanimously offered to grant Kṛṣṇa a boon. A sovereign god, albeit of obsolete sovereignty, offering a boon to a king, who was also a sovereign god reigning over sovereigns. At the time Arjuna hadn't even noticed the oddity and irony of what was going on. What he did remember, though, and very clearly, was the boon Kṛṣṇa had asked for: Arjuna's friendship, forever.

It was Draupadī, princess of the Pañcālas, the people of the figure Five and of the Dolls, who first brought Kṛṣṇa and Arjuna together. Born from the sacrificial fire, Draupadī had the dark, almost black skin of charred logs (which was why they also called her Kṛṣṇā). She smelled like blue lotuses. Her father, King Drupada, proclaimed for her a *svayaṃvara:* this was the ceremony during which a bride selected her husband. The suitors were to compete with their bows. Disguised as brahmans, guests at a potter's house, the Pāṇḍavas braced themselves for the challenge. There were fifteen days of sumptuous and exhausting festivities. No one had seen Draupadī yet. The sixteenth day the princess appeared in the arena, adorned with a golden garland that shone out between dark skin and bright white robe. The suitors all got to their feet, shouting: "Draupadī will be mine." Hundreds of earrings flashed in the sun. Among the guests who had come to watch was Kṛṣṇa, at the head of the Vṛṣṇis. He was the only one in the crowd who immediately recognized the Pāṇḍavas among the brahmans. And, of the Pāṇḍavas, it was Arjuna who attracted his attention. For how long had they perched on opposite branches of the *aśvattha* tree that spans the worlds, for how long had they drifted together over the endless waters, for how long (a thousand years?) had they sat together in that niche of rock in Badarī, one with his right leg crossed, the other with his left, the roaring of a river in the distance?

Now they would meet as men lost in a throng of men. Meanwhile, the other princes had missed the target. Kṛṣṇa saw Arjuna's left arm slowly drawing back his bow. He thought: "Not the forest, but the tree. Not the tree, but the bird. Not the bird, but the head. Now . . ." There was a mighty shout. The target: pierced through. Draupadī turned radiant eyes on Arjuna. She had already chosen the man who had won her. She went toward him with a chaplet of white flowers.

Draupadī didn't have long to enjoy feeling that she was wife to the man she had chosen: Arjuna. She knew she was marrying into an unusual family, with those five brothers as different and interlinked as the fingers of a hand. She found them all extremely charming, but, when she looked at Arjuna, she needed no more. And at once the others were right there beside him: Yudhiṣṭhira, solemn and authoritative, something dark in the background; Bhīma, whom the others called Wolf's Belly and who looked like a tower; Nakula and Sahadeva, the twins, two thoroughbreds. "Who keeps them together? Their mother, Kuntī," thought Draupadī. She feared the moment she would have to meet her.

They left the city. Draupadī walked in Arjuna's footsteps, dreaming of her new life. Little did she know that she was never to recover that lightness and euphoria again. There was a tangle of cane. Their feet sank in the mud. Those who met them on the way thought they were a group of pilgrims. Arjuna was up front. He wanted to be the first to go to his mother. He came out of the forest in front of a low house surrounded by jars. They went into a huge, dark room and sensed a presence. "Mother, look what we've brought for you . . ." Without even looking up to where the door was filled with light, Kuntī said, "Share it out among yourselves." She meant whatever offering they had brought. But a mother's word is final: thus, Draupadī became the bride of all five brothers, shared equally among them. An inexhaustible bowl of rice. When night came, she lay at the feet of those five men she hardly knew, like a cushion.

. . .

They decided for how long and in what order Draupadī was to live with each of the brothers. Then they added just one rule: if one of the Pāṇḍavas disturbed Draupadī when she was alone with another of them, he would have to go off into the forest for twelve months. It happened to Arjuna.

He burst into the room to get the weapons beside the bed and interrupted Yudhiṣṭhira and Draupadī as they were making love. It was a conscious violation. If he hadn't done it, he wouldn't have been able to defend an unarmed brahman who was asking for his help. Yudhiṣṭhira tried to keep his brother from leaving, citing possible cavils that would have allowed him to get around the punishment. It was Arjuna who insisted on going. He wanted to find out what it meant to be alone in the world. To get away from brothers, cousins, mother. And even from that wonderful wife, whom he could hardly get near. He was looking for something exotic and out of the ordinary: experience, any experience, exposing himself to chance.

The spiteful said that no one had visited so many holy places and so many pretty women on the Island of the Jambū as Arjuna in the months of his travels. He wandered around like one of the many *brahmacārins*, students of *brahman*, devoted to purity and chastity. He bathed in the waters of the Utpalinī, the Alakanandā, the Kauśikī, the Gayā and the Gaṅgā, where Ulūpī, daughter of the King of the Nāgas, drew him underwater in a delirium of desire. Arjuna overcame his scruples when Ulūpī convinced him that the only thing that could save her was sex with himself. But then he immediately felt reassured when he saw that even on the bed of the great river, in the palace of the Nāgas, rites were being celebrated before the brahmanic fire. He didn't say, but he thought that the *dharma* could not survive unless allied to the Nāgas. Behind the visible hostility between spirit and serpent, the most ancient of pacts holds good. Then it was intriguing to spend a night of liquid love with a snake-girl. And he was to have another watery adventure too. One day in the swamps of the deep south, he found himself locked in a fight to the death with a crocodile. Then he saw the horrifying creature clutched in his arms turn into an Apsaras, who immediately spoke to him: "There are five of us. We are proud and beautiful, irreverent and cursed by an ascetic. My name is Vargā. We have been waiting for you to pay our ransom . . ." "Even a crocodile turns into a girl in his arms," the spiteful were quick to mock once more, as soon as word of this story began to make the rounds.

Arjuna's wanderings brought him to the shores of the western ocean. Kṛṣṇa found him at Prabhāsa. They embraced and sat down in the forest. As yet they had never spoken alone together. First Kṛṣṇa asked: "Why are you visiting all the holy places?" And Arjuna told him. They might have been friends swapping stories after a long separation. But Arjuna realized, and wanted to take his time over the realization, that Kṛṣṇa was the eye that watched his eye, the mind at the bottom of his own mind, that already knew everything Arjuna was seeking to know. With this companion, whether visible or invisible, his whole life changed. It wouldn't be enough now to be a warrior who excelled with his bow. Nor to fight for *dharma*, the Law. Before doing that, his mind must open out wide toward those two focal points. A sense of calm, unlike anything he had felt before, spread through Arjuna: now he knew that, whatever he did, Kṛṣṇa would never do anything against him, even if he were to oppose—and how often that was to happen—his thinking, his gaze, his words. And now those words seemed more and more spaced out, as if in the intervals between them Arjuna were being absorbed into the other watching him in the silence. Kṛṣṇa broke into his reflections: "Let's go up to Mount Raivataka. There's a big festival on, with actors and dancers."

. . .

The mountain was lit up by torches like a huge hall. The young Vṛṣṇis were milling around, showing off garlands and bracelets. Arjuna wandered among them, cheerful and intrigued, Kṛṣṇa behind him. Suddenly he saw Subhadrā and stopped stock-still in the throng. She was beauty incarnate. But something else too: she was a propitious creature. Time opened up before her. Behind him Arjuna heard Kṛṣṇa's quiet, suggestive voice ask: "Why on earth is a powerful ascetic like yourself, someone accustomed to the forest, suddenly getting mixed up in love? That is Subhadrā, my sister."

Now everything happened very quickly. Arjuna said: "When I look at her, the earth smiles at me." Kṛṣṇa had already assumed an absorbed, pensive expression, as when he used to speak of the art of government. He said: "For a *kṣatriya*, the rules recommend a *svayaṃvara*. But one can never be quite sure which suitor will win. Someone else might be preferred to yourself. However, a *kṣatriya* may resort to abduction. That is also allowed. Carry off the beautiful Subhadrā. That's my advice. I'll look after everything else."

At the end of twelve months, Arjuna went back to his brothers and Draupadī. He had Subhadrā beside him, dazzling in a red silk robe. Draupadī looked at Arjuna and said: "When you undo a bundle, it's the oldest knot that comes loose first." Arjuna tried to object, as though duty bound to do so. Proud and tough, Draupadī seemed not to hear.

Some time later, Arjuna went to Draupadī again with Subhadrā. He had got her to dress as a *gopī*. If possible, she was even more beautiful. She refracted a distant happiness: that of her brother Kṛṣṇa's infancy. This time it was Subhadrā who spoke to Draupadī. She said: "I am Subhadrā, your servant." Draupadī smiled at her: "May your husband at least be without rivals . . ." In an earnest voice, Subhadrā answered: "So be it . . ." From then on the women quarreled no more. A few months later Subhadrā gave birth to Abhimanyu.

. . .

Nothing ever generated so much curiosity in Indra's heaven as the imminent arrival of Arjuna. "His son! His son! His favorite!" was the general murmur. Meanwhile Arjuna looked around, among the peaks, moraines, and dark blue valleys of the Himālaya, where he had discovered terror and absolute solitude. Now he greeted the mountains, at once grateful and moved. "I have been happy among you . . . ," he said. "It was here I discovered *tapas* and practiced it until the forests began to steam. Here I sat motionless for months, eating the wind. Here countless ephemeral creatures passed before my eyes, creatures with no *karman,* obedient only to the one imperative: "Live! Die!" Here I fought a wild hunter who reduced me to a bloody lump of sacrificial meat before giving me the weapon that surpasses all others, the severed head of Brahmā, a weapon that can be wielded with a thought, with a glance of the eyes, with a word or with a bow." He went on with a meticulous list of his solitary adventures. Heaven didn't seem to hold much attraction for him.

It was then that Mātali, the charioteer, burst out of the clouds unfurling the deep blue Vaijayanta standard above a chariot waving with snakes. "Your father is calling you," he said. "He wants all the Celestials to welcome you . . ." As the chariot rose with him on board, Arjuna saw thousands of other chariots wandering in the air. They shone brightly, so that already the sun and the moon seemed superfluous. Mātali acted as his guide, pointing them out to him, telling him the names of those they belonged to. For the most part they were sages of olden times, whose names Arjuna barely knew. He realized the chariot was getting close to the divine residence when a vast, white, four-tusked elephant appeared. "It must be Airāvata . . . ," thought Arjuna, and suddenly there before him was Amarāvatī, city of Indra. A noisy, colorful crowd had gathered to greet him. It wasn't so much the gods, whom he gradually began to recognize, that struck him as the multitudes of Gandharvas and Apsaras. Airy, vibrant, and fickle, more beautiful than the gods perhaps, these beings seemed to him the natives of the sky. Then he saw his father, under a tall, white umbrella, screened by a fan that gave off perfume. The Gandharvas' hymns rose and fell frenetically, while the Apsaras swayed slowly on their hips. No one had ever seen so much tenderness in Indra's eyes. He went to Arjuna, took him by the hand, stroked his cheeks and long arms. Then as, cautiously, almost incredulously, the king of the gods moved a hand toward Arjuna's chest, at the same time breathing in the smell of his head, his open palm could be seen to bear the scars left by thunderbolts. Indra led his son toward the throne and sat down beside him. For Arjuna this was perhaps the first moment of unthreatened beatitude in his life. Nothing was asked of him. The weight of duty was lifted. The sky was a spectacle decked out for this occasion.

He watched the Gandharvas busying themselves with basins full of water to wash his feet and refresh him after his long trip. Arjuna's eyes took in the seething circle of the Apsaras. In a low voice he asked Mātali, who had stayed close beside him, what their names were. Mātali listed them: "Ghṛtācī, Menakā, Rambhā, Pūrvacitti, Svayaṃprabhā, Urvaśī, Miśrakeśī, Ḍuṇḍu, Gaurī, Varūthinī, Sahā, Madhurasvarā . . ." And he went on. Arjuna couldn't follow. Some of the names evoked stories he had heard as a child, of princesses, *ṛṣis*, warriors, hunters. But these heroines seemed to have returned to their places in a chorus of dancers, as if together they made up just one single story, one single face, happy to merely refract and sparkle. "I must learn how to recognize them . . . ," thought Arjuna. And his eyes went on running tirelessly across those faces, those bodies. In their exultation, their splendor, the eyes he met had something vacuous and jaded about them, as though they were no more than inset stones. Even the swelling breasts held high in pearl bodices, even the soft thighs seemed painted. Until Arjuna's eyes were compelled to settle on those of one Apsaras among many. "High cheekbones, like mine," he thought. And he realized his gaze was sinking into eyes as remote and unruffled as the surface of a lake. "Who is that Apsaras with the high cheekbones?" he asked Mātali. "It's Urvaśī," said the charioteer.

"What to do in heaven?" wondered Arjuna in his rooms, his thoughts already turning to the brothers he had left behind. "Receive gifts of arms," his father would soon explain. Indra trained him in the use of the *vajra*, the thunderbolt. "But that's not everything," he said. "Now you must learn the dances and hymns that men don't know." He nodded to a Gandharva who was following him. "This is Citrasena. He will be your friend and teacher. Trust him."

Arjuna soon learned to sing and dance the way they do in Indra's heaven, something men know nothing of. Every day he practiced along with the Gandharvas and the Apsaras. But he couldn't relax. He kept thinking of his brothers, homeless and persecuted back on earth. Citrasena understood and was good at distracting him. "What's the name of that Apsaras who just went by and turned to look at us?" Arjuna asked one day. "It's Urvaśī," answered Citrasena. Meanwhile, he was thinking: "If anyone can keep Arjuna in heaven, it's Urvaśī." Citrasena went straight off to talk to Indra. And he was given the task of acting as go-between and bringing Arjuna and Urvaśī together as lovers.

Urvaśī welcomed him as if she already knew the mission Indra had given him. "Citrasena, no need to waste words. I've seen how handsome Arjuna is. And you know I love men," she said with a joyless smile. Then, in a lower voice, as though speaking to herself: "I'm compelled to love men . . ." That very evening, smelling sweetly of sandalwood paste and with a faint tinkling of anklets, a slightly tipsy Urvaśī went to Arjuna's rooms. Far from being delighted, Arjuna was overcome by a new kind of terror. Without thinking, he lowered his eyes and whispered a few deferential words. In her contralto voice, Urvaśī said: "When you arrived and had hundreds of celestial beings all around you, you looked at me just once, with your unyielding eyes. I remembered that look. I've known it for hundreds of years. Then Citrasena came to visit me and said that you had remembered it too. Now I am here . . ." The more Urvaśī spoke, the more terrified Arjuna seemed to be. He stuffed his fingers in his ears like a child. Then he said: "It's true that I looked at you. But then I realized: you are the mother of the lunar dynasty. And I am the last of the children of the lunar dynasty. You are my mother. How could I embrace you?" Urvaśī's eyes were sorrowing and cold. She said: "We Apsaras know no bonds. Our realm is emotion. We abhor usefulness. Yet if you men have fire on earth, it is only because one day long ago I left the man who desired me and was your ancestor. It was my absence that unleashed fire in the world. It still burns today. It will burn forever. This time it is I who follow you. Don't reject me." Arjuna had grown more obdurate: "I owe you nothing but respect." Urvaśī was livid now. "You are insulting a woman your father has offered you. You are rejecting a woman you desire. Well then, you will live like a woman among women, and you will dance with them. You are not fit for anything else." Then Urvaśī vanished in the night.

Still pale with anger, Urvaśī undressed mechanically, scornful syllables on her lips. Then she lay on her bed and recovered that expression that many admired so much and said was hers alone: one of immense distance and sadness. She thought: "But no one looks more like Purūravas than Arjuna." Then once again, as had happened countless times before and for hundreds of years, she withdrew into the lake of memory.

No sooner had Urvaśī gone than Arjuna felt annoyed with himself. He knew he would never see her astonishing beauty again. And why have so many scruples and be so nervous over an ancestor of fifteen generations back? Yet some powerful instinct had ordered him not to touch her. As he was thinking, he had a hand on his right thigh. Something tingled under his fingertips, like an ancient wound. With it came the fleeting vision of a scene, though he couldn't remember when or where. Two young, almost identical men sitting on a rocky seat. Air bright, as in a mirror. In the distance, the roar of rushing waters. All around, a whirl of perfumes, of Apsaras. But the two men were unimpressed. Suddenly one of them slapped his thigh. A tiny female figure popped out, ornate and perfect. Then it grew bigger and pointed up to the sky. He recognized her, and murmured: "Urvaśī, you from the thigh, *ūru* . . . You are also my daughter . . ." But he wasn't able to articulate that thought and fell fast asleep.

For a year Arjuna lived as a eunuch in the court of King Virāṭa. His hair hung down on his shoulders, long earrings twinkling in his curls. His wrists were circled by gold bracelets encrusted with mother-of-pearl. He kept his arms covered to hide the scars that came from using his bow. Virāṭa couldn't believe it when he saw him. This strikingly feminine figure, he realized, was the warrior himself. Indeed, with senile rashness he offered to grant him his kingdom, thus cutting out his son. But Arjuna insisted: "I am a eunuch. All I want is to teach music and dance to your daughter Uttarā."

It was a year of subtle, ceaseless rapture, and an arduous, exhausting trial. In the evenings Arjuna told stories of monsters, princesses, and warriors to a small group of girls who adored him as soldiers do their leader. The days he spent in the dance pavilion. Virāṭa's kingdom was rich and troubled. Blind and deaf to the spirit, life followed physiological rhythms. The only people Arjuna saw were girls who imitated his movements. The torture was Uttarā. Arjuna immediately promised himself he would never so much as touch her. Yet both had the impression of being constantly glued together, as when Arjuna sang and Uttarā's voice sang over his. "Uttarā, Uttarā . . ." Arjuna found himself murmuring in the long stillness of the afternoons, immersed in the sticky air as though in an amniotic liquid.

"The Extreme, the Ultimate, She-who-comes-from-the-north, She-who-takes-us-across, Uttarā, Uttarā . . ." He knew that all he could do as far as his pupil princess was concerned was fantasize, feverishly. And he imagined her as a creature come down from Uttarakuru, that square land no one had ever trod but which everyone always told stories about, in the far north. His wanderings had brought him to its borders. Indeed now that he had visited both the watery depths and Indra's heaven, and had had his fill of both of them, Uttarakuru was the only name still pregnant with the unknown for Arjuna. And then he recalled one of the many stories he had heard about the place as a child, a story that hadn't meant much to him at the time but that now came irrepressibly back. It was the story of two lovers who are born together and die together too, in each other's arms, after eleven thousand years—and those last thousand intrigued him. Then a flock of Bhāruṇḍa birds lifted the two bodies with their powerful beaks and laid them down in huge mountain caverns. Not a trace or memory was left of them. And it was this—not their immensely long lives—that elated him, as if for a moment he were putting down the burden of the impending war, of the *dharma,* of his brothers, of the reputation one was obliged to leave behind. Fascinated, he went on repeating: "Eleven thousand years and not a trace."

For Uttarā it was an even more tormenting time. Still barely more than a child, she was about to emerge from the cocoon of her invisible lovers. "The first to have her was Soma, then came the Gandharva. The third husband was Agni, the fourth is he who is born of man." The female mind knows no state without lovers but only a succession of states, where the son of man can only come fourth. Without knowing it, Uttarā had lived with Soma, with the Gandharva, with Agni. Now she was waiting for a man, any man. And she found him in Arjuna, this eunuch who was teaching her to sing, who passed on his voice to her like a shiver, and withdrew from every contact. "You are more elusive than a Gandharva, more distant than all the gods, yet I am inside you, modulated in your voice . . . ," murmured Uttarā, sobbing with happiness.

Then Arjuna understood just how far—and it was far indeed—Urvaśī's revenge would go. Because he had rejected her, as if she were his mother, now he must reject Uttarā, as if she were his daughter. Arjuna remembered some words Kṛṣṇa had once hurriedly spoken: "Even the curses we undergo must be of use to us." And slowly he thought up a plan. There was something about Uttarā that went beyond beauty. Something that was the beyond itself. Her pores emanated an odor he'd never come across before, a briny smell, the secret sign that she could ferry one to another world, the world that would come after the one about to be swallowed up. So Arjuna set about getting Uttarā to marry his adolescent son, Abhimanyu. That way he and she could go on exchanging lovers' glances without ever touching each other. Uttarā would give birth to the last of the Pāṇḍavas: Parīkṣit, who was born dead but then brought back to life by Kṛṣṇa. He then fathered Janamejaya, who would be the first to hear tell the adventures of his own ancestors: the *Mahābhārata*.

As a king, Janamejaya went to extremes. The powers of sacrifice and storytelling were stretched to the breaking point in him. It was Janamejaya who celebrated the sacrifice of the snakes, which was more an attempt at extermination than anything else. It was Janamejaya who encouraged Vaiśampāyana to get Vyāsa to tell him the story of the *Mahābhārata* so that Vaiśampāyana could then tell it to Janamejaya himself and to the many brahmans who took part in the sacrifice of the snakes. The extermination of the snakes was thus to alternate with the story of the extermination of the heroes. Each explained the other. Each became the other. And if both failed, it was because in each case something, someone, was left over, a residue: Janamejaya himself, last survivor of hero stock, who fought furiously to exterminate the snakes but didn't succeed, because once again one snake survived, the very moment it was about to fall in the fire. That snake was Janamejaya's archenemy, Takṣaka, who had already survived the burning of the Forest of Khāṇḍava. And two survivors will suffice to ensure that the stories go on, that they mingle with further sacrifices, further wars, further exterminations, to make sure that that interwoven and sovereign couple, king and snake, will go on propagating their kind. Until such time as they launch themselves on the waters once again, one supine on the other, god and snake, Viṣṇu and Śeṣa.

Janamejaya and his three brothers were crouched down during a *sattra*, one of those interminable sacrifices that obliged officiants, among other things, to creep rather than walk. They got down on the soil of Kurukṣetra that three generations before had been drenched in the blood of their forefathers on every side of the family, and that many more generations before had been trodden by the gods when celebrating their own different sacrifices there before escaping to the sky. It was a sultry day, the air quite still. Oppressed, the four brothers exchanged glances. A dog came up to them, a stray. It was shy, hesitant in its approach. Not only did it not dare to go and lick the offerings at the center of circle but it was even afraid to look at them. It moved sideways, head down. All of a sudden, as if in response to a sign given among them, Janamejaya's three brothers got up and began to beat the dog. Their long, thin sticks came down hard on its skinny flanks. The dog yelped and squealed, its only defense. Then it limped off and disappeared.

All that had happened for thousands of years in Kurukṣetra poured down on that moment, that scene, in a cataract of time. It was the moment the seer Vyāsa chose when he began to retrace the long stream, tell the story of all that had happened in Kurukṣetra. He chose the most futile moment and the most obscure so that something "immeasurable, sanctifying, purifying, atoning and blessing" might spread out from it, something "at whose expense the best of poets would live, as ambitious servants live at the expense of a noble patron."

Meanwhile the wounded, beaten dog had crept back to his mother, Saramā, she-dog of Indra, and was complaining to her. "You must have done something wrong," said Saramā. "I didn't do anything. I didn't lick the offerings. I didn't even look at them. But Janamejaya's brothers beat me." Then Saramā thought that Janamejaya, who had only looked on, deserved punishment. She paid no attention to his brothers. Watching the crime was worse than having done it.

There is no story so complicated as the *Mahābhārata.* And not just because of its length: three times as long as the Bible, seven times as long as the *Iliad* and the *Odyssey* put together. But why did Vyāsa choose this of all ways to tell the tale of a war fought between cousins in a plain of northwest India? Why is the frame in which the narrative is set so complicated that it alone would be enough to generate a sense of vertigo? Was it an artifice to allude to the infinite complication of existence? That would be banal—and wouldn't have required such an enormous effort. Even a tenth of the stories would be enough to generate the same impression. And the rest? Whatever happens in the Island of the Jambū, there's always a residue, an excess, something that overflows, goes beyond. Never the sharp profile, carved in the air, but long friezes, strips of stone bursting with action. They could have gone on forever. They are crests on the waves of a "migration," *saṃsāra.* The war between the Pāṇḍavas and the Kauravas is a "knot" (and the books that make up the *Mahābhārata* are called *parvans,* "knots"), just one of the innumerable stitches in the weave of everything with everything. Going back in time to what came before it, or forward a little, after it ended, we encounter a net that brushes against us on every side—and immediately we are struck by the conviction that we will never see the edges of that net, because there are no edges. And already this is a less obvious reflection: that end and beginning, terms the mind is ever toying with, don't, in themselves, exist at all. When the seers speak of the beginning, and push as far back as they can to where the existent and the nonexistent hadn't as yet been separated, even this point is not a beginning but a consequence. A residue. Something happened before—a whole other world happened before—in order to bring about that lump that drifts like flotsam on the waters. The beginning is a shipwreck. Such was the unspoken premise of the seers. And likewise of the *Mahābhārata.*

It was as if everybody were suddenly tired of doing things that had meaning. They wanted to sit down, in the grass or around a heap of smoldering logs, and listen to stories. And often the stories described the same rites the listeners were performing. But now those rites had become episodes inside long and bloody adventures, pretexts for skirmishes and treachery. The stories were no longer a breathing space within the ritual sequence, but the rite itself became an event within the stories, in the same way as a duel or a night of passion might be. So where did meaning lie? Did the rite give meaning to the stories? Or was it only the stories that meant something—using the rites as their material? And what if both rite and stories were meaningful—but their meanings opposed to each other? There was a back-and-forth between a clutter of too many meanings that canceled each other out, to the point of paralysis. The rites—it was well known—served to conquer the sky. And the stories? What were they for? After all, the whole tale of the *Mahābhārata* looked forward, as though to its final consequence, to the sacrifice of the snakes, the sacrifice that Janamejaya, the only surviving heir of the poem's heroes, had so much desired. That sacrifice was a long act of madness, not so much a ceremony as an attempt to wipe out a race—the snakes—at once more ancient than men and quite likely destined to survive them, since what are men in the end if not the dream of a god as he drifts around on a snake's coils? So was it that the meaning of the stories could only emerge within a meaningless sacrifice? But wasn't the meaninglessness of that sacrifice precisely the secret meaning that only someone who had followed the whole story of the *Mahābhārata* could grasp? And how had it come about that the fullness of ritual meaning ended up by bubbling over into meaninglessness? Whatever the answers, there was something new to come to terms with: gesture was no longer enough on its own. Now it had to be recounted too, along with other gestures—not all of them ritual. Now, as the times grew dark, as everything was turned upside down and inside out, one would have to begin—and end—with the stories of one of the many dynastic quarrels, one of the many wars that had taken place in an area that was really quite small, albeit long frequented by the gods. It was precisely this reckless profusion of random events and adventures that formed the cocoon that allowed the preceding body of knowledge, no longer able to exist alone, to be saved. Thus the *Mahābhārata* was called the Fifth Veda—and at its outset one reads these proud words: "A brahman who knows the Four Vedas with their branches and likewise the Upaniṣads but who does not know this poem possesses no knowledge whatsoever."

There came a day, as the times grew dark, when it became evident that the Four Vedas did not exhaust every form of knowledge. The hymns and ritual gestures went on, self-sufficient in their meaning. But, in the space between one ritual act and another, time was penetrated by the act of someone telling a story. Sitting in the ritual enclosure, people listened. For months and months, while the sacrificial horse wandered freely around, the king listened to stories. Then the horse was led back to him so that it could be killed, so that its lifeless body might lie a night with its hooves intertwined between the naked legs of the *mahiṣī*, the first queen. In the beginning, stories were no more than appendices to knowledge, but gradually the time given over to them grew in the gaps in that knowledge like grass between the bricks of the altar of fire, expanded and multiplied in stories that generated more stories, until they covered the whole construction of knowledge in which they had made their first furtive appearance as no more than an intermezzo. Thus literature began. Literature is what grows in the intervals of the sacrifice. First a grass, then a creeper that slips into the joints between the bricks and breaks them from within.

And there came another day when the bard Ugraśravas took advantage of a break in a twelve-year sacrifice celebrated in the Forest of Naimiṣa to begin the story of the war between the Kauravas and the Pāṇḍavas, a story he had heard Vaiśampāyana tell during a break in the sacrifice of the snakes celebrated by King Janamejaya, great-grandson of Arjuna and last descendant of the Pāṇḍavas, in the place later to be known as Taxila. And Vaiśampāyana had heard the story from Vyāsa, who had had an overall vision of the tale and was also involved in it himself, being grandfather to both the Pāṇḍavas and the Kauravas and likewise their counselor. Thus was the *Mahābhārata* told.

In the beginning the Āryas celebrated rites that were also hymns of praise that illuminated those rites. Then at a certain point they found themselves celebrating the same rites, but with their attention now concentrated on the intervals between the various phases of the rites, during which long stories of kings and warriors were told, stories in which the very rites that they were now celebrating played a part. The ancient hymns of praise were brought together in the Ṛg Veda, which is the knowledge of "praise," *ṛc*. The stories told in the intervals within the rites made up the *Mahābhārata*, the longest epos the world has ever known. As to how and why they passed from the one form to another, never a word was said. But though dates slither back and forth across a range of hundreds and hundreds of years, one can safely say that the two forms were separated by at least a thousand years. What happened in that time? Why were the hymns established and settled once and for all? Why did the stories of kings and warriors go on multiplying?

They moved on to the epic, which is the threshold of history, when they recognized that the system of ritual was producing aberrant results. Once it had been ritual that absorbed history: the *rājasūya*, the ceremony that consecrated the king, was full of hints of ambushes and forays and duels. But now the opposite was true. One began the celebration of a rite, Yudhiṣṭhira's *rājasūya*, for example, or, three generations later, Janamejaya's sacrifice of the snakes (during which Yudhiṣṭhira's sacrifice was already being recounted), and something escaped one's grasp: the consequences of the rite became facts now—a crude, poisonous category of events. And facts that were horribly visible. Draupadī abused, the Pāṇḍavas exiled, Arjuna cut down by his own son. Not only was ritual no longer able to contain violence but it multiplied it, like a machine—not of desire now but of disaster. Indeed, might not ritual itself, this faith in the absolute precision and truth of gesture, be the very thing, in the end, that was provoking the worst of evils?

Should they say all this? It would be a wicked notion, like so many others making the rounds of the city streets. Could they show it perhaps? But how does one show something? By having it happen. There is a point at which having something happen and recounting something converge: they both leave an impression on the mind. Telling a story is a way of having things happen at the highest possible speed, that of the mind. What was needed was a story that would bring all this out—that would itself be everything, since ritual deals with everything there is. But stories are always strictly referential, they are stories about one person or a few people in a certain segment of time, in a certain combination of circumstances that could not have occurred previously. So they needed a story that would bring together everything, going back in time and pointing forward in time, and have it run in a single channel, like the water that ran from a stone *yoni*. It was the story of five brothers in a kingdom of the plain that lies between the Gaṅgā and the Yamunā. Thus Vyāsa, who composed the story (who saw it), and played a part in it himself (after all, those five princes were his grandsons), said from within this story: "Whatever is here, on Law, on Profit, on Pleasure, and on Salvation, that is found elsewhere. But what is not here is nowhere else." It was the first of those "works that are too complete, works in which everything is expressed," that from then on were to present themselves from time to time, and imperiously so—right up to Wagner's *Ring* and Proust's *Recherche*—as somehow unavoidable, and that would quickly arouse not only admiration but also a certain intolerance, because they mean too much, even though, once one has listened to them, every other story "will sound harsh as the crow sounds to one after hearing the cuckoo sing."

The story of the last battles beneath the walls of Troy was told by Homer, a blind poet; the battle of Kurukṣetra was handed down to us as told to a blind king by someone to whom Vyāsa, the author of the narrative and likewise a participant in it, had granted the gift of total vision: the omniscience of the narrator. At some point of the act of narration, a point that may be moved but not eliminated, we find blindness. Is this simply because he who sees too much, as Tiresias did, is punished with loss of sight? Or is it a hint at something beyond that, something that has to do with storytelling itself? Narration presupposes the loss of the reality narrated. It makes no sense to tell a story to someone who witnessed it. But when the real has sunk away in space and time—and such is its most usual state—all that is left is a dark room where words ring in the ear. Whether that dark room be that of the author, as with the *Iliad*, or the first listener, as with the *Mahābhārata*, is hardly important: in the beginning, author and listener merge. All that is really required is a scene of blood confined in a perpetual light, and a gaze that follows fleeting signs forming against a shadowy backdrop.

. . .

Satyavatī was dark, beautiful, dressed in rags. She gave off a subtle odor of fish and musk. She didn't know it, but she was a princess. Every day she ferried pilgrims across the Yamunā. It seemed to her her life had always been made up of these monotonous gestures. She could recall nothing different in her infancy. The only thing the fisherman who had brought her up had told her was that she came from the river. Satyavatī felt this herself. But the fisherman hadn't explained exactly how he found her: on opening up the belly of a big fish that had swallowed the seed of King Uparicara. Satyavatī rarely spoke. She held out her hand to take the pilgrims' coins. She knew every inch of the Yamunā's banks: the canes, the mud, the stones. She had no desires and never thought of herself as any different from her boat or the water beneath it. One evening, toward sundown, she brought her boat to the bank to pick up her last cargo of pilgrims. But this time there was no one there. Then she saw a brahman detach himself from the shadows. His eyes were bright, and he carried a stick. Without a word he climbed into her boat. Satyavatī didn't wait and pushed off into the open water. As on hundreds of other occasions, she was gazing at the other bank, sensing the boat slide lightly along beneath her bare feet, when she felt two hands on the nape of her neck. A thread of fire darted up her back: or that was how she described this shiver she had never felt before. She didn't even turn her head as the brahman ran his hands slowly over her. Thin, strong fingers slipped inside her rags. They lay down on the bottom of the boat, which, without veering off course, was drifting toward the further bank. The two bodies mingled with the puddles and scraps of food on the bottom of the boat. They said nothing. Suddenly they found themselves looking up toward the overarching sky suffused by the last light of the sun, already set. Backs on the damp wood, like leaves on a stream, they thought, without telling each other, that they had never known such happiness—that every further happiness must be measured against this. The prow touched the shore. Satyavatī got to her feet to tie up. She held out her hand to the brahman as he left the boat. Her fingers closed on a coin. The brahman looked at her, without saying good-bye. Soon the forest's thick curtain had swallowed up his vigorous back. Thus was Vyāsa conceived, author of the *Mahābhārata* and grandfather of its protagonists.

If we go back to the origin of that imbalance that led to the war between the Pāṇḍavas and the Kauravas—and this is problematic, since anything any of the characters does reminds us of something their ancestors in various branches of the family did before them; and if then we restrict ourselves to following the line of Pāṇḍu, putative father of the Pāṇḍavas, each of whom bore the traits of one of five gods, we appreciate that that long convulsion of the lunar dynasty that lasted three generations and ended in massacre was triggered by the strange, unreasonable insistence of the king of the fishermen that the offspring of his adoptive daughter, Satyavatī, an abandoned orphan found in the belly of a fish and hence unable to claim any recognizable lineage, should prevail over all others. And, since Vyāsa later took Vicitravīrya's place when it came to generating children, it was he who championed the privilege of the *unknown line*. For if Satyavatī presented herself as an abandoned orphan, Vyāsa was the fruit of an illicit love between Satyavatī and an unknown brahman. As the decisive crisis approaches, two orphans, offspring of unknown fathers, assert themselves within the lineage that must save the *dharma*. The irony receives further and glorious confirmation when five gods take the place of Pāṇḍu, Vyāsa's son, as procreator, to generate the five princes who will fight in Kurukṣetra. Remote and legitimate, the lunar dynasty lurches toward the spasm of fratricidal war in a multiplication and exaltation of clandestine fathers, who endow it with impenetrable, shadowy powers, as though a slowly and laboriously achieved order needed to nullify itself in a welcoming darkness, the better to regenerate itself in the unknown.

• • •

Lying on a bed of arrows that passed right through his body and stuck deep in the ground, his head resting on yet more arrows that Arjuna had shot out of a sense of pity; tortured by hundreds of mortal wounds, which would not kill him until he himself decided to die, until, that is, fifty-six days had passed and the sun began its journey northward, Bhīṣma talked. He talked for hours and days. Around him, in a circle, were his Pāṇḍava nephews, Kṛṣṇa, a few princes, a few brahmans. Worn out, they took turns listening. Bhīṣma talked and talked. Nothing was too big, nothing too small to be named. The encyclopedia of encyclopedias flowed calmly from the mouth of the venerable warrior.

Bhīṣma talked without looking at his listeners. He kept his eyes fixed on the sky, on its blessed neutrality, which mirrored his own. He let the rains wash his bloody scabs. He exposed his old and withered skin to constant sunshine. The doctrines he had to set forth before dying were many and complex. They would be of service to those who had beaten and shot him: the Pāṇḍavas. And above all the greatest of them, Yudhiṣṭhira, who was overcome by anguish and kept saying: "This victory feels like a defeat." But the only essential thing was this: that the doctrines be set forth for a last time in every detail. Bhīṣma didn't expect that they would be understood in every detail. He knew that his function was first and foremost that of recapitulating an interminable sequence of truths and precepts that was already melting away in much the same manner as his life, the last hours of which were now trickling from his body. He was perfectly aware of being at the origin of everything that had happened at Kurukṣetra. For if his nephews had fought each other to the death, luring whole tribes and peoples to their deaths with them, if from now on all claims to legitimacy would forever be accompanied by the mocking shadow of doubt, then this was simply because one day he, Bhīṣma, fruit of King Śāṃtanu's love of a goddess, Gaṅgā, and hence legitimate and indisputable heir to the kingdom, had agreed to renounce not only his birthright but likewise the right to procreate, in order to allow his father to keep by his side that obscure ferry-girl Satyavatī, with her subtle odor of fish and musk, who had usurped the role of his mother and, obedient to the inflexible will of the king of the fishermen who had adopted her, was to become the mother of Śāṃtanu's successor. At the time Bhīṣma was called Devavrata. But when he made a public declaration to the effect that he was simultaneously renouncing both sovereignty and offspring, after uttering this denial at once so unnatural and unreasonable, depriving him as it did of what almost everyone yearns for, power and women, while nevertheless leaving him in the midst of power and women insofar as he was to continue to carry out his work as chief counselor—after uttering this denial Bhīṣma heard a sigh and a word: "This man is terrible, *bhīṣmo 'yam!*" And from then on, he was simply called Bhīṣma, the Terrible. Why did he do it? Was it just an excess of filial devotion? If so, why was he so determined later on to ensure that the heirs of Satyavatī should in their turn have descendants? Why did he go so far as to abduct the three princesses of Kāśī with their enchanting and childish names—Ambā, Ambikā, Ambālikā—to marry them to one of those heirs? And how was it that he attracted the savage hatred of one of those girls, Ambā, who thought him the most vile of rapists, when on the contrary he observed a strict vow of chastity? And why, finally, when Vicitravīrya, Satyavatī's last son, died, worn out by his pleasures but childless all the same, did Bhīṣma, again obedient to his vow, refuse to take the place of his half brother, agreeing instead that the queens should accept the repellent embrace of Vyāsa, Satyavatī's illegitimate and neglected son, to bring forth their offspring with his seed?

No one knew. Least of all Bhīṣma himself, despite the fact that everybody bowed down before his knowledge, elusive as it was. "The moment comes," thought Bhīṣma, "when the sky no longer touches the earth, just as my head and back, resting on these arrows, are not touching it now. It is a terrible moment, it is Bhīṣma's moment. The words of the sky are still there, but they no longer touch the grass. Then the sky may seem empty. Yet its power is intact and unappeased. But it is no longer recognized. And, unrecognized, it becomes even more cruel. That is why no war was ever so bloody and treacherous as the war fought between my noble nephews. And I lived here and walked this earth so that all this could be prepared, so that it might come to pass." He thought this in the last watch of the night, with the sky graying in a first hint of dawn and the group around him much thinned out. Weary with standing still, those remaining looked on with solemn faces, while Bhīṣma stared at the sky and his mind wandered far away to where no one wished to follow, nor he himself wished to be followed.

An invocation may one day become a person. "Ambā! Ambikā! Ambālikā!" groaned the *mahiṣī,* thighs tightly pressed to those of the sacrificed horse. That tortured cry to "mother," *ambā,* to her diminutives, *ambikā, ambālikā,* and to the waters as surging wave, *ambhas,* was embodied, thrice embodied, in the princesses of Kāśī abducted by Bhīṣma to become the queens of a king who secretly tormented women's hearts but did not procreate: Vicitravīrya. One night, after Ambikā and Ambālikā had been widowed, they saw a shaggy, smelly man coming to their bed. Stiff and silent, they suffered his embrace. They could no longer groan, calling out to a lost mother, because they themselves were that mother. The world had shrunk: there was no other to call out to anymore.

Ambika closed her eyes in coitus—and conceived a blind boy: Dhṛtarāṣṭra. Ambālikā turned white when Vyāsa penetrated her—and conceived a disturbingly pale child: Pāṇḍu. Neither of the women recognized the dead horse or the compiler of the Vedas, in Vyāsa. This outrageous expedient was the method the *dharma* had chosen for avoiding extinction. More and more, paradox, trickery, and horror had to be treated with prudence, and even delicacy. They might always turn out to be the last resource for saving the *dharma.*

. . .

More than love or war, what really set stories going were curses, and, though these were of secondary importance, the vows and boons that often served to ease a curse. It wasn't only men's lives that teemed with curses but the gods' too. Destiny's turning points, a little attention shows, occur at the moment when a great caster of curses—and they are generally brahmans, and in particular seers—pronounces the fatal words. Whether anybody realizes a curse has been cast or not makes no difference at all. Śakuntalā suffered the pains of lost love for many years as a result of a curse she was quite unaware of. For those who told these stories—Vyāsa, for example, who was himself in a position to pronounce terrible curses—cursing was obviousness itself, life's bedrock, and above all precious, the most precious formal artifice for rendering life complex in a way consonant with its nature. The same texts that spend pages over every single action, describing everything down to the last detail, have nothing at all to say about the curse that prompted it, as if this were self-evident. And it is not just individual destinies that depend on curses but likewise the destiny of the world. More often than not a cosmic cataclysm is unleashed by some futile gesture that nobody has noticed.

Despite their ability to resort to metamorphosis when, for all their overwhelming powers, they find themselves in trouble, the gods can do little or nothing against a curse. Before they can free themselves, they must suffer like the merest of mortals. And when they appear among men, it is usually not to come to their aid but to free themselves from a curse. Even Viṣṇu's various *avatāras,* generally presented as those great deeds that periodically saved the world, were, as some saw it, first and foremost something he was condemned to by a curse.

The defining characteristic of the curse, or so it seemed, was this: that it always worked. As one approaches the realm of the curse, one comes up against the invisible wall of certainty. But what is invulnerable certainty? The supremacy and pervasiveness of the mind. The curse is a purely mental act. And while one day this kind of act would be considered by definition ineffective, in those days it was precisely its mental character that made it seem efficacy itself. That is why the custodians of the curse are mostly brahmans, creatures of the mind. They owe their authority, their power, and even their name to their contact with *brahman*—and to nothing else. *Brahman* strikes more swiftly than the sword. So the brahman has no need of the sword. For a word articulated in his mind already conceals "a sharp-bladed razor." More than their internal quarrels or their perpetual war with the Asuras, what most frightened the gods were certain encounters, above all with solitary old men who might very well appear to be the merest beggars or pilgrims, but would then all at once start darting flames from their eyes if something should irritate them. More terrifying and impenetrable than all the others was the brahman Durvāsas.

Durvāsas was a "portion," *aṃśa,* a splinter, a glowing coal of Śiva. He too was a *ṛṣi,* but not a master of mind and gesture, like Yājñavalkya, or one of those who saw the hymns, like Viśvāmitra, or a weaver of plots and poetry, like Vyāsa. Durvāsas's realm lay beyond the word, in the fury and excess that lie behind the many-colored curtain of the world of appearance. Curses and boons were the only ways he showed himself, as if in him the world were reduced to but two elements: prodigy and punishment. Everything was a source of offense for Durvāsas. There was nothing that might not spark his retaliation. Once he met Indra and offered his elephant, Airāvata, a garland of flowers. But the garland bothered the animal. Slowly, using his trunk while Indra looked on, Airāvata got the garland to slither to the ground. Immediately Śrī, the Splendor of the World, plunged into the ocean. Indra sensed that he was about to be stripped of his power. He looked around and saw nature desolate, buckling under some obscure burden. The garland rejected by the sluggish elephant had been consigned to Durvāsas directly from heaven. That garland was Śrī. Now the world would be bereft of splendor. It went back to being an arid wasteland. It was because of this petty incident that the gods had to undertake the toughest of all their labors, the enterprise that was supremely theirs: the churning of the ocean.

If Durvāsas showed himself at all, the meaning was clear enough: something ferocious and devastating was about to happen. In this emaciated brahman the gods were obliged to recognize spirit in its most remote and rugged form: flare, willfulness, devouring fire, at once out of control and inexhaustible. Every time history tightened in a noose, Durvāsas was there. Whether wayfarer or guest, the more casual his involvement, the greater the crisis it provoked. Thus when time was ripe for the massacre at Kurukṣetra, Durvāsas arrived at the court of Kuntibhoja. Everybody served him eagerly, but they were faking. And Durvāsas never failed to recognize haste and ill will behind apparently abject deference. Only one little girl came to wait on his orders as if nothing in all the world could be more gratifying. But that wasn't enough, because Durvāsas "more than anything else enjoyed putting people to the test." One day, climbing out of his bath, Durvāsas found his boiled rice served in a scorching hot bowl. Without so much as a word, he raised impatient eyes to the little Kuntī. Then Kuntī got down on all fours, like a stool, to let Durvāsas put the bowl on her back. The muslin cloth she was wearing quickly burned through, exposing the skin. Kuntī suffered in silence. Durvāsas ate his rice, slowly.

At last the day came when Durvāsas was ready to set off again. He called Kuntī and said: "Child, listen to this *mantra.* One day, you will be able to use these words to evoke the gods. You will be able to touch them. Those whom others cannot even see will be your lovers, if you like." As soon as Kuntī had learned the *mantra,* Durvāsas was gone, without saying good-bye. Years later, Yudhiṣṭhira, Bhīma, and Arjuna formed in Kuntī's womb, each conceived from divine seed. In order for the twins Nakula and Sahadeva to be conceived, Kuntī revealed the Aśvins' *mantra* to Mādrī, Pāṇḍu's second wife.

Nārada had barely said good-bye, and already Kṛṣṇa was nostalgic for that old gossip who knew everything about everybody in every inch of the Island of the Jambū, and other worlds too, and went from one world to another as if they were different parts of the same town, cunning and curious, infatuated by detail, hardly interested in exercising his own power, so entertaining did he find it to watch others exercising theirs, intrigued above all by stories involving women. Stories without women, he maintained, got boring after a while, perhaps because he had once been a woman himself, not to mention a worm and a monkey, and this explained why, whatever the subject under discussion, he was never reduced to amazement and debated with great precision, as if delicately shaking the dust from some past experience or other.

Nārada had barely said good-bye when another brahman arrived at Kṛṣṇa's palaces. He couldn't have been more different from the one who had just left. Dressed in rags, he stepped gloomily forward on legs thin and long as a wading bird's. His skin was burnished with a hint of dirty green. His lips moved in a dismal cadence. "Who will welcome the brahman Durvāsas to their home?" These were the only words anyone could make out. They were spoken with a malevolent chuckle. No one volunteered. They sensed the brahman's unreasonable rage and didn't want to provoke him. But Kṛṣṇa went to speak to him, offering a calm welcome, as if unaware of anything out of the ordinary. Meanwhile he was thinking: "The Guest again. This will be the hardest of all trials. No vow could be so strict. The Guest is the unknown. He takes precedence over all else, prevails over all else." Kṛṣṇa at once called for Rukmiṇī, first among his wives. Rukmiṇī appeared in all her splendor and asked the guest to order everything that would give him pleasure. Durvāsas didn't even seem to notice her. His eyes wandered among the ornaments, as if through a break of dry bush. When they offered him all kinds of delicious food, he ate with inhuman voracity. He haunted the palace, paying no attention to anybody, Kṛṣṇa not excepted. Every now and then a servant would find him laughing at nothing in a corner, making a sound like dried leaves. But others found him weeping copious tears.

When he lay on the ground, they mistook him for a heap of rags. He would go for days without eating. Kṛṣṇa had given the strictest orders: everybody must obey him in everything. Once, a thick smoke spread through the corridors. It was coming from Durvāsas's room. When they got there, they found the brahman had set his bed alight and gone off. Some hours later, they caught sight of him again in the shadow of an alcove, deep in thought, as if he had never moved. No one asked him anything. On other days he would go into a room and hurl anything he could lay hands on against the walls. Finally there came the morning when he wanted to sit at Kṛṣṇa and Rukmiṇī's table. The conversation was desultory but apparently normal enough. Then he wanted rice cooked in milk. Immediately the servants offered him this common food, the *pāyasa*, that Kṛṣṇa had ordered to be kept ready along with countless others to satisfy Durvāsas's every whim. The brahman then ordered Kṛṣṇa to undress. His tone was brusque. "Come here," he said. Kṛṣṇa stood naked in front of him. Durvāsas ordered him to smear the white mush all over himself. Kṛṣṇa maintained an unworried expression. He was thinking of when, as a child, he used to climb on the kitchen stool to steal butter, and how some would always be left on his face. He avoided looking toward Rukminī. Kṛṣṇa's body turned white, smeared all over.

Now every pore of Kṛṣṇa's skin was covered. Only the soles of his feet on the cold floor had not been spread with cream of rice. Durvāsas's eyes were veiled, absent. In a hoarse voice he ordered Rukmiṇī to undress. Rukmiṇī couldn't help sneaking a resigned glance at Kṛṣṇa, who paid no attention. He stood beside her like a puppet. One by one Rukmiṇī removed her delicate, sumptuous clothes. Durvāsas didn't even look at her body. Meticulously, he began to spread the *pāyasa* over her. The cream was still dripping from her nipples when Durvāsas ordered a cart to be prepared. The servants obeyed. Then Durvāsas yoked up Rukmiṇī, cracked his whip, and set off south. Kṛṣṇa walked behind. Now and then Durvāsas would yell out like a rude cart driver and bring down his whip on Rukmiṇī's shoulders, leaving pink welts that mingled with the white of the rice and trickles of sweat. Then he got off the cart and started walking in the same direction. Naked, white, impassive, Kṛṣṇa and Rukmiṇī followed him. All at once Durvāsas stopped and turned to them. He saw they were bowing slightly in his direction. He said: "Now go back. You will find everything I broke is whole again. You"—this to Rukmiṇī—"will ever give off a fragrant odor. Your beauty shall not wither. You will follow Kṛṣṇa even after death." Then he spoke to Kṛṣṇa: "You will die like any other man, because you didn't smear the soles of your feet. But what does it matter? You have understood. Go in the company of this *mantra*, which you must recite in silence." He murmured some formula or other. "As long as there is food, you will be loved. As long as there is a just man, you will have glory." They were his last words. Already he was veiled in flame. Then he disappeared.

Kṛṣṇa and Rukmiṇī walked back to the palace in silence, their bodies encrusted with dust and rice. They found everything intact, as if Durvāsas had never stayed with them.

The approach of the last age began to make itself felt. This was the Age of the Losing Throw, the *kaliyuga*, when one development became clear to all: sacrifice was no longer effective. Risk par excellence, first of all voyages, and hence with every chance of becoming first of all shipwrecks, sacrifice, this undertaking within which exactitude and truth might be measured, could no longer hold up on its own, in its keen-edged abstraction. It turned into war. But that wasn't all. War and sacrifice easily become two sides of the same coin. Sacrifice became the failed war. An inexact, fraudulent war, and necessarily so, a war that ended up looking like pure massacre. That was what took place between the Pāṇḍavas and the Kauravas.

What used to happen before an *avatāra*, before these "descents" of the god upon the earth in time of disorder? The rites. And they were enough. But what were they? Reality elaborated in thought to the point of exhaustion, everything, every moment, every nook and cranny, articulated in the mind. A constant preoccupation that distracted one from any other conquest. But clearly something eluded this thinking. Something bubbled over. Or sifted down like some poisoned, indestructible dregs. So it was that one day gods or men or the earth itself, oppressed by the sheer weight of too many creatures, went to Brahmā to ask for help. Upon which Brahmā declared himself impotent. Impotence had dogged him from the beginning—perhaps precisely because he was a creator god. Brahmā relied too much on thought, thought was his element, as other gods had their elements in some power of nature. And what Brahmā thought immediately became ritual formula. But that didn't mean its effectiveness was assured. Brahmā was the first to have doubts about the efficacy of the rites. His mind frequently dwelled on the problem. He realized that he tended to associate it with certain episodes of his life: the flight of his born-of-the-mind children, his desire for a girl's body, Śiva's severed fifth head. All stories that made a mockery of him. He looked on those seeking his help, and they were many, with feelings of detached sympathy. He felt sorry for them, petitioners to a helpless king. Then one day he gestured toward Viṣṇu and said: "Ask him. He will find a way to do what I cannot." Then he fell back into his lucid melancholy.

During the first seven *avatāras*, events followed a coherent sequence: an evil king (though he might just as well be a saint) achieved excessive power, disturbed Indra's love-making, and hounded him out of heaven. Order was overturned. A figure of even greater power had to come to establish a new order. The *avatāra.* The repertory of possible events offered a great variety of plots, but the decisive steps were always duels, challenges, curses, boons, escapes, exile. Only when one arrives at Kṛṣṇa, and then the Buddha, in the eighth and ninth *avatāra,* does everything become irrevocably complicated and far more ambiguous. There are still duels and cosmic contests. But they are no longer decisive. What is decisive is what takes place in the spectator of the duels, that is Kṛṣṇa, with Arjuna fastened to him. And with the Buddha a further and more disquieting level is reached. Now, seen from without, nothing happens at all. Life goes on in all its mediocrity, a mere succession of unimportant events. There is no longer a cosmos, nor even an empire, just a provincial backwater. There is the usual grating comedy between rich and poor. Some begging monk or other in the midst of it. Of duels and wars not a mention now. Everything seems to be portrayed in the mind of a monk, the Buddha, whom one may come across in the shade of a tree or walking some beaten track along with everybody else. Yet the duel goes on with new names, different gestures—in the sealed chamber of that mind.

Thus began the age of Kṛṣṇa: men yearned for stories, interwoven stories, characters who needn't always be the Devas, the Asuras, and the *ṛṣis.* They could no longer sustain Vedic abstraction, nor the fact that the entire world and everything that happened in it should end up as glosses on an everlasting ritual. Not everything, they thought, frightened almost by their own blasphemous boldness, could converge in the construction of the altar of fire. Now the bricks would be so many stories, and to bake them, to give them substance, the gods agreed to come down to the earth again, injecting a "portion," *aṃśa,* of themselves into those heroes who would fight at Kurukṣetra, on that great open space, that battlefield that reminded the gods of something else, for in a remote past they had held a sacrifice there. Or was it from there perhaps that they had ascended to heaven, and won their immortality? They couldn't rightly remember, so much time had gone by.

"Ritual is dangerous," Vyāsa reminded Yudhiṣṭhira before the ceremony that would consecrate him as king. It was a warning that might seem pointless, obvious. The *ṛṣis* had always spoken of ritual as a voyage over which shipwreck ever loomed. But that danger had to do with some eventual shortcoming in precision of thought and gesture. Whereas now Vyāsa was alluding to a new danger: in one phase of the *rājasūya*, the regal consecration, there was a game of dice that the king had to win, by cheating if necessary. In a game one is aware of tension, yet the rite is still, as always, detached from the world of fact, as if keeping itself two palm breadths above the ground. It cannot allow itself to be invaded. But with Yudhiṣṭhira the opposite happened. He lost his game and everything else with it. Or rather: he really lost twice. What went wrong? Like capricious demons, the dice had smashed the ritual order from within. They were no longer a prescribed act, but agents of the invading *daiva*, of that "fate" that operates wherever and however it will, both outside and inside the rite. No finery of thought could stop it. It was a wild horse. Now the *daiva* acted alone: all it needed were those tiny, rolling nuts. One day, in a sudden rage, King Virāṭa hurled the dice in Yudhiṣṭhira's face. Blood began to drip from his nose. Draupadī hurried to collect it in a golden cup to prevent it from touching the ground. But this was the warning that soon blood would touch the ground, and drench it too. The last barrier between game and blood was down now.

In the immensity of its structure the *Mahābhārata* can be seen as an overwhelming demonstration of the futility of conflict. Of every conflict. Was the *dharma* really renewed when the Pāṇḍavas at last, and at a cost of countless dead, succeeded in defeating the Kauravas? Hardly. Peace was a half life, still oppressed by memory. The *dharma* did reign again, but as it were for a fleeting interval. There was still something brooding that would have to burst out. Thirty years after the end of the war, the Vṛṣṇis, Kṛṣṇa's people, wiped themselves out in a massacre that began as the merest drunken brawl. It was as though the war that had come before, conducted as it was along the lines and rhythms of a complex ceremony, had only served to offer a pretext for this stupid slaughter.

Throughout, the *Mahābhārata* is the story of the *dharma*'s being sick, exhausted, weighed down by the impediments that history accumulates along its way. It is not the victory of the *dharma* over the *adharma* but their near equality and convergence in a disaster that is prelude to the world's taking a new breath, in a desert scenario, where only the tiniest residue will testify, through the word, to past vicissitudes. Every victory of Hero over Monster or Order over Disorder or Good over Evil is ingenuous when set against this vision, because this alone accommodates Kāla, Time, which generates constant inequalities, but only as a stratagem for arriving later at a leveling on a vast scale. While the only irreversible inequality is the one that only now became clear: detachment, the doctrine that Kṛṣṇa passed on to Arjuna before his hostile relatives, lined up for battle.

"The Law is subtle, great king, and we do not know its course," said Yudhiṣṭhira when obliged to persuade Draupadī's father that his daughter be shared equally among the five Pāṇḍava brothers instead of belonging to the one, Arjuna, whom Draupadī had chosen at the *svayaṃvara*. And how many more times, later on, and on how many other occasions, many of them bloody, would he return to that observation concerning the subtlety of the *dharma*. Excessively subtle, hard to follow, or even simply to recognize, and this for the man who was Dharma's son: Yudhiṣṭhira. It was as if the *dharma* were being woven, thread after thread, since time began—and now those threads entangled everyone, on every side, like an oppressive net. Once caught in the net, anyone who moved too brusquely risked being strangled by its threads. Yudhiṣṭhira's normal state of mind was this: he was always speaking of the *dharma,* but he was always thinking of something that lay beyond it: death or liberation. Which was why his remarks about the *dharma* were so often the prelude to Yama's devastations, as if for him law and death tended to merge, to the point of coinciding. There was something distant and melancholy about Yudhiṣṭhira—something that was never more obvious than when he eagerly joined in the fatal game of dice with the Kauravas, loving to play but not knowing how. That game was the "lesion," *bheda,* that would never be healed: the proof that fate may not only ignore the *dharma* but even hold it in contempt. Perhaps all Yudhiṣṭhira wanted was to arrive at that irreparable evidence.

In the war of the enemy cousins, the heartrending figures, those who generate the most pathos, are the ones who abandoned the roles assigned to them by birth: Bhīṣma, the *kṣatriya* who behaved like a brahman, pronouncing the loftiest of thoughts while stretched on a bed of arrows; Droṇa, the brahman who became master of arms to both the Pāṇḍavas and the Kauravas and taught them how to eliminate all around them, hence the world, so as to concentrate on one tiny point, the target; and Karṇa, the obscure *sūta,* the charioteer who didn't know he was the son of Sūrya, the Sun, and who became an invincible warrior, the only one who was a match for Arjuna. They had been the first to sense that delicate distortion of the *dharma* which ushers in every new era and is sealed by every new *avatāra.* For order to continue to have a sense, they had to be the first to damage it. There was something in their behavior that went beyond occasion and passions. An unspoken imperative compelled them to make manifest, in what they did, something nobody else had dared point to, a form, an uncommon combination of elements. Each invented his own style. They were artists of the gesture, who ended up—and there was a subtle cruelty to it—suffering the consequences of their artistry, as though a surplus of torture necessarily went hand in hand with those new forms they had chosen to experiment in.

Bībhatsu, He-who-feels-repugnance: of all Arjuna's many epithets, this one stands out on its own, offers decisive significance. The figure of the *kṣatriyas,* those determined, powerful warriors who do not even know what doubt is, who smash through every obstacle, who fight with wild beasts—men who can only affirm, ever avid of new strength, men who breathe fire, was seen for the last time and most perfectly of all in Arjuna. Yet he never managed to free himself from a feeling of nausea. About what? The monotonous duty of killing? Or something else too? Arjuna was eaten up with repugnance for the world: not for certain aspects of the world but for its very existence. This creeping nausea gripped him as soon as he passed the peak of affirmation—and from that moment on it spread a delicate, irreversible coloring over everything. It showed in his eyes as a sporadic absence, a perennial distance from whatever was happening to him. Arjuna said nothing of all this, except in his secret conversations with his charioteer, with Kṛṣṇa. Others knew nothing about it. They saw him as the exemplary warrior, the seductive young man, the just man. Yet very often the ringing, authoritative words he would find himself pronouncing sounded vacuous and worn out to Arjuna.

It was difficult to be flexible, on the Island of the Jambū. Every path was lined with vows, boons, curses. Every step was a precept. If life was to become more fluid again, more diffuse and confused, then a god was required, an *avatāra,* an unclouded, far-seeing mind: Kṛṣṇa.

Nothing could be more subtly contrary to the law than

some of Kṛṣṇa's shrewd counsels, betrayals, and deceptions during the war between the Pāṇḍavas and the Kauravas. Nothing could be more subtly damaging to people's faith in the gods than some of the Buddha's doctrines. Yet Kṛṣṇa and the Buddha were both Viṣṇu's *avatāras*, come down to earth to heal the wounded *dharma*, reduced as it was to a quarter of itself. Nothing of the kind had happened with the previous *avatāra*: the Dwarf, the Boar, the Man-Lion had appeared, done what they were supposed to do, and then melted away, leaving the world ready for another cycle. But in the last cycles, when the smell of the *pralaya*, the general dissolution, was already in the air, everything got mixed up and the rules were turned upside down. Defeating an Asura who had in his turn defeated Indra was no longer enough. There was something infantile and empty about those sovereignty games now. Rather than beating one's enemy, the important thing these days was to imitate him, to assume some of his gestures: but this had to be done *in a certain way*, superimposing this new knowledge over the old and allowing the two to live together in the energy of their collision. This, perhaps, was the peculiar mystery of the *kaliyuga*, the obscure age much favored by women and those without caste, who, in the general confusion, might seize a chance for liberation otherwise denied them. In the flagrancy of contradiction, there was no longer any cult that could act as axis and lodestone, only *bhakti*, the heart's devotion, that addresses itself to anything, is ready for anything, a perennial emotion whose first messengers were Kṛṣṇa's *gopīs*, wandering around alone with their herds.

King Śiśupāla was saved by the chemical purity of his hatred for Kṛṣṇa, saved because he didn't repent. He too will enter into the body of Kṛṣṇa, he too will be liberated in Kṛṣṇa. Kṛṣṇa penetrates the ranks of his enemies and does not seek to avoid their wiles, or trickery, with the result that his enemies open a breach in him. All this would be in complete violation of the Law, were it not for the fact that the

Law itself demands it, the new Law Kṛṣṇa gave first to the *gopīs* before showing it to the warriors. Thus, in the successive *avatāra*, the Buddha's, the doctrine of the *anattā*, of the "non-Self," of the emptiness of every element, the proclaimed inexistence of the intrinsic, the doctrine that dealt an ax blow to the sovereignty of the *ātman*, of the Self, and hence of the *brahman*, which is coincident with it, and hence of everything, this doctrine was not only not rejected but welcomed. Why this and not another of the many heresies that were making the rounds? It was welcomed because of the cruel and drastic purity of its opposition to everything the *ṛṣis* had taught. Yājñavalkya and the Buddha sat face-to-face, but not as enemies. They lived in the same mind now, and each went on pronouncing his own words, without moderating them at all.

Before the battle of Kurukṣetra, Kṛṣṇa enlightened an Arjuna paralyzed with anguish as to the nature of what is. During the battle most of the help he gave Arjuna had to do with the art of deception. And perhaps he never exercised that art so treacherously as in the duel between Arjuna and Jayadratha. A curse hung over whoever killed Jayadratha. His father, Vṛddhakṣatra, had proclaimed that whoever brought his son's head to the ground, that man's own head would split into a hundred pieces. The two warriors were fighting it out as the sun's tawny disk sank in the sky. The moment it was hidden behind the horizon, Arjuna's word would lose all contact with the truth, because his vow to kill Jayadratha before sunset would have been shown to be vain. "If the truth is lost to Arjuna, it is lost to the world," thought Kṛṣṇa. It was then that he whispered a few feverish words of advice to his friend: "Cut off Jayadratha's head cleanly, so that it flies into his father's lap." With his supreme ability as an archer, Arjuna aimed the fatal arrow (which he had saved up, honoring it with perfumes and flowers, to kill the killer of his own son, Abhimanyu) so that Jayadratha's head would fly away from him—right to where Vṛddhakṣatra was sitting at the edge of the forest, absorbed in the ceremony of twilight. Like a stone from the sky, his son's head, ornamented with extravagant earrings, fell on his knees. Vṛddhakṣatra didn't even notice. He was a severe *ṛṣi,* capable of blocking out the world. As soon as his prayer was over, he got up. Jayādratha's head rolled to the ground, upon which Vṛddhakṣatra's head was seen to burst into a hundred pieces. The last rim of the sun was sinking down.

What happened in India, from the Vedas to the Buddha, belonged to the trunk of a single tree, the immense *aśvattha* rooted in the sky, that spread its branches everywhere, covering the earth. What was inside that trunk? *Brahman.* And what was *brahman?* The "unique that awakes," says the *Maitri Upaniṣad.* The *brahman* was consciousness and what brings consciousness to birth: the Awakening One. In the end, a solitary monk came to sit at the foot of the tree, which on this occasion was a common fig tree, in Bihar. He told himself he wouldn't get up until awakening passed from the tree to himself. It was the Bodhisattva who was about to become the Buddha. The tree he was sitting under was called the Tree of Awakening (*bodhi*), and it grew in Gayā, later to be known as Bodhgayā. Many were the pilgrims who went to visit it, for centuries. What they saw was a *nyagrodha,* a banyan tree with aerial roots, the tree that strangles its guests, but they went on depicting it as an *aśvattha,* the fig tree that contains within it the seed of fire.

The Tree of Life and the Tree of Knowledge looked like a single tree: when the branches rustled, that was the Vedas who were its leaves, speaking; when the air was still, *soma* dripped from its trunk, offering life without end. Looking at that huge plant carefully, you saw that there were in fact two trees, inextricably twisted together. One thrust its branches upward, the other toward the ground. They were a *śamī* and an *aśvattha.* It was hard to see which was which.

On two opposite branches, at the same height, two birds could be made out, "inseparable friends." One was eating a berry, the other was watching it intensely. To light a fire, you need to rub a twig (*araṇī*) of *aśvattha* against a twig of *śamī*. Pushing out its aerial roots, the *aśvattha* slowly strangles the *śamī*. Consciousness slowly strangles life. But life exists—or is perceived to exist—only to the extent that it allows the parasite of consciousness to grow upon it.

The first of all stories is vegetable and has no plot. It is the twining of two trees, their perennial and motionless coitus. One's roots stretch off into the sky; the other's into the ground. Their branches mingle, some pointing up, some down. Every image of a god embracing his partner—Śiva with Pārvatī, Viṣṇu with Lakṣmī—recalls the shape of the two entwined trees, as if two figures with human limbs had been expelled from those tangled branches, and, joining together, strove to recompose them once again. The many heads, arms, legs, feet, hands that so shocked and frightened travelers when they first discovered the idols of India all testify to the fact that before being what it is now, the human figure was a tree with many branches. There was a time when the thirty-three gods lived not in celestial palaces but among the leaves and branches of that tree. Perched on those branches, they fought enemy snakes coiled around lower branches—and what they were fighting for was the liquid oozing from the trunk that fed all of them, Devas and Asuras alike.

In every story, if you go back, as far back as you can, to the point where every horizon disappears, you find a snake, the tree, water. It's either a snake that covers a spring of water with its coils or a lump, a knot drifting on the waters, a circular cushion bearing a divine figure as it slithers across the waves. Or a snake coiled around a trunk growing out of the water. And you can also find all this by looking inside yourself, as the *Kaṭha Upaniṣad* claims some people did long ago ("a certain wise man who was seeking immortality looked inside himself by turning the globes of his eyes back to front"). The snake is coiled around the trunk from which the essence, the *rasa,* dribbles down, just as the Twisted Goddess, Devī Kuṇḍalinī, wraps her coils three and a half times around the *suṣumnā,* the vertical stream that crosses the *meru,* the spine, but also Mount Meru, emerging below the vault of the skull or the cosmos, where Śiva on his lotus throne awaits the awakening call. The stolen cows, the imprisoned oceans, the lost *soma*—they're all hidden away in an anatomical recess, where a stream is blocked and begins to seep up through the coils of a snake. Devī awakens, arches up from her residence in the *mūlādhāra,* the "stool root," between phallus and anus, climbs the *suṣumnā,* the rootstock of the lotus, follows the royal way that leads upward, punches through the six *cakras,* the "wheels" that she finds in her path, like so many archons, becomes Śiva's sheath, and from their coitus drips *amṛta,* the "immortal" liquid that irrigates and inebriates every dendrite.

The two birds of the Vedic hymn turn up again in Kṛṣṇa and Arjuna. No longer on the two opposite branches of the same tree but on a war chariot. Kṛṣṇa is the charioteer, Arjuna the archer. Arjuna was the bird that ate "the sweet berry." But now eating meant shooting the lethal arrow. Kṛṣṇa watched, like the other bird, "without eating."

With its seething tangle of human, animal, and divine adventures, its proliferation of words, the *Mahābhārata* was an attempt to impose a silence in which the dialogue between those two birds perched on opposite branches of that unique tree composed of an *aśvattha* and a *śamī* might once again be heard. It was the oldest dialogue, and unceasing. But time's concretions, ritual's weave, divine and human chatter had almost suffocated it. The real challenge was not to find it again in the rustling of the forest.

That was too easy—and almost a profession. No, but to be able to hear it once more amid the clash of arms, in the moment of pure terror, in the mind's disarray and to cause that battlefield, which had once been a clearing where rites were celebrated, a place of such dense silence as is a precondition of ritual—to cause it to be invaded by an even denser silence now, a deafening silence, until once again one might hear as it were for the first time the shrill voices of the two birds who that day presented themselves dressed up as warriors, and were called Kṛṣṇa and Arjuna.

Nara and Nārāyaṇa were two *ṛṣis* unlike others but very like each other. Brahmā saw them pass by one day, side by side. "Those two are older than I am," he thought—and already they had gone. "But how can it be that I, who am progenitor of everything, feel that I come after someone else?" Gnawed by doubt, he turned to Kaśyapa, who said: "Whether the existent world be made of mind or fire or some aggregate called matter is, in the end, hardly important. It only exists if consciousness perceives it as existing. And if a consciousness perceives it, within that consciousness there must be another consciousness that perceives the consciousness that perceives. They are inseparable friends. They are Nara and Nārāyaṇa. You can spread yourself across ten thousand worlds, but without them you don't exist. One day Śiva said of them: 'The world is held up by the splendor of the two of you.' That is why they are continually appearing and disappearing. They were the two birds on the *aśvattha* tree. They will be Kṛṣṇa and Arjuna. Nara is Man and Water, as his name suggests. He is the one and the other, when he is not torn apart, when he is the single wave. It is through Nara that we have knowledge, but our knowledge would be limited, no greater than the knowledge of a muscle that contracts and relaxes, if it were not reflected in Nārāyaṇa's eye. In which, what's more, we lose ourselves: to pass from one eye to the other is to pass from a river to the sea. Thus true knowledge is cloaked in uncertainty. But that is enough to live with. The supreme, ultimate relief is to know that Nara is indissolubly tied to Nārāyaṇa. And it was Nārāyaṇa, Kṛṣṇa at the time, who when granted a boon by Indra asked for the perennial friendship of Nara, Arjuna at the time. The boon was asked of Arjuna's father, against whom, together with Arjuna, Kṛṣṇa had fought and won. Friendship prevails over kinship. Every family dies out, but the tie between the mind and his Guest does not. When men feel dumb and afflicted, they remember what Nārāyaṇa once said through Kṛṣṇa: 'I cannot look at this world even for the briefest instant without Arjuna.' Then there is a detail that betrays all the kindness, the almost studied carelessness of the god: Nārāyaṇa is a patronymic. As if the god who has no name had, in choosing a provisional name, decided to give precedence to man, to the point of having himself pass for his son. You, with all your children born-of-the-mind, would not have been capable of this."

When the five Pāṇḍavas showed themselves, they dazzled the eye. But only so long as they had Kṛṣṇa beside them, that relative, friend, counselor who never bore arms himself. As soon as Kṛṣṇa left them, a veil of dust fell on their faces. Their words became dull, lifeless. They would launch into redundant oratory, like actors who have played a part once too often. One day, Arjuna realized he could no longer bend his bow. He thought of time and how it corrodes. He didn't know that at that very moment Kṛṣṇa lay dying.

This is how Kṛṣṇa died: he was lying down, eyes closed, back resting on a tree trunk. The soles of his feet were propped up on a clump of grass. Jara, an Asura hunter, was chasing an antelope. Dazzled by the sudden light of the clearing, he shot an arrow at the soles of Kṛṣṇa's feet, which he had mistaken for the antelope's ears. It was the only part of his body on which, one day long ago, while obeying the orders of the brahman Durvāsas, Kṛṣṇa had not spread the cream of rice.

. . .

Everything begins with an arrow shot in perfect consciousness at two copulating antelopes; everything ends with an arrow shot in perfect unconsciousness at the sole of a foot mistaken for an antelope. In the beginning: everything emerged from the indistinct wave. Later: everything was suddenly submerged by another indistinct wave. In the middle: a devastating war, won by the five Pāṇḍavas, only in name sons of Pāṇḍu, who had been cursed by a brahman he had shot in the hunt while, in the form of an antelope, the brahman was copulating. "As soon as you penetrate a woman, you will die" were the brahman's last words. From that moment on Pāṇḍu committed himself to a life of chastity. One day he was in the forest with Mādrī, his favorite wife. He lifted his eyes in a look of desire and farewell. He died the moment he penetrated her.

When Pāṇḍu's funeral rites were over, Vyāsa went to his mother, Satyavatī, who was "blinded by the pain of sorrow." He delivered a lofty speech, full of pathos, which he would later insert in the *Mahābhārata*: "The happy days are gone, now there are horrors in store. Tomorrow after tomorrow, each day will be worse. The earth has lost its youth." This epitaph for Pāṇḍu was also an epitaph in advance for the Pāṇḍavas, and it resounds throughout the poem like the tolling of a bell. Yet Ānandavardhana, who knew more than anyone of *dhvani*, of "poetic suggestion," maintained that the dominant *rasa*—the flavor, the taste, the tonality—of the *Mahābhārata* was the *śāntarasa*, the "peace *rasa*." To many this claim seemed paradoxical and provocative. Where was peace to be found in that appalling chain of events? None of the poem's protagonists could be considered an appropriate bearer of such a *rasa*. Who could feel peaceful upon hearing of a succession of slaughters framed by a general disaster? Yudhiṣṭhira himself, who was the very stuff of *dharma*, would remain unappeased, even in Indra's heaven. But Ānandavardhana was right. Peace was there, in the tone of the narrative voice that never wavered, never buckled. A voice as willing to reveal the "most secret knowledge of the secret" as to list the members of a Nāga dynasty, or press on with a story told within a story and creating a frame for other stories, or to give us the most minute details of a massacre. The most immediate objection to Ānandavardhana's theory might be this: the introduction to the poem "expressly states that the *Mahābhārata* gives instruction on all purposes of life and contains all the *rasa.*" How could anyone deny it? And how can we subordinate the many *rasa* of the *Mahābhārata* to that "peace *rasa*" which, what's more, was not included in the original list of the *rasa,* written down in the *Nāṭyaśāstra* of Bharata? Ānandavardhana was aware that the fate of his whole theory, according to which the noblest poetry does not admit of mixture but is based on one dominant *rasa,* depended on the answer to that question. And he wrote: "An essential meaning generates even greater beauty if made manifest without being directly explicit. This is common custom when refined and cultured people meet together: the thought they have most at heart is made manifest implicitly, not directly and explicitly."

The old blind king, Dhṛtarāṣṭra, so fearfully thin; his wife, Gāndhārī, blindfolded since their marriage; the Pāṇḍavas' mother, Kuntī, widowed now, were walking together toward the Gaṅgā. Behind them was the vast forest where they had spent three years in silent wandering. They sat down to look back at it. An evil wind was shaking the foliage. Then flames leapt above the tops of the trees. Scorching waves licked over them. Shrieks, trumpetings, and howls came from the forest. The animals rushed out of the vegetation to save themselves. They rushed past the three witnesses, who sat motionless, wrapped in clouds of smoke. Dhṛtarāṣṭra was a pole clad in rags. To each side, as though escorting him, were the two women and beyond them the fire that had reduced majestic trees to ash burned up the grass of the clearing, and their bodies too.

When Vyāsa told Yudhiṣṭhira how his mother, Kuntī, Dhṛtarāṣṭra, and Gandhārī had died, the man who was the

Law wept like a child. "Oh, Fire, oh, Agni, so it's not true that you were assuaged that day by the endless arrows Arjuna loosed against his father's waters while the Forest of Khāṇḍava burned . . . Oh, Agni, you chose to seize the mother of your benefactor . . . He who had a hundred sons has seen them all die . . . He who was once fanned by a hundred palm fronds waved by the beautiful hands of young girls is fanned now by a hundred vultures' wings . . . The march of Kāla, of Time, is subtle and hard to understand . . . We are alive, and yet we are dead." Then Yudhiṣṭhira looked at Vyāsa to ask him a question, as if behind his pain he sensed a torment at once fiercely intense and ceremonial, a torment for which only the great *ṛṣi* could offer relief: "There were many sacred fires in that forest . . . How can it be that Dhṛtarāṣṭra and my mother were burned by a wildfire?" Calmly, Vyāsa answered: "It's true, there were many sacred fires, and Dhṛtarāṣṭra tended them. They celebrated their rites with those fires in the most remote part of the forest. Then he decided to abandon them. The brahmans who were with him didn't check to see that the fires had gone out. They followed the blind king. So the fires spread through the forest. I was told as much by the ascetics who live nearby, on the banks of the Gaṅgā."

They walked slowly, at a good distance from each other, along the narrow climbing path. To their right, boulders and shale, steep and dazzling. Before them, a barrier of rocks and snow, thrust into an enamel sky. There were six of them plus a dog. Five brothers, their common wife, the dog. The long and lanky Yudhiṣṭhira led the way, followed by the black mongrel that they had found wandering around the western slopes and that had followed them ever since. They called the animal Dharma, because it was always at Yudhiṣṭhira's feet.

They never spoke and rarely stopped. They had trudged along interminable beaches, then headed for the highest peaks, crossed the Himālaya and the desert that stretches beyond, and now were climbing again toward Mount Meru, which joins the earth to the sky, toward Indra's paradise. They were wearing faded rags held together with strips of bark. But their steps were warriors' steps. Their minds met in memory and mourning. They counted the dead of that single family that had fought against itself to the point of extinction. The appalling carnage of Kurukṣetra was the central vortex. It was there that the chains of earlier events converged, from there that the chains of future events emerged. The links were welded together with boons and curses that went far, far back, intertwining with other stories that distracted them as they tried, sometimes in vain, to reconstruct their every twist and turn. "Time! Time!" were the only words that Arjuna answered when Yudhiṣṭhira in a tone of sober acknowledgment told him that everything was over now. "It is time that cooks each creature in its pot," said Yudhiṣṭhira. And now it was time to leave the world. The others had agreed with a nod of their heads. And as they stubbornly climbed on and up like tiny parasites hugging the world's back, everything that had happened, the shame and the glory, the rancors and the spells, seemed to level out and break up, blending their colors in one knotted, worn-out drape.

The still beautiful Draupadī brought up the rear. As always she emanated a scent of lotus, mixed with sweat. Every so often she would raise her head and narrow her proud, bright eyes, a delicate embroidery of wrinkles forming on the burnished skin at their corners, to look at the strong shoulders of those five men among whom her body had been equally shared. She dwelled just a little longer on Arjuna, who, with his strange, high cheekbones, still looked like a boy and a foreigner. From the depths of the silence came the roar of a distant stream, hidden in a gorge. The occasional muffled thud. Ice breaking up. No birds in the air here. No animals on their path. No one noticed when Draupadī missed her footing and fell. But the brothers turned together and saw something dark, like a bundle of rags, rolling down through the boulders till it disappeared. They said nothing, gathering around Yudhiṣṭhira. "You know why it happened? Because in her secret heart Draupadī always preferred Arjuna to the rest of us," said Yudhiṣṭhira. No one answered. They set off again. Every day the sun followed its obsessive course, ever nearer. Sometimes they would be beset by fogs. Then even their feet were lost to them. One by one they fell, even Arjuna. Each time, with a few terse words, Yudhiṣṭhira would explain why. When Bhīma fell, and he was the last, as he lay dying he managed to ask: "Why?" "Because you were too greedy, when you were eating you never asked yourself whether there was enough for others," said Yudhiṣṭhira. Then he walked on along the path, without turning back. Now there was only the dog behind him.

Yudhiṣṭhira walked on for days and days. When he slept the dog stretched out at his feet. They were only ever apart when they came across running water. Then the dog crouched down in the freezing stream. His dusty coat became shiny and smooth again. As he watched Yudhiṣṭhira on the bank, his tongue hung down from happiness.

Yudhiṣṭhira had always hoped that the Law would not be suffocated by life's tumultuousness. Now that all the others had fallen, the Law shone within him like a crystal, but it had nothing in which to be reflected. The mountains don't ask anyone to defend the *dharma*. They have no need of it. Yudhiṣṭhira's Law had survived, the only living being in an immense void. No voice could ever answer him again, save the dog's timid bark. When Yudhiṣṭhira had called it Dharma, he never thought that one day he would find himself conversing with the animal as though with himself.

As he went on climbing, Yudhiṣṭhira noticed that from a certain point upward there was an alteration in the air's transparency: beyond that invisible barrier, the very rocks, snows, and those unlikely plants that still grew at this height took on a different consistency, a graphic presence they had never had anywhere else.

Yudhiṣṭhira was curious to see how the air would part at that point. But he wasn't able to. As soon as he got there,

Indra's resplendent chariot descended on him with a sudden boom. "Welcome to my heaven, Yudhiṣṭhira. You are about to enter with your body." "All the others have fallen, my brothers and Draupadī. Without them I have no desire for heaven," said Yudhiṣṭhira, his voice distant and weary. "You will find them again here," said Indra, with hurried cordiality. "They got here before you." "But they are not here with their bodies," said Yudhiṣṭhira. "So it is decreed," said Indra, suddenly serious. "But you can ascend with your body."

Yudhiṣṭhira was silent. At that moment the dog jumped awkwardly, happily, onto Indra's chariot. Violently, Indra kicked it out. Yudhiṣṭhira felt a sudden rush of anger. "That dog is devoted to me. He must come with me. My heart is full of compassion for him," he said. Indra immediately returned to his more coaxing tone: "Yudhiṣṭhira, today you have become immortal like myself. The happiness of heaven is yours. Why bother about this dog? Get rid of it." "I spent my life on earth practicing justice," said Yudhiṣṭhira. "I cannot cross the earth's borders by committing an act of injustice." Indra could not conceal his impatience. "There's no room in heaven for people who arrive with their dogs. Just leave it behind. Here and now, it's not an act of cruelty." "It was once said that to abandon a creature devoted to you is a crime as great as the murder of a brahman. I shall never be able to abandon someone who is frightened, who is devoted to me, who is weak and who asks for my help." Indra made an effort to behave with a patience and politeness hardly natural to him. He explained: "Here in heaven, the fact that a dog looks at a sacrificial flame is enough to take away all value from the ceremony. Hence dogs are not allowed. Yudhiṣṭhira, you have renounced everything, lost everything, including your brothers, including Draupadī, whom you loved in earnest. Why do you not renounce this dog?" "The others are all dead, and I can do nothing to resurrect them," said Yudhiṣṭhira. Then he added: "But this dog is alive."

Indra fell silent. His eloquent persuader's expression fell like a scale from his face. The dog was playing at Yudhiṣṭhira's feet. They had nothing more to say to each other. Then they realized that another being, of sovereign authority, was standing between them, as if he had been listening to what had been said from the beginning. "I am Dharma," he said. "I am your dog. And you, Yudhiṣṭhira, are a portion of me. I take pleasure in you. You have survived many difficult trials, but none so difficult as this. You have refused to climb on the Celestials' chariot without your dog. Because of this, you are now one of the Celestials yourself."

XIV

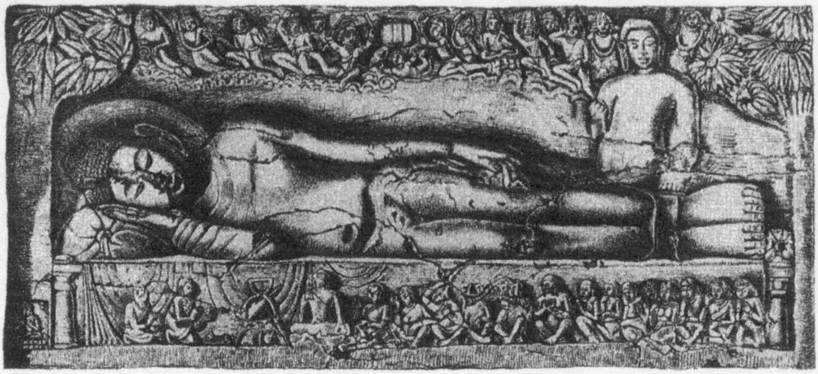

Shortly before the Bodhisattva entered into his last existence, the house of the noble Śuddhodana, chief of the Śākyas in Kapilavastu, suddenly appeared "free from weeds, free from dead tree trunks, free from thorns, free from gravel, free from sand, free from waste, well watered, well purified, free from eddying dust, free from darkness, free from dirt, free from gadflies, mosquitoes, moths, free from snakes, full of flowers, smooth as the palm of a hand." It seemed everything was preparing to take on its definitive form. The countless and the shapeless were put to one side, like a crowd of extras waiting in the wings. A small number of elements, not further reducible, prepared to submit themselves to the gaze of the great decomposer of the existent world.

Māyā was lying on her left side. Numerous metal rings circled her ankles, wrists, and arms. An embroidered cloth was wrapped around her hips. A round breast rested on the back of one hand. It pushed out as though from a balcony. The other hand was bent back behind her head. A small, white elephant came down through a crack in the ceiling. It sank through the air toward Māyā's uncovered right flank. Then it slipped in there, opening a passage for itself in the soft, smooth surface. When he was inside his mother's body, the Bodhisattva settled down in contemplation. He looked through the transparent skin. He never moved until he was born. Meanwhile, Māyā dreamed of an immense white elephant, experiencing a pleasure she had never known before.

The Bodhisattva was born the way a king descends a flight of stairs. Contemplative and knowing in the heaven of the Tuṣitas, he descended mindful and knowing into Māyā's body. During the months of pregnancy, when she was alone, his mother watched him in the crystal casing of her womb. And she always found him motionless, composed, attentive. When Māyā felt her hour approaching, she wanted to go home to her parents. She traveled on a chariot drawn by young girls. Halfway there she ordered the procession to stop in the woods at Lumbinī. She could feel the first pains of labor. She sought out the shadow of a tall *śāla* tree and gripped a branch. Eyes staring into the void, she remembered a white elephant she had dreamt of one night. Her maids hung an embroidered veil on the branches of the *śāla,* as a screen. The only sound was the humming of bees on a hedge thick with flowers. Māyā gave birth to the Bodhisattva standing up. The child was laid on an antelope skin, then a silk cushion, then the ground. They protected him with a white parasol. From then on, wherever he went, a white parasol always went with him. After the birth, Māyā, the baby, and their entourage went back to Kapilavastu. Seven days later, Māyā was dead.

Remembering his childhood and youth, the Buddha said: "I was delicate, monks, extremely delicate, too delicate. They laid out three lotus ponds for me in my father's house: blue lotuses in one, red in another, white in the third. I wouldn't use any sandalwood that did not come from Vārāṇasī, my clothes—my tunic, my robe, my cloak—were made of Vārānasī cloths. Night and day I was protected by a white parasol to keep me from the cold and heat and dust and weeds and dew. I had three palaces, one for the cold season, one for the hot season, one for the rainy season. During the rainy months, I would shut myself high up in the top of the palace and never come downstairs. The only people around me were minstrel girls. I didn't even think of leaving the palace. And, while in other houses people offer a broth of rice husks to slaves and laborers, in my father's house we gave the slaves and laborers bowls full of rice and meat."

Eighty thousand girls could claim to have been born the same day as the Bodhisattva. They took turns in his three palaces, became his lovers and musicians, for thirteen years, as earlier they had taken turns as his playmates. His chosen wife was called Gopā. One thing we know about her is that she refused to wear a veil of any kind. Nobody could understand why. It was an allusion to the preceding age: when Kṛṣṇa's *gopīs* heard his flute approaching, their plaits would come undone of their own accord and the veils supporting their breasts fell away. Yet something kept the memory of Kṛṣṇa at bay. For everything that happened to the Bodhisattva happened, as it were, at a remove, was the merest copy. He belonged to the many who are called on not to invent gestures but to repeat those of others. But he was also the only one who would be called upon to extinguish gesture itself. By the time the Bodhisattva appeared, all events of whatever kind seemed to have lost their epic profile. Their only value was as a pretext for thought. And it was there, perhaps, that something new was about to happen. There, ever since time began, something had been awaiting the arrival of the Buddha.

The Bodhisattva's life was coated by a uniform film, like the thin walls his father, Śuddhodana, had had built around the palace park. Whatever happened, there was always something slightly artificial and suspect about it. Why did the Bodhisattva only meet creatures of his own age? Why, whenever he approached the boundaries of the park, did the path veer off into thick vegetation that hid any trace of the walls and turn back? Was this the world—or a piece of temporary scenery whose real purpose was to hide the world? One day the Buddha would sum up those years in a single sentence: "Once, before I left my father's house, I could easily obtain the five qualities of sensory pleasure." That was all he said. Characters, faces, adventures, emotions: all smoothed out in just one sentence—cold, technical, quite without resonance.

The Bodhisattva was twenty-nine before he saw an old man. Then he saw a sick man. Then he saw a dead man. Three separate occasions, one soon after the other, in three corners of the park. Another day, in the fourth corner of the park, he saw a renouncer begging. He hurried back to the palace. He was nearly there with his escort, when he realized that Kṛśā Gautamī, his playmate of old, was watching him from the roof. She shouted something, but the words were muddled when they reached him, a slight, mad vibration. Then, as he came nearer, he understood: "Happy the mother, happy the father, happy the wife who has such a husband." Why was Kṛśā speaking like this? The Bodhisattva was fascinated, almost stunned—and only one word, "happy," sank in to his mind. He had the impression that for the first time its meaning flashed alight for him, precise and distinct as any object. Then he took off a magnificent necklace and told a servant to take it to Kṛśā Gautamī as a gift.

Kṛśā's hands trembled: she looked at the necklace, moved. "Finally," she thought, "a message of love. Perhaps I won't have to waste away just looking at his almost violet hair." Her friend hadn't been paying her any attention for quite some time. She wept for joy, not realizing that the necklace was a gift of farewell.

That night the Bodhisattva woke alone in his high bed. Moonlight bathed the summer palace pavilion. It lay on the bodies of the minstrels huddled on the floor, as though on a landscape of low hills. Carafes, cushions, shawls, sandalwood. Arms clasping lutes and drums like lovers. The Bodhisattva went on gazing into the half dark. Suddenly he saw reality ablaze.

As he had been returning to the palace, an excited messenger had come toward him to tell him that Gopā had given birth to a son. "Rāhula is born, a tie is born," murmured the Bodhisattva. He hadn't wanted to see the child. He had immediately withdrawn to the most remote part of the palace, a place open to the breeze. Now, in the silence of the night, he thought that before leaving he would like to see his son this once. He gently pushed the door of the room where Rāhula's mother lay sleeping. A perfumed oil lamp spread a faint light. One of Gopā's hands was covering the little Rāhula's forehead. "If I move Gopā's hand, she will wake up, and that will make it difficult for me to go." Thus the Bodhisattva left the haunts of his childhood and youth in silence. His horse's hooves didn't touch the ground, because every time they came down a large and loyal Yakṣa slipped his back beneath.

Śuddhodana was not surprised by his son's sudden departure. Behind every other, life offered but two possibilities: to be sovereign over the world—or to free oneself from it. Siddhārtha Gautama had already savored the first. There were numerous—and much admired—examples of those who, from the earliest times, had chosen the second. There were men, often powerful men, who one day disappeared. One said of them that "he has gone into the forest." From that day on no one ever saw them again, except by chance perhaps. They were called *saṃnyāsins*, "renouncers." They renounced what had made up their lives before that day. And having spent their lives celebrating the rites with impeccable propriety, they now practiced them no more, or at least not visibly. Having parceled out their days in obligations and precepts, they now had no habits at all. Having provided the wherewithal for huge families, they now kept no provisions. Having sought to attain herds, children, and long life, they now made no plans. For years they had built themselves up in an architecture of actions cemented one upon another. Now they sought immobility, because that way they could at least escape from every visible gesture. But the more subtle masters soon discovered that action, *karman,* went on accumulating, even in silence and immobility. They would have to go right down to the secret chamber of the mind and flush it out. But how could they get in there? And how could one act to extinguish whatever it is that acts? "Many have tried . . . ," murmured Śuddhodana, his thoughts turning nostalgically to his son. "Many have tried . . . ," said Siddhārtha, already wandering through the forest. "This will be my achievement," he added, in the silence.

There were sixty-two schools of thought when the Bodhisattva left his father's house. And six eminent masters. Pūraṇa Kāśyapa claimed that actions do not give rise to retribution. Maskarin Gośālīputra claimed that the course of existence is already established and that effort of any kind is pointless. Ajita Keśakambalin claimed that a human being is made up of four elements, which come apart at death. Kakuda Kātyāyana claimed that the human being is made up of seven permanent elements and that, when someone is murdered, there is no murder or murderer or murder victim. Saṃjayin Vairaṭīputra claimed that there is no definitive answer to any metaphysical inquiry—and thus they called him "the eel." Jina Mahāvīra claimed that in each life one must do severe penance to expiate the crimes committed in previous lives.

The Bodhisattva sought out, followed, then left two masters. He realized they would turn him into a charred log, while one ought to be a leafy tree. He wandered around alone for a long time. He thought: "The life of those who live without a home is rubbed smooth as a seashell." He found his *locus amoenus* in Uruvilvā. "Then I thought: 'Truly this is a delightful spot, a fine forest; clear and pleasant runs the river, with pretty places to bathe; there are villages round about where one can go; this is a good place for a noble man in search of salvation.' " Two thousand, four hundred years later, when Hermann Oldenberg visited, Uruvilvā still looked "delightful," and, even if it was less densely wooded, there was still a scattering of majestic trees. It was winter, the river almost dry in its wide, sandy bed. Another scholar, Karl Eugen Neumann, had compared the place with the lower regions of the Main. Oldenberg did not agree.

How did Buddha behave in Uruvilvā? He was like a gazelle in the forest, an antelope, a fawn. "When I saw a cowherd or a goatherd or someone going to cut wood or to gather grass or to work in the forest, I would run from thicket to thicket, bush to bush, valley to valley, peak to peak. Why so? So that they wouldn't see me and so that I wouldn't see them."

The turning point in the Buddha's life did not come when he left his father's house. From Annapūrṇā to Cape Comorin, from the thickest forests to the promontory's ocean plunge, the country was crawling with renouncers. To don the ocher robe and set off along the road, begging bowl in hand, was considered an entirely normal thing to do, scarcely less so than living as the father of a family celebrating the rites around the domestic hearth. It was the way of the forest. And "forest" had never referred merely to the place that surrounds—how far?—the place where men live, but to the secret doctrine. To understand the world of men, and indeed every other world, one's point of observation must be out there in that harsh, dense realm where only animal voices were to be heard. It was the metaphysical place par excellence. He who thinks out in the forest is left entirely to himself; there he touches bottom, the baseline otherwise hidden beneath human chatter, there he goes back to being like a wild animal, which is the closest approximation to pure thought.

No, the turning point in the Buddha's life came six years later. It was then that Śuddhodana's son, a Śākya from Kapilavastu, provincial noble, renouncer, disciple of various masters, began to consider himself with an uneasy smile. He had felt his breathing come like the bellows of a furnace. He remembered the time well. Then the ferocious headaches that followed, the hot flushes that overwhelmed him. Then there were long periods of fasting, his scalp turned wrinkly as a wind-dried pumpkin. Two masters had attracted and then disappointed him. None of this had helped him to see what is as it is. Why not? He didn't know, but an image came to his mind. Two sticks of green wood. He tried to rub them together to start a fire. Nothing happened. Then he took two other sticks: they weren't damp but were still full of sap inside. He tried to start a fire. Nothing happened. Then, excited, he thought: "It takes two dry twigs . . ." Those childish words brought him an odd happiness, somehow allusive, though to what he couldn't say. He wasn't thinking of his life as a wandering monk now. But another, more distant memory came to him.

His father, Śuddhodana, was working in the fields. Perhaps he was plowing. Under the *jambū*, a rose-apple tree, left lying there like some bundle or other, his son watches. He's a little boy, scarcely more than a baby. He looks around and senses how pleasant the air is, and the hills, the shade, the grass, the branches. There is nothing else on his mind. His father is absorbed in his work and doesn't turn to look at him. Nobody is looking at him. The world pays no attention. The boy's eyes slowly scan the whole scene. There is no resistance, there is no tension, there is no desire. Everything is completed, self-sufficient. There is nothing to add, nothing to subtract. Cautiously, the mind penetrates itself, then, almost playing, formulates these words: "Perhaps this is the way that leads to awakening." And a question forms: "Are you afraid of this happiness?" He thought: "I'm not afraid of this happiness." Then the boy became a man. He was alone and disheartened. He thought: "What lies hidden in this memory?" He realized he was whispering two words: "Dry twigs."

Later he resumed his thinking: "Those doctrines they taught me, those harsh exercises, there's still too much desire in them. That's the sap that drips. These motionless, rigid wise men would like to become pieces of wood. But it is wet wood." Supple, loose-jointed, that boy under the tree had wanted nothing. But dry twigs were rubbing together in his mind. He went on thinking: "That obstinate striving does not lead to awakening. It's a curtain that cloaks the mind. When the curtain is moved aside and happiness flashes out, it frightens us like the sudden movement of a wild animal. And why does that happiness frighten us? Because it isn't born of desire." Inside himself he added: "Then it is unlikely that that happiness will flash out if one's body is exhausted."

Then Śuddhodana's son, whom few would now have recognized in this solitary, emaciated monk, got to his feet and set off on his way again. When he went through a village, he asked for the same food everybody else ate, as if he were a normal traveler. Thus the Tathāgata—He-who-came-thus—came down to us, the Buddha.

The Buddha rarely uses images—and when he does so they are very simple, to be cherished like talismans. They said what analytic dissection was unable to say. Often they alluded and referred back to Vedic images, to those times when everything that was said was imagery. But the allusion was not meant to be noticed, as though the images were now being discovered for the first time. The "dry wood" of correct meditation is the *araṇi,* the twig that serves to start a fire, that conceals Agni and is the first of all sexual creatures. That friction of one wood against another had once lain at the origin of every kindling, cosmic and erotic. Now, as used by the Buddha, what stood out most in the image was this dryness, this draining away of every drop of sap, which made the wood precious. Even the images were dried out.

Tathā, "thus," was the Buddha's favorite word. Not just because he liked to go by the name of Tathāgata, He-who-came-thus. But because the Buddha taught others to see the *tathatā*, the "thusness" of all that is.

When the Buddha taught people the Middle Way, the only way that is free from error, he also said: "One should speak quite slowly, not hurriedly, one should not affect the dialect of the countryside, one should not deviate from recognized parlance." Only what is neutral, free from glaring features, only what blends in with all that is common, only what least departs from "thusness" can save us.

It was May. There was a full moon. That night the Bodhisattva had five dreams. Upon waking, he thought: "Today I will achieve the *bodhi*, the awakening. Everything will be exactly as before, as now when I woke up. But I will consider all that happens as now my mind is considering those five dreams."

A girl, Sujātā, stepped forward. The Bodhisattva had met her before in Uruvilvā. Shyly, she held a golden bowl, brimful. Without a word, she offered it to the Bodhisattva. The Bodhisattva took the bowl to the riverbank. He sat and ate. Then he tossed the bowl in the river. Meanwhile he was thinking: "If the bowl floats upstream against the current, I will become a Buddha today; if that doesn't happen, let the bowl follow the current." No one knows how much doubt he felt, if any at all. The bowl drifted to the center of the stream. Then all at once it darted like a horse across the surface of the water. It was racing upstream on the crests of the waves. Further upriver there was a whirlpool that sucked everything down into itself. A Snake lived there, a

Nāga. The bowl sparkled a moment on the eddies, then disappeared. On the bottom it bumped against three other bowls, covered in waterweed. They had been there for thousands of years and had once belonged to three other Buddhas. The new arrival settled on the muddy bed, a little further down from the others.

If we translate *bodhi* as "illumination," as most people do, the word is, like it or not, metaphorical and points toward the world, the light that pours down upon the world. If we translate *bodhi* as "awakening," the word corresponds exactly to its early usage in Sanskrit, from the root *budh-*, "to wake," and points exclusively to the mind, to what happens in the mind and has *no* counterpart in the manifest. It is only by enhancing this characteristic, which the mind shares with nothing else, that one can achieve that detachment from the existent world, that separation from what is given, that irreversible caesura: the *bodhi* that transforms Prince Gautama into the Buddha, into the Awakened One.

During the second quarter of the night of awakening, the Buddha remembered his previous lives. First one, then two, then five. Soon he stopped counting. Names appeared—and he would say: "That was me." He saw places—and said: "That was me." He saw passions flare and fade. He saw people dying—and said: "That was me." A throng of faces, clothes, towns, animals, merchandise, roads. He went on watching. He had stopped repeating "That was me." And suddenly he realized he was watching the lives of others. He didn't notice any fundamental difference. He pressed on, amazed, but amazement was a constant in these migrations through time. True, he could no longer say: "That was me." But was that really so important? He could still recognize the joy—and above all the suffering. The scenes he had lived through and those he had not lay side by side, each attracting the other, like leaves in a pond.

The light they emanated fused into one. As soon as the eye retreated, they became a thread of beads, each with a slightly different color, and here and there a small chip.

For seven days after the awakening the Buddha remained seated. Then he got up and gazed long at the fig tree that had protected him. He looked over every inch of it with an elephant's eye. After fourteen days the Buddha got up again and began to walk. He wasn't going anywhere in particular. Not far away, Māra collapsed, defeated. He wrote on the ground with his stick. Tantrī and Aratī, his daughters, came to read: "Gautama has escaped from my clutches." Devoted to their father and used to seeing him triumph, the two girls eagerly asked: "But who is this man? Do you want us to bring him to you in chains? He will be your slave." Māra shook his head and nodded to the signs he had traced in the dust. Then he said: "He has routed my armies with a cough. He has put my roaring troops to flight by skimming the palm of his hand over the ground." Then Tantrī and Aratī decided to seek out this stranger. They found him walking slowly along. They followed him, furtively, to get his measure. He was a man—they told themselves—and they knew how to deal with men.

All at once they stepped out from a bush and came gracefully, obsequiously, to meet him. "We would like to adore your feet, O happy creature," they whispered. The Buddha kept on walking. Then the two girls started following him, walking right beside him so that they were almost brushing against him. "Many are the desires of men. Many are the desires of men . . . ," they repeated, concentrating on their words. The Buddha showed no sign of having heard them. The two girls stopped to consult. "Let's transform ourselves. Let's each become a hundred fifteen- or sixteen-year-old girls," said Tantrī. Gravely, Aratī agreed. Now the Buddha was walking in the midst of a procession of girls, all making one of the twenty-three gestures of female seduction. They all kept saying: "We would like to adore your feet, O happy creature." The forest was full of tripping chatter. The Buddha kept right on walking. Soon the girls disappeared.

The Buddha was sitting under a tree. Tantrī and Aratī reappeared. This time Aratī spoke in a cold, sober voice: "Are you in the forest because you are overwhelmed by some grief? Do you plan to pass your life in thought? Have you insulted the inhabitants of your country and are unwilling to make peace with them? What other reason is there for being so alone?" The Buddha answered as if picking up an old conversation: "I have torn up the roots of grief. I have no thirst for life." Then Aratī remembered that adulation can prove the supreme weapon. She started again, wheedling this time: "If that is so, many will follow you. Already I see multitudes behind you." The Buddha interrupted her: "You are scratching a mountain with your nails. You are biting on iron. Why are you following me, if not out of envy?" The two girls stood up, pale and beautiful. They went back to their father. Aratī said: "Father, today I was defeated." Māra looked up: "He brushed you off like a ball of cotton." Then he got up and, still gloomy, left his daughters alone.

The Bodhisattva's first five companions left him because they disapproved of his decision to eat normal food. They were convinced that this amounted to giving way to the world. One day they were sitting beside the road when they saw him reappear, some time after his awakening. They were already thinking of something sarcastic to say when his expression froze them. Throats tight, they were about to utter his name and nothing more: Gautama. The Buddha sketched the barest of gestures with his hand to stop them, and said: "I am the Tathāgata, He-who-came-thus. That is the name you must call me by."

Śāriputra and Maudgalyāyana were young, rich, handsome, and noble. Together they experienced the feeling that the world is vanity. Together they set out to seek the truth of the matter. They agreed that the first to find it would tell the other. Thus one day, in the narrow streets of Rājagṛha, Śāriputra met a monk who immediately made an impression on him. He had an enchanting way of moving, of going forward and backward with his beggar's bowl. A way of holding his arms, of always looking at a point some distance away on the ground, and always the same distance. All his gestures were as if supported by threads. Śāriputra followed him for a long time before speaking to him, and when he did so it was with the politeness of someone who has been tempered by a strict education. "How long is it since Your Lordship left his family?" he said. "Not long," answered the monk. It was Aśvajit, the slowest to understand of the Buddha's first five companions. With due respect for good manners, which abhor questions that are too direct, but at the same time urged on by an impulse that demanded he find out, Śāriputra continued to converse with the monk. He wanted to know what doctrine could lead to such gracious behavior. For it must be a perfect doctrine.

Aśvajit was cagey. He was well aware of his own inadequacy. He had never been able to reconstruct the Buddha's doctrine in all its various steps. He remembered his four companions, who had been illuminated before him. He thought how he always got there late, and was always plagued by a sort of blur, which, however, he now accepted without fuss. Looking at the ground he whispered: "I shall never be able to expound the doctrine in all its vastness. All I can do is hint at its spirit." For a moment Śāriputra dropped his wary, delicate manners. With great excitement in his eyes, he simply said: "That is what I want." So then Aśvajit said: "The Master has shown how phenomena spring from one cause. He has said what the cause is and what the cessation of the cause." At that very instant, immaculate, free from any speck of dust, the eye of the Law opened in Śāriputra.

Immediately, the monk and Śāriputra set off on their separate and opposite ways. Śāriputra was desperately eager to find Maudgalyāyana. He was proud to be in a position to keep their pact. He searched far and wide for a long time, but without success. He stared at all the travelers as if in a daze. But it was Maudgalyāyana who saw him one day from a long way off along a flat road. He immediately sensed a change in his friend's face. His skin was as if brightened by serenity. As soon as he was within earshot, Maudgalyāyana said: "You've found it." "I've found it," said Śāriputra. "Now I'll tell you." Śāriputra then recounted his meeting with Aśvajit in every detail. He stopped a moment before repeating the monk's words on doctrine. As had happened with Śāriputra, the eye of the Law opened in Maudgalyāyana. Now they walked along together, in silence. When the Buddha saw them approaching, and while they were still far away, he told the monks around him: "You see those two who are coming toward us? They will be my two best disciples." And he welcomed them. People who had known Śāriputra and Maudgalyāyana in the past said: "They have set out on the path of that monk who steals children. A path full of widows. A path that destroys families." The Buddha ordered the monks to answer only that it was the *dharma* that had taken away Śāriputra and Maudgalyāyana. Say no more. The murmuring would end after seven days.

Śāriputra and Maudgalyāyana were illuminated by two sentences. "Phenomena spring from one cause" is the first. There are those who might pass over this sentence as obvious. But it is a continent. Śāriputra immediately saw something new in those words. The world is a throw of the dice. And the worlds that follow are successive throws of the dice. They are phases of the *līlā*, the cosmic game. From infancy on, Śāriputra had been picking up this doctrine here and there, the way one gets to know the secrets of sex. But how can one recognize *one* cause, *one* origin, in a sovereign game that unfolds in the totality of things? Now someone was teaching: "Phenomena spring from one cause." And then immediately afterward opening vistas on a further continent: "He has said what the cause is." So it was possible, then, to have a vision of the precise point from which dependence arose, the way one can see, on the ground, the place where a spring of water rises. But perhaps the most momentous words for Śāriputra were those that followed: "He has said what is the cessation of the cause." Cessation, extinction, *nirvāṇa*: the most popular, the most abused, and the most mysterious word the Buddha used. Śāriputra was still thinking how wonderful it was to be able to say what the cause is, when he heard that one could also announce the cessation of the cause. But had anything ever really ceased in this world, this perennial, endlessly repeated buzz? Such a doctrine was truly unheard of.

The Buddha's life was ever tinged by colors of sunset and uncertainty. He wanted nothing better than to appear, announce the doctrine, and disappear. For him, everything sprang from the casual occasion, from what he encountered along the road. As for the doctrine, he decided to announce it only on the insistence of an unknown brahman with whom he had fallen into conversation one day—and who turned out to be Brahmā himself. The Buddha let events take him to the point where the word dropped from the branch. Thus even what was soundest seemed precarious, chancy. The epoch demanded it. Things had changed from the days of the preceding Buddhas, when life was long and men accumulated merits. The Law's sun still shone, but the light it spread was weak now. As the venerable Mahākāśyapa said: reality was sick.

It took an immense effort for the world to achieve the ingenuousness, the improvidence of Locke, who spoke of the human mind as a *tabula rasa*. But then the dizzying gadgetry of the modern needed a perfectly flat surface to stand on. And that was the *tabula rasa*. In India, at the time of the Buddha's birth, people's assumptions could not have been more different. Every being was born as a tally of debts—a quadruple debt, according to Vedic doctrine: to the gods, to the *ṛṣis,* to his ancestors, to other men. But—and this doctrine became increasingly obsessive as time went by—every being was also born weighed down by actions already performed and attracted to others yet to be performed. We are born old, of an age that dates back to the beginning of time. Every life is a segment in which certain actions fade and others blossom. More than anyone else, the Buddha appreciated the mass of pain stored up in time by the accumulation of one act after another. Perfection is achieved when someone is about to put an end to the long series of actions. Then that person is surrounded by a sudden lightness, an emptiness.

When the Buddha was born, he was close to that perfection. He just had to finish "doing what had to be done," as one formula common among his disciples put it. Hence his whole life was a gesture of farewell. Hence it was overlaid with a patina of melancholy and absence. The loves of his youth—his father, his mother, his wife—these figures are barely sketched in. They have no features. They perform their functions and disappear. Perhaps this partly explains why the oldest depictions of the Buddha show him as an empty space in the middle of a scene, or at most represented by one of his attributes. As for the doctrine: it was a wheel between two antelopes.

From the first discourse in Vārāṇasī on, the Buddha's words are analytic and repetitive. Everything seems to dissolve, except numbers. There are four noble truths, the path is eightfold, the objects of grasping are five. Whatever the subject under discussion, the Buddha takes it apart and reduces it to the elements, whose number he later established as seventy-five. A single word, *dharma,* is now used to designate both the "Law" and the "elements." It is as if a discriminating eye had penetrated every nook and cranny, leaving nothing out, dividing everything up. And the procedure begins over and over, the same formulations endlessly repeated. All the more impressive, then, is the one omission: *sacrifice*—the word that in the past had been repeated more than any other, the word that had always been there at the beginning and end of every discussion, indeed had sometimes seemed to be the only object of discussion and the only theater of action.

Omission and substitution were the weapons the Buddha used to oppose those who came before him. He did not say a word against sacrifice (nor for that matter against the castes that derived from it). But if we consider the space the word "sacrifice" takes up in his teachings, we find it is minimal. Before him, it was immense. It is as if the prolixity of the Buddhist texts sought to make that omission the more momentous, to occupy all available space in order to deny that unspoken word any place of refuge, however small.

The Buddha made himself understood first and foremost through contrast. His strongest form of denial is not to mention something. He did not deign to name what others evoked and reiterated with every new day in an intrusive, all-pervasive murmuring. For the Buddha, not mentioning sacrifice was like ignoring the air he breathed, the ground he trod. The Buddha never quoted, in a land where every leaf that trembled was a quotation.

There was an obsessive attention to action. It went back to the very first actions—which were not even human, but divine. *Yajñéna yajñám ayajanta devā́s*, "with the sacrifice the gods sacrificed to sacrifice": so said the texts—then, to make it clear that nothing had happened before that, they added: "Such were the first institutions." The gods had appeared, surrounded on all sides by sacrifice. Sacrifice was the tool, the object, the recipient of action. And any action accomplished was sacrifice. Would there ever be anything that was not sacrifice? Hence it came as the result of immense effort when people began to speak of *karman*: a neutral, generic word to indicate all actions. At first it was a secret. Then, with the Buddha, it became a ceaselessly declared and repeated secret, while sacrifice was now implicit, silently understood as action par excellence. But the most daring and devastating rebellions come when someone decides to ignore something implicit.

The Buddha undid the knot that tied the victim to the sacrificial pole. But at the very moment he was undoing it, he explained that everything is a knot. From their vantage point in the heavens, the spies of Varuṇa, god of knots, were watching.

One of the many things the Buddha did not speak of was the cosmos. How the heavenly mechanics came into being, how it worked. Of what substances life was made and how composed. None of this seemed to interest him. With the exception of one invisible element: time. Of everything he said that it rose up and died away. That must suffice. He also said how something rose up and through what transitions it came to die away. But he was always referring to things of the mind. Outside the mind, he didn't mention so much as a blade of grass. He rarely used similes, and when he did they were always the same, and almost always had to with poor materials. Sometimes he mentioned the lotus plant. Animals he mentioned were the elephant and the antelope. Yet the Buddha was fond of certain natural locations. What he loved best were the parks near towns. They were quiet, suitable for gathering one's thoughts. And it was easy to leave them and find roads where one could beg. Around those parks and their silence, like a frame on every side, you could still sense the city's roar and babble. The Buddha's wanderings were punctuated by the rests he took in these parks. Some were donated to the communities of monks. Often they settled down there, stayed for some centuries. When the imperious believers of another faith sought to subdue India, such places proved easy to find and destroy. Behind them they left heaps of stone, smothered in vegetation.

What would one day be called "the modern" was, at least as far as its sharpest and most hidden point is concerned, a legacy of the Buddha. Seeing things as so many aggregates and dismantling them. Then dismantling the elements split off from the aggregates, insofar as they too are aggregates. And so on and on in dizzying succession. An arid, ferocious scholasticism. A taste for repetition, as agent provocateur of inanity. Vocation for monotony. Total lack of respect for any prohibition, any authority. Emptying of every substance from within. Only husks left intact. The quiet conviction that all play occurs where phantoms ceaselessly substitute one for another. Allowing the natural algebra of the mind to operate out in the open. Seeing the world as a landscape of interlocking cogs. Observing it from a certain and constant distance. But what distance exactly? No question could be more contentious. Adding this last doubt, then, to a trail of other gnawing uncertainties.

One becomes what one knows: that was the premise of the *ṛṣis.* "Men become like unto that by which they are intoxicated." That was the premise of the Buddha. Why seek to know the world, if knowing it means being possessed by it? The thinking of the *ṛṣis* embraced the implicit risk that the-thing-one-becomes-like-through-thinking-it will take us over entirely, obscuring any further investigation, dominating the mind the way a Gandharva or an Apsaras will toy and sport with the person who hosts them, and whom they possess. This doesn't just happen sometimes, but always and inevitably if one no longer accepts the immensity and continuity of the *ātman,* if consciousness is seen as the result of mere aggregation. The Buddha's gesture was meant to counter a secret enemy: possession. That mental life is continually invaded—by what? powers? call them what you will, in any event elements that agitate—was revealed to the Buddha as the ultimate slavery, that bondage to which all others lead back. Mental life: objects looming before us, without respite, taking over, obsessing us. The gesture of grasping, of reaching out, like the monkey's lean paw. This is the most precise image of mental life: restlessness, the pathetic tension of the monkey among the branches of a big tree. He who reaches out to grasp is himself grasped, possessed by the mental object that looms up and imposes itself. There is only one circumstance in which this doesn't happen: if one is able to recognize a common trait in all those objects: emptiness.

The Buddha turned the Upaniṣad formula *tat tvam asi* on its head. "You are that" tells us that, whatever appears to us, "you are that": that thing is within you, is in the Self, which—immensely larger than any thing, spreading out from the barley grain hidden in the heart—includes within itself, little by little, every shape that appears. Nothing is alien to it. And being everything that appears gives us the basis for understanding everything that appears. "As if the universe was captive, lost in the midst of my consciousness," as one Vedantic master, though unaware of being such, would one day remark.

There are shapes that can equally well be seen as convex or concave. An instantaneous adjustment of the eye will do the trick. The Buddha's doctrine is concave. *Pūrṇa,* "full"; *śūnya,* "empty." Fullness drawn from fullness: this is the Vedic doctrine. Emptiness drawn from emptiness: this is the Buddha's doctrine. The transition from the Upaniṣads to the Buddha is one from fullness to emptiness. But the shape is the same. What opposition cannot do, affinity may. They are not hostile shapes, unless perhaps in the way the case is hostile to the razor it conceals.

For the *ṛṣis* the pivotal word was *tapas,* "heat." For the Buddha it was *nirvāṇa,* "extinction." Perfect correspondence, poles apart. Inversion. In the land they lived in, extinction was thought of as fire going home, withdrawing into its dark dwelling. Premise common to both the *ṛṣis* and the Buddha: what happens in fire, with fire, is crucial.

The boldest character of all, he who took the irreversible step, origin of every deviation, first subversive, was the renouncer. A solitary figure silently sets out from the village and disappears into the forest. From the Buddha to the individual, in the purest Western sense, all are descendants of the renouncer. It was the first gesture of detachment, of cutting loose, from society camouflaged in nature—and from nature camouflaged in the cosmos. It was the first recognition of a world beyond yet still within this world, and of the possibility of setting up home there, of observing the horizon from there. An order that might be the shadow and counterpart of the other order. Or of which the other order might be itself the shadow and counterpart. One served mostly for living. The world beyond mostly for thinking, without restraint. The world beyond was the forest, thought cut loose from any doctrinal obedience, form released from any ceremonial obligation.

Wrapped in robes of ocher and white, Jainist and Buddhist monks migrated throughout the world. Others, faithful to the Devas, recognized them as heirs of the Asuras. It was a question of their being not enemies now but heretics. People heard them teach severe doctrines that ridiculed ceremonial practices and shook the world as though it were no more than a rag doll. But time's slow grind changed this too. There came a point where one could no longer say whether these doctrines really were incompatible with those of the ancient gods—and many figures reappeared in the Buddha's halo, crouching in the light. Brooding, intertwined, dancing. The divine wheel reemerged, as if fished up from deep waters.

. . . . .

If there was something that frightened them right from the start, it was the mind's dispersion. Passing rapidly and without respite from one point to another, the mind sought to duplicate the world, superimposing its own spider's web over the web of the visible. In the end this diminished its power rather than enhancing it. The world remained intact, sovereign—outside the mind and inside it too. To overcome the world (and this demands a first step: seeing it), the mind must gather itself up, the way the hand must gather a clump of grass before the sickle can cut it. The sickle is "wisdom," *prajñā*. The hand that gathers is attention.

The thirty-three gods, they say, are immortal—or, more precisely, they live an extraordinarily long time, many millions of years—or, even more precisely, they were originally wretched and vulnerable like normal men, then one day they won immortality through sacrifice, but not a full immortality, since at some time, however remote, it must end. In any event, their long lives did not grant them metaphysical supremacy, which belongs to knowledge alone, and above all to being conscious of knowledge. Which is why the Buddha—at the end of time—and the *ṛṣis*—at the beginning of time—treated the thirty-three gods in such an offhand, impatient, and condescending fashion, as immature and muddled beings, not to be taken entirely seriously. The *ṛṣis* and the Buddha Śākyamuni knew that up in the heaven of the Tuṣitas the gods were abandoning themselves to supreme pleasures. But in the end, what difference can it make whether a pleasure lasts millions of years or just an instant? The only thing that makes a difference is the discrimination that creeps into pleasure's veins.

The most radical attack ever leveled at analogy was conducted by the Buddha. It wasn't that he denied its existence. On the contrary, he accepted it as something obvious that reaches out to everything there is. The world, of course, was a fabric, a thin, metallic mesh. But it wasn't the individual, ever-different shapes from one link to the next that mattered. What mattered was that it was a net, something that covers, that tightens, that can suffocate. *This* was the true, dominant, omnipresent analogy. An expert eye could sense it in all the variegated diversity of the apparent world. And one day it would sense *only* that, discarding the individual shapes as irrelevant. But if that was the case, then every stitch could be substituted by any other. And at this point, where everything was analogy, mightn't one more exactly say that everything was substitution? The unending net of the *bandhus,* of the "connections," became a single lace, whose various parts had no distinctive features save that of reinforcing the general constriction. It was called *pratītyasamutpāda,* the interlinking of everything that arises.

The Buddha breaks the analogical pact. He ignores correspondences. He doesn't deny their existence, but he belittles them. Why concern oneself over echoes of like and like when all elements are anyway linked together in the same chain, in the way they manifest themselves, and for the mere fact that they do manifest themselves?

The tragic is the unique and irreversible act. To elude the tragic, the Buddha dilutes every action in a series of actions, every life in a series of lives, every death in a series of deaths. Suddenly everything loses its consistency. Whatever is multiplied is also extenuated. Simultaneous with this gesture came the epistemological denial of the existence of the Self, now reduced to a series of elements that can be added together and unified in conventional fashion.

Convention, the supreme power of the modern, proceeds along a path cleared before it by a dry, cautious, analytic monk, who drained away the energy of the divine figures without even taking the trouble to remove them.

"The animate universe, like sand in the fist," said the Buddha. A multiplicity of tiny elements, all entirely alien to one another. Trapped in the same grip. But this is their one affinity. In every other respect, each grain is on its own, unconnected with the others, even though the substance is always the same.

The Buddha was in no hurry to go back to Kapilavastu. But one day he did reappear in the place where he had spent his infancy and youth. His son, Rāhula, was there, whom he remembered as no more than a shadow in his mother's bed, the night he had left her. When she got news of the Buddha's return, Rāhula's mother said to her son: "Now go to your father. Go and ask him for your inheritance."

While the Buddha was wandering around northeast India, stopping from time to time to expound the doctrine to his followers, history went on just the same. So the day came when the Śākyas were massacred. That morning the Buddha told his monks that he had a bad headache, as if a stone were pressing down on his head, a stone that was a mountain. Meanwhile, one by one, his relatives were being exterminated, and with them the entire tribe of the Śākyas. Virūḍhaka, king of the Kosalas, had launched a surprise attack. Following an ancient tradition, the Śākyas were excellent archers. But because they had heard the words of the Buddha, they were no longer willing to kill. Hence, though their arrows were able to slow down the massacre, they could not stop it. Virūḍhaka had brooded long over his vendetta, ever since those wretched provincials at Kapilavastu, who spoke as if they were guardians of the *dharma* when in the end they were just his subjects like anybody else, had called him "son of a slave." He wanted that arrogant, unarmed tribe to die in agony. He had a large number of pits dug and ordered that the men and women be piled in them, packed tight. Then he had them trampled on by elephants. There were only a few, desperate survivors. They reached the Buddha in the forest and told him what had happened. When they left, they asked if they could take some relics with them. The Buddha gave them a few hairs and nail parings. After that, he never saw them again. It is said that they founded a kingdom in Vakuḍa, a place no one has ever seen.

The Buddha was alone now. He had no relatives, nor any home to go back to. Kapilavastu had been razed to the ground—and likewise his much loved Park of the Banyans. Of his family, his cousin and constant shadow, Ānanda, was the only survivor. Together they made no comment. Not even when a few days later they heard that Virūḍhaka and his troops had been drowned in a torrent of floodwater that had swept down the stony bed of the Aciravatī River. Gloating over their loot, the Kosalas had camped there for the night.

Like Kṛṣṇa, the Buddha can only appear close to the "dissolution," the *pralaya*. Behind these two there is always a massacre. Before them, a stretch of water swollen with wreckage. At least Kṛṣṇa had fought, and intrigued, though he never bore arms. The massacre came about just the same. Not so the Buddha. He did not intervene. And once again the massacre took place. Had they stood in its way somehow? Had they instigated it? Had they let it happen? Perhaps the massacre was just a premonitory sign of the real and inevitable event: the rushing floodwater that would dissolve all, wipe away the profile of a world and return it to what it had originally been: a residue. And among those residues, among the uprooted trees, the sodden timbers and washed-out rags, barely distinguishable from the endless watery surface, a coiled snake, soft as a cushion, would one day emerge. An adolescent body lay on that bed, carmine lips opening to the sky.

Why was the residue granted this privilege? Why, rather than representing the insignificant, did it become the place that conceals the essential? When the *vrātyas* played in the *sabhā,* first with heaps of nuts, later with two dice, the winning throw was *kṛta*: a number divisible by four with nothing left over. After that came *tretā* and *dvāpara;* respectively the throws that gave remainders of three and two. The losing throw, *kali,* the "dog's throw," was the throw that gave a remainder of one, the irreducible remainder. The names of these throws were then transferred to the different eras, or *yugas*: *kṛta* was the perfect age; *kali* the age of conflict and ruin, which continues to this day, ever more vividly prefiguring the "dissolution," *pralaya,* the longer it goes on. Even when they divided up time into the calendar, they realized that there was always a remainder, an intercalary period that obliged them to make adjustments and new, more complicated calculations. The game, in which destiny is decided, and time: following these two trails, they reached a conclusion: one can only eliminate any residue in the realm of the discontinuous. The continuous, by contrast, is ever elusive. The discontinuous rests, drifts, on the continuous. Through the residue, the continuous forcibly reminds us of its existence. However subtly broken up, the discontinuous never quite manages to superimpose itself over the continuous. The difference is the surplus: that which must be sacrificed, in order for the equation, if only for a while, to come out. For a while: that is, until a new residue forms and is noticed. Obliging us once again to bow down before the continuous.

Something does get transmitted from one *avatāra* to another: a weak trace of the history that went before, the disaster that went before. The peculiarity of an aeon just concluded is passed on to the next aeon as a flavor, a tone, a veiled memory. Being ripens, is streaked, speckled, made anew with pieces that are already worn out. And much is lost. Something of Kṛṣṇa the negotiator, the military adviser of the Pāṇḍavas, ever absorbed in a plan obscure to all but himself, gets rubbed off on the prince of the Śākyas who left his home: the Buddha. Something unites them, even if the words they used were now so different, as likewise the things they did. Their detachment unites them. Their turning away from the fruit.

Following the Buddha, a throng of monks was approaching Vaiśālī. There were one thousand, two hundred and fifty of them. They were dumbstruck when the Buddha led them into the Park of the Mango Trees, a vast area of thick and silent woodland. The monks lined up between the plants, like schoolboys. They knew the Buddha liked to stay in parks not far from the towns, but not too near either, with plenty of entrances, not too busy by day, quiet at night. They had been to many others, given as gifts to the Buddha by sovereigns or merchants. But none possessed the subtle enchantment of the Park of the Mango Trees, this place where they entered as if into their own home, where only the odd ribbon or bead dropped along the paths showed that someone had passed that way before them.

Then the Buddha began to speak: "Monks, be ardent, perfectly conscious and attentive. Āmrapālī, the courtesan, is coming. Her beauty is without equal in the universe. Yoke your minds and do not produce false notions. The body is like a fire covered by ashes that a foolish man walks on." Āmrapālī, Guardian of the Mango Trees, was mistress of the park. To spend a night with her cost fifty *kārṣāpaṇas,* equivalent to a value of five dairy cows. People had immediately whispered to her the news of the arrival of the Buddha and his monks. "The Buddha is staying here among my mangoes," said Āmrapālī, thoughtfully. Her son, Vimalakauṇḍinya, offspring of a regal love, had left her to become a monk. "Now I will see," Āmrapālī said to herself. She chose the finest clothes she had and ordered her pupils—there were five hundred of them—to put on their finest clothes. She set out at once in a welter of subdued murmurings. The procession penetrated the park like a dagger plunged to the speckled hilt. How often they had laughed together along those paths, among those trees.

The Buddha was finishing what he had to say to his monks. Āmrapālī got down from her carriage and bowed at his feet. The one thousand, two hundred and fifty monks lowered their eyes, to protect themselves. "Why have you come?" the Buddha asked Āmrapālī. "Because you are venerated in heaven," said the courtesan. She had sat down on a stool beside the Tathāgata. The Buddha went on asking her questions. Did she like her work? "No," said Āmrapālī. "The gods ordered me to do it." "Who ordered you to gather together your five hundred pupils?" the Buddha asked. "They are poor girls, and I protect them," said Āmrapālī. The Buddha said nothing. The silence was total. The ocher patches of the monks mingled with the colorful patches of the courtesans. "That's not true," said the Buddha in a soft voice. Āmrapālī bowed and said she wanted to become a follower of the Buddha. Then she felt she could say no more. She put the palms of her hands together in a sign of farewell and mustered up the courage to say one last thing: "My only desire is that the Buddha and the community of monks accept an invitation to my house." Saying nothing, the Buddha accepted.

On their way back to Vaiśālī, Āmrapālī's pupils, who couldn't keep their voices down now, ran into another, even more sumptuous procession, made up of the Licchavis, the eminent families of Vaiśālī. They were going to meet the Buddha. Everyone stood to one side to let them pass. Not so Āmrapālī. Her carriage and the five hundred pupils behind it refused to move from the center of the road. The procession of courtesans collided with the procession of nobles. Wheel against wheel, hub against hub, Āmrapālī's carriage pressed on, while others tumbled down the bank. In the melee, the courtesan brushed right past the angry faces of the Licchavis. They asked: "Why are you behaving like this?" "I've got to get back in time to prepare myself to receive the Buddha," said Āmrapālī scornfully. Then they offered her all kinds of treasures to concede the honor of the invitation to them. "Why should I accept?" said Āmrapālī. "Perhaps I shall be dead before tomorrow morning. I would only accept if the Buddha were to remain among us forever." And she ordered two of her pupils to whip the oxen pulling her carriage.

Having finally reorganized themselves, the Licchavis reached the Buddha. The dignitaries got down from their carriages. Their servants stood behind them. They bowed and lay their gifts at the Buddha's feet. The Licchavis women followed, heaping up precious fabrics. The Licchavis asked the Buddha to do them the honor of letting them invite him. The Buddha answered: "Āmrapālī has already invited me."

Veṇuvana, Jetavana, Āmravaṇa, Kalandakanivāpa: these names punctuate the uniform, uneventful life of the Buddha, his dusty progress from place to place, begging bowl in hand. They are enameled islands, quiet paddocks furrowed by trickling streams. It was here that the Buddha loved to talk to his monks. None was more dear to him than the place he stayed last of all, Āmravaṇa, the Park of the Mango Trees, the most enchanting of all Vaiśālī's seven thousand, seven hundred and seven parks. Āmrapālī begged the Buddha to accept it as a gift, out of pity for her.

Ānanda was the Buddha's cousin. In his name we find "joy" (*ānanda*), a promise of happiness. He was preparing for his marriage to Janapadakalyāṇī when, together with six other young nobles of Kapilavastu and the palace barber, Upāli, he ran off to join the Buddha's disciples. For twenty years he followed him, anonymous among the other faithful. Then the Buddha named him as his servant. From then on, for the next twenty-five years, they were never apart. Ānanda mended the Buddha's cloaks. He went to find water for him. He introduced visitors. It is said he listened to eighty-two thousand statements of the Buddha. A further two thousand were told him by others. He came to be called Bahuśruta, "He who has heard much." But he remained a "white robe," never took ordination, like a student forever *on the way*. Later he would be severely reproached for this. He kept no account of the mind's states and conquests, unlike many of those around him. One supreme privilege, denied to all the others, was enough for him: the constant company of the Buddha, for he was the only one who could see him all the time. The only one who stayed with him during those long periods when the monks would split up into small groups, scattered around desert places, with only the pelting of the rain for company as they awaited the Buddha's return.

No one knew the Buddha as well as Ānanda did. Often he said nothing at all. "Was not the Buddha the Master? What need was there for me to speak?" he would say one day in his defense. All the same, he could be pushy too. More than once he had seen how the Buddha might refuse something twice and then agree at the third time of asking. Ānanda was accused, among other things, of having taken advantage of this. It is thanks to Ānanda's insistence that women were admitted to the Order. "The doctrine would have lasted a thousand years, now it will only last five hundred," said the Buddha on that occasion. But he did agree.

Ānanda never worried about always being *on the way*, because he was next to the Buddha, and he thought that for this reason alone he was nearer to the goal than anyone else. If others claimed to have reached it, what did that matter? It was better to be continually on the brink. This thought that had so long consoled him, filled him with terror when the Buddha told him that he would be dead three months hence. Ānanda wept. "I'm not ready yet, I never will be. And if I'm not ready living near the Buddha, how can I ever be when he is gone?"

It is true that Ānanda sometimes took advantage of his proximity to the Buddha. He could pass quite suddenly from his habitual silence to a petulant wheedling, of the variety he had seen other monks indulge in. On these occasions he was possessed by a demon who shook him like a puppet. One day he questioned the Buddha about what had happened after death to twelve people he had known. The Buddha gave prompt answers about each of the people concerned. He explained when they were to be reborn, how many times, and in what form. He was as calm as ever. Then he added: "Ānanda, it is not an unusual thing for a man to die. If you go asking questions of the Tathāgata every time a man dies, the Tathāgata will wind up a weary man. I had better reveal to you a chapter of the doctrine that will allow you to work out on your own what we can expect after death." As the Buddha talked on, illustrating this new chapter of the doctrine, Ānanda's mind was clouded by an immense sense of shame. The Buddha's words flowed over him and evaporated into the air. He could never remember them.

Ānanda looked up at the Buddha and asked him the question he had been putting off for days and days: "How can awakening come about?" The Buddha was tracing signs on the ground with a stick. He went on doing so. In a flat voice he said: "In many ways. Looking at a peach blossom. Hearing a stone strike bamboo. Hearing the drum announcing dinner. Walking on a bamboo stick. Looking at the forest and the mountains. Looking at yourself in a barber's mirror. Falling to the ground in a cloister. Tying a noose around your neck. Pouring water on your feet and watching it being soaked up by the dry earth."

. . .

The Buddha once said that Ānanda was like a house that leaked when there was a storm. The water that got in was women. The image of the delightful Janapadakalyāṇī, left behind in Kapilavastu, would come to him from time to time, when he was preparing the Buddha's bed or meditating or going to look for water, and bring on the sharpest of pangs. They left him exhausted and vulnerable. The Buddha reminded him of their previous lives when Ānanda was an ass, Janapadakalyāṇī a she-ass, and the Buddha their master—a poor peasant who would goad them on from time to time with a stick. Such subtlety wasn't enough. So the Buddha took Ānanda like a baby and flew up into the sky, showing him an immense forest fire. He pointed to the disfigured body of a monkey on a charred trunk. Ānanda looked away. They flew on. In some heaven or other—and how was Ānanda supposed to know which?—in a noble but abandoned palace, they saw a marvelously shapely Apsaras looking into the void. "She's waiting for you," the Buddha said. They flew on. They saw five hundred amazingly beautiful Apsaras. "Beautiful, aren't they?" said the Buddha. "Janapadakalyāṇī looks like a monkey in comparison," said Ānanda. "You'll have them all," said the Buddha. Then he added: "But for the moment you mustn't leave the monks." Ānanda wasn't sure whether he had been rewarded or humiliated. In silence they flew back down through the heavens.

The Buddha knew Ānanda was wavering and vulnerable. He watched him from the corner of his eye as he busied himself with the chores. A feverishness in Ānanda's eyes betrayed his turmoil. There was a witch's daughter who was mad about Ānanda. She asked her mother to throw some brilliant *arka* flowers on a brazier to attract him. Ānanda left the other monks like a sleepwalker. More than a woman, it was a flower he was following. A fog hid the rest.

Then the Buddha was forced to resort to the *satyavākya*, the "word of truth." He wasn't pleased that the absolute of the truth must come up against a sorcerer's spells. Of course the true word would win, but it would be diminished by the clash. Truth does not compete with facts. Truth is not a tool. But the Buddha wanted to win Ānanda back. One evening, he saw him returning to the monks. He looked like a mule with saddle sores. Without a word he fell to the ground and slept for a long time.

"And women?" said Ānanda. "Don't look," said the Buddha. "But what if we see some?" said Ānanda. "Don't say anything," said the Buddha. "What if we do speak?" said Ānanda. "Be vigilant," said the Buddha.

That life is "sweet" (*madhura*, deriving from *madhu*, "honey") the Buddha announced when he was eighty years old, a few days before dying. It was the beginning of the rainy season. The Buddha said to his monks: "Split up and go your ways. Go wherever you have friends, in small groups. The land is prosperous toward Śalavatī. Around Vaiśālī there is famine. I will stay here with Ānanda. He will look after me."

When they were alone, the Buddha was afflicted by a violent bout of sickness. He felt pains all over his body. Ānanda was in a state of constant agitation. Two questions echoed over and over in his confused mind: "What if the Buddha is utterly extinguished now? If the community is left without instructions?" All at once he realized he had asked the questions out loud. The Buddha replied: "What more can the community expect of me? I preached the doctrine without holding back." And what he meant was, the esoteric no longer exists. Everything has been declared. All you have to do is listen. He went on: "I'm an old cart, vainly held together by thin belts. But even the diamond bodies of past Buddhas melted away. Even the gods of unconsciousness, who live for many *kalpas*, for millions and millions of years, die one day. Therefore, Ānanda, you must all stay on your islands, in your retreats—the islands and retreats of the doctrine."

As soon as he was feeling better, the Buddha told Ānanda that he wanted to go back and see a few places near Vaiśālī that were dear to him. They reached a clearing that opened out toward a vast horizon. The Buddha asked Ānanda to stop. He had pains in his back again. Ānanda laid out the Buddha's mat under a mango tree. Then he sat down next to him. The Buddha looked into the distance. He said: "Splendid and many-colored is the Island of the Jambū, and sweet the life of men." They went down to Vaiśālī, to ask for alms. As they were leaving, the Buddha turned back, to his right. With elephant's eyes, he looked at the city gate and smiled. "Why are you smiling?" asked Ānanda. "In twenty-five years I have never seen the Buddha turn to a city gate and smile." "If a Buddha turns back and smiles, it must mean something. This is the Tathāgata's last look at Vaiśālī," said the Buddha.

There were three times in those last days when Ānanda omitted to ask a question. He did not ask the Buddha why man's life is "sweet." Another day, the Buddha three times remarked: "The interior of the Island of the Jambū is very pleasant." Ānanda said nothing. Finally, shortly after the Buddha was feeling better, Ānanda heard him talk about the four "bases of magical powers" (*ṛddhipādas*), which, if developed, allow one to live for a whole *kalpa*, a whole cosmic cycle. Then the Buddha had added: "The Buddha now possesses those powers. Could he not, then, live for as long as the *kalpa* lasts? It would bring great good to the world, and the shadows would disperse. Gods and men would achieve peace." Stubbornly, eyes steadily staring, Ānanda said nothing. It was his great, perhaps his only crime, certainly the only one he was reproached with, not just by the community of monks but by the Buddha himself. If at that critical moment Ānanda had asked the Buddha to exercise his powers and stay for a whole cosmic cycle, the Buddha would have stayed.

But why didn't Ānanda say anything? He was possessed by Māra, who had ensconced himself in his belly. It was out of spite that Ānanda did not speak. "You did not grasp the sense of my words because you were possessed. I saw two horns on your head. Why did you let Māra get into your belly?" the Buddha asked him some time afterward. Those words buried themselves forever in Ānanda's mind. Later, when he found himself alone before the monks, his inquisitors, still dressed in white before that huge splash of ocher robes, Ānanda admitted that he had been possessed by Māra. But then he added: "If the Buddha had stayed in the world for a whole *kalpa,* how could the Buddha Maitreya, who is to come after him, the venerable perfect one, ever appear?" Silence reigned among the holy gathering. Ānanda waited, terrified. A voice was raised: "Go back to your place. Repeat in their entirety the words you heard from the Buddha."

That the compound disintegrate after eighty years or after three thousand was a matter of no importance to the Buddha. What matters is that the compound does disintegrate. Even the diamond Bodhisattva had disintegrated. So it was out of provocation that the Buddha let slip those words Ānanda would forever regret not having taken him up on: "There are those who have developed the four bases of magical powers (*ṛddhipādas*) and can live for a whole *kalpa.* I have developed them." Ānanda said nothing. Was he distracted, confused? Or did he keep silent out of an excess of zeal? Or great wisdom? If Ānanda had asked the Buddha to exercise his powers, the world would have benefited immensely. But in so doing Ānanda would have shown that the important thing for him was the Buddha's presence, not the truth of the doctrine, according to which it is irrelevant when a compound disintegrates, the crucial point being that the compound does disintegrate. By not asking the Buddha to stay—something that seemed the greatest of crimes to the monks and to himself—Ānanda had been faithful, perhaps too faithful (but can one ever be too faithful?) to the doctrine.

These were the Buddha's last days. The Tathāgata said: "When I am no longer here, the monks can be happy even if they do not observe the lesser and least important of the rules." Ever beside him, Ānanda said nothing. This was the moment in which the history of Buddhism was decided. Why didn't Ānanda immediately ask the Buddha to specify which were "the lesser and least important of the rules." When the implacable Mahākāśyapa—and the four hundred and ninety-nine monks meeting in the council of Rājagṛha—asked him to explain this omission, Ānanda said: "I didn't want to pester the Buddha." Yet he had pestered him so many times before . . . Now, as a result of that omission, the monks were obliged not to follow the Buddha's advice. Had they announced that they were choosing not to observe "the lesser and least important of the rules," everybody would immediately have said that the Order was degenerating, that now that the Master was gone, the monks were taking things easy. And how could they decide on their own which rules were "the lesser and least important" ones? The sixth and the ninth, in a list of rules? Or the fourth and the seventh? Or just the twelfth? Who could decide that? Ānanda observed a sad silence.

"But," they went on, "if we obey all the rules just as they are, we will still be acting against the Buddha's will. We will never know the happiness that he allowed us to glimpse when freed from the 'lesser and least important of the rules.' " There was no way out. They decided they would go on following all the rules the Buddha had given them with equal zeal, even the ones that might seem obscure and irrelevant. Thus an invisible burden weighed on the monks. Sometimes they thought of that lightness that they would never now be able to achieve.

After the Buddha's funeral there was a stasis in the air. A dull curtain was drawn across everything. The community of monks were looking to make a gesture. They wanted a scapegoat, someone to punish. Among the hundreds of ocher robes, one white robe stood out: Ānanda. He who had heard more of the Buddha's teaching than anybody else, who knew the doctrine like the palm of his hand. He who had failed to persuade the Buddha to stay alive. He who had omitted to ask him to stay at the right moment. Omission: what crime could be worse? Every gesture can be redeemed by the mental state in which it is made. But omission is a defeat of the mind, makes a mockery of vigilance, which should be constant, always. "It didn't occur to me," Ānanda blurted out, with that effrontery which so exasperated the older monks, when they began to question him.

Four hundred and ninety-nine monks were arranged in a semicircle. Before them stood Ānanda, alone. In the center of the semicircle was Mahākāśyapa, the chief inquisitor. He had not witnessed the great events of the Buddha's life. He was the last of the latecomers, but he came from farther away than the others. With the Buddha gone, the monks had been seized by the frenzy to follow him. They thought: "When the great elephant goes, the little ones follow him." Mahākāśyapa stopped them with a voice that demanded obedience: "Monks, do not go! It is imperative that we all unite to prevent the Law from falling into ruin." Then he sounded the gong to summon everybody to a gathering. And he warned the monks: "Before composing the supreme meaning, you must not give up life for extinction." Now he was presiding over the assembly. He called Ānanda a "mangy jackal." No one objected.

. . .

Gathered together at Rājagṛha, the monks reminded Ānanda that with his stubborn impudence he had always been one for the women, right to the end, as though in complicity with them. After his death, the Buddha's feet, like the rest of his body, had been coated with gold. Yet the tears of some unknown woman had turned them white, as if the liquid of suffering were corrosive. It was Ānanda who had allowed this outrage.

And there was another, even more scandalous episode. Surrounded by a group of women, Ānanda had lifted the robes of the dead Buddha, thus revealing his phallus. Now everybody knew that the Buddha's phallus was like that of those stallions with hidden testicles—or at least so it ought to have been to conform with the thirty-two *lakṣaṇas,* or "tokens" of perfection. But how dare Ānanda expose it to the adoration of those bigoted, or perhaps incredulous women? When they reproached him with this crime, Ānanda muttered something about the "nakedness of the Buddha." But no one was convinced. Alone among the monks, even after the Buddha's death, even in a now empty world, Ānanda went on plotting with the womenfolk, in the teeth of all criticism.

The line of monks moved along the road to Rājagṛha. Lost in their midst was a restless Ānanda. His hair was gray, but there were still those who called him "boy," *kumāraka.* He thought: "Among all these *arhats*, I feel like a still unweaned calf among big oxen. My studies are still not over." Before him and behind him, heavy, purposeful footfalls. It was a very different business from when he had walked along with the Buddha and the forest closed behind them as if they had never passed. Now he felt like one particle in a swarm, only he wasn't sure whether of friends or enemies. Perhaps they set such store on keeping him with them the better to enjoy the moment when they would throw him out.

There were many paradoxes in the story of Ānanda. He

was a servant who, while living among monks, never thought of becoming ordained himself, yet it was to him more than anyone else that the Buddha's teaching was entrusted. Being alone, for the Buddha, meant being with Ānanda. Cut off by the rainy season, unable to move around, the monks would wonder what the Buddha in some other place might be saying to Ānanda, words they would never hear perhaps, words that might constitute the secret from which they were to be forever excluded. Thus they nursed a silent and growing rancor toward Ānanda, this eternal adolescent, albeit with a web of wrinkles around his eyes, who always seemed to be waiting for something, who fed on the words of the Buddha, close to him as his jugular, and thus never became "he who has done what must be done" (*kṛtakṛtya*). Then there was another paradox: the most serious crimes Mahākāśyapa accused Ānanda of, the ones that had had the gravest consequences, were a number of omissions. But at the same time, the community of monks depended on Ānanda and Ānanda alone if they were not to commit the most serious omission of all: ignoring or passing on incorrectly the Buddha's words. Ānanda was the only one who had heard all those words. Would he agree to reveal the wonderful and hidden words, or would he jealously try to keep them for himself? At that moment, with the monks all assembled, their eyes converging on him and his crimes, and with Mahākāśyapa listing those crimes one by one, Ānanda was the body of the Law, which was entirely gathered together in his mind, just waiting to be recorded and divided up into the Three Baskets. The charges all leveled, the feeble answers of the accused all heard, Mahākāśyapa ordered: "Now get up. We shall not gather the essence of the holy words with you." But then a monk called Anuruddha whispered what the whole community was thinking: "What shall we do without Ānanda, who has heard the Law in its entirety?" Ānanda went off, sadly, and the monks were left arid and abandoned in their uncertainty. Ānanda wandered around, in the forest again now, solitary and cheerless. What if he were unable to achieve that level of awakening which alone would allow him to present himself to the assembly of monks once more? What if he failed yet again to reach that goal he had never sought with real determination while living with the Buddha? There had been a reason for his not seeking it, a reason he had just confessed to Mahākāśyapa: if he had become an *arhat*, like other monks, he would not have been able to serve the Buddha, because an *arhat* cannot serve anyone. And that was the only thing Ānanda had wanted: to serve the Buddha. But was that really the only reason? Or had the ferocious Mahākāśyapa had good grounds for not believing him? Ānanda was well aware that contemplation was not his strong suit. He was too restless and anxious, there was always something distracting him. Now for the first time he was on his own, with no Buddha to serve. Nothing could hide his inadequacy now. He walked up and down, asked people the way. All of a sudden he thought he glimpsed liberation, but far away—and immediately it vanished. Nothing happened. Toward dawn he was overcome by a feeling of faintness that blurred his sight. He collapsed on his pallet. A moment before his head touched the pillow, he was dazzled. It was the awakening, which for him came together with sleep. And then he remembered. One day the Buddha had told him some words he hadn't understood: that he would be able to still the currents thanks to extreme tiredness.

Ānanda got up from his pallet. It was still dark outside. He walked through the forest until it opened out on the clearing where the monks slept. He approached the door that Mahākāśyapa had shut behind him only a few hours ago, but as though forever. Ānanda knocked. Mahākāśyapa's strong and vigilant voice answered at once: "Who is knocking?" "It's me, Ānanda." "Why have you come here?" "Last night I finally stilled the currents." "We won't open the door for you. Come in through the keyhole." Ānanda went in through the keyhole. In the darkness he recognized the eyes of the monks, all staring at him. He fell down before them and confessed his crimes. Then he looked at his accuser and said: "Mahākāśyapa, do not reproach me." "Do not harbor rancor toward me," said

Mahākāśyapa. "I did it all so that you might find the way. Now go back to your place."

When Ānanda was welcomed back among the monks, when they asked him to repeat all the words of the Law he had heard and explain when and where he had heard them, a subtle distress disturbed the serenity he had just achieved. "The doctrine is incommensurable," he thought. "Who could ever collect it and arrange it for display?" As far as he could remember, there had never been any order to the Buddha's teachings. He waited for whatever came up. Then he spoke, perhaps for a long time, but using all kinds of forms. His words might be the Law, or rules, or stories, or treatises. As long as the Buddha was there, no one had bothered to link the doctrine together in order. The monks recited the *sūtras* beginning at the tenth section, then going on to the third or the eighth or any of the others. The next time the sequence would be different. And thus it had always been. Now the forest of words loomed up like a great wall. There was nothing left but that forest. The Buddha's teaching had always been dense. Now they would have to disentangle it, divide it up. "But how?" wondered Ānanda. And finally four sections appeared to him, which in his mind he called what everybody was then to call them: the One-and-more, the Middle-length, the Long, and the Mixed. Those names evoke that element of formlessness of which the Buddha's teaching ever partook. As if it were a substance that could shrink and expand without limit. So those who came to seek the doctrine asked for the Long Discourses and the Short Discourses, because the doctrine could consist of a few syllables or of vast, effusive treatises.

The gamble the Buddha took was far more radical than a mere challenge to the order of sacrifice. Sacrifice had produced the renouncers, the renouncers had reproduced sacrifice. Brahmā was the first of the renouncers. Śiva is the sacrifice made in every moment in the world, even when there are no longer any places of sacrifice. "Viṣṇu is the sacrifice." To strike Brahmā then was not the most arduous of undertakings, nor was it the last. One then had to strike Viṣṇu. The Buddha was a renouncer who wanted to strike the one from whom he had arisen: Viṣṇu. But how can one strike he who protects everything and keeps everything in existence? The Buddha concentrated on just one point. He wanted to take away Viṣṇu's pallet, eliminate the residue. When he spoke of *nirvāṇa,* what was essential was that this state be defined as "without residue," such, that is, as to guarantee escape from the cycle. This was the gamble then: to break the circle of existence. What lay in that place beyond any residue could be called neither life nor death, because life and death can only be known as powers within the cycle—and hence are always a new life and a new death. We have no way of saying what life and death might be outside the realm of repetition. Thus the Buddha refrained from defining them.

Yet the Buddha chose not to take his struggle against residue to the limit. Right to the end he kept Ānanda beside him, and Ānanda was his residue. He couldn't live without him. And to this day it is only through Ānanda that we have access to his doctrine.

Ānanda, ananta: "joy," "infinite." The difference between the two sounds is minimal. Ananta is the bed of serpentine coils Viṣṇu sleeps on as he drifts around the waters. That bed is also called Śeṣa, Residue, what is left over—dissolved, submerged, burned up—from the previous world: what another world will one day rise from. Ānanda is enlightened as his head touches the pillow. That is the moment when Ānanda discovers himself. Because Ānanda is the pillow, the amorous, still sleepy vagueness. But also the Buddha's only support, the man who for twenty-five years made the master's bed.

The Buddha's hidden challenge was directed at *śeṣa,* the "residue." *Nirvāṇa* is his most drastic attempt to wipe it out. Residue signifies rebirth. Yet the Buddha did allow the

Nāgas, the remote and sovereign serpents, to protect him. And Ānanda was his *śeṣa.* Ānanda was the "residue" that history leaves—and that allows history to reach its conclusion. The difference the Buddha introduced can be found in the opposite attitudes of Ānanda and Gavāṃpati. Summoned to the assembly at Rājagṛha, the powerful Gavāṃpati, a man given to solitary rumination, refused to come down from his mountaintop: he was afraid they were calling him because they were already fiercely divided over the doctrine. And it was true. But Gavāṃpati wanted nothing more than to join the Buddha in *nirvāṇa* as soon as possible. Like the ancient *ṛṣis,* he disappeared in a blaze of fire that burst from his chest. All that was left of him were his cloak and his bowl. A mute residue. These two objects were the only things that would testify on his behalf at the assembly. If the monks had followed Gavāṃpati's example, the Three Baskets of the Law would have remained empty and the Buddha's teaching been lost. But there is more: if the only impure one of all the monks, Ānanda, had not agreed to recall the Buddha's teachings in their entirety, the Law would have been forever incomplete.

Nanda and Ānanda. The attractive, fatuous brother. The obliging and tenacious cousin. Sometimes their stories get mixed up, overlap. They were counterweights to the Buddha: the terrestial twin, the Residue, Śeṣa. The Buddha could never exist alone. Even when he sits to meditate, his lotus seat is a coiled snake. The Buddha never sets foot on the bare earth. His foundation (*pratiṣṭhā*) is a flower and a snake. They have taken the place of the black antelope skin. But how could the Buddha sit on himself? And the antelope presupposes sacrifice. The Buddha wishes to presuppose the world and no more: flower and snake. Then, when he preaches, he is supported by his friend and faithful servant, his cousin Ānanda. Thus the two birds of the great *aśvattha* live on, "inseparable companions," through transformation after transformation.

. . .

In the woods of Kuśinagara the Buddha stopped by twin *śāla* trees, each growing as a mirror image of the other. He told Ānanda that he wanted his bed made here. And he added: with the head toward the north. Ānanda prepared the Buddha's bed just as he had been doing for twenty-five years. But he knew that toward the second watch of this particular night, the Buddha would enter the *nirvāṇa* without residue. He was gripped by terror. The Buddha lay on his right side, his legs slightly bent, feet together, like a lion. He looked ahead, with the same expression he always wore. Before lying down, the only thing he said was that he was very tired. Meanwhile the branches of the two *śāla* trees had bent toward each other a little, and though it was not the season, soft flowers began to fall on the Buddha's body and the ground around him.

An old monk, Upavāṇa, came by. Sitting next to the Buddha, he fanned him. Ānanda, who had gone off somewhere for a moment, recognized him immediately: he had been the Buddha's servant before him. Now he had turned up again without even asking to be introduced to the Buddha. What cheek! He was waving a large fan in a dense, heavily charged silence. Then Ānanda was amazed to see the Buddha send Upavāṇa packing with just a few curt words. The Buddha had never treated anyone like that, Ānanda thought. And a torrent of questions flooded his mind: "How can the Buddha, on the very night he is about to enter into extinction, mistreat a monk who is trying to do him a kindness? How can the Buddha, at this of all moments, do something that I might do? What inaccessible stores of anger lurk within the Buddha? Or is it just me again not understanding what's going on?" "For twelve *yojanas* around, this place is thick with gods, their heads knocking against each other; they have all come here to watch, and they are complaining because Upavāṇa's fan is preventing them from seeing what is happening," said the Buddha, answering the thoughts of his bewildered servant.

Then Ānanda suddenly felt he was onstage in an immense theater, with thousands of eyes staring at him from the darkness. Numbed, he thought: "The Buddha hasn't told me everything." And so it was. A little later the Buddha went on in a lower voice: "Of course Upavāṇa isn't only that foolish monk whose place you so proudly took. It's a long story. All stories are long stories. One day, thousands of years ago, in the times of the Buddha Kāśyapa, Upavāṇa was left alone in the monastery to sweep the floor and prepare the fire for the other monks. That blaze was so intense that it still illuminates him today. The gods are disturbed, dazzled by the light that shines from Upavāṇa's face. And they are afraid they won't ever see the Buddha again, because Buddhas are unpredictable, no one knows when they will appear, the way no one knows when the *udumbara* will flower. But that's still not the end of the story: because Upavāṇa is just one of many gods, who chose to come along ahead of the others by assuming the form of the monk who lit the fire. But as far as I'm concerned, all the gods have to be kept at the same distance. That's why I sent him packing," said the Buddha, and he went back to gazing into the still air where the *śāla* petals were silently falling.

During the Buddha's last night, Ānanda went about his duties as always, the most important being to decide who could be introduced to the Buddha and when. Lying between the twin *śāla* trees, the Buddha was gradually being covered by the petals of the two trees that had blossomed out of season, and by other petals falling slowly from the sky. Nearby, among the hovels of Kuśinagara, Ānanda had had to announce that in the third watch of the night the Buddha would be extinguished without residue. Already a large number of Mallas were crowding into this little village hidden away in the forest—and many others were arriving from the five nearby towns. They brought with them their children, their womenfolk, their servants. They wanted them all to be able to say one day: "I saw the Buddha." They kept together in groups, as though afraid of losing each other in the confusion of a caravansary. Ānanda thought: "If I admit them to the Buddha's presence one by one, I'll never get them all to see him." With all the experience he had accumulated in twenty-five years with the Buddha, he gave simple, straightforward instructions. They would be brought to the Buddha family by family. Ānanda led each family. The children stared wide-eyed, understanding nothing. Dozens and dozens of Malla folk filed by the two *śāla* trees, Ānanda introducing every one of them. The Buddha looked at them and was silent. They too were silent, huddled together in one dark clump, like a heap of rags. Behind every family, the huddle of another could be seen, waiting motionless in the darkness. The only sound was the shuffling of new arrivals. As so often in the past, Ānanda directed everybody's movements. He went from one group to the next. He was always present.

The last Malla family was leaving. The only sounds now were those of the animals in the forest. Ānanda felt tense and exhausted. A slim shadow materialized from the trees. A solitary figure, a wanderer with no faith, Subhadra. He had passed by the village and heard the news. He said to Ānanda: "They told me that the Tathāgata will be extinguished in the last watch of the night. I feel uncertain about something. Perhaps the *śramaṇa* Gautama can free me from this uncertainty. I would like to be allowed to see him, Ānanda, like the others." Imagining the Buddha wouldn't hear him, Ānanda whispered: "It's late, Subhadra, my friend. Don't disturb the Tathāgata. The Blessed One is tired." But Subhadra insisted. Then, soft and clear, came the Buddha's voice: "Enough, Ānanda. Don't keep Subhadra away. Whatever he wants to ask me, it will be for knowledge. And he will understand what I tell him." Then Ānanda said: "Come this way, Subhadra. The Tathāgata will receive you." After greeting him in accordance with the rules, Subhadra sat down next to the Buddha. He spoke as though taking up an old, unfinished conversation, starting in the middle: "Did the old masters," said Subhadra—and he listed some illustrious names, including those of Ajita and Saṃjayin—"did the old masters understand or not? Or did some of them understand and others not?" "That's enough, Subhadra," said the Buddha. "Let's leave aside the question of whether they understood or not. Now listen to me. Whatever the discipline, if the noble eightfold path can be found within it, then likewise to be found there is the person who understands. Everything else is meaningless. For fifty years, ever since I left my father's house, I have been a pilgrim in the vast realm of doctrine. There is no other knowledge. But within it the brotherhood can live the perfect life." Subhadra kept his eyes on the ground. He said: "The Tathāgata has shown me the truth in many ways. I too wish to find refuge in the doctrine. I too wish to enter the Order." "Anyone," said the Buddha, "who wishes to enter the Order after following another doctrine must submit to a trial period of four months." Subhadra went on staring at the ground. "I will submit to it. I hope that after four months they will accept me." Then the Buddha called Ānanda and said: "Ānanda, welcome Subhadra into the Order." "It shall be done," said Ānanda. Then Subhadra rose to his feet and thanked Ānanda. He was the last disciple converted by the Buddha. He went on living a solitary life.

When Subhadra left, the Buddha saw Ānanda was puzzled. The Buddha said: "Ānanda, don't be surprised that I spoke to Subhadra. One day, when I was king of the deer, the forest where we lived was set on fire. All we could hear around us was the desperate bellowing of our relatives and friends scorched by the flames. All the deer crowded together—and there was only one way out. Someone would have to lie down and form a bridge so that the others could escape by running over him. I lay down to make a bridge for them. Subhadra was the last of the deer to pass over me. There will be no more now."

The Buddha's last words were: "Act without inattention."

XV

The earth, a lotus leaf, drifted on the waters. The "flower," *puṣkara,* is also a "stronghold," *pūṣkara,* say the gods, "who love what is secret" and thus play with the sounds of words. And it is also the "nest of the waters." Life: an intermittent fever between long lapses of quiet, when the leaf wandered on the liquid surface. That leaf was a bed, a pallet. Who slept on it? The drowsy god, who had just created or fought his enemy or descended into the world in some form or other. The vegetable filaments could become a snake's coils, twined together as though in a basket. Softly stretched upon them was Viṣṇu.

The beginning: something not to be found in nature. The first distinct image was that of Viṣṇu drifting on the waters, his head reclined on Śeṣa. In the image that precedes all others, Viṣṇu was already resting on the past. The first world was always at least the second, always concealed within it another that had come before.

Śeṣa was also *śeṣa,* the "residue" one meets every day: food leftovers, remainders in division, the remnants of our actions, which are still there even when the fruit of the action has been consumed, on the earth and in the sky. From that residue new life develops. The new is an old, old lump, which refuses to dissolve.

Residues are ubiquitous. They hem us in on every side. The crucial thing is how we deal with them: do we eliminate them? cultivate them? Sometimes they contaminate, sometimes they enhance. "On the residue are founded name and shape, on the residue is founded the world." Not only is the world founded on the residue but the world is the first of all residues, broken off from something immensely more vast that in its overabundance could not bear to remain whole. "This is the world," thought the *ṛṣis*.

"In the beginning, only the Self (*ātman*) was this (*idam*, the world). Nothing else flickered an eyelid." If we don't really know, and we can never really know, what the *ātman* is, what the Self is, here we find a hint. Only what is conscious blinks, only what is inhabited by a mind. Thus "this," and hence the world, was the mind, before it came to be called "the world." Rather than a laborious process, the passage from what happened before creation to what happened afterward was a flickering of eyelids. It separated the quiescent world from a world that was looking at something. Creation was the looking. To measure life on earth one had to know the relationship between the lotus leaf and the waters. The liquid expanse was the iris, which surrounded the pupil: the flower. When Urvaśī appeared in the form of a swan, on the waters of the pond Anyataḥplakṣā, one of the six Apsaras escorting her was called Hradecakṣus, the Eye of the Pond.

Viṣṇu's belly was bare, burnished. One day a lotus stalk sprouted from his navel. That stalk belonged to him, just as much as his pink nails. It had the same porosity as his skin. It grew from his body, up to its flower. Everything else was a consequence. With something incongruous and disconnected about it, like all consequences, like all worlds, forgetful of their origin.

An unexpected excess of *sattva*, of "being"—like a shove, a spurt, a sigh—awoke the young Viṣṇu as he drifted in silence, aimlessly. It was enough to let him see that the world was empty. Again that nameless thrust. Amazed, eyes half closed, Viṣṇu realized that a stalk had grown in the void. Where from? He looked down, following the stalk. Then Viṣṇu saw that that strange filament, upright and slightly curved, was sprouting from his navel. His eye followed it up to where, at the top, lotus petals were opening to the sky. And there, sitting on the corona, he caught sight of Brahmā with his four heads, looking puzzled. He too was gazing around, like a ship's topman. And he could only confirm that the world was indeed empty. Except for that body supine on the waters, whence arose—Brahmā thought—his own delicate, hanging abode. Viṣṇu and Brahmā ignored each other, each believing he was everything.

Brahmā said: "Interrupting a deep sleep is like interrupting two lovers in their coitus." The world begins with the interruption of a sleep. Which is why wakefulness is the only proof of existence. And why the world is fragmented and cannot achieve fullness. And why it constantly seeks to reconstruct fullness. In vain, because the discontinuous will never pass over into the continuous. Mathematics tells us that, last outpost of all that is.

The watery expanse was endless in all directions. Only in one remote point could something be seen rising from it. Getting closer, you could make out a tree, but so thick and huge as to look like a mountain. Hidden among its branches, which formed an enameled pavilion, Garuḍa awoke. In his claws he held hymn number 121 of the tenth book of the Ṛg Veda. His eye settled on the very syllable from which everything had issued forth. Ka. But when had that happened? And was it still happening? A moment ago, or in another aeon? The rest followed from it. And then the same question came back: who is who? He lifted his beak, sucked in the air that filtered through the foliage. Once again it was time to take flight.

A Note on Sanskrit Pronunciation

The vowels are given their full value, as in Italian, with the exception of the short *a,* which is more like the *u* in *but.* Thus long *ā* is pronounced like the *a* in *father, i* as in *fit, ī* as in *machine, u* as in *put, ū* as in *rule, e* as in the Italian *nero, o* as in the Italian *tenore, ai* as *i* in *bite, au* as *ou* in *found.* *Ṛ* and *ḷ* are also vowels and are generally pronounced as *r* followed by a very short *i* or *u,* somewhat like *re* in *pretty,* and as *le* in *little,* or in the French *table.*

The aspiration of the aspirated consonants should be heard distinctly. Thus *th* and *ph* must never be pronounced as in English *thin* and *telephone,* but as in *hothouse* and *upheaval.* The same for *kh, gh, ch, jh, ṭh, ḍh, dh, bh. G* is sounded as in *get,* and *ṅ* as *n* in *king; c* is similar to *ch* in *church,* and *j* is pronounced as in *join. Ñ* sounds like *n* in *punch,* but the combination *jñ* may be pronounced somewhat like *dny* or *gny.* The difference between the retroflex *ṭ, ṭh, ḍ, ḍh, ṇ* and the dentals *t, th, d, dh, n* is that the former set is pronounced with the tongue turned rather back along the palate, while the latter is produced by bringing the tip of the tongue against the very edge of the front teeth. *S* sounds like *s* in *sin, ṣ* like *sh* in *shun,* while *ś* is something midway between the two.

Ḥ is in India generally pronounced as a hard *h* followed by a faint echo of the preceding vowel, while *ṃ* is a nasalization of the preceding vowel, rather in the way some French vowel sounds are nasalized. The stress is laid on a long penultimate (Kālidā́sa), on the antepenultimate when followed by a short syllable (Himā́laya, Gótama), and on the fourth from the end when two short syllables follow (*kā́rayati*). A syllable is long if it contains a long vowel (*ā*, *ī*, *ū*, *e*, *o*, but also *ai* and *au*), or a vowel followed by more than one consonant. It should be noted that the aspirated consonants are considered single consonants in the Sanskrit alphabet. In a few words which are typically Vedic the musical accent called *udātta* has been marked. This stress, which consisted in a higher pitch of the voice, has disappeared in Classical Sanskrit.

Glossary

Abhimanyu	Son of Arjuna and Subhadrā; marries Uttarā, 301, 308, 334
Aciravatī	River in the Bihar region, 374
adharma	Disorder, illegality, illegitimacy, violation of *dharma*, 330
adhvaryu	Chief priest of proceedings, one of four basic kinds of officiants in the sacrifice of the *soma;* the others are the *hotṛ*, the *udgātṛ*, and the *brahmán*. The priest who, more than any other, performs the liturgical actions; he moves around continually, handles the sacrificial implements, cooks the oblations, tends the fire. "The *adhvaryu* is the eye of the sacrifice" (*Bṛhad Āraṇyaka Upaniṣad*, 3.1.4), 132–36, 139, 143, 146, 147, 149
Āḍi	A demon hostile to Śiva, 113
Aditi	Boundless, She who loosens bonds; mother of the Ādityas through her union with Kaśyapa, 70, 219, 220, 227
Ādityas	The twelve sons of Aditi and Kaśyapa: Viṣṇu, Indra, Vivasvat, Mitra, Varuṇa, Pūṣan, Tvaṣṭṛ, Bhaga, Aryaman, Dhātṛ, Savitṛ, Aṃśa, 17, 25, 32, 70, 135, 189, 194
Agastya	A *ṛṣi* born with Vasiṣṭha from the bowl where Mitra's and Varuṇa's sperm fell; sometimes considered one of the Saptarṣis, husband of Lopāmudrā, 160, 178, 209, 210, 261
Age of the Losing Throw	*Kaliyuga*, 326
Agni	Fire, 24, 33, 50, 85, 119, 123, 124, 131, 181, 190, 194, 195, 197, 228, 243–46, 253, 255, 260, 292–94, 307, 342, 357

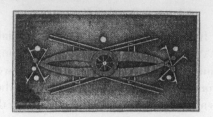

agnīdh He who lights the fire; an officiant who tends the fire, 141, 142, 145

agnihotra Offering to the fire; the simplest and most important of the solemn rites. The head of every family of the three upper castes must offer this sacrifice all his life, morning and evening, shortly before the rising of the sun or the appearance of the first star, 28, 33, 133

agre Forward; Agni's secret name, 194

Ahalyā Unplowable One; wife of the *ṛṣi* Gotama, 180–81

aham I, 225

āhavanīya Fire into which one pours the offering; one of the three sacrificial fires, together with the *gārhapatya*, "belonging to the sacrificer," a domestic fire, and the *dakṣiṇāgni*, "fire of the south." The *āhavanīya* is lit with a flame taken from the *gārhapatya*, 133

ahiṃsā Not to wound; nonviolence toward living beings. A lizard defined it as "the supreme law of all creatures that breathe" (*Mahābhārata*, 1.11.12), 151

Airāvata Born of the ocean; a white elephant ridden by Indra, 115, 302, 322

Ajita Keśakambalin Philosopher who lived at the time of the Buddha, 354, 396

Akūpāra Cosmic turtle, immersed in the waters, 231

Alakanandā River that rises in the Himālaya and flows into the Ganges, 299

Albertine A character in Proust's *Recherche*, 259, 260

Aldebaran A star in the Taurus constellation; it corresponds to Rohinī, 29, 55, 56

All-gods Viśve Devas, 140

amāgadho māgadhavākyaḥ Man-not-from-the-Magadha called man-from-the-Magadha, 200

Amarāvatī Indra's celestial city, 302

Ambā A princess of Kāśī, carried off by Bhīṣma with her sisters, Ambikā and Ambālikā, 319, 320

amba Mother, 320

Ambālikā A princess of Kāśī, marries Vicitravīrya, mother of Pāṇḍu through her union with Vyāsa, 319, 320 *ambālikā* An affectionate form of *amba*, "mother," 320

ambhas Water, billow, 320

Ambikā A princess of Kāśī, marries Vicitravīrya, mother of Dhṛtarāṣṭra through her union with Vyāsa, 319, 320

ambikā An affectionate form of *amba*, "mother," 320

Āmrapālī Guardian of the Mango Trees, courtesan of Vaiśālī, 376–78

Āmravaṇa Park of the Mango Trees, one of the Buddha's favorite parks, 378

amṛta Immortal; liquid of eternal life, drunk by the gods, which surfaces during the churning of the ocean (*amṛtamanthana*) and coincides with the substance that men call *soma*, 42, 231, 232–36, 254, 337

Aṃśa Portion; one of the Ādityas, 17, 70

aṃśa Portion. The gods can descend into certain human beings with a part of themselves. Thus, of the Pāṇḍava brothers, Bhīma has a portion of Vāyu, Yudhiṣṭhira of Dharma, Arjuna of Indra, Nakula and Sahadeva of the Aśvins, 296, 322, 328

ānanda Joy, beatitude, 278, 391

Ānanda Joy; Buddha's cousin, 374, 378–96

Ānandavardhana A poet and writer of treatises, author of the *Dhvanyāloka*, "The Light of Poetical Suggestion," perhaps the most important Indian work of literary criticism; lived in Kashmir in the ninth century A.D., 340, 341

Ananta Infinite; another name of the snake Śeṣa, 391

ananta Infinite, without limit, 391

Anasūyā Without envy; daughter of Dakṣa and Vīriṇī, wife of Atri, 69

anattā Non-Self; a Pāli term of Buddhist doctrine (equivalent to the Sanskrit *anātman*) that denies the existence of a Self, *ātman*, 334

Andrée A character in Proust's *Recherche*, 259

Aṅgiras A group of *ṛṣis*, their guide is also called Aṅgiras, 47, 69, 93, 107, 189, 190, 247, 249, 250

anirukta Inexpressible, unexpressed, implicit; describes those verses and rites in which the divinity of whom one is speaking is not named; also describes formulas that are murmured or pronounced mentally, 31

Annapūrṇā — Full of food; a peak in the Himālaya, 355

Antelope — Mṛga, name of the constellation Orion, 56

Antelope Park — Mṛgadāva, park of the king of Vārāṇasī, 54

Anumati — Consent; daughter of Aṅgiras; also the fifteenth day of the lunar cycle, when the gods look favorably on sacrificial offerings, 17

Anuruddha — A Buddhist monk present at the Council of Rājagṛha, 388

Anyataḥplakṣā — A pond in Kurukṣetra where Urvaśī appears with her following of Apsaras, 264, 400

āpaḥ — Waters, from *āp-*, "to pervade," 258

aparimita — Boundless, 31

apauruṣeya — Not from man; of nonhuman origin, 161, 168

Apollo — Son of Zeus and Leto, twin brother of Artemis, 248

Apsaras — Flowing in the waters; celestial nymphs, 72, 92, 101, 115, 140, 159, 181, 182, 233, 258, 260–62, 265, 278, 300, 302–6, 368, 381, 400

apuṃścalū puṃścalūvākyā — "Not-whore called whore," 200

araṇī — A twig of *aśvatthu* with which the ritual fire is kindled and with which Purūravas first unleashed fire in the world, 336, 357

Aratī — Dissatisfaction; a daughter of Māra, 360, 361

Archer — Śarva; one of Rudra's names, 44–46, 52–53, 56, 57

arhat — Worthy; the fourth level of sanctity in Buddhist terminology; refers to those who have freed themselves from *karman*, 387, 389

Arjuna — White One; one of the Pāṇḍavas, born of the union between Indra and Kuntī, first wife of Pāṇḍu, his putative father, 152, 291–308, 313, 314, 318, 324, 328, 330–32, 334, 337–39, 342–44

arka — Brilliant; *Asclepias gigantica;* a hymn of praise; the mystic name of the holy fire in the *agnicayana* and the *aśvamedha*, 381

Ārtabhāga — A brahmanic master, contemporary with Yājñavalkya, 191

Artemis — Daughter of Zeus and Leto, twin sister of Apollo, 56

Aruṇa Son of Kaśyapa and Vinatā, Sūrya's charioteer, 4–5

Arundhatī One of the Kṛttikās, wife of Vasiṣṭha, 124

Aryaman One of the Ādityas, an ancestor of the Āryas, 17, 70

Āryas Noble Ones; used by the Vedic texts to refer to members of the three upper castes, 52, 166–73, 313

as- To gain, 226

Aśani Flash (of lightning); one of Rudra's names, 46

asat That which is not (*a-sat*), the unmanifest, 164, 195

āśrama Hermitage, 179, 202

Asuras Gods, the first-born sons of Prajāpati; when they oppose the Devas, the gods par excellence, they become antigods, 6, 100, 168, 224, 231, 232–36, 238, 243, 254, 256, 257, 322, 328, 333, 336, 339, 370

aśva Horse, 30, 130, 226

Aśvajit One of the first five companions of the Buddha, 362, 363

Aśvala Priest (*hotṛ*) of King Janaka, 183

aśvamedha Sacrifice of the horse, 129, 134, 141, 142, 150, 153

aśvattha *Ficus religiosa,* peepul tree, 30, 139, 267, 297, 335–38, 392

Aśvins Divine twins, sons of Vivasvat and Saraṇyū, 50, 140, 213–16, 218, 222, 224–28, 240, 296, 324

atirikta Overflowing, 31

ātman Self, 21, 28, 46, 109, 149, 189, 224–25, 334, 368, 400

Atri Devourer; one of the Saptarṣis, to whom are attributed a number of the hymns of the fifth *maṇḍala* of the Ṛg Veda and one hymn of the tenth *maṇḍala*, 69, 71, 93, 160, 162, 166, 173–75, 182, 190, 192–94, 198–99

avabhṛtha Ritual bath, 153

avatāra Descent; a periodic apparition, under a different form on each occasion, of Viṣṇu upon earth. The most widely accepted list gives the ten main *avatāras* as follows: Matsya, Kūrma, Varāha, Narasiṃha, Vāmana, Paraśurāma, Rāmacandra, Kṛṣṇa, Buddha, Kalkin, 278, 279, 321, 327–28, 331–34, 375

Avimukta	Cremation ground in Kāśī, 95
Awakened One	The Buddha, 359
Awakening One	The *brahman*, according to the *Maitri Upaniṣad*, 6.4, 335
Āyus	Life's duration; son of Purūravas and Urvaśī, 17, 266
Badarī	A place of pilgrimage, sacred to Viṣṇu, in the upper Ganges valley on the slopes of the Himālaya, 297
Bad Creation	Creation of Ahriman in Avestic theology, 52
Bahuśruta	He who has heard much; epithet of Ānanda, 379
Balbec	A seaside town where certain episodes of Proust's *Recherche* take place, 259
Balzac	Honoré de Balzac, 1799–1850, 31
bandhu	Connection, 50, 61, 195, 372
Banyan Park	Nyagrodhārāma, a park in Kapilavastu, 374
Baudhāyana	Traditionally recognized as the founder of the school of the "black" Yajur Veda (Taittirīya school), author of numerous Sūtras, 151
Bear	*Ursa major; ṛkṣāḥ;* residence of the Saptarṣis, 93, 190, 249
Bengal	A region in northeast India, 283
Betelgeuse	A star in the constellation Orion, 56
Bhaga	Dispenser of riches; one of the Ādityas, brother of Uṣas, 17, 70, 85
Bhairava	The Tremendous One; epithet of Śiva, 67
bhakti	Devotion, 61, 278, 333
bhaṅgā	*Cannabis indica*, 112
Bharadvāja	One of the Saptarṣis, to whom are attributed a number of hymns of the sixth, ninth, and tenth *maṇḍala* of the Ṛg Veda, 160, 162, 165, 195–98
Bharata	Author of the *Nāṭyaśāstra;* may have lived in the third or fourth century A.D., 341
Bhārhut	Place in Madhya Pradesh holy to Buddhism, 173
Bhāruṇḍa	Mythical birds who live in Uttarakuru, 307
Bhava	Existence; one of Rudra's names, 46
bheda	Lesion, fracture, difference, 331
Bhīma	One of the Pāṇḍavas, born of the union between Vāyu and Kuntī, first wife of Pāṇḍu, his putative father, 295, 296, 298, 324, 331, 344

Bhīṣma — Terrible; son of Śāṃtanu and Gaṅgā, 318–20

Bhṛgu — A *ṛṣi,* head of one of the clans founded by a *ṛṣi*, 69, 208

Bhūmi — Earth; *śakti* of Viṣṇu, 140

Bībhatsu — He-who-feels-repugnance; epithet of Arjuna, 332

Bihar — Region in east India, bounded by Bengal, Orissa, and Nepal, 335

bilva — *Aegle marmelos,* tree sacred to Śiva, 80

Bindusaras — Lake of Drops; formed from drops of Gaṅgā fallen to earth, 119

Black One — Kālī, 112

Black One — Kṛṣṇa; also an epithet of Śiva, 112

Blessed One — Epithet of the Buddha, 395

Boar — Varāha; the third *avatāra* of Viṣṇu, 333

bodháyantī — The Awakening One, 55

Bodhgayā — The name of the place (near Gayā) where the awakening (*bodhi*) of the Buddha took place, 335

bodhi — Awakening, 54, 335, 358, 359

Bodhisattva — A being destined to the awakening; the name used for those destined to become Buddhas as well as for those who have chosen not to reach the state of Buddha immediately, out of compassion for other beings. Before achieving awakening, Siddhārtha Gautama is a Bodhisattva, 53, 54, 335, 349–55, 358, 361, 384

Born-in-a-reed-marsh — Śaravaṇodbhava, 124

Boy — Kumāra; one of the names of Rudra, 46

Brahmā — All the unresolved disputes that revolve around the term *brahman* can equally well be applied to the meaning of this name. His antecedent is Prajāpati, 6, 12, 61–71, 75, 76, 81, 82, 85, 87, 88, 94, 100, 101, 160, 161, 178, 182, 193, 260, 286, 327, 338, 364, 390, 391, 401

brahmacārin — He who behaves according to brahman; the name of those in the first stage of human life, that of a pupil under the guidance of a *guru*, characterized by chastity and the observance of special rules, 299

Brahmāhatyā — Fury of the Brahmanicide; a girl who pursues those who have killed a brahman, 87, 94–95

brahman	The St. Petersburg Dictionary (Böhtlingk-Roth) offers seven meanings in the following order: prayer, magic formula, sacred discourse, sacred knowledge, sacred way of life, the absolute, the caste of the brahmans. The debates over this word have gone on since the beginning of Indological studies. Each of the seven meanings has its supporters, who believe it to be prevalent. Numerous hybrid meanings have also been proposed, as have further translations, for example, "connective energy compressed in enigmas" (Renou); "power of language" (Staal); "powerful word" (Kramrisch); "link between life and death" (Heesterman). A whole literary genre, the Brāhmaṇas, was given over to the interpretation of *brahman*. In the *Atharva Veda*, 10.8.37, we read: "He who knows the thread of the thread knows the great essence of *brahman*," 36, 64, 69, 134, 142, 143, 167, 173, 175, 183, 184, 186, 188, 197, 299, 322, 334, 335
Brāhmaṇas	Prose texts of ritual exegesis, written between 800 and 600 B.C., 61
brahmodya	A dispute through enigmas, 142, 157
Bṛhaspati	Lord of the sacred discourse; the chief priest, *purohita*, of the Devas, 14, 17, 247, 249, 250
Brilliant	Vivasvat, 219
Buddha	Awakened; the Buddha Śākyamuni, Siddhārtha Gautama, son of Śuddhodana and Māyā; according to Viṣṇuite tradition, the ninth *avatāra* of Viṣṇu. The dates of his life are still a matter of controversy, but usually considered as straddling the sixth and fifth centuries B.C., 54–55, 137, 173, 278, 328, 333, 334, 350–52, 355–96
Buddha Kāśyapa	The Buddha who precedes the Buddha Śākyamuni, 394
Buddha Maitreya	The Buddha of the future, who appears after the Buddha Śākyamuni, 384
Buddha Śākyamuni	Siddhārtha Gautama, the Buddha, 371
Bušyanstā	Avestic demon of morning-time inertia, 52
cakra	Wheel; in Tantrism, the name of the centers through which Devī Kuṇḍalinī ascends; also referred to as lotuses (*padmas*). Their

	number varies with the traditions; in the *haṭha yoga* there are seven, 337
Cape Comorin	Southernmost extremity of the Indian subcontinent, 355
Castle, The	Franz Kafka's novel, 31
Celestials	The Devas, the Apsaras, and the Gandharvas, 302, 346
chandas	Meter, 149, 196
Chāndogya Upaniṣad	Together with the *Bṛhad Āraṇyaka,* the oldest and most important of the Upaniṣads, 151
Chāyā	Shadow; another name for Saraṇyū, 219–21
cit-	To think intensely, 34
citi	Brick, 34
Citrasena	A Gandharva and music and dance master in Indra's heaven, 304, 305
Coomaraswamy	Ananda K. Coomaraswamy, indologist, 1877–1947, 52
Cow of Desires	Kāmadhenu, magic cow possessed by Vasiṣṭha; one of the gems, *ratnas,* that appeared during the churning of the ocean, 235
Cows	*Go;* a term in the language of enigmas: cows have twenty-one secret names, 51, 158, 246, 248–50
Craftsman	Tvaṣṭṛ, 194, 218–19, 241
Creator	Brahmā, 87
Cyavana	A *ṛṣi* of the Bhṛgu clan, 208–14, 227–28, 240
Dadhikrāvan	In the Ṛg Veda, the name of a regal horse, 148
Dadhyañc	Son of the primordial priest Atharvan; knows the *pravargya,* a ceremony incorporated in the cult of the *soma*, 213–25, 227
Daityas	Sons of Kaśyapa and Diti, enemies of the Devas, 70
daiva	Fate, 329
Dakṣa	Skillful (*dexter*); born from Brahmā's right thumb. Also "Dakṣa was generated by Aditi and Aditi was generated by Dakṣa" (*Ṛg Veda,* 10.72.4); father of Satī, 5, 68–71, 75–78, 80–86, 93
dakṣiṇā	Ritual fee, 203
Dānavas	Demonic beings, enemies of the Devas, sons of Kaśyapa and Danu, 70, 294
Danu	Daughter of Dakṣa, wife of Kaśyapa, mother of the Dānavas, 70

dīkṣita	Initiate; one who submits himself to the rites of the *dīkṣā*, "consecration," 54
Dinkas	A Nilotic tribe, 168
Dīrghatamas Māmateya	Long Darkness, son of Mamatā; the *ṛṣi* to whom hymns 140–164 of the first book of the Ṛg Veda are attributed, 151–52
Disorder	*Adharma*, 330
Diti	Limit; daughter of Dakṣa, wife of Kaśyapa, mother of the Daityas, 70
Draupadī	Daughter of Drupada, king of the Pañcālas, born from the sacrificial fire, marries the five Pāṇḍava brothers, 292, 297–99, 301, 314, 330, 343–45
Droṇa	Master of arms of both the Pāṇḍavas and the Kauravas, born of the seed of Bharadvāja, father of Aśvatthāman, an ally of the Kauravas, 331
Drupada	King of the Pañcālas, father of Draupadī, 297
Ḍuṇḍu	Name of an Apsaras, 303
Durvāsas	A brahman and *ṛṣi,* a portion (*aṃśa*) of Śiva, 322–26, 339
Dusk	Sandhyā, 50
dvāpara	When playing dice the throw that gives a remainder of two. In the sequence of the *yugas,* it follows the *kṛtayuga* and the *tretāyuga*, and comes before the *kaliyuga*, 375
Dvārakā	City where Kṛṣṇa reigns, on the northeastern coast of India, 286–88
dvitīya	Second, 24
Dwarf	Vāmana, the fifth *avatāra* of Viṣṇu, 333
Earth	Pṛthivī, 25
Elephant	Airāvata, one of the *ratnas* "gems," that appeared during the churning of the ocean, 235
Eleusis	Place of the eponymous mysteries, 158
Enchantress	Mohinī, 236
Everything	Sarva; one of the names of Rudra, 46
Evil of Death	*Pāpmā mṛtyuḥ*, 47
Existence	Bhava; one of the names of Rudra, 46
Extreme	Uttarā, 307
Eye of the Pond	Hradecakṣus, 400
Father	Prajāpati, 32, 41, 46, 53, 163
Father Time	Prajāpati, 22
Fénelon	French theologian, 1651–1715, 280
Fifth Veda	One of the definitions of the *Mahābhārata*, 312

Fire	Agni, 24, 342
Forest of Cedars	Devadāruvana; a place inhabited by *ṛṣis* and their wives, on the slopes of the Himālaya, 88–91, 94, 102, 182
Forest of Khāṇḍava	A forest near Indraprastha; or Sugar Candy Forest, 292, 295, 296, 309, 342
Forest of Naimiṣa	Naimiṣāraṇya; the forest where Ugraśravas recited the *Mahābhārata* for the first time, 313
Four Vedas	The Ṛg Veda, Sama Veda, Yajur Veda, and Atharva Veda, 312
Fury of the Brahmanicide	Brahmahatyā, 87
Gaṇas	Genies who follow Śiva, 85, 86, 102, 105, 111, 122
Gandhamādana	A mountain east of the Himālaya, 11
Gāndhārī	Wife of Dhṛtarāṣṭra, mother of the Kauravas, 341
Gandharvas	Celestial demons, 236, 237, 256, 261, 266, 302–4, 307, 308, 368
Gandhi	Mohandas Karamchand Gandhi, 1869–1948, 151
Gāṇḍīva	A prodigious bow, given to Arjuna by Agni, 293, 296
Gaṇeśa	Lord of the Troops; son of Pārvatī; has an elephant's head, 112–15, 125, 162
Gaṅgā	Sister of Pārvatī; the river Ganges, 95, 104, 105, 113, 116–20, 124, 286, 299, 315, 318, 341, 342
Gārgī	Woman theologian of the Kuru-Pañcālas, 184–87
gārhapatya	Belonging to the sacrificer; domestic fire; one of the three sacrificial fires. It is from the circular *gārhapatya* that one takes the flame to light the *āhavanīya*, 133, 239
Garuḍa	Immense eagle, son of Kaśyapa and Vinatā, 3–17, 256–58, 401
Gaurī	Name of an Apsaras, 303
Gautama	Name of the clan into which the Buddha was born, 359–61, 395
Gavāṃpati	A *ṛṣi* contemporary with the Buddha, 392
Gayā	A place in the Bihar region near which the awakening of the Buddha occurred, 299
Gāyatrī	Daughter of Brahmā
gāyatrī	A Vedic meter made up of three lines of eight syllables, 14, 32, 65, 191
Geldner	K. F. Geldner, indologist, 1853–1929, 52

Gemini	A constellation between Canis Major and Orion, 56
Genie	Yakṣa, 81
Genies	Ones who drink words; Rākṣasas, 65
Genies	Following Śiva: Gaṇas, 65, 82, 84, 102
Ghṛtācī	Name of an Apsaras, 303
Gilda	The protagonist of *Gilda* by Charles Vidor, 1946, 51
Goddess	Devī, 77, 116, 120, 121, 273
Gokula	A village near Mathurā, 271, 272, 275
Good Creation	Creation of Ohrmazd, in Avestic theology, 52
Gopā	Wife of Siddhārtha Gautama, the Buddha, 351, 353
gopī	Cow girl, 271, 272–83, 285, 286, 288, 291, 301, 333, 334, 351
Gotama	Or Gautama; one of the Saptarṣis, author of hymns 74–93 of the first *maṇḍala* of the Ṛg Veda, 93, 160, 162, 165, 167, 180–82
Grace-Done-to-Antelopes	Became the name of King Vārāṇasī's Antelope Park after the Buddha, in one of his earlier lives, passed through it in the form of an antelope, 54
grāma	Village; temporary settlement of nomad shepherds, 200, 201
grāvastut	Praiser of stones; officiant in the rite of the *soma*, 254
Great Bear	Or Great Chariot; a northern constellation of seven stars, 160–62, 202
Great Black One	Mahākāla; epithet of Śiva, 112
gṛhapati	Leader, guide of the officiants who takes the place of the sacrificer, *yajamāna*, in the *sattra*, 239, 240
Gṛtsamada	A *ṛṣi* attributed with the authorship of the second *maṇḍala* of the Ṛg Veda, 162
Guardian of the Mango Trees	Āmrapālī, 376
Guardians	*Phúlakes;* to whom Plato entrusts control of the city, 100, 163
Guṅgū	The new moon, 17
Harappa	With Mohenjo-daro, one of the two main centers of civilization in the Indus valley, which flourished between 2500 and 1700 B.C., 170
Hastināpura	A city of the Pāṇḍavas and the Kauravas, near the present Delhi, 296

Head of the Antelope	Mārgaśīrṣa; month corresponding to November–December, 95
Hegel	G. W. F. Hegel, 1770–1831, 167
He-who-came-thus	Tathāgata, the Buddha, 137, 357, 361
He-who-feels-repugnance	Bībhatsu; epithet of Arjuna, 332
He-who-has-the-blue-neck	Nīlakaṇṭha; epithet of Śiva, 234
He-who-holds-the-bowl	Kapālin; epithet of Śiva, 68
Himālaya	Himavat, 75, 99, 105, 118, 302, 342
Himavat	Himālaya; father of Pārvatī, 99–101, 103, 106, 107
hiṃs-	To wound, 151
Hindukush	A mountainous region between Afghanistan and the west of India (Pakistan and Kashmir), 194
Hipparchus	Hipparchus of Nicea, second century B.C., astronomer who identified and described the precession of the equinoxes, 56
Hoffmann	Karl Hoffmann, indologist, 1915– , 263
hotṛ	He who pours the oblation; one of the four main officiating priests, whose duty is to recite hymns and ritual formulas, 137, 143, 144, 183, 199, 203, 245
Hradecakṣus	Eye of the Pond; one of the six Apsaras who escort Urvaśī, 400
hṛdyá samudrá	The ocean of the heart, 246
Hrī	Modesty, 140
I	*Aham*, 225
idam	This, 28, 400
idaṃ sarvam	All this, 23, 28
India	The Island of the Jambū, 48, 65, 157, 167, 173, 336, 364, 368
Indo-Aryans	Āryas, 166
Indra	King of the Devas and one of the Ādityas, 12, 14–17, 36–37, 51–52, 70, 93, 100, 140, 180, 181, 197, 199, 203, 215, 217, 224, 228, 241–50, 294, 296, 303, 310, 322–23, 328, 343, 345, 373
Indrāṇī	Indra's wife, 224
Indraprastha	A city of the Pāṇḍavas, corresponds to the present Delhi, 291, 294
Indus	Sindhu, 75, 170
Iran	Ērānšahr, "Land of the Āryas," 52
Īśāna	Lord; one of the names of Rudra, 46

Island of the Jambū — Jambūdvīpa; ancient name of the Indian subcontinent, 299, 310, 332, 383

iva — "In a certain sense"; "so to speak." "The particle *iva* stresses indetermination, evokes latent values" (L. Renou and L. Silburn, "*Nírukta* and *ánirukta,*" in *L. Sarup Memorial Volume*, Hoshiarpur, 1954, p. 76), 21

jagatī — A Vedic meter made up of three lines of twelve syllables, 14, 32, 191

Jamadagni — Devouring fire; a *ṛṣi,* descendant of Bhṛgu, according to some traditions, one of the Saptarṣis; introduced the *virāj* meter, 160, 165, 177–78, 191–92, 195, 198

jambū — Rose-apple tree, *Eugenia jambos;* Island of the Jambū, Jambūdvīpa, is the ancient name of India, 356

Janaka — Generator; king of Videha, 183

Janamejaya — One who makes men tremble; son of Parīkṣit, 308–11, 313

Janapadakalyāṇī — The beauty of the land; girl betrothed to Ānanda (or, according to some, to Nanda), 378, 381

jarāyantī — Awakening, making one grow old, 55

Jayā — Maid of Pārvatī, 103

Jayadratha — One who has victorious chariots; king of Sindhu, ally of the Kauravas against the Pāṇḍavas, 334, 335

Jena — City in Germany, 167

Jetavana — One of the Buddha's favorite parks, 378

Jina Mahāvīra — A spiritual master at the time of the Buddha, founder of Jainism, 354

K. — Josef K. in *The Trial* and K. in *The Castle,* novels by Franz Kafka, 31

ka — Who? Secret name of Prajāpati, 17, 31, 37, 149–50, 152, 401

Kadrū — Daughter of Dakṣa, sister of Vinatā, mother of a thousand Nāgas; according to the *Śatapatha Brāhmana,* 3.2.4.1, she and Vinatā were *māyās,* "magic forms," evoked by the Devas to win the *soma,* 4, 5, 7–9

Kafka — Franz Kafka, 1883–1924, 31

Kailāsa — A mountain in western Tibet on whose slopes the Indus, the Ganges, and the Brahmāputra rivers all flow, 81, 82, 85, 86, 88, 90, 108, 116, 122

Kakuda Kātyāyana	A philosopher at the time of the Buddha, 354
Kāla	Time; one of the names of Śiva, 330, 342
Kālakūṭa	The poison of the world, drunk by Śiva during the churning of the ocean, 234
Kālandakanivāpa	Offered to the squirrels; one of the Buddha's favorite parks, 378
Kalāvatī	Sister of Menā, 100
kali	When playing dice the losing throw, "the dog's throw," which gives a remainder of one; in the sequence of the *yugas,* it comes after the *kṛtayuga,* the *tretāyuga,* and the *dvāparayuga*, 375
Kālī	Black One, Dark One; an epithet of Devī, and hence of Pārvatī, 112
Kālidāsa	An Indian poet and playwright who lived between the fourth and fifth centuries A.D., 109
kaliyuga	Age of the Losing Throw, 132, 326, 333
kalpa	A cosmic cycle corresponding to a day of Brahmā; divided into four aeons, *yugas,* it ends with the *pralaya,* "dissolution," also known as the "night of Brahmā", 383, 384
Kāma	Desire, son of Brahmā, 66, 101, 102, 104, 105, 110
kāma	Desire, 284
Kāmarūpa	Form of desire; ancient name of Assam, 86
Kāñcī	A city in Tamil Nadu, 111, 194
kapāla	Bowl, 68
Kapālin	He-who-holds-the-bowl; epithet of Śiva, 68
Kapilavastu	The Buddha's birthplace; presumably corresponds to Piprāwā, in Uttar Pradesh, 349, 350, 356, 373, 374, 378, 381
Kārapacava	A bend in the Sarasvatī River, 240
Karkoṭaka	Name of a Snake, son of Kadrū, 8
karman	Action; initially, sacrificial action, 302, 354, 366
Karṇa	Son of Sūrya and Kuntī abandoned at birth, adopted by Adhiratha and Rādhā, 331
kārṣāpana	A coin of the Bihar, 376
Kārttika	Month of the Kṛttikās, the Pleiades; October–November, 286
káśā mádhumatī	Honey whip; used by the Aśvins, 227
Kāśī	The Splendid; ancient name of Vārāṇasī (Benares), 94, 185, 319, 320

Kaśyapa	Turtle; one of the Saptarṣis. He always has two wives—either Aditi and Diti or Kadrū and Vinatā. Or he marries thirteen of Dakṣa's daughters, including Aditi, Diti, Kadrū, and Vinatā, 4, 9–13, 69, 70, 160, 163, 165, 189, 228
Kaṭha Upaniṣad	An upaniṣad almost entirely in verse; contains the instructions given by Yama to a young brahman, Naciketas, 336
Kātyāyanī	Epithet of Durgā, the Inaccessible One; manifestation of Devī, 273
Kātyāyanī	Wife of Yājñavalkya, 187–88
Kauravas	Descendants of Kuru; the name usually used for the hundred sons of Dhṛtarāṣṭra and Gāndhārī, cousins of the Pāṇḍavas, 157, 294–96, 310, 313, 317, 327, 330, 331, 333
Kauśikī	River in Bihar, frequently called Kosi, 299
Kaustubha	Gem that appeared during the churning of the ocean, 216
kavi	Poet, 195
Kāvya Uśanas	Chief priest of the Asuras, 232
Khyāti	Daughter of Dakṣa and Vīriṇī, 69
Kosala	A principality of the Bihar region, 373, 374
Kratu	Will; a *ṛṣi* of the second list, 69, 93
Kṛśā Gautamī	Companion of the Buddha in his youth; in Pāli: Kisā Gotamī, 352
Kṛśānu	A footless archer, guardian of the *soma*, 14
Kṛṣṇa	Black One, Dark One; Obscure One; son of Vasudeva and Devakī, adopted by Nanda and Yaśodā; eighth *avatāra* of Viṣṇu, 152, 271–88, 291–94, 296–98, 300, 301, 308, 318, 324–26, 328, 330, 332–34, 337–39, 351, 374, 376
Kṛṣṇa	Black One; epithet of Draupadī, 297
kṛta	A winning throw when playing dice; a number divisible by four, leaving no remainder; name of the perfect age, 375
kṛtakṛtya	He who has done what must be done, 388
Kṛttikās	The Pleiades, the wives of the Saptarṣis; six of them carry Skanda in their wombs and give birth to him, 55, 124
Kṣamā	Daughter of Dakṣa and Vīriṇī, 69
kṣatriya	Warrior; noble; the second of the four castes, 301, 331, 332
Kumāra	Boy; one of the names of Rudra, 46

kumāraka Boy, 387

Kumbhayoni He whose womb was a pot; epithet of Vasiṣṭha, born together with Agastya from the sperm simultaneously squirted into a pot by Mitra and Varuṇa upon seeing Urvaśī, 160

Kuntī Adopted daughter of Kuntibhoja; mother of Karṇa by Sūrya; wife of Pāṇḍu, mother of Yudhiṣṭhira by Dharma, Bhīma by Vāyu, and Arjuna by Indra, 295, 296, 298, 323–24, 341

Kuntibhoja King of the Kuntī and the Bhoja peoples; adoptive father of Kuntī, 323

Kūrma Turtle; second *avatāra* of Viṣṇu, 278

Kurukṣetra Field of the Kurus; about a hundred and fifty kilometers north of Delhi; place where the gods made sacrifices; site of the battle between the Pāṇḍavas and the Kauravas narrated in the *Mahābhārata*, 264, 278, 309, 315, 317, 318, 323, 329, 334, 343

Kuru-Pañcālas Collective name of the Kuru and Pañcāla peoples, who settled in the "middle region" (*madhyadeśa*), brahmanic par excellence, in the northwestern part of the Ganges plain. The territory of the Kurus was the Kurukṣetra, 183

Kurus Inhabitants of the Kuru-Pañcāla region, 214, 278

Kuśinagara Capital of the Malla people; in a wood near Kuśinagara the complete extinction (*parinirvāṇa*) of the Buddha took place, 393, 394

Lake of Drops Bindusaras, 119

lakṣaṇa Token of perfection; the Buddha has thirty-two *lakṣaṇas* that distinguish his body from those of other beings, 387

Lakṣmī Consort and *śakti* of Viṣṇu, 336

Last Uttarā, 306–308

Law Dharma, 300, 315, 330, 333–34, 342, 344, 362–65, 388, 390, 392

Laws of Manu *Manusmṛti;* according to tradition, a text in which the *ṛṣi* Bhṛgu described the institutions of the sacred law as proclaimed by Manu; believed to have been written down between the second century B.C. and the second century A.D., 53, 151

Licchavis	The dominant clan in the city of Vaiśālī, 377–78
līlā	Game, 363
liṅga	Sign, token, phallus, 111, 118, 259
Locke	John Locke, 1632–1704, 364
Long	*Dīghanikāya*, "group of long [discourses]"; name of one of the five sections into which the *Suttapiṭaka*, one of the Three Baskets of the Buddha's discourses, is divided, 390
Long Discourses	The doctrine of the Buddha expounded in long treatises, 390
Lopāmudrā	Wife of Agastya, 209–11
Lord of the Animals	Śiva, 87, 93–94
Lord of the Creatures	Prajāpati, 31
Lord of the Herds	Paśupati, 121
Lord of the Mountain	Parvata, Himavat, 103
Lords of the Ornament	Śubháspátīs, 226
Lord of the Residues	Vastupa; epithet of Śiva, 208
Lumbinī	The place Māyā gave birth to the Buddha, a small wood on the road between Devadaha and Kapilavastu; identified with a village in Terāi (Nepal) not far from Gorakhpur (India), now known as Rummindei, 350
Mada	Intoxication; a demon, 228
madhu	Honey, 382
madhura	Sweet, 382
Madhurasvarā	Name of an Apsaras, 303
mādhurya	Sweetness, 284
madhuvidyā	Doctrine of the honey, 256
Mādrī	Second wife of Pāṇḍu, who, by her union with the Aśvins, gives birth to Nakula and Sahadeva, 296, 324, 340
Magadha	Ancient name for the present southern Bihar, 200, 203
Mahābhārata	Epic poem attributed to Vyāsa, said to have been written down sometime between the third century B.C. and the third century A.D., 132, 138, 162, 308, 310–13, 315, 317, 329–30, 337, 340, 341
Mahādeva	Great God; one of the names of Rudra, 46
mahaduktha	Great recital; chants intoned by the *hotṛ* on the day of the *mahāvrata*, during the mid-day squeezing of the *soma*, 199
Mahākāśyapa	Great Turtle; one of the first sixteen *arhats*, led the Buddhist community after the death of the Buddha, 364, 385, 386, 388–90

Mahākośī	A river that rises in the Himālaya, 107
mahāvīra	A clay pot made during the *pravargya* rite, used for heating milk, 130
mahāvrata	Great vow; a ceremony that forms part of a *sattra* lasting a year; at its center is the *mahaduktha*, 199, 200
mahiṣī	Consecrated One; the first in rank of the king's wives; she who married him first, 133, 145–48, 312, 320
Main	Name of the region around Frankfurt, where the Main flows
Maitreyī	Wife of Yājñavalkya, 187–88
Maitri Upaniṣad	An Upaniṣad in which the sage Maitri appears, 335
Mallas	At the time of the Buddha, the dominant clan in the north of Bihar, 394–95
manas	Mind; Latin: *mens*, 21
mānasaputras	Sons born of the mind, 65
maṇḍala	Circle; the books that make up the Ṛg Veda are known as *maṇḍalas*, 160–61
Mandara	A mountain used by the Devas and Asuras for the churning of the ocean, 231–33
Man-Lion	Narasiṃha, fourth *avatāra* of Viṣṇu, 333
mantra	Incantatory formula, metric unit; the hymns of the Ṛg Veda are composed of *mantras*, 103, 323, 324, 326
Manu	Son of Vivasvat and Chāyā, progenitor of men, who are thus known as *mānavas*. Or the son of Brahmā and Śatarūpā, 67, 220, 221, 226, 261
Māra	Killer; prince of demons, enemy of the Buddha, 360, 361, 384
Marcel	Name of the narrator in Proust's *Recherche*, 259
Mārgaśīrṣa	Head of the Antelope; the month corresponding to November–December, 95
Marīci	A *ṛṣi* of the second list, 93
Mārtāṇḍa	Dead Egg; the name of the Sun, shapeless son of Aditi, 219, 220–21
Maruts	Darting Ones; Rudra's children, born "from the laugh of the lightning" (*Ṛg Veda*, 1.23.12), 228
Maskarin Gośālīputra	Philosopher at the time of the Buddha, 354
Mātali	Charioteer and messenger of Indra, 302–4
Mathurā	A city of Uttar Pradesh, on the Yamunā River; birthplace of Kṛṣṇa, 271
Maudgalyāyana	A disciple of the Buddha, 361–63

māyā	Enchantment; also illusion, deception, magic; from the root *mā-*, "to measure," 110, 111, 119
Māyā	Mother of the Buddha, 349–50
Memory	Smara, 110
Menā	Wife of Himavat, mother of Pārvatī and Gaṅgā, 100, 103, 106, 107
Menakā	Name of an Apsaras, 303
Meru	The mountain that is also the axis of the world, 6, 63, 179, 272, 337, 342
meru	Spine, 337
Middle-length	*Majjhimanikāya*, "group of middle-length"; the name of one of the five sections into which the *Suttapiṭaka*, one of the Three Baskets of the Buddha's discourses, was subdivided, 390
Middle Way	*Madhyamā pratipad;* term used to define the teaching of the Buddha and the Eightfold Path he preached, 358
Milky Way	Flow of celestial waters; the whitish band that crosses the celestial vault, including about 100 billion stars; identified with Gaṅgā, 56, 117–18, 240, 254
Miśrakeśī	Name of an Apsaras, 303
Mitra	Friend; one of the Ādityas; a divinity who has a dual relationship with Varuṇa, 17, 70, 159, 160, 260, 261
Mixed	*Saṃyuttanikāya*, "mixed group"; the name of one of the five sections into which the *Suttapiṭaka*, one of the Three Baskets of the Buddha's discourses, was divided, 390
Mohenjo-daro	A city in the Indus valley; center of the eponymous civilization, which flourished between 2500 and 1700 B.C., 170
Mohinī	Enchantress, She who deceives; celestial courtesan, female manifestation of Viṣṇu, 91–93, 236
Moon	Soma; one of the *ratnas*, "gems," that appeared during the churning of the ocean, 233, 235
Mother of the Universe	Pārvatī, 123–24
Mountain Girl	Pārvatī, 197
Mṛga	Antelope; name of the constellation Orion, 56
Mṛtyu	Death; sometimes male, sometimes female, 25, 27, 62, 63, 140, 222

muhūrta — A unit of time, equivalent to about forty-eight minutes, 34

mūlādhāra — First of the *cakras,* "wheels," through which Devī Kuṇḍalinī ascends the body; situated at the base of the spine, 337

Muralī — Kṛṣṇa's flute, 277, 280–82

Nāgas — Snakes; name of the sons of Kadrū and of all snakes, 293, 299, 341, 359, 392

Nakṣatras — Houses of the Moon, 70

Nakula — One of the five Pāṇḍavas, twin brother of Sahadeva, whose parents were Nāsatya, one of the Aśvins, and Mādrī, Pāṇḍu's second wife, 295, 296, 298, 324

Nanda — Herdsman, Kṛṣṇa's adoptive father, 273

Nanda — Brother of the Buddha Śākyamuni, 392

Nandin — The bull that Śiva rides, 82, 85, 86, 102, 106, 108, 112–15, 122, 125

Nara — Man from whom the waters, *nāras,* are born; a *ṛṣi,* brother of Nārāyaṇa; appears as Arjuna in the *Mahābhārata,* 338–39

Nārada — A *ṛṣi,* son of Brahmā, 65, 103, 104, 166, 196, 286–88, 324

Nārāyaṇa — He who moves in the waters; dwelling place of man; epithet of Viṣṇu; a *ṛṣi,* brother of Nara, 338–39

Nāṭyaśāstra — Treatise on the Theater, attributed to Bharata; the first and most important Indian text on the theater, sometimes considered a Fifth Veda, 341

Nawāb Ja'far Khān — Ruler at whose court in Bengal in 1717 a dispute took place between supporters of *svakīyā* love and *parakīyā* love in the cult of Kṛṣṇa and Rādhā, 283

neṣṭṛ — Priest who leads the wives of the king in the *aśvamedha,* 145

Neumann — Karl Eugen Neumann, 1865–1915, scholar of Buddhism, 355

Night — Ratri, 113

Nīlakaṇṭha — The Blue-Necked One; epithet of Śiva; refers to the stain that appeared on the god's neck after he drank Kālakūṭa, 234

nīpa — *Nauclea cadamba,* a tree of scented, orange-colored flowers, 274, 276

Nirṛti — Dissolution, 140

nirvāṇa — Extinction, 364, 369, 391–93

Niṣādas — Population of India; according to the *Laws*

	of Manu, 10.8, "a Niṣāda is born from a brahman and the daughter of a *śūdra* [the lowest caste]," 8–10, 295
Noble Ones	Āryas, 166
nyagrodha	*Ficus indica*, the banyan tree, 335
Nymph	Apsaras, 182, 235, 253, 258
Oldenberg	Hermann Oldenberg, indologist, 1854–1920, 355
Olympus	Seat of the Greek gods, 258
Omniform	Viśvarūpa; epithet of Tvaṣṭṛ and of his son Triśiras, 219, 241
One-and-more	*Aṅguttaranikāya;* a group of discourses made up of one or more lines; name of one of the sections into which the *Suttapiṭaka*, one of the Three Baskets of the Buddha's discourses, is divided, 390
Order	The Buddhist community (*saṅgha*), 379, 396
Order	*Ṛta*, 158, 330
Orion	A constellation between Gemini and Taurus; Prajāpati in the sky, 56, 57
Orissa	A region of northeastern India, 283
Oṣadhiprastha	A city in the Himālaya, birthplace of Pārvatī, 107
pālāgalī	Daughter of the Herald; fourth in rank of the king's wives, of a lower caste than the others, 133
Pāñcālas	People who share a border with the Kuru people, 297
Pañcaviṃśa Brāhmaṇa	The twenty-five-chapter Brāhmaṇa; similar in theme to the *Jaiminīya Brāhmaṇa*, 240
Pāṇḍavas	The five brothers born of Kuntī and Mādrī, and held to be the sons of Pāṇḍu, cousins of the Kauravas, descendants of the lunar dynasty, 7, 157, 294–97, 299, 308, 310, 313, 314, 317, 318, 327, 330, 331, 333, 339–41, 376
Pāṇḍu	Son of Vyāsa and Ambālikā, putative father of the five Pāṇḍavas, 56, 278, 296, 317, 320, 324, 340
Pāṇini	The greatest Indian grammarian, who lived around 500 B.C. in Śalātura in northwest India, 172
parakīyā	Another's woman; the object of an adulterous, illegitimate love, 283, 284
parakīyādharma	Law of the illegitimate one, 285

Parīkṣit	Son of Abhimanyu and Uttarā, father of Janamejaya, 308
pāriplava	Circular story, 138, 139
parivṛktā	Neglected One; the third in rank of the king's wives, 133, 148
Parjanya	Cloud; Indra's younger brother, 140
Park of the Mango Trees	Āmravaṇa; a park in Vaiśālī, 376, 378
parvan	Knot; used of the books that compose the *Mahābhārata*, 310
Pārvatī	Daughter of the Mountain; her father, Himavat, is also called Parvata, 99–117, 119–20, 122–25, 197, 234–35, 336
paśus	Domestic animals (including man); animals that can be sacrificed, 159
Paśupati	Lord of the Herds; one of the names of Rudra, then of Śiva, 46, 121
pāyasa	Rice cooked in milk, 325, 326
pecus	Herd; primordial form of wealth, from which comes *pecunia,* "money," 159
Person	Puruṣa, 163
Person in the Eye	Indra and Indrāṇī appear as Persons in the Eye, he in the right, she in the left, 224
Physician	Dhanvantari; one of the *ratnas,* "gems," that appeared during the churning of the ocean, 235
Place of the Hunter	The celestial region between Sirius and Aldebaran, including the constellations Gemini and Taurus, 56
Plakṣa Prāsravaṇa	A place forty-eight days' march from where the Sarasvatī silts up; the center of the earth is a span (*prādeśa*) to the north of it, 239, 240
Plato	427–347 B.C., 163
Pleasure	Rati, 101, 315
Pleiades	Kṛttikās; a group of seven stars in the Taurus constellation, 55, 56, 124, 125
Prabhāsa	A city in Gujarat, 300
pradakṣiṇā	Ritual circumambulation around a statue, a temple, or a person, in a clockwise direction, that keeps the object of veneration on one's right (from *dakṣiṇā*, "right hand"), 65
Prajāpati	Progenitor; Lord of the Creatures; antecedent of Brahmā, 17, 21–37, 41–47, 53, 55–57, 61, 130–31, 140–42, 149–51, 163, 224, 231
prajñā	Wisdom, 371

prakṛti	Nature's fabric, made up of three threads (*guṇas*); the female counterpart of Puruṣa, in the Sāṃkhya doctrine, 110, 123
pralaya	Cosmic dissolution, which occurs at the end of every *kalpa*, 164, 333, 374, 375
prāṇa	Vital breath; man has seven of them, 199
prāśitra	First portion; when the portions of the sacrificial food are distributed, the first to be cut is a morsel no bigger than a barley grain, which is offered to the brahman on a wooden plate with a handle; it corresponds to the piece of flesh torn from Prajāpati when he was wounded, 190–91
prati-	Prefix that indicates, among other things, a coming toward, typical of Uṣas, 49
pratiṣṭhā	Foundation, base, 23, 392
pratītyasamutpāda	"Production (*utpāda*) converging (*sam*) in function of (*pratītya*)" (L. Silburn); "law of interconnection" (T. Stcherbatsky), 372
Precious Stone	Kaustubha; one of the *ratnas*, "gems," that appeared during the churning of the ocean, 235
preman	Love, 284
Prisonnière	*La Prisonnière;* the third-to-last part of Proust's *Recherche*, 259
Prīti	Daughter of Dakṣa and Vīriṇī, 69
Progenitor	Prajāpati, 24, 25, 29, 63, 163
Progenitors	The Saptarṣis, 160
Propitious	Śiva, 118
Proust	Marcel Proust, 1871–1922, 259, 315
Pulaha	A *ṛṣi* of the second list, 69, 93
Pulastya	A *ṛṣi* of the second list, 69, 93
punarmṛtyu	Repeated death, 94
púr	Most commentators interpret the word as "walls"; W. Rau gives it as "livestock corral," 170
Pūraṇa Kāśyapa	Philosopher at the time of the Buddha, 354
Purāṇas	Ancient Ones; texts that tell the stories of the gods and, in relation to them, deal with any other matter, cosmic or human; composed mostly between the fourth and fourteenth centuries A.D., 61
pūrṇa	Full, 369
Purūravas	Lover of Urvaśī, father of Āyus, 261, 262–67, 305
Puruṣa	Person; primordial man, who is broken up in the world, 161, 163

puruṣa Person, 225

pūrvácitti First thought, 49

Pūrvácitti Name of an Apsaras, 303

pūrváhūti First ritual call, 49

Pūṣan Nourisher; one of the Ādityas, brother (or husband) of Sūryā, 17, 50, 70, 85

puṣkara Blue lotus, 399

pūṣkara Rock, 399

Pūtanā Fetid; a demon, 282

Python Snake of Delphi, 248

quincunx The shape in which the number five is displayed on dice, 254

Rādhā Kṛṣṇa's most celebrated lover, a *gopī*, 277, 282, 283, 285, 286

Rāhula Son of the Buddha and Gopā, 353, 373

Raivataka A mountain near Prabhāsa, 300

Rājagṛha A city in Bihar where the first Buddhist council was held shortly after the Buddha's death, 362, 385, 387

rājasūya Rite in which the king was consecrated, 314, 329

Rambhā Name of an Apsaras, 303

rasa Juice, flavor, emotion, essence, 280, 284, 337, 340, 341

rāsalīlā Game of the dance; a circular dance, 282, 283

Rati Pleasure; Kāma's consort, 101, 102

ratilīlā Game of pleasure, 112

ratnas Gems; visions that appeared during the churning of the ocean; including Sun, Moon, the Apsaras, Uccaiḥśravas, Śrī, Airāvata, Dhanvantari, Kāmadhenu, and Kaustubha, 233

Rauhiṇa An immense tree from whose branches hang the Vālakhilyas, 10, 14, 16

ṛc Praise, hymn, 313

ṛddhipāda Basis of magic power, 383, 384

Recherche *À la recherche du temps perdu* by Marcel Proust, 259, 315

Renou Louis Renou, indologist, 1896–1966, 52

Residue Śeṣa, 193, 391, 392

Ṛg Veda Wisdom made up of hymns; A collection of 1,028 hymns divided into ten books (*maṇḍalas*), belonging to the eponymous Veda. It is believed to have been put together between 1200 and 1000 B.C., 17,

48, 50, 61, 138, 160–62, 169, 172, 248, 313, 401

Ring — *Der Ring des Nibelungen*, by Richard Wagner, 315

riṣ- — To consume oneself, 163

rocaná — Space of light, 255, 256

Rohiṇī — Tawny One; Aldebaran, 29, 55, 57

Romance of the Horse — Narrative implicit in the course of the *aśvamedha*, 138

ṛṣi — Seer, 52, 69, 70, 81, 90, 92–94, 99, 102, 108–9, 157–64, 166, 167, 172, 173, 175, 178–82, 189, 197, 202, 210, 227, 228, 238, 246–48, 255, 256, 259, 261, 303, 322, 328, 329, 334–35, 365, 368–71, 392, 400

Ṛśyaśṛṅga — Son of the *ṛṣi* Vibhāṇḍaka; hermit, 182

ṛta — Order, truth; Heinrich Lüders dedicates a considerable part of his two-volume *Varuṇa* (unfinished) to a demonstration of how and why the two meanings are copresent, 158, 248

ṛtávan — Endowed with truth, 248

Rudra — Yelling One or Tawny One, according to the ancient etymologists; antecedent of Śiva, 42–48, 53, 55, 56, 61, 190–91, 201, 232, 237

Rudras — Eleven divinities who, with the Vasus, the Ādityas, and the two Aśvins, make up the thirty-three Vedic gods, 17, 25, 32, 140

Rukmiṇī — First wife of Kṛṣṇa, 324–26

rūpa — Form, 136

ruvan — Roaring, 261

sabhā — Meeting place, assembly hall, 148, 157, 158, 163, 166, 375

sāhā — The girl who takes part in the rite of the *aśvamedha*, 148

Sahā — Name of an Apsaras, 303

Sahadeva — The youngest of the five Pāṇḍavas, twin brother of Nakula, whose parents were Dasra, one of the Aśvins, and Mādrī, Pāṇḍu's second wife, 295, 296, 298, 324

Śākalya — A brahman of the Kuru-Pañcālas, 187

śakti — Power; the *śakti* par excellence is Śiva's consort, 110

Śakuntalā — Daughter of Viśvāmitra and the Apsaras Menakā; from her union with King

Duṣyanta she gives birth to Sarvadamana, later known as Bharata, emperor of India, 321

Śākyas The royal clan to which the Buddha belonged, hence his name Śākyamuni, "Wise man of the Śākyas," 349, 356, 373, 376

śāla *Shorea robusta, Vatica robusta,* a resinous tree common in India, 350, 393–95

Śālavatī An area of the principality of Kosala, 382

Śālva A tribe settled on the banks of the Yamunā, 240

Śāmaśravas Disciple of Yājñavalkya, 183

śamī *Acacia suma, Mimosa suma, Prosopis spicigera,* a tree of the acacia family, 335, 336, 337

Saṃjayin Vairaṭīputra Philosopher living at the time of the Buddha, 354, 396

saṃjīvanī vidyā The science of resurrection, 232–33

Sāṃkhya One of the six schools of thought fundamental to Indian philosophy, 161

saṃnyāsin Renouncer, 353

sampad That which falls together, equivalence, 25, 27

saṃsāra Migration; the circle of rebirth, becoming of phenomena, 310

Śāṃtanu King of the lunar dynasty, father of Bhīṣma, husband of Satyavatī, and father of Vicitravīrya, 318–19

saṃtati Continuity, 136

Sāñcī A place in Madhya Pradesh sacred to Buddhism, 173

Sandhyā Conjunction, dusk; daughter of Brahmā, 50

Sannati Daughter of Dakṣa and Vīriṇī, 69

śāntarasa Flavor of peace, 340

Saptarṣis The seven *ṛṣis* who reside in the stars of the Great Bear, also known as *ṛṣis* of the first list, partly to indicate that they came before all the other *ṛṣis* and partly because of the antiquity of the tradition that bears witness to them: Bharadvāja, Kaśyapa, Gotama, Atri, Viśvāmitra, Jamadagni, and Vasiṣṭha. The *ṛṣis* of the second list, predominant in the epics, are Marīci, Atri, Aṅgiras, Pulastya, Pulaha, Kratu, and Vasiṣṭha. Bhṛgu is sometimes included in

	the second list, 107, 160–62, 165, 177, 199, 203
Saramā	Indra's she-dog, 249, 250, 310
Saraṇyū	Daughter of Tvaṣṭṛ, twin sister of Triśiras, wife of Vivasvat, mother of Yama and Yamī and of the Aśvins, 216, 218–22
Sarasvatī	Flowing One; wife of Brahmā, sacred river of the Punjab, whose waters sink into the sands of the Rajasthan, 17, 65, 75, 85, 178, 179, 211, 213, 238–40
Śaravaṇodbhava	Born-in-a-reed-marsh; name of Skanda, 124
Śāriputra	Disciple of the Buddha, 361–64
Sārnāth	Place where the Buddha began to preach, near Vārāṇasī, 54
Sarva	Everything; one of the names of Rudra, 46
Śarva	Archer; one of the names of Rudra, 46
Śaryāti	King, son of Manu, father of Sukanyā, 207, 208, 225–26
Śatapatha Brāhmaṇa	The Brāhmana of the hundred paths; the most important and complex of the Brāhmaṇas, attributed to Yājñavalkya, 208
Śatarūpā	She who has a hundred shapes; daughter and consort of Brahmā, 65–67
Satī	She-who-is; daughter of Dakṣa and Vīriṇī, consort of Śiva, 75–89, 91, 93, 105, 116
sattra	Sitting; a rite without *dakṣiṇā*, which can last from twelve days to, in theory at least, a hundred years, 202–3, 309
sattva	Being, purity; one of the three threads (*guṇas*) that make up the world, 400
satya	Truth, 151
satyavākya	Word of truth; ordeal of the word, 382
Satyavatī	Born from the seed of King Uparicara swallowed by a fish who was the Apsaras Adrikā; mother to Vyāsa through her union with the brahman Parāśara, wife of Śāṃtanu, 316–17, 319, 340
Savitṛ	He who gives impulse; shape of the Sun, one of the Ādityas, 17, 70
Sāvitrī	Daughter of Savitṛ, consort of Brahmā, 65
Sāyaṇa	Commentator of the Vedas who lived in the fourteenth century, 178
Self	*Ātman*, 21, 28, 46, 79, 149, 189, 204, 224–25, 334, 369, 372, 400

Soma	Divine king, made up of the substance called *soma*, 17, 70, 75, 77, 119, 197, 237, 243, 244, 253–59, 307
soma	Squeezed, juice; an intoxicating plant that has been identified over the centuries with numerous botanical varieties, both in India and by Western indologists. From the Brāhmaṇas on, the *soma* is replaced in the rites (because it is no longer available) by *Ephedra, Sarcostemma,* and other epiphytes. In 1968, R. Gordon Wasson claimed to have identified the *soma* as the hallucinogenic mushroom *Amanita muscaria.* According to D. S. Flattery, on the other hand, it is another hallucinogenic plant, *Peganum harmala*, 6, 14–16, 33, 45, 105, 139, 159, 165, 170, 171, 199, 213, 215, 218, 226, 228, 231, 236, 238, 241, 245, 247, 254–58, 260, 335, 337
Splendor of the World	Śrī, 322
Squirt	Skanda, 124
śraddhā	Trust, faith, 36, 193
śramaṇa	Ascetic, 395
Śrī	Splendor of the World; appeared during the churning of the ocean and became the consort of Viṣṇu, 234, 322–23
sṛj-	To squirt, 44
śruti	That which one hears; revelation, a term used to designate the Vedas as a whole, 168
Sthūra	*Gṛhapati* of a group of officiants of a *sattra* that was celebrated along the banks of the Sarasvatī, 240
Styx	Infernal river, 258
Subhadra	A wanderer; the last disciple converted by the Buddha, 395, 396
Subhadrā	Fortunate One; sister of Kṛṣṇa, wife of Arjuna, mother of Abhimanyu, 291, 292, 301
Śubháspátīs	Lords of Ornament; epithet of the Aśvins, 226
Submarine Mare	Vaḍavā, 294
Śuddhodana	Nobleman of the Śākya tribe in Kapilavastu, father of Siddhārtha Gautama, later called the Buddha, 349, 351, 353, 354, 356, 357
Sugar Candy Forest	Forest of Khāṇḍava, 292

Sujātā	Well born; a girl from Uruvilva who lived at the time of the Buddha, 358
Sukanyā	Good daughter; daughter of Śaryāti, 207–9, 211–12, 214, 226
Śunaḥśepa	Son of the *ṛṣi* Ajīgarta Sauyavasi, 50
śūnya	Empty, 369
Suparṇī	Aquiline One; another name of Vinatā, 5
Sūrya	Sun; son of Aditi and Kaśyapa, 5, 17, 214, 226, 227
Sūryā	Daughter of the Sun, 50, 119, 331
suṣumnā	Central channel, inside the spinal cord, along which Devī Kuṇḍalinī ascends, 337
sūta	Caste of charioteers, heralds, and bards, 331
sūtra	Thread, rule enounced with a minimum number of words, in somewhat algebraic formulas, often with no verb; in Buddhism, the word takes on the larger connotation "discourse" of the Buddha, 172, 390
sva-	From self, of self, auto-, one's own, 64
svakīyā	One's own woman, legitimate wife, 283, 284
svargaloka	Bright world, 239
svásṛ	Sister, 50
Svasti	Well-being; one of the names of Devī, 17
svayamātṛṇṇa	Term for the "naturally perforated" stones used in the altar of fire, 37
svayaṃbhū	Self-existing, 22
Svayaṃprabhā	Name of an Apsaras, 303
svayaṃvara	Independent choice; ceremony in which the future bride chooses one of her suitors, after they have undergone a trial of ability, 301, 330
Takṣaka	King of the Nāgas, lives in the Forest of Khāṇḍava, 309
Tāṇḍava	Śiva's cosmic dance, 86
Tantrī	Daughter of Māra, 360, 361
tapas	Heat; ardor; from the Indo-European root *tap-*, which gives the Latin *tepeo.* Long translated with a range of terms (*austérités, penance, Kasteiung, ascèse*), *tapas* means at once the cosmic heat and the heat within the mind, that which broods, in the sense of incubates (*Brütung*, occasionally, in Deussen), 21, 25, 66, 70, 72, 75, 78–80, 84, 90, 93, 102–5, 112, 113, 115, 116, 118, 120, 125, 133, 134, 161, 162, 168,

	177–79, 181, 182, 185, 197, 210, 216, 220, 232, 302, 369
tapasvinī	A woman who practices *tapas*, 91
Tāraka	A powerful Asura, 100–101, 105, 121, 122, 125
tathā	Thus, 358
Tathāgata	He-who-came-thus; name the Buddha gave himself, 137, 357, 358, 361, 377, 380, 395, 396
tathatā	Being thus, 358
tat tvam asi	"You are that" (*Chāndogya Upaniṣad*, 6.8.7); one of the "great sentences," *mahāvākyas*, of the Upaniṣads, 269
Taurus	A constellation between Orion and the Pleiades, 56
Tawny One	Rohiṇī, Uṣas, 29
Taxila	Takṣaśilā, a city in northwest India, now Pakistan, near Rawalpindi, 313
tejas	Flame; luminous force, manifestation of *tapas*, 67, 177
telestērion	Rectangular building, with columns, where part of the Eleusinian mysteries were enacted, 158
Ten Sisters	The ten fingers, 253, 254
Thirty-three	The Devas: the twelve Ādityas, the eight Vasus, the eleven Rudras, and the two Aśvins (or, in other traditions, Dyaus and Pṛthivī, Sky and Earth), 122
Three Baskets	*Tripiṭaka,* into which the teaching of the Buddha is divided, 388, 392
Time	Kāla, 45, 330, 342, 343
Tiresias	Seer of Thebes, 315
Tolstoy	Leo Tolstoy, 1828–1910, 31
Tree of Awakening	The fig tree in Gayā under which the awakening, *bodhi,* of the Buddha occurred. Today the place of the awakening is known as Bodhgayā, 335
Tremendous	Bhairava; epithet of Śiva, 67
tretā	When playing dice the throw that gives a remainder of three; in the sequence of the *yugas,* the *tretāyuga* follows the *kṛtayuga*, 375
Trial, The	Franz Kafka's novel, 31
Tricephalous	Triśiras, 218
Triśaṅku	King of the solar dynasty, favorite of Viśvāmitra, 202

Triśiras	The Tricephalous; son of Tvaṣṭṛ, twin brother of Saraṇyū; also called Viśvarūpa, 218
triṣṭubh	A Vedic meter made up of four verses of eleven syllables, 14, 17, 32
Truth	*Satya; ṛta*, 158
Turtle	Kūrma, 121
Tuṣita	Celestial home of the various Bodhisattvas, 350, 371
Tvaṣṭṛ	Carpenter, Craftsman; father of Saraṇyū and Triśiras, one of the Ādityas, 17, 70, 194, 218–19, 221–22, 241–43
Twelve	The Ādityas, 194
Twisted Goddess	Devī Kuṇḍalinī, 337
tyád	That, 173
Uccaiḥśravas	He who neighs loudly; the White Horse, one of the *rutnas*, "gems," that appeared during the churning of the ocean, 6, 8, 233
udgātṛ	One of the four main officiants; the chanter, his task is to sing the ritual hymns (*stotrus*) of the Sama Veda, 140
udgītha	The second and most important part of the *stotra;* a trio for voices sung by the *udgātṛ* and his assistants, 140
udumbara	*Ficus glomerata;* according to legend, it flowers every three thousand years, 188, 199, 394
Ugradeva	Terrifying God; one of the names of Rudra, 46
Ugraśravas	A bard who tells the story of the *Māhābhārata,* which he hears from Vaiśampāyana, 313
Ulūpī	Daughter of the king of the Nāgas, wife of Arjuna, 299
Umā	From *u mā*, "oh, no"; another name of Pārvatī, 104, 111, 197
Unlimited One	Aditi, 227
Upāli	Palace barber at Kapilavastu, who joins the Buddha's disciples, 378
Upaniṣads	Treatises around correspondences; metaphysical texts, the oldest of which are in prose, the later in prose and verse, 312, 369
Uparicara	King from whose seed, swallowed by a large fish, Satyavatī is born, 316
Upavāṇa	Monk, disciple of the Buddha, his servant before Ānanda, 393–94
Ūrjā	Daughter of Dakṣa and Vīriṇī, 69

ūru Thigh, 306

Uruvilvā Locality in Magadha, near Bodhgayā, 355, 358

Urvaśī The first of the Apsaras, ancestor of the lunar dynasty, into which the Pāṇḍavas and the Kauravas were born, 159, 160, 260–67, 303–306, 308, 400

Uṣas Dawn, 17, 41–44, 46, 48–55, 57, 226, 227

Uttarā Extreme; daughter of Virāṭa, wife of Abhimanyu, 306–308

Uttarakuru A fabulous and inaccessible country in the far north, 307

Vāc The goddess Word, 24–25, 118, 191, 236–39, 256

vāc Word, voice (Latin: *vox*), 133, 191

Vaḍavā The Submarine Mare; from her mouth issues a blaze of heat, *vāḍavāgni*, that ends up consuming the waters of the ocean, 195

Vaijayanta Indra's standard, 302

Vaiśālī The ancient city of the Licchavi clan, in Bihar, 376–78, 382, 383

Vaiśampāyana A *ṛṣi*, disciple of Vyāsa, 308, 313

vajra Thunderbolt; supreme weapon forged by Tvaṣṭṛ for Indra, 113, 163, 304

Vakuḍa Place where the last of the Śākyas find refuge, 374

Vala Cave; the rock that conceals the Cows and the Waters, 247, 250

Vālakhilyas A race of *ṛṣis* the height of a thumb, born from Prajāpati's hair; Hymns 49–59 of the eighth book of the Ṛg Veda are attributed to them, 10–12

Varāha Boar; third *avatāra* of Viṣṇu, 278

Vārāṇasī The capital of the kingdom of Kāśī, whence derived the Hindi Banāras, later anglicized to Benares, 54, 283, 350, 365

Vāraṇāvata City where the Pāṇḍavas live before fleeing the burning of the lacquer house, 295

Vargā Name of an Apsaras, 300

varṇa Color, caste, 178

Varuṇa All-embracing; one of the Ādityas, 17, 30, 51, 70, 100, 140, 157–60, 246, 258, 260, 261, 367

Varūthinī Name of an Apsaras, 303

vasatīvarī Overnight waters; used in the *soma* rites, 260

Vasiṣṭha Born from the seed of Mitra and Varuṇa squirted into a bowl, one of the Saptarṣis, author, as tradition has it, of the seventh *maṇḍala* of the Ṛg Veda, 69, 72, 93, 158–60, 162, 165, 175, 178–80, 193–94, 196–97, 202, 204, 261

Vāstoṣpati Lord of the Place, Lord of the Sacrificial Residue; one of the names of Rudra, 46

Vāsuki Snake, one of the kings of the Nāgas, used by the Devas and the Asuras in the churning of the ocean, 115, 232

Vasus Group of eight divinities, including Soma, Agni, and Vāyu; with the Ādityas, the Rudras, and the Aśvins, they make up the thirty-three Vedic gods, 17, 25, 32

vāvātā Favorite One; the second in rank of the king's wives, 133, 148

Vāyu Wind; the god who generates Bhīma through his union with Kuntī, 113, 197, 296

veda Knowledge, 168

Vedas A collection of texts including the books of hymns, the Brāhmaṇas, the Araṇyakas, the Upaniṣads, and the Sūtras. They are divided into the Ṛg Veda, Sāma Veda, Yajur Veda, and Atharva Veda (the latter is sometimes excluded, in which case one speaks of the Three Vedas), 8, 16, 17, 52–54, 105, 110, 132, 139, 160, 161, 170, 173, 196, 237, 241–43, 259, 280, 294, 320, 328, 335, 337, 357, 365, 369

vedi Altar, 143

Veṇuvana Bamboo Wood, one of the Buddha's favorite parks, 378

vi- Prefix indicating separation and pervasiveness, 44

Vicitravīrya Son of Śāṃtanu and Satyavatī, husband of Ambikā and Ambālikā, 317, 319, 320

Videhas A people in northeast India, 183, 185

Vidura Son of Vyāsa and one of Ambikā's maids, uncle of the Pāṇḍavas and the Kauravas, 295

Vijayā Maid of Pārvatī, 103

Vikrampur A city in Bengal, 283

Vimalakauṇḍinya Son of Āmrapālī, 376–77

vīṇā A musical instrument with strings, emblem of Sarasvatī, 286, 292

Vinatā — Daughter of Dakṣa, sister of Kadrū, mother of Garuḍa and Aruṇa; according to the *Śatapatha Brāhmaṇa*, 3.2.4.1, Kadrū and Vinatā were two *māyās*, "magic forms," evoked by the Devas to conquer the *soma*, 3–8, 12–13, 16, 258

Vināyaka — Without husband; epithet of Gaṇeśa, born from Pārvatī alone, 114

Vipāśā — A river in the Punjab, 179

vipras — Vibrant; epithet of the *ṛṣis*, 161

Vīrabhadra — Terrifying manifestation of Śiva, 85, 86

viraha — Separation, 284

virāj — A Vedic meter of four lines of ten syllables, 161

Virāṭa — King of the Matsyas (Fishes), father of Uttarā, 306, 329

Vīriṇī — Wife of Dakṣa, 69, 78

Virūḍhaka — King of the Kosalas, 373–74

Viṣṇu — All-pervasive One; from *viś*, "to enter," or *vy-aś*, "to penetrate," "to pervade." "For he penetrates in everything" (*Vāyu Purāṇa*, 5.36). One of the Ādityas, 6, 17, 70, 86, 91, 100, 101, 122, 182, 198, 216–17, 232, 234–36, 260, 278, 309, 321, 327, 333, 336, 391, 399–401

visṛj- — To expand, to emit, 44

Viśvāmitra — Friend of everyone; one of the Saptarṣis; according to tradition, author of most of the third and fourth *maṇḍala* of the Ṛg Veda, 160, 162, 165, 175–76, 178, 179, 194–95, 199–204, 322

Viśvarūpa — Omniform One; another name of Tvaṣṭṛ and of his son Triśiras, 219, 241

Viśvāvasu — Beneficent to everyone; a Gandharva, 236

Viśve Devas — The All-gods, 140

Vivasvat — Irradiant, Brilliant One; the Sun, one of the Ādityas, 17, 70, 219–22

Voice — Vāc, 238

Vraja — Vṛndāvana; the forest where Kṛṣṇa would meet the *gopīs*, near Mathurā, 276, 278

vrata — Way of life, vow, 200

vrāta — Band, fraternity, group of initiates, 200

vrātya — Member of a wandering band (*vrāta*) bound by a vow, *vrata*, 200–204, 375

Vṛddhakṣatra — Father of Jayadratha, 334–35

Vṛndāvana — Forest where Kṛṣṇa and Rādhā pleasure each other; there is a celestial Vṛndāvana

yojana A unit of length, corresponding to about fifteen kilometers, 393

yoni Vagina, womb, spring, 314

Yudhiṣṭhira The eldest of the Pāṇḍavas, born of the union between Dharma and Kuntī, first wife of Pāṇḍu, his putative father, 132, 295, 296, 298, 299, 314, 318, 324, 329–31, 340–46

yuga Aeon, 375

yūpa Pole to which sacrificial victims are tied, 159, 190

Zodiac Celestial band corresponding to the ecliptic, 272

Sources

The first number in the left column refers to the page, the second to the line on which the quotation ends. When specific translations are cited, in some cases the wording has been adapted.

21,2 *Śatapatha Brāhmaṇa*, 10.5.3.1
21,8 *Aitareya Brāhmaṇa*, 2.40 (tr. by A. B. Keith)
22,4 *Ṛg Veda*, 10.129.3 (tr. by L. Renou)
22,6 *Śatapatha Brāhmaṇa*, 11.1.6.1
22,7 *Bṛhad Araṇyaka Upaniṣad*, 4.3.32
22,16 *Śatapatha Brāhmaṇa*, 11.1.6.1
22,17 *Ṛg Veda*, 10.129.3 (tr. by L. Renou)
22,19 *Śatapatha Brāhmaṇa*, 11.1.6.1
24,29 *Pañcaviṃśa Brāhmaṇa*, 20.14.2
24,32 *Pañcaviṃśa Brāhmaṇa*, 20.14.2 (tr. by W. Caland)
29,27 *Śatapatha Brāhmaṇa*, 7.1.2.1 (tr. by J. Eggeling)
30,12 *Śatapatha Brāhmaṇa*, 10.5.2.3 (tr. by J. Eggeling)
31,13 *Śatapatha Brāhmaṇa*, 13.5.3.3
36,10 *Śatapatha Brāhmaṇa*, 7.3.1.42
37,1 *Aitareya Brāhmaṇa*, 3.21 (tr. by A. B. Keith)
47,27 S. Kramrisch, *The Presence of Śiva* (Princeton: Princeton University Press, 1981), p. 76
48,8 *Ṛg Veda*, 4.3.1
48,32 *Ṛg Veda*, 7.75.7 (tr. by L. Renou)
48,33 *Ṛg Veda*, 3.61.3 (tr. by L. Renou)
49,1 *Ṛg Veda*, 1.124.8 (tr. by L. Renou)
49,4 *Ṛg Veda*, 1.113.9 (tr. by L. Renou)
49,12 *Ṛg Veda*, 7.80.2
49,13 *Ṛg Veda*, 1.124.4 (tr. by L. Renou)
49,16 *Ṛg Veda*, 1.123.10 (tr. by L. Renou)
49,17 *Ṛg Veda*, 6.64.2 (tr. by L. Renou)
49,19 *Ṛg Veda*, 5.80.6 (tr. by L. Renou)

49,23 *Ṛg Veda*, 1.122.2
49,24 *Ṛg Veda*, 1.112.1
49,31 *Ṛg Veda*, 1.123.4 (tr. by L. Renou)
49,32 *Ṛg Veda*, 1.123.12 (tr. by L. Renou)
51,15 *Ṛg Veda*, 1.30.20 (tr. by J. Varenne)
52,11 *Atharva Veda*, 4.16.5
52,17 K. F. Geldner, note to *Ṛg Veda*, 4.30.8–11
52,22 L. Renou, *Études védiques et pāninéennes*, vol. 3 (Paris: Boccard, 1957), p. 8
52,33 *Ṛg Veda*, 10.61.8 (tr. by K. F. Geldner)
52,34 *Ṛg Veda*, 10.61.8 (tr. by K. F. Geldner)
53,21 *Manusmṛti*, 2.23 (tr. by W. Doniger)
54,29 *Ṛg Veda*, 1.124.7 (tr. by L. Renou)
54,33 *Ṛg Veda*, 7.75.2
55,12 *Ṛg Veda*, 1.113.12
55,18 *Ṛg Veda*, 1.113.11 (tr. by L. Renou)
65,7 *Vāyu Purāṇa*, 65.128
65,20 *Matsya Purāṇa*, 3.30
65,30 *Matsya Purāṇa*, 3.33, 36, and 38
103,2 Kālidāsa, *Abhijñānaśakuntala*, 5.2
109,7 *Bṛhad Araṇyaka Upaniṣad*, 4.3.21
114,14 *Śiva Purāṇa*, 2.4.13.5
131,35 *Baudhāyana Śrauta Sūtra*, 15.16
132,18 *Mahābhārata*, 14.87.13
132,22 *Mahābhārata*, 14.90.22
132,33 *Śatapatha Brāhmaṇa*, 13.1.1.4
133,5 *Śatapatha Brāhmaṇa*, 13.4.1.7
134,2 *Vādhūla Sūtra* (fragment 70 Caland)
134,10 *Āpastamba Śrauta Sūtra*, 20.1.17 (tr. by P.-E. Dumont)
134,13 *Āpastamba Śrauta Sūtra*, 20.1.17 (tr. by P.-E. Dumont)
134,18 *Āpastamba Śrauta Sūtra*, 20.3.2 (tr. by P.-E. Dumont)
134,24 *Śatapatha Brāhmaṇa*, 13.1.6.3
135,3 *Vājasaneyi Saṃhitā*, 22.3 (tr. by P.-E. Dumont)
135,33 *Śatapatha Brāhmaṇa*, 13.1.6.2
136,7 *Śatapatha Brāhmaṇa*, 13.4.2.16
136,9 *Śatapatha Brāhmaṇa*, 13.1.3.7
137,7 *Baudhāyana Śrauta Sūtra*, 15.23
137,25 *Śatapatha Brāhmaṇa*, 13.4.2.17
139,4 *Śatapatha Brāhmaṇa*, 13.4.3.15
139,26 *Bṛhad Araṇyaka Upaniṣad*, 1.3.28
139,32 *Śatapatha Brāhmaṇa*, 13.2.3.1
140,5 *Āpastamba Śrauta Sūtra*, 20.13.7 (tr. by P.-E. Dumont)
141,12 *Śatapatha Brāhmaṇa*, 13.4.2.17; 13.4.1.10; 13.4.2.17; 13.5.1.15; 13.5.3.9
141,17 *Śatapatha Brāhmaṇa*, 13.2.4.3
141,23 *Śatapatha Brāhmaṇa*, 13.2.4.1
141,32 *Śatapatha Brāhmaṇa*, 13.2.4.3 (tr. by J. Eggeling)
142,25 *Śatapatha Brāhmaṇa*, 13.2.4.3

143,2 *Baudhāyana Śrauta Sūtra*, 15.29 (tr. by P.-E. Dumont)
143,5 *Baudhāyana Śrauta Sūtra*, 15.29 (tr. by P.-E. Dumont)
143,7 *Baudhāyana Śrauta Sūtra*, 15.29 (tr. by P.-E. Dumont)
143,12 *Baudhāyana Śrauta Sūtra*, 15.29 (tr. by P.-E. Dumont)
143,17 *Baudhāyana Śrauta Sūtra*, , 15.29 (tr. by P.-E. Dumont)
144,15 *Vājasaneyi Saṃhitā*, 29.1 (tr. by P.-E. Dumont)
144,19 *Vājasaneyi Saṃhitā*, 29.5 (tr. by P.-E. Dumont)
144,31 *Ṛg Veda*, 1.162.20–21 (tr. by K. F. Geldner)
145,18 *Śatapatha Brāhmaṇa*, 13.2.8.1
145,19 *Śatapatha Brāhmaṇa*, 13.2.8.2
146,2 *Śatapatha Brāhmaṇa*, 13.2.8.4
146,11 *Vājasaneyi Saṃhitā*, 6.15 (tr. by P.-E. Dumont)
146,24 *Vājasaneyi Saṃhitā*, 23.20 (tr. by P.-E. Dumont)
146,30 *Vājasaneyi Saṃhitā*, 23.21 (tr. by P.-E. Dumont)
147,11 *Taittirīya Saṃhitā*, 7.4.19 (tr. by P.-E. Dumont)
147,28 *Vājasaneyi Saṃhitā*, 23.25 (tr. by P.-E. Dumont)
147,36 *Śatapatha Brāhmaṇa*, 13.5.2.9
148,5 *Vādhūla Sūtra*, 3.93 (tr. by H. Falk)
148,12 *Ṛg Veda*, 4.39.6
148,14 *Śatapatha Brāhmaṇa*, 13.5.2.10 (tr. by J. Eggeling)
148,17 *Śatapatha Brāhmaṇa*, 13.5.2.9
148,28 *Śatapatha Brāhmaṇa*, 13.2.10.1
148,31 *Vājasaneyi Saṃhitā*, 23.35 (tr. by P.-E. Dumont)
148,32 *Vājasaneyi Saṃhitā*, 23.37 (tr. by P.-E. Dumont)
149,25 *Vājasaneyi Saṃhitā*, 23.39 (tr. by P.-E. Dumont)
150,5 *Śatapatha Brāhmaṇa*, 13.4.1.1
150,8 *Śatapatha Brāhmaṇa*, 13.4.1.1 (tr. by J. Eggeling)
150,14 *Śatapatha Brāhmaṇa*, 13.4.1.1
150,16 *Śatapatha Brāhmaṇa*, 6.6.3.1
151,15 *Varaha Śrauta Sūtra*, 1.4.4.14 (tr. by H. Falk)
151,33 *Vādhūla Sūtra*, 3.94 (tr. by H. Falk)
152,12 *Vādhūla Sūtra*, 3.94 (tr. by H. Falk)
153,5 *Āpastamba Śrauta Sūtra*, 20.22.9 (tr. by P.-E. Dumont)
158,29 *Ṛg Veda*, 7.88.2
160,4 *Ṛg Veda*, 7.33.11
164,8 *Śatapatha Brāhmaṇa*, 6.1.1.1
165,20 *Atharva Veda*, 10.8.9 (tr. by W. D. Whitney)
169,11 *Ṛg Veda*, 9.87.3
171,8 W. Caland and V. Henry, *L'Agniṣṭoma*, vol. 2

(Paris: E. Leroux, 1907), p. 469

172,8 *Ṛg Veda*, 10.30.4 (tr. by K. F. Geldner)

172,26 C. Malamoud, *Cuire le monde* (Paris: La Découverte, 1989), p. 243

175,3 *Bṛhad Āraṇyaka Upaniṣad*, 1.4.10 (tr. by É. Senart)

175,4 *Bṛhad Āraṇyaka Upaniṣad*, 1.4.10 (tr. by É. Senart)

175,13 *Bṛhad Āraṇyaka Upaniṣad*, 1.4.10 (tr. by É. Senart)

175,17 *Bṛhad Āraṇyaka Upaniṣad*, 1.4.10 (tr. by É. Senart)

175,22 *Bṛhad Āraṇyaka Upaniṣad*, 1.4.10 (tr. by É. Senart)

178,4 *Ṛg Veda*, 1.179.6

184,24 *Bṛhad Āraṇyaka Upaniṣad*, 3.6.1 (tr. by É. Senart)

185,5 *Bṛhad Āraṇyaka Upaniṣad*, 3.6.1 (tr. by É. Senart)

185,36 *Bṛhad Āraṇyaka Upaniṣad*, 3.8.10 (tr. by É. Senart)

186,10 *Bṛhad Āraṇyaka Upaniṣad*, 3.8.12 (tr. by É. Senart)

187,6 *Śatapatha Brāhmaṇa*, 11.6.3.11

187,30 *Bṛhad Āraṇyaka Upaniṣad*, 1.4.3 (tr. by É. Senart)

188,21 *Bṛhad Āraṇyaka Upaniṣad*, 2.4.1; 4.5.2 (tr. by É. Senart)

188,28 *Bṛhad Āraṇyaka Upaniṣad*, 2.4.2; 4.5.3 (tr. by É. Senart)

188,30 *Bṛhad Āraṇyaka Upaniṣad*, 2.4.2; 4.5.3 (tr. by É. Senart)

188,33 *Bṛhad Āraṇyaka Upaniṣad*, 2.4.3; 4.5.4 (tr. by É. Senart)

188,36 *Bṛhad Āraṇyaka Upaniṣad*, 2.4.4; 4.5.5 (tr. by É. Senart)

188,38 *Bṛhad Āraṇyaka Upaniṣad*, 2.4.5; 4.5.6 (tr. by É. Senart)

189,16 *Bṛhad Āraṇyaka Upaniṣad*, 4.5.15 (tr. by É. Senart)

189,27 *Ṛg Veda*, 10.130.6 (tr. by W. Doniger)

190,1 *Śatapatha Brāhmaṇa*, 1.6.2.2 (tr. by J. Eggeling)

191,6 *Śatapatha Brāhmaṇa*, 1.7.4.22 (tr. by J. Eggeling)

195,25 *Ṛg Veda*, 10.129.7 (tr. by W. Doniger)

196,23 *Chāndogya Upaniṣad*, 1.4.3

202,29 *Devībhāgavata Purāṇa*, 6.12.26 (tr. by J. E. Mitchiner)

204,12 *Maitri Upaniṣad*, 6.34

204,32 *Śatapatha Brāhmaṇa*, 11.2.3.6

208,1 *Śatapatha Brāhmaṇa*, 4.1.5.1 (tr. by J. Eggeling)

210,3 *Ṛg Veda*, 1.179.1 (tr. by P. Thieme)

210,21 *Ṛg Veda*, 1.179.6 (tr. by P. Thieme)

210,25 *Ṛg Veda*, 1.179.3 (tr. by P. Thieme)

210,26 *Ṛg Veda*, 1.179.5 (tr. by P. Thieme)

210,28 *Ṛg Veda*, 1.179.4 (tr. by P. Thieme)

211,3 *Ṛg Veda*, 1.179.4 (tr. by P. Thieme)
213,35 *Ṛg Veda*, 5.74.5
214,3 *Mahābhārata*, 3.123.18
214,9 *Mahābhārata*, 3.123.23
220,2 *Ṛg Veda*, 10.17.2
225,5 *Chāndogya Upaniṣad*, 8.7.1 (tr. by É. Senart)
226,21 *Śatapatha Brāhmaṇa*, 4.1.5.16
226,22 Yáska, *Nirukta*, 12.1
227,17 *Ṛg Veda*, 1.118.5 (tr. by K. F. Geldner)
228,18 *Jaiminīya Brāhmaṇa*, 3.159 (tr. by W. Doniger)
228,20 *Śatapatha Brāhmaṇa*, 3.6.2.26
233,19 *Ṛg Veda*, 4.58.1 (tr. by K. F. Geldner)
236,18 *Śatapatha Brāhmaṇa*, 3.6.2.2
237,24 *Aitareya Brāhmaṇa*, 1.27 (tr. by A. B. Keith)
238,3 *Śatapatha Brāhmaṇa*, 3.2.4.6 (tr. by S. Lévi)
238,11 *Ṛg Veda*, 10.125.5 (tr. by K. F. Geldner)
238,14 *Ṛg Veda*, 1.164.10 (tr. by W. Doniger)
238,34 *Jaiminīya Brāhmaṇa*, 2.298 (tr. by W. Caland)
239,8 *Jaiminīya Brāhmaṇa*, 2.298 (tr. by W. Caland)
239,13 *Jaiminīya Brāhmaṇa*, 2.298 (tr. by W. Caland)
239,28 *Jaiminīya Brāhmaṇa*, 2.298 (tr. by W. Caland)
239,38 C. Baudelaire, *Bohémiens en voyage*, in *Les Fleurs du mal*, XIII
240,34 *Pañcaviṃśa Brāhmaṇa*, 18.10.10 (tr. by W. Caland)
243,36 *Ṛg Veda*, 4.18.2
244,37 *Śatapatha Brāhmaṇa*, 1.6.3.17
245,12 *Ṛg Veda*, 10.51.4
246,28 *Āśvalāyana Śrauta Sūtra*, 10.9.2 (tr. by H. Lüders)
246,32 *Ṛg Veda*, 4.58.5
253,18 *Ṛg Veda*, 9.68.6 (tr. by H. Lüders)
253,20 *Ṛg Veda*, 9.73.1 (tr. by H. Lüders)
255,13 *Bṛhad Āraṇyaka Upaniṣad*, 1.4.6
255,21 *Ṛg Veda*, 9.9.4 (tr. by H. Lüders)
255,21 *Ṛg Veda*, 9.44.3 (tr. by K. F. Geldner)
257,26 *Śatapatha Brāhmaṇa*, 11.1.8.1–2
258,12 *Śatapatha Brāhmaṇa*, 3.3.3.1
258,20 *Ṛg Veda*, 10.129.4 (tr. by W. Doniger)
259,19 *Bṛhad Āraṇyaka Upaniṣad*, 4.3.32
259,30 M. Proust, *Albertine disparue*, in *À la recherche du temps perdu*, vol. 4 (Paris: Gallimard, 1989), p. 189
261,16 *Bṛhaddevatā*, 2.59
263,22 *Ṛg Veda*, 10.95.5
296,36 *Mahābhārata*, 1.134.5 (Bombay)
307,30 *Ṛg Veda*, 10.85.40 (tr. by K. F. Geldner)
310,2 *Mahābhārata*, 1.2.242 (tr. by J. A. B. van Buitenen)
310,5 *Mahābhārata*, 1.2.241 (tr. by J. A. B. van Buitenen)
312,25 *Mahābhārata*, 1.2.235
315,7 *Mahābhārata*, 1.56.33
315,8 M. Proust, *Sodome et Gomorrhe*, in *À la recherche du temps perdu*, vol. 3 (Paris:

Gallimard, 1988), p. 210
315,16 *Mahābhārata*, 1.2.236 (tr. by J. A. B. van Buitenen)
318,22 *Mahābhārata*, 12.1.15
319,17 *Mahābhārata*, 1.94.90
322,13 *Mahābhārata*, 1.3.132
323,24 Somadeva, *Kathāsaritsāgara*, 3.2.36 (16.36)
330,29 *Mahābhārata*, 1.187.28 (tr. by J. A. B. van Buitenen)
335,14 *Maitri Upaniṣad*, 6.4 (tr. by A.-M. Esnoul)
336,2 *Ṛg Veda*, 1.164.20
337,3 *Kaṭha Upaniṣad*, 4.1 (tr. by L. Renou)
337,25 *Ṛg Veda*, 1.164.20
337,26 *Ṛg Veda*, 1.164.20
338,26 *Mahābhārata*, 3.41.2 (tr. by J. A. B. van Buitenen)
339,11 *Mahābhārata*, 7.56.24
340,18 *Mahābhārata*, 1.119.5 (tr. by J. A. B. van Buitenen)
340,22 *Mahābhārata*, 1.119.6
341,1 *Bhagavad Gītā*, 18.63
341,8 Ānandavardhana, *Dhvanyāloka*, 4.5 (tr. by V. Mazzarino)
341,20 Ānandavardhana, *Dhvanyāloka*, 4.5 (tr. by V. Mazzarino)
349,9 *Lalitavistara*, V (tr. by P. E. de Foucaux)
351,6 *Aṅguttara Nikāya*, I.145
358,15 *Majjhima Nikāya*, III.230 (tr. by I. B. Horner)
366,27 *Ṛg Veda*, 1.164.50
366,29 *Ṛg Veda*, 1.164.50
368,23 *Mahāvastu*, 2.418 (tr. by J. J. Jones)
369,22 M. Proust, notes for his review of *Les éblouissements* by Anna de Noailles, in *Contre Sainte-Beuve* (Paris: Gallimard, 1971), p. 932
373,3 Aśvaghoṣa, *Saundarananda*, 15.35 (tr. by A. Passi)
386,32 *Kia-ye kie king*, 4 (tr. by J. Przyluski)
386,34 *Vinaya of the Māhāsāṃghikas*, 33a (tr. by J. Przyluski)
391,2 *Śatapatha Brāhmaṇa*, 1.7.1.21
392,35 *Ṛg Veda*, 1.164.20
396,36 *Dīgha Nikāya*, II.156
399,2 *Śatapatha Brāhmaṇa*, 7.4.1.13
399,3 *Śatapatha Brāhmaṇa*, passim
399,5 *Taittirīya Saṃhitā*, 5.6.4 (tr. by A. B. Keith)
400,5 *Atharva Veda*, 11.7.1
400,11 *Aitareya Upaniṣad*, 1.1 (tr. by L. Silburn)

Akṣamālā

As in an *akṣamālā*, a necklace of "nuts," or *akṣas*, which were used for playing and sometimes likened to *akṣaras*, "syllables," I string together here some of the names of those who helped this book to become what it is:

V. S. Agrawala; A. H. Anquetil-Duperron; André Bareau; Émile Benveniste; Abel Bergaigne; Madeleine Biardeau; Maurice Bloomfield; H. W. Bodewitz; J. F. K. Bosch; W. Norman Brown; J. A. B. van Buitenen; Eugène Burnouf; Wilhelm Caland; Jarl Charpentier; A. K. Coomaraswamy; Alain Daniélou; René Daumal; Hertha von Dechend; Joachim Deppert; Paul Deussen; Wendy Doniger; Georges Dumézil; Louis Dumont; P.-E. Dumont; Julius Eggeling; Robert Eisler; Harry Falk; Maryla Falk; Alfred Foucher; K. F. Geldner; Raniero Gnoli; Jan Gonda; René Guénon; Hermann Güntert; J. W. Hauer; J. C. Heesterman; G. J. Held; Victor Henry; Alfred Hillebrandt; Karl Hoffmann; E. W. Hopkins; Hermann Jacobi; K. F. Johansson; P. V. Kane; A. B. Keith; Willibald Kirfel; Stella Kramrisch; Hertha Krick; F. B. J. Kuiper; Sylvain Lévi; Heinrich Lüders; A. A. Macdonell; Charles Malamoud; Marcel Mauss; Manfred Mayrhofer; Armand Minard; J. E. Mitchiner; Max Müller; Paul Mus; Boris Oguibenine; Hermann Oldenberg; Jean Przyluski; Walpola Rahula; Wilhelm Rau; Louis Renou; Claudio Rugafiori; Giorgio de Santillana; Leopold von Schroeder; Émile Senart; D. D. Shulman; Lilian Silburn; Frits Staal; Theodor Stcherbatsky; Heinrich von Stietencron; Paul Thieme; Edward Thomas; L. B. G. Tilak; Jean Varenne; R. G. Wasson; W. D. Whitney;

Stig Wikander; Moritz Winternitz; Michael Witzel; Heinrich Zimmer Jr.; Heinrich Zimmer Sr.

Roberto Donatoni and Giovanna Ghidetti have looked after the text from start to finish, watching over every detail.

They all have my deep gratitude.